The Declining
Significance of Gender?

The Declining Significance of Gender?

Francine D. Blau, Mary C. Brinton, and
David B. Grusky, editors

Russell Sage Foundation ◆ New York

The Russell Sage Foundation

The Russell Sage Foundation, one of the oldest of America's general purpose foundations, was established in 1907 by Mrs. Margaret Olivia Sage for "the improvement of social and living conditions in the United States." The Foundation seeks to fulfill this mandate by fostering the development and dissemination of knowledge about the country's political, social, and economic problems. While the Foundation endeavors to assure the accuracy and objectivity of each book it publishes, the conclusions and interpretations in Russell Sage Foundation publications are those of the authors and not of the Foundation, its Trustees, or its staff. Publication by Russell Sage, therefore, does not imply Foundation endorsement.

Library of Congress Cataloging-in-Publication Data

The declining significance of gender? / Francine D. Blau, Mary C. Brinton, and David B. Grusky, editors.
    p. cm.
    Includes bibliographical references and index.
    ISBN 0-87154-092-4
       1. Sex discrimination in employment. 2. Pay equity. 3. Sex discrimination against women. I. Blau, Francine D. II. Brinton, Mary C. III. Grusky, David B.

  HD6060.D43 2006
  331.4'133—dc22   2005055256

The paper used in this publication meets the minimum requirements of American National Standard for Information Sciences—Permanence of Paper for Printed Library Materials. ANSI Z39.48-1992.

Text design by Suzanne Nichols.

RUSSELL SAGE FOUNDATION
112 East 64th Street, New York, New York 10021
10 9 8 7 6 5 4 3 2 1

Contents

Contents

Contributors

FRANCINE D. BLAU is Frances Perkins Professor of Industrial Relations and Labor Economics at Cornell University, research associate of the National Bureau of Economic Research, and research fellow at IZA and CESifo.

MARY C. BRINTON is Reischauer Institute Professor of Sociology at Harvard University.

DAVID B. GRUSKY is professor of sociology and director of the Center for the Study of Poverty and Inequality at Stanford University.

PAULA ENGLAND is professor of sociology and an affiliate of the Institute for Research on Women and Gender at Stanford University.

CLAUDIA GOLDIN is Henry Lee professor of economics at Harvard University and director of the Development of the American Economy program at the National Bureau of Economic Research.

HEIDI HARTMANN is an economist and president of the Institute for Women's Policy Research and research professor at The George Washington University.

ROBERT MAX JACKSON is professor of sociology at New York University.

LAWRENCE M. KAHN is professor of labor economics and collective bargaining at Cornell University, and research fellow at IZA and CESifo.

VICKY LOVELL is study director for employment and earnings at the Institute for Women's Policy Research in Washington, D.C.

EVA M. MEYERSSON MILGROM is visiting associate professor in the Department of Sociology and senior research scholar at Stanford Institute for Economic Policy.

TROND PETERSEN is professor in the Haas Organizational Behavior and Industrial Relations Group and in the Department of Sociology at the University of California, Berkeley.

Contributors

SOLOMON W. POLACHEK is distinguished professor of economics and political science at the State University of New York at Binghamton and fellow at the Institute for the Study of Labor (IZA) in Bonn, Germany.

CECILIA L. RIDGEWAY is Lucie Stern Professor of Social Sciences in the Department of Sociology at Stanford University.

STEPHEN J. ROSE is senior research economist at ORC Macro in Washington, D.C.

Preface and Acknowledgments

Countless books on gender inequality have been published in recent years. Why did we decide to publish yet another? We cannot claim that the particular topic we take on, the future of gender inequality, has gone largely unstudied. To the contrary, there is a growing industry of commentary on precisely this question, with some authors arguing that a backlash against egalitarian change is unfolding and others referring to the inevitability of continuing egalitarian change.

We ourselves are avid consumers of this literature and are very appreciative that smart people are thinking seriously about the future of one of the most important egalitarian revolutions of our time. At the same time, what is currently available tends to be either journalistic in style and fails to fully engage with the massive scientific literature on the topic or, alternatively, is narrowly disciplinary in orientation and does not take into account the variety of social-scientific approaches. This line of reasoning motivated us to bring together scholars representing different scientific disciplines and methodological approaches and ask them to weigh in on the sources and future of the gender revolution.

The intense public interest in this subject and the multiplicity of points of view held, both within the academy and more broadly, make for a complicated ideological environment in which scholars of gender must operate. How does one craft a credible book about gender inequality in such a context? The first answer, and one which we find only partly satisfactory, is that the scientific method insists on engagement with the empirical world under rigorously objective and documented protocols that force scholars to shed their extra-scientific commitments. This is an obvious point but nonetheless one worth stressing. As we see it, too much of the contemporary discussion about the future and trajectory of gender inequality has taken the form of journalistic reports and public commentary, neither of which typically involves the same type of explicit confrontation with empirical data. To be sure, public discussion and good journalism is crucially important (not the least for saving academics from their own excessively arcane debates), but it works best when complemented by scientific research that is deeply empirical in orientation and that accordingly provides the extra-scientific community with a firm base upon which to ground their debates.

The second, and equally important, point is that a credible book about gender and its future has to appreciate that there is a diversity of scientific approaches on offer, a diversity that is best featured rather than concealed. We have therefore made every effort to bring together scholars with heterogeneous backgrounds and orientations. The roster of editors and contributors includes economists and sociologists, experimentalists and survey analysts, and academics and practitioners.

In writing our own introductory essay, we spent much time and effort debating and critiquing each other's work, thus forcing us to come to terms with at least some commitments that had before gone unquestioned. We likewise subjected most of the chapters to interdisciplinary reviews and asked the authors to engage, whenever possible, with the other contributors. The resulting book is therefore less affected by the idiosyncrasies of biography or discipline than is generally the case, and comes closer, we would argue, to an unadorned exposition of precisely what science can and cannot tell us about the dynamics of gender inequality.

This project was begun when we were all faculty members at Cornell University. We are grateful to the Russell Sage Foundation, the Center for the Study of Inequality, and the Cornell Careers Institute for providing the funding that made our interdisciplinary effort possible. This funding allowed us to invite leading scholars of gender inequality to present their research at Cornell University in a lecture series titled, "The Declining Significance of Gender?" These talks were expertly organized by Jessica Henning and Elizabeth Heitner and were co-sponsored by the Mario Einaudi Center for International Studies, the Program on Gender and Global Change, the Feminist, Gender and Sexuality Studies Program, and the Feminism and Legal Theory Project, all at Cornell University. We are also grateful to the School of Industrial and Labor Relations at Cornell University for providing space and administrative support for the lecture series. In addition, portions of this project were completed while Francine Blau was a visiting fellow in the Economics Department at Princeton University, supported by the Industrial Relations Section. She very gratefully acknowledges this support.

We are also grateful to the production and marketing staff at the Russell Sage Foundation, especially Genna Patacsil and David Haproff, for their excellent work and their patience in tolerating our long delays in assembling an edited volume. Most inconveniently, we cannot blame our anonymous reviewers for these delays, as their comments were not just excellent but also timely. We especially thank Suzanne Nichols of the Russell Sage Foundation for her support throughout the project.

Finally, we gratefully acknowledge the role of our own children, Daniel Blau Kahn, Lisa Blau Kahn, Emma Brinton, and Max and Dashiel Szelényi Grusky, in serving not just as unwitting data points but also as active, if sometimes irritated, informants about how gender has played out in their lives so far. We have quizzed them frequently and, we would like to think, to good effect. We accordingly dedicate this book to them.

Francine D. Blau

Mary C. Brinton

David B. Grusky

Part I

Introduction

Chapter 1

The Declining Significance of Gender?

Francine D. Blau, Mary C. Brinton, and David B. Grusky

I n the typical life history of a social revolution, the initial revolutionary ardor proves to be sustainable for only so long, and gradually sentiment grows that the revolution has stalled or run its course. We appear to be entering just such a period of pessimism about the future of the ongoing "gender revolution." After a half-century of dramatic reductions in the gender pay gap and other forms of gender inequality, we now find ourselves poised at a crossroads in which two very plausible futures appear before us, an "optimistic scenario" which assumes that the remaining (and very substantial) gender inequalities will continue to erode, and a "pessimistic scenario" which treats the gender revolution as stalling and regards contemporary institutional arrangements as an equilibrium.

The optimistic vision rests on the straightforward premise that the forces making for change over the last half-century remain in play and will bring about further substantial reductions in gender inequality. The scholars who advance this vision emphasize that egalitarian values continue to spread unabated and to produce a growing commitment among parents to provide their daughters with the same opportunities as their sons. These egalitarian values also undergird a shared political commitment to such powerful legal interventions as antidiscrimination legislation and may lead ultimately to more ambitious and far-reaching forms of legal intervention (for example, paid parental leave legislation, expanded provision of government-provided child care). At the same time, gender equality is further advanced by the continuing diffusion of women-friendly organizational reforms, most notably on-site child care, guaranteed family leaves, and rigorously enforced bureaucratic rules that provide formal guarantees of equal treatment. Finally, because women are disproportionately located in economic sectors that are growing (especially the white-collar and service sectors) and men are disproportionately located in economic sectors that are shrinking (especially blue-collar and manufacturing sectors), there is continuing downward pressure on the gender pay gap. The foregoing forces for change are all ongoing and, one might argue, can be anticipated to carry the gender revolution forward.

The pessimistic vision rests on an equally diverse array of counter-arguments that have appeared with increasing frequency in popular magazines (Louise Story, "Many Women at Elite Colleges Set Career Path to Motherhood," *New York Times*, September 20, 2005; Lisa Belkin, "The Opt-Out Revolution," *New York Times*, October 26, 2003), popular books (Barash 2004; Faludi 1991), and scholarly outlets (chapters 8 and 9, this volume). This work often emphasizes that the gender revolution has been a profoundly asymmetric one, a revolution in which females have increasingly assumed male-typed jobs, but males have not to the same extent moved into female-typed jobs. If, as proponents of this view argue, most of the gains that asymmetric change can generate have now been reaped, any further gains will have to rest on the unlikely prospect that the revolution develops a more symmetric cast to it (see chapter 8, this volume). For other commentators, it is equally troubling that there has been no great rush among men to take on child care and other domestic duties, an outcome that is entirely in keeping with the asymmetric dynamic observed elsewhere. It is argued that the persistence of this deeply gender-based division of labor in the family reduces the incentives for women to further invest in their human capital or to acquire work experience, thus dampening the rate of change in gender inequality. The final set of pessimistic arguments, again closely related to the foregoing ones, emphasizes that a rather constricted form of egalitarianism has been diffusing, one that rests on a formal commitment to "equal opportunity" without any corresponding commitment to ensuring that women and men will be similarly oriented toward taking up such opportunities. By this line of argument, a narrow commitment to purely formal guarantees of equal opportunity leaves much room for "essentialist" ideologies to flourish, ideologies that regard women and men as fundamentally different, having very distinctive skills and abilities, and therefore unlikely to avail themselves of the formally equal opportunities in the same ways (see Charles and Grusky 2004).

It is possible, then, to put forward two quite contradictory predictions about the future of gender inequality, both of which have at least a surface plausibility. How well do these scenarios stand up under closer scrutiny? How does the pattern of change over the last half-century accord with each of these visions? What are the proximate mechanisms at work that might move us toward the optimistic or pessimistic visions? How, if at all, might ongoing and new political interventions make the optimistic or pessimistic visions more or less plausible? Are there other, more complicated visions of the future that might be realized? To address these issues, we have assembled eminent scholars in the field of gender inequality, scholars who span many approaches and disciplines. Although impassioned arguments in defense of the optimistic or pessimistic visions have frequently been advanced, to date we have not seen a serious and sustained attempt to consider dispassionately the forces that might lead to either of these outcomes or to some yet more complicated outcome. We present such an attempt in the pages that follow.

The precursor to this volume was a series of colloquia at Cornell University, sponsored by the Center for the Study of Inequality, on recent declines in the gender pay gap and in gender differences in other labor-market outcomes. The participating scholars were asked whether such declines, which are among the most spectacular forms of social change in the twentieth century, can be expected to continue apace as we move into the twenty-first century. The chapters in part II, "Making Sense of Change and Stability in Gender Inequality," focus on understanding change and stability in gender inequality in the past, while also giving some attention to prospects for the future. The chapters in part III, "Possible Futures of Gender Inequality," consider and build on analyses of what has happened in the past, but to a great extent focus on the implications of this past for the future.

We shall here explore the central themes that play out in these chapters by providing an organizing frame through which they may be usefully viewed. We focus our comments on the United States because understanding this case is very challenging in itself and is a useful preparation for the more daunting task of making sense of the future of gender inequality throughout the world.

As noted, the principal motivation for the colloquia and volume was the considerable dissensus among scholars over the future of gender inequality, a dissensus that is all the more striking because the empirical record of change over the last half-century is, for the most part, well established and is not a matter of much debate. Why is there nonetheless so much disagreement about the future? We think that it arises for three reasons:

1. Some forms of gender inequality, such as the pay gap and the level of female labor-force participation, have changed more rapidly than others, such as women's representation in top managerial positions and the division of labor in the family. This makes it possible for scholars to develop projections that implicitly feature extrapolations of different time series and stylized facts.

2. The evidence that scholars feature and the projections they develop are themselves undoubtedly affected by differences in their political orientations, in their personal experiences with gender inequality and discrimination, and in their disciplinary worldviews.

3. The causal forces underlying change and stability in the data remain unclear, making it possible for different scholars to weave stories that feature different causal forces and, as a result, different outcomes.

We shall elaborate briefly on each of these three sources of dissensus. On the matter of the empirical record, it bears emphasizing that some stylized facts suggest an impressive decline in gender inequality in the United States, whereas others suggest that gender inequality will not wither away completely, at least not in the near term. The various facts are well known (see, for example, Blau 1998; Blau, Ferber, and Winkler 2002; Charles and Grusky 2004) and need not be covered in great detail here. The evidence that leads commentators to emphasize changes in gender inequality includes the dramatic growth in female labor-force participation, especially that of married women, from the middle to the late twentieth century; the reduction and even reversal in gender differentials in educational attainment; a notable decline in occupational sex segregation, beginning in the 1960s and proceeding more rapidly over the 1970s and 1980s; a marked decline in the gender wage gap beginning in the late 1970s; and a small but notable reallocation of housework between husbands and wives, a change that was especially prominent in the 1980s.

However, commentators can also readily draw on less favorable evidence, including a rate of change in the sharing of household tasks within the family that lags behind the dramatic rise in female labor-force participation and that is slower than many social scientists would regard as necessary for further progress in reducing market inequalities; the slowing rate of decline in the gender wage gap and in occupational sex segregation and the slowing rate of increase in female labor-force participation; the continued underrepresentation of women in the upper echelons of corporate America, government, and academia; the persistence of discriminatory practices in hiring and other aspects of employment (though there are indications that such discrimination has been reduced); and the seeming intractability of the essentialist presumption that skills, proclivities, and tastes tend to be gender-specific, an especially insidious source of inequality that appears, like employment discrimination, to have been reduced but not eliminated.

The simple point that we wish to make is that the empirical record encompasses time series that are changing at varying rates and cadences, making the future difficult to predict. Will the forces underlying past change continue to operate unabated until full equality is achieved? Or does the slowdown in the rate of change in a number of important time series suggest that we have reached a plateau and that further change in gender relations will now occur comparatively slowly?

This ambiguity in the data makes it possible for scholars to interpret the evidence in ways consistent with their favored causal models, political orientations, and various other predispositions. We are not arguing that individuals engage in conscious distortions or selection in their interpretation of the evidence. Rather, the lens through which inequalities are described and interpreted is inevitably refracted by values, orientations, and predispositions of which we are sometimes only faintly aware. This makes even straightforward description—let alone analysis—difficult to achieve. For example, most scholars are committed to equalizing opportunities for women and men (though there are obvious disagreements as to how this objective might be achieved), a commitment that can color how evidence is presented or discussed. In some cases, this shared commitment to equalization motivates scholars to downplay evidence of decline in gender inequality, presumably out of concern that undue emphasis on the progress achieved so far will make it appear that the remaining level of inequality is acceptable or unproblematic. Because of this concern, a conventional rhetorical strategy is to emphasize that much inequality remains and to assure the reader that the goal of perfect equality has by no means been achieved. That is, rather than focusing on how much progress has been made over the last half-century or longer, most scholars emphasize how far contemporary societies truly are from reaching the condition of gender equality.

Finally, because none of the disciplines is operating with a wholly consensual causal model of inequality, scholars often focus on different sources of change and consequently arrive at different conclusions about the likely trajectory of change.

If, instead, they could agree on a single causal model, it would reduce debate to disagreement about the trajectory of the independent variables that are presumed to drive change. In the absence of a consensual model, the debate is complicated by differences of opinion as to which variables are most relevant as sources of change—an additional source of uncertainty in forecasting change. We aim to develop a more comprehensive narrative that recognizes the manifold causal forces underlying change and stasis and that clarifies why more specialized narratives can lead to such diverse assessments.

The search for an improved narrative underlies many of the book's chapters. We seek here to clarify the discussion in these chapters and in the field at large by introducing a distinction between the proximate and distal causal mechanisms that affect gender inequality. It is hoped that this distinction will motivate readers to think expansively about the different types of processes that affect gender inequality in economic life and about the often complex relationships among these processes. Throughout this introduction we apply this distinction for the purpose of explaining trends in the wage gap and in occupational sex segregation, as these two outcomes are fundamental to gender inequality and illustrate the many processes at work that either sustain or weaken gender inequality.

DISTINGUISHING PROXIMATE AND DISTAL MECHANISMS

The conceptual distinction that we seek to make is between proximate mechanisms of change, such as declining employer discrimination, and more distal "macro-level forces," such as economic competition or bureaucratization, that affect gender inequality via the proximate mechanisms. In past analyses, the tendency has been to focus on proximate mechanisms alone and to either ignore distal ones altogether or to mix them indiscriminately with proximate ones. This conventional approach can lead to incomplete analyses that beg the more fundamental question of why the proximate mechanisms are themselves undergoing change. It is not entirely satisfying, for example, to explain declines in gender inequality by simply noting that employer discrimination now occurs less frequently or that the gender gap in occupational aspirations is declining. To be sure, it is crucial to understand the proximate mechanisms at work, and indeed much fundamental research in the field is oriented toward precisely that task. However, once the proximate mechanisms have been established, one should then ask why discrimination is abating, why women are increasingly aspiring to hold formerly male-typed occupations, and why the household division of labor has changed more slowly than other forms of gender inequality. These types of questions require us to consider the macro-level forces that affect gender inequality via proximate mechanisms.

In table 1.1 we list the five proximate forces and the four distal, or macro-level, forces that the contributors to this volume identify either explicitly or implicitly. We organize our discussion by considering each of the macro-level forces—eco-

TABLE 1.1 / Macro-Level Forces and Proximate Mechanisms Generating Gender Inequality

Proximate Mechanisms	Macro-Level Forces			
	Economic	Organizational	Political	Cultural
A. Discrimination				
1. Tastes	X	X	X	X
2. Statistical	X	X	X	X
3. Institutional	X	X	X	X
B. Internalization				
1. Preferences				X
2. Self-evaluation				X
C. Labor-force commitment				
1. Domestic division of labor	X	X	X	X
2. Workplace adaptations	X		X	X
D. Cultural Devaluation				
1. Pollution		X	X	X
2. Cultural devaluation		X	X	X
E. Feedback effects				
1. Expectations of discrimination	X	X	X	X
2. Expected sanctions				X

Source: Authors' compilation.

nomic, organizational, political, cultural—in turn and the proximate mechanisms through which they exert their effects. We shall show how some of the proximate mechanisms are linked to all or nearly all of the forces at the macro-level, whereas others are more narrowly linked to a small number of macro-level forces. In each of the following sections, we first describe a particular narrative in positive and sympathetic terms and then we discuss the countervailing or inertial forces that may prevent the stylized account from playing out as straightforwardly as its adherents presume. In this way we seek to provide a comprehensive discussion of the forces making for change as well as stability.

THE ECONOMIC NARRATIVE

We begin with the well-known narrative of market competition (see Becker 1957/1971; Arrow 1973; chapters 2 and 7, this volume). In this narrative, it is assumed that labor-market practices that disadvantage women are often (but not always) inefficient, implying that a competitive market will select for firms that eschew women-disadvantaging practices. We review the three classes of proximate mechanisms through which market forces may reduce gender inequality: discrimination, labor-force commitment, and feedback effects. We then turn to the countervailing forces and conditions that may undermine the putatively equalizing effects of the market.

The Positive Case

In his original formulation of the "taste for discrimination" model (see table 1.1, line A1, "Tastes"), Gary S. Becker (1957/1971) argued that employer discrimination would be eroded by competitive market forces because it requires employers to pay a premium to hire members of the preferred class of labor, whether these be males, whites, or individuals identified by other ascriptive characteristics that employers consider desirable.[1] This taste is "discriminatory" because it rests on exogenous preferences for a certain category of labor that cannot be understood as arising from some larger concern for maximizing profitability, market share, or another standard economic outcome. That is, when managers make hiring decisions in accord with discriminatory tastes, their firms will not be competitive with nondiscriminating firms because they must pay extra to secure labor from the preferred class, without any compensating increase in productivity. In standard renditions of this account, it is presumed that such discriminating firms will gradually be selected out by the market, although it is of course also possible that some discriminating firms will change their hiring practices to remain competitive. For example, managers with tastes for discrimination may shed these tastes, may no longer feel free to act upon them, or may be replaced by individuals without such tastes.

We further interpret this model as suggesting that competitive forces should operate against institutionalized organizational practices that involve discrimination and thus hinder firms from minimizing their labor costs or using labor efficiently. These types of discriminatory practices, which we term "institutional discrimination" (line A3, "Institutional"), may be deeply embedded in organizational routines and hence can be perpetuated quite independently of individual tastes for discrimination. To the extent that these routines are inefficient,[2] market competition should again root them out, either by selecting against the offending firms or obliging them to reform their ways by eliminating the routines themselves. If, for example, the institutionalized assignment of women to a dead-end "mommy track" compromises a firm's efficiency, the economic narrative tells us that it will ultimately be selected out by market forces. To be sure, firms are complicated bundles of many discriminatory and nondiscriminatory practices, implying that the market effect on any particular practice may be indirect and potentially slow to register. This complication may be one reason why discrimination has tended to persist over time in the face of competitive forces.

The situation with respect to statistical discrimination (line A2) is more complex. Where there is considerable uncertainty and poor information about worker performance, firms may be tempted to treat sex or other ascriptive characteristics as a low-cost source of information about an individual worker's productivity. The resulting statistical discrimination entails making hiring, promotion, and pay decisions on the basis of group performance, such as the average productivity of all women at a given job, rather than individual performance (see Aigner and Cain 1977).[3] If employers are correct in their assessments of average group differences in productivity, we cannot count on competitive forces to eliminate statistical discrimination. That is, competitive forces will eliminate statistical discrimination when it is based on *erroneous* inferences about group differences or when other screening devices are more cost-effective, but not when it is based on correct and cost-effective judgments.[4]

The "taste for discrimination" model and at least one form of the statistical discrimination model (erroneous beliefs) may be couched, then, as a narrative about how discriminatory firms, managers, and practices gradually disappear under the force of market competition. It may be argued this narrative not only has market forces rooting out inefficient firms, managers, and practices, but also has such forces positively selecting for new practices that make firms more efficient in an ever-changing environment. In the contemporary context, one of the main environmental changes to which firms must respond is the dramatic increase in the size of the female labor force, and various inequality-reducing workplace adaptations (line C2) to this environmental change might well prove to be efficient and hence be positively selected by market forces. For example, policies that facilitate the integration of work and family responsibilities, such as maternity and parental leave, employer-provided child care, or child-care subsidies, have become increasingly prevalent in recent years. Although such policies can be government-mandated and hence proliferate for reasons other than their efficiency, some employers have voluntarily offered such policies to attract employees who may regard them as desirable nonwage benefits and may be willing to forgo some wages in exchange, and also to retain employees in whom they have made substantial investments.

The provision of such benefits probably will increase in the future as women continue to be integrated into the workforce at all levels. Moreover, employers have an additional incentive to provide such benefits because, insofar as household responsibilities in the family are increasingly shared, family-friendly policies are attractive to men as well as women.[5] Widespread adoption of family-friendly policies should in turn promote a more equal division of labor in the household, since such policies make it possible for women to compete more successfully in the labor market and thus increase their incentive to invest in human capital with a market payoff instead of specializing in domestic labor. It is of course difficult to predict the extent to which such a "benign circle" will develop.[6]

The latter point leads us directly to a discussion of "feedback effects" (see especially chapter 2, this volume). As indicated in line E1, the foregoing economic forces should have indirect positive effects on women's human capital and other job-related investments, since they encourage firms to become family-friendly and thereby increase the anticipated payoff to women for making such investments. Because human-capital theory posits that individuals make investments in light of their anticipated future gain, their perception of the extent of employer discrimination and family-friendliness may affect these investment decisions. If women have historically made lower investments in their human capital than men partly because employer discrimination and other women-disadvantaging practices have caused them to anticipate a lower payoff to their investments, the erosion of discriminatory tastes and practices in the labor market should reduce this expectation of a payoff differential and lead to more-similar investment decisions by men and women (line E1, "Expectations of discrimination"). This decline in the payoff differential likewise should act to undermine an important rationale for the intrafamilial division of labor in which men are regarded as principally responsible for market labor and women are regarded as principally responsible for domestic labor. If the economic rationale for this division of labor begins to disappear, one might anticipate that the cultural support for such an arrangement, including norms about female domesticity, may likewise begin to falter.

This discussion implies that the economic narrative is perhaps more far-reaching than has usually been appreciated. Although the "tastes for discrimination" argument is well known, economic forces may also operate to root out other institutionalized forms of discrimination, decrease some forms of statistical discrimination, positively select for women-friendly workplace adaptations, motivate women to increase their investment in human capital as the anticipated payoff to such investment rises, and help to promote a more equal division of labor in the family. These effects all depend on the presumptions that women-advantaging reform is efficient and profit-maximizing and, moreover, that the forces of competition are sufficiently strong so as to lead to these results. We now address these presumptions more directly.

Limitations

As has long been recognized, the claim that competitive forces will erode gender discrimination, particularly discrimination based on employers' tastes, is arguably at odds with empirical evidence that such discrimination has persisted for some time and shows no sign of having been eliminated. Some commentators have argued that, because gender inequality has persisted, the economic narrative cannot provide a very compelling account of the evolution of inequality. We note, however, that the intractability of gender inequality is a double-edged sword that has led other social scientists to doubt that labor-market discrimination is responsible in whole or in part for gender inequality in economic outcomes. The very persistence of gender inequality is regarded by such commentators as presumptive evidence that it is efficient and that pure discrimination cannot account for it. We shall suggest below that this defense of the economic narrative fails to recognize that there are cogent economic reasons for expecting that the forces of competition may not eliminate all forms of gender discrimination.

The economic narrative can be undermined by at least two general types of problems: first, the competitive market will not eliminate forms of gender inequality that are consistent with or even increase firm efficiency; and second, the competitive forces that play out in real economies are imperfectly developed and cannot always be counted upon to completely eliminate even those forms of gender inequality that *reduce* firm efficiency. We consider each type of problem in turn.

The first class of problems arises from the unfortunate possibility that, much as gender inequality is morally troubling to most of us, some of its manifestations may actually solve organizational problems. The classic illustration of this dilemma is statistical discrimination. The strategy of making predictions about future productivity on the basis of group averages may be efficient if there is not much individual-level variability around such averages, and if more reliable forms of information gathering, such as forms that capture this residual individual-level variability, are unduly expensive. If these two tests are met and statistical discrimination is accordingly an efficient adaptation to the high costs of gathering information, competitive forces may not penalize firms that deploy it (see, for example, Aigner and Cain 1977; Blau, Ferber, and Winkler 2002). Likewise, many inequality-enhancing adaptations, such as "mommy tracks," could be interpreted as forms of statistical discrimination in which firms presume, with a tolerable amount of error, that women have more substantial domestic duties and therefore are efficiently assigned to less-demanding positions. (This reference to mommy tracks is purely illustrative and is not intended to suggest that they are indeed efficient adaptations.)

In the foregoing discussion of statistical discrimination, we have referred to the compatibility of the competitive market with gender inequality. As Aigner and Cain (1977) have pointed out, whenever women are less productive in a particular job and employers accurately perceive this productivity differential and set wages accordingly, women's wages will be reduced, but as a group women will be paid their expected productivity. This does not constitute labor market discrimination as economists define it because, at the group level, gender differences in pay are accounted for by gender differences in productivity. It does mean, however, that a woman who performs above her group mean will nonetheless be treated as a member of her (gender) group and hence not be paid according to her individual productivity. From a normative perspective, the practice of basing employment decisions on characteristics like sex—a characteristic that the individual cannot change—is a form of discrimination because it does not accord with the standard of paying *individuals* based on their *individual* productivity. Indeed, the practice of judging an individual on the basis of group characteristics rather than on his or her own merits seems the very essence of stereotyping or discrimination, and such behavior is certainly not legal under antidiscrimination laws and regulations.

It must further be recognized that "enlightened" employers who ignore the sexist tastes of their clients or customers may be penalized for imposing their views on a recalcitrant public. For instance, discrimination may not be incompatible with economic efficiency if customers or clients strongly prefer not to deal with women and threaten to take their business elsewhere if the firm places women in positions where the public expects to find men, such as airplane pilots, and heart-transplant surgeons. These potential sources of discrimination were elucidated by Becker in his initial formulation (Becker 1957/1971; also Arrow 1973 and Sunstein 1991).

Further, Francine D. Blau (1977) has pointed out that some forms of occupational sex segregation within the firm can be efficient if they reduce the amount of worker heterogeneity within an occupation and thereby allow firms to treat occupational incumbents in an undifferentiated and hence cheaper way.[7]

The second class of problems to which we alluded above is arguably more troubling, as it involves a fundamental failure of modern economies to deliver efficiency. This class of problems arises when departures from competition in product or labor markets weaken or eliminate the discrimination-eroding effect of competitive forces. For example, Becker (1957/1971) has pointed out that discrimination may be more likely to persist in monopolistic industries, such as some utilities, where employers are to some extent shielded from the forces of competition in the market for their product. As another example, Dan Black (1995) has developed a model in which workers face substantial search costs in locating new jobs, which can have an inequality-preserving effect because search costs give employers more market power over wage determination than they would have in a competitive labor market. To the extent that labor-market discrimination raises the search costs of female or minority employees above those of their male and white counterparts, these groups can safely be underpaid by an amount that is just less than what would induce them to search further. Finally, we note that the market cannot in all cases be expected to work expeditiously in selecting out inefficient organizational practices, given that firms are complicated and ever-changing bundles of practices, some of which may be optimizing and others not. In this context, the market verdict on any particular practice may be slow in coming—indeed, by the time a verdict is reached, the environmental conditions under which it holds may well have changed. Thus, there is nothing in the economic model that specifies a time frame within which inefficient practices will be selected out. If particular inefficient practices are so widely diffused as to be universal, one might well be faced with a long wait before a particular firm breaks with convention and subjects such a practice to a test.

In our view, these examples make it clear that the persistence of some gender inequality can be plausibly understood within the context of the economic narrative. There is no need to question the narrative in its entirety merely because gender inequality persists. Although these illustrations suggest that some forms of discrimination and gender inequality may solve organizational problems, it bears emphasizing that this need not imply that these female-disadvantaging practices will necessarily persist into the twenty-first century and beyond. However, it may be necessary to rely upon processes invoked in other, noneconomic narratives to understand why they might not persist.

THE ORGANIZATIONAL NARRATIVE

A second narrative of interest emphasizes the diffusion of modern personnel policies in the form of universalistic hiring practices and bureaucratized pay scales and promotion procedures (Meyer and Rowan 1977; DiMaggio and Powell 1983;

Dobbin et al. 1993; Jackson 1998; Reskin and McBrier 2000; Charles and Grusky 2004). The essence of bureaucratic personnel practices is a formal commitment to treating all workers equally, and to meritocratic hiring and promotion on the basis of credentials. In its ideal-typical form, bureaucracy is not about substantive rationality involving the maximization of productivity or output but about a formal commitment to a bundle of organizational practices, such as universalistic hiring and a reliance on credentials, that are regarded as normatively desirable and are typically presumed, rightly or wrongly, to be efficient. We will proceed again by first outlining this narrative in its positive form and then discussing why it may not play out as straightforwardly as some scholars have assumed.

The Positive Case

From the start, we note that the economic and organizational narratives have identical implications insofar as bureaucratic organizational forms are indeed as efficient as many managers, employers, and organizational scholars presume. In this context, the economic narrative implies that such forms will diffuse by virtue of their intrinsic efficiency, and the organizational and economic narratives therefore overlap. But the two narratives diverge to the extent that bureaucratic forms may not embody strictly efficient practices and the diffusion of bureaucratic forms is accordingly attributable to cultural stories about their efficiency rather than their actual efficiency. The widely held belief that bureaucratic practices are modern and efficient will itself serve to further diffuse such practices, either because managers have been socialized into this modern belief in colleges or business schools and will seek to implement it in their own organizations, or because managers pragmatically realize that, in an environment that regards bureaucratic practices as modern and efficient, there are real costs involved in setting up organizations along some different, nonbureaucratic model (Meyer 2001). In this sense, firms that eschew bureaucratic forms will not only forgo the productivity gains that bureaucratic hiring may generate but will also incur various social and even legal penalties.

If neo-institutionalist and economic neoclassical accounts are fused in this way, it becomes apparent that the costs of exercising discriminatory tastes may vary depending on the particular legal, institutional, and cultural environment in which employers operate.[8] Indeed, it is plausible that the diffusion of beliefs about legitimate organizational forms independently contributes to the costs of discriminating, beyond the efficiency costs discussed above in connection with economic forces. In an environment that has delegitimated discriminatory practices, a firm that nonetheless persists in discriminating faces real social costs, not just the legal costs that arise in such environments but also the public relations costs of becoming branded as an unfriendly employer for women. The long persistence of many discriminatory practices throughout the nineteenth and early twentieth centuries suggests that employers may need to incur additional social costs of this sort before fundamentally rethinking their hiring and promotion practices. This inference is consistent with the evidence that the enactment of federal antidiscrimination legislation and regulations in the United States in the mid-1960s contributed to the subsequent reduction in the gender pay gap, although these laws and regulations appear to have had a less dramatic effect on the gender pay gap than on the black-white pay gap.[9]

Thus, a decline in pure discrimination (lines A1 and A3) may be driven in part by institutional forces as well as economic competition. Does the same argument apply to statistical discrimination (line A2)? We think it does. This is because statistical discrimination is inconsistent with a formal bureaucratic logic that treats all individuals equally and without concern for such ascriptive group memberships as race, ethnicity, and gender. In their purest form, bureaucratic personnel practices delegitimate gender-based hiring, firing, and promotion even when it would be efficient to treat gender as a signal in these decisions (see chapter 7, this volume). As we have argued, competitive forces will only undermine those instances of statistical discrimination that are based on *erroneous*, and thus inefficient, inferences about group differences in productivity, whereas the diffusion of bureaucratic practices should erode all forms of discrimination, even those that are efficient. There is little scope within the context of ideal-typical bureaucratic systems to discriminate against women merely because it is believed that they tend on average to perform more poorly at the job in question or are more likely to quit than are men. When institutionalized in ideal-typical form, bureaucratic practices thus undermine both the "strong form" of statistical discrimination in which, on average, there are objective gender-based differences in productivity, and the "weak form," in which beliefs about objective differences are incorrect but nonetheless persist because stereotyping blinds employers to disconfirming evidence or because feedback effects influence women's incentives to invest (see Blau, Ferber and Winkler 2002; Lundberg and Startz 1983).[10]

Although negative prohibitions on ascription are fundamental to bureaucratic systems, these systems additionally involve a positive commitment to hiring and promoting on the basis of formally meritocratic criteria. In practice, this means that positions are typically awarded on the basis of credentials, especially those secured in schools or through vocational training. Does the diffusion of such meritocratic practices work to reduce gender inequality? Again, we think it does. The rise of credential-based hiring allows high-achieving women to substantiate their claims to high status, claims that might otherwise be challenged and undermined by men or women who hold negative stereotypes about women. For example, a woman credentialed at Harvard Law School has considerable legitimacy, which makes it more difficult for men at her law firm to challenge her abilities and reduces their interest in trying to doing so. In chapter 3, "The Rising (and Then Declining) Significance of Gender," Claudia Goldin proposes a "pollution theory" of discrimination in which men in high-status segregated occupations are concerned that the prestige of their occupations would be "polluted" by the entry of women, who are presumed to be less qualified.[11] Just as residents of high-status, all-white neighborhoods are often concerned that property values will fall when African

Americans move in, male incumbents of traditionally male high-status occupations may be concerned about the effects of gender integration on the prestige of their "occupational neighborhood." This so-called polluting effect may be at least partially countered if formal credentials serve to certify that newly entering women are as qualified as their male counterparts (see chapter 3, this volume). If bureaucratization does in fact increase credential-based hiring and promotion, one can conclude that it could undermine the perceived polluting effect of women and allow integration to occur more readily.

Finally, we note that the organizational narrative, like the economic narrative, can be embellished with feedback effects. Indeed, whenever there is an equalization in the payoff to male and female human capital, the incentive for women to invest in such capital increases. This dynamic plays out regardless of whether the macro-level source of changing payoffs is economic competition or the diffusion of bureaucratic personnel systems. Two types of feedback effects should emerge: the reduction in discrimination that bureaucratization engenders should trigger an increase in human-capital investments by women and an associated decline in occupational sex segregation and in the pay gap (see table 1.1, line E1); and the bureaucracy-induced equalization in the human-capital payoffs for women and men diminishes the rationale for a domestic division of labor (line C1). The organizational narrative is therefore a powerful story that is consistent with many of the same proximate processes that have conventionally been associated with the economic narrative.

Limitations

The organizational narrative arguably has an internal logic as compelling as that of the economic narrative. Just as the economic narrative marches ineluctably forward once one conditions on a competitive market, so too the organizational narrative plays out quite straightforwardly insofar as organizational change takes the simple form of bureaucratization. The main critiques, therefore, of the organizational narrative involve questioning whether bureacratization of this simple type is indeed in ascendancy. In reviewing these critiques, we may distinguish in particular between impediments to equalization that emerge within bureaucratized workplaces and those that emerge within newer or smaller organizational settings that have not been bureaucratized.

Within bureaucratized workplaces, there is ongoing debate as to what constitutes modern and legitimate organizational forms, and the particular vision of "bureaucracy" featured in the conventional organizational narrative is surely not the only possible vision. There is in fact a tension between bureaucratic visions in which all forms of gender inequality are regarded as illegitimate and those in which gender inequality is deemed acceptable insofar as it is efficient. Although the organizational narrative outlined above presumes that the first vision is dominant (implying, for example, that statistical discrimination based on correct perceptions of gender differences will come to be delegitimated), it is hardly obvious that this vision of equity will triumph over those that instead permit gender inequality whenever it is—or is perceived to be—efficient.

This contest between competing visions is revealed when one considers the gender inequality that internal labor markets (ILMs) typically produce. In an ideal-typical ILM, the main prerequisite for promotion is accumulating relevant firm-specific human capital (for example, performing feeder jobs), and men will typically accumulate such capital more quickly than women because they are freed from pregnancy, childrearing, and other domestic work that have historically tended to lead to women's intermittent labor supply. The question here is whether the resulting gender inequality will be delegitimated, even though it is presumably efficient. In the standard organizational narrative, a radically egalitarian vision is assumed to be diffusing in ways that delegitimate such inequality and motivate efforts to overcome it. But there is also much cultural support for an alternative bureaucratic vision that enshrines efficiency and treats all inequality emanating from an efficiency imperative as wholly unproblematic. This efficiency rationale is therefore an inertial force that reduces support for certain types of equality-enhancing organizational reform.

Meanwhile, some forms of inefficiency that clearly disadvantage women may nonetheless persist because they are subtle, difficult to detect, and hence unlikely to be exposed to challenge. The formally gender-neutral regulations, procedures, and institutions within bureaucratized settings may offer ample room for informal decision making that remains gender-biased (Baron 1984). For example, bureaucratic rules about open job posting and hiring can create the appearance of gender-neutral competition, but the actual hiring and promotion decisions that are made within this context may not be truly gender-neutral. We do not mean to suggest that managers and other decision makers merely "go through the motions" of open competition, but in the end cynically make decisions that are consistent with their overt tastes for discrimination. Rather, the typical mechanism is likely less Machiavellian than this, with managers discriminating in subtle and unconscious ways that proceed from deeply internalized essentialist presumptions about the types of jobs for which men and women are best qualified. Because subtle and unconscious forms of discrimination are difficult to detect and prove, further progress in combatting these residual forms of discrimination may occur less rapidly than in the past, when efforts could be focused on more obvious and overt forms.

These subtle processes also appear in more dynamic organizational settings in which bureaucratic forms have yet to emerge or are undergoing change. As Cecilia Ridgeway (chapter 9, this volume) points out, modern bureaucratization remains limited in its reach, given that contemporary economies are highly dynamic and that new organizations and occupations are constantly being formed. The dynamism of modern economies may in some cases generate increasing elaboration, specialization, and differentiation within the division of labor, leading to the creation of new jobs that are subdivisions of older ones. How are these subdivisions implemented? Although this topic remains underresearched (for one of the few studies, see Reskin and Roos 1990), we suspect that at least on occasion the new subdivisions are defined upon partly essentialist lines, with the "essentially female" aspects of the old job amalgamated into one subclass of occupations and the "essentially male" aspects of the old job amalgamated into another subclass of occupations. For example, the occupation of lawyer was once quite undifferentiated, but it has gradually subdivided into a host of specializations. As women streamed into this occupation, they appear to have moved disproportionately into various "essentially female" specializations, such as family law.[12] In this particular case, the occupation differentiated in advance of the encroachment of women, although it is possible that some types of differentiation among lawyers emerged in part as a response to the influx of women.

If segregative processes of this sort are more generally at work, they would be operating on the margins of a larger pattern of quite significant occupational integration over the last half-century (Blau, Simpson, and Anderson 1998; Charles and Grusky 2004). We believe that such integrative trends will continue as a result of the various proximate processes outlined in table 1.1 and discussed here. In noting that countervailing forces are also at work, we are pointing out that the proximate processes itemized in table 1.1 do not operate altogether unopposed, that the occupational gender segregation that remains may be actively generated by essentialist and other processes, and that one cannot treat it as a simple residue of old institutional practices that will quietly fade away.

THE POLITICAL NARRATIVE

In turning to the political narrative, we shift the focus to collective action that is explicitly oriented toward changing the laws, institutions, and norms that govern labor-market practices. We again lead off by outlining how gender inequality may be reduced through political action and then follow up with a discussion of the complexities and limitations of the political narrative.

The Positive Case

While economic and organizational narratives treat change in gender inequality as an unintended by-product of macro-level forces, political narratives concern instrumental action that is explicitly oriented toward effecting a decline in gender inequality. In theory, such political action could engage any of the proximate mechanisms listed in table 1.1, but historically the main emphasis has been on legislation aimed at reducing the three types of discrimination listed in lines A1 to A3. The United States implemented its antidiscrimination legislation before most other advanced industrial countries (Blau and Kahn 2003) and may therefore be viewed as the home ground of the political narrative. The centerpiece of this legislative approach has of course been title VII of the Civil Rights Act of 1964. As noted previously, the evidence strongly suggests that the federal government's antidiscrimination effort has played a role in reducing gender inequality in the labor market.

The federal government's effort has been driven primarily by an emphasis on equal opportunity rather than the equalization of outcomes. The main possible exception to this generalization is affirmative action, which has been defined as "proactive steps . . . to erase differences between women and men, minorities and nonminorities, etc." in the labor market (Holzer and Neumark 2000, 484). The affirmative-action approach may be contrasted with laws and regulations that solely require employers not to discriminate against these groups. However, affirmative action is legally required under quite limited circumstances, generally as a result of the implementation of an executive order impacting government contractors and very occasionally as part of a court order in cases where employers have lost or settled discrimination suits. Although some commentators argue that affirmative action leads to inefficient and nonmeritocratic hiring and promotion decisions, in fact the available evidence strongly suggests that such claims are off the mark and that so-called "reverse discrimination" is not widespread in the labor market (Holzer and Neumark 2000).

If anti-discrimination legislation constitutes a major political success of the late twentieth century, comparable-worth initiatives have fared considerably less well. These initiatives are directed at equalizing pay for predominantly male and predominantly female occupations that are deemed to have comparable skill requirements. The pay differences that motivate comparable-worth initiatives potentially arise from a number of sources:

1. Employers may exclude women from higher-paying male jobs and relegate them to female occupations that are relatively poorly paid because of the resulting "overcrowding" and wage competition (Bergmann 1974).

2. A preference among women for "female" occupations and among men for "male" occupations has the effect of crowding women into relatively few occupations and thereby lowering their wages.

3. Employers may undervalue and underpay female-dominated occupations because they internalize the societal assumption that any task assigned to women cannot be very important or useful (table 1.1, line D2; see England 1992).

4. Higher pay in predominantly male jobs may also reflect compensation for higher skills, longer or more complicated training, or less favorable working conditions.

The last mentioned cause of pay differentials is deemed legitimate by most advocates of comparable worth and is not the target of equalization efforts. The objective of comparable-worth reform is instead to equalize pay in male-dominated and female-dominated occupations that are *equivalent* in skill demands, training requirements, and working conditions. Despite the best efforts of comparable-worth advocates to control for such variables, it is always possible that the metric through which "comparability" is ascertained is flawed and that pay differences that are judged to be problematic under this metric are in fact attributable to differences in skill, training, or working conditions (Polachek 1981; Macpherson and Hirsch 1995).

Whatever the sources of the pay gap, the objective of comparable-worth remediation is to achieve pay parity without the necessity of eliminating occupational segregation. This form of remediation has been proposed as a legal interpretation of title VII of the Civil Rights Act of 1964, but such an interpretation has not been ratified by the Supreme Court, which has not issued a definitive ruling on the matter. Nor is there much evidence that comparable worth has been widely adopted in the private sector, although some state and local governments have implemented or begun to implement some version of it.[13] In addition, some unions, particularly those in the public sector, have pressed for pay equity as a collective-bargaining demand.

There has also been some political work oriented toward establishing family-friendly programs as a type of "workplace adaptation" (line C2). As suggested previously, such family-friendly policies may spread not only because of the economic payoff associated with them but also because political pressure on behalf of these policies is brought to bear on firms, either through explicit laws mandating these policies or in the form of more diffuse public opinion. In the end, this political effect may be partly mediated through economic incentives, as firms presumably factor in the cost of violating the law or inflaming public opinion in deciding how and in what ways to modify their personnel practices. It is useful to distinguish between cost calculations that reflect the political climate firms face and thus are part of the political narrative and those that reflect more narrowly drawn concerns about attracting and motivating the best workers, implicating the economic narrative.

Although the United States has been an innovator in antidiscrimination legislation, it has lagged behind its counterparts abroad in implementing other types of organizational reform. By international standards, the United States has a relatively weak entitlement to parental leave: a federally mandated twelve-week unpaid leave, introduced in 1993. In contrast, other OECD (Organization of Economic Cooperation and Development) countries implemented mandated leave earlier and most have a much longer period of leave, usually paid (Ruhm 1998). Similarly, the United States tends to have a smaller share of young children in publicly funded child care than many other OECD countries, although it does provide relatively generous tax relief for child-care expenses (Gornick, Meyers, and Ross 1997).

Like the economic and organizational narratives, the political narrative encompasses a number of unintended feedback effects, but in this case such effects may play out in inequality-enhancing ways. Three classes of unintended effects are of special interest here. First, Eva M. Meyersson Milgrom and Trond Petersen (chapter 6, this volume) point out that family-friendly programs not only ease the work-family conflict for currently employed workers but also may motivate new workers with substantial child-care responsibilities to enter the formal labor force. As family-friendly programs diffuse, the female labor force may therefore become less stringently culled, with women's labor-market outcomes suffering on average as a result. Second, if firms implement "comparable-worth" adjustments to their pay scales, occupational segregation could intensify as improved pay encourages women to remain in female-typed occupations. In theory, men should also be attracted to the increasing pay of female-typed occupations, yet the evidence suggests that they are more resistant to entering such occupations than women are to entering male-typed occupations (see chapter 8, this volume). Third, if government-mandated policies such as parental leave raise the costs of labor beyond any increase in benefits to the firm, employers could seek to avoid these costs by discriminating against women at the point of hiring.[14]

In all three cases, the core problem is that policy interventions can have inconsistent effects on the various outcomes of interest, increasing inequality on some outcomes, such as choice of occupation, while diminishing inequality on others, such as pay. This means that it is impossible to make good policy recommendations without first settling on some master metric that establishes how much of a loss on one dimension should be exchanged for a gain on another (see Bourguignon 2006). Moreover, a further challenge arises because policy decisions are often gradational rather than binary in character, meaning that potentially consequential judgments about the size or extent of the program must be made. For example, mandating long parental leave that is generously remunerated by the employer could end up being a significant deterrent to hiring women into highly responsible positions, whereas the hiring deterrent under more modest mandates might be offset by the benefits of promoting women's attachment to the firm and the enhanced investment in firm-specific skills that may result.

In reality, it is unlikely that the success of political reform depends entirely on its costs and benefits. Instead, the outcome of reform efforts probably depends at least in part on the actions of powerful actors, such as politicians and capitalists, who presumably attend to their own interests as well as to those of the larger collectivity. According to Jackson (chapter 7, this volume), inequality-reducing political reform has been successful because males as a group are no longer deeply committed to their privileged status and have not exerted themselves in its defense. We will argue below that the success of such reform is also due to cultural changes that affect the tastes and interests of women as well as men.

Limitations

The reach of political reform in the United States has been limited by its liberal egalitarian premises. As noted, political activism in the United States has focused on equalizing opportunities (access) rather than outcomes (wages), meaning that little reform effort has been targeted toward either equalizing the aspirations of men and women or equalizing their pay. The main objective of reform has been to reduce discrimination in employment, an objective that is consistent with liberal egalitarianism. If government intervention continues to be oriented toward reducing discrimination, the pace of future declines in inequality may gradually slow as the residual of discrimination-induced inequality grows ever smaller and more difficult to address due to the increasingly subtle and even unconscious form contemporary discrimination is likely to take. It follows that upward trends in gender equality may stall because reform remains oriented toward sources of gender inequality that are becoming less important and increasingly hard to identify.

How might this pessimistic view be countered? First, it is possible that reform efforts focused on employment discrimination will have a "jump-starting" effect, triggering changes in human-capital investments and the domestic division of labor. The "benign circle" that we outlined earlier implies that reductions in discrimination will encourage further shifts in the amount and type of women's human-capital investments and promote continued reallocation of household responsibilities between partners. It follows that a relatively small intervention at any point in the circle could precipitate self-generating change.

Second, political reform may develop in new, more ambitious ways that create momentum for change. Although liberal egalitarianism undergirds most contemporary reform efforts, it is not outside the realm of possibility that other logics may ultimately come to the fore and provide an expanded foundation for reform. The ongoing public interest in the gender pay gap is suggestive in this regard because it does not seem to stand or fall on any complicated analysis of whether the gap is attributable to employment discrimination or other conventional targets of liberal egalitarian reform. Rather, at least some of the interest in the pay gap appears to signal a more generic concern with inequalities in *outcome*, no matter how such inequalities have been generated. This generic interest in the pay gap motivates the research of Heidi Hartmann, Stephen J. Rose, and Vicky Lovell (see chapter 5, this volume).

In the past, such interest in unequal outcomes has been the impetus for comparable-worth initiatives intended to eliminate, by legal or organizational fiat, inequalities of pay prevailing between comparable male-typed and female-typed occupations. As stated, the comparable-worth effort did not meet with much legal support in the past, nor are there any obvious signs of revived support for it. If there is growing public attention to unequal outcomes in the future, we suspect that it will instead lead to increased political support for workplace adaptations that go beyond conventional antidiscrimination guarantees.

THE CULTURAL NARRATIVE(S)

The cultural narrative rests on the argument that egalitarian beliefs are grounded in Western ideals of justice and equality that continue to be endogenously worked out through a cultural logic that to some extent operates independently of the economic efficiency of such ideals. These ideals may lead to increasing "tastes" for equality and for egalitarian practices, tastes that might at the limit be honored in the labor market even with some loss in profits or efficiency.

The Positive Case

The cultural narrative thus makes tastes endogenous to fundamental cultural forces. Although none of our contributors outlines a cultural narrative in such stark terms, Robert Max Jackson's line of argument (chapter 7) hinges on changes in cultural expectations of this general sort. Similarly, Solomon W. Polachek (chapter 4) suggests that "societal discrimination" may ultimately weaken, not because of the economic costs of discrimination but because of egalitarian cultural change that erodes the conventional domestic division of labor.

The cultural narrative can be straightforwardly distinguished from the economic narrative because tastes are not presumed to change merely because of the cost of exercising discriminatory tastes. Likewise, the cultural narrative is distinct from the organizational narrative by virtue of focusing on the spread of tastes for equality and equality-enhancing practices, not the spread of organizational forms such as bureaucratization that are deemed efficient, normatively desirable, or both. In the last analysis, the diffusion of organizational forms and practices may be understood in cultural terms, yet the "culture" that is diffusing is principally a story about the efficiency or normative desirability of bureaucracy. The cultural narrative, by contrast, pertains to the diffusion of tastes for equality rather than the diffusion of beliefs about the efficiency of bureaucracy.

The cultural and political narratives are closely related because political commitments to equal opportunity, affirmative action, and comparable worth may be partly motivated by tastes for equality. The political narrative may ultimately be driven by these more fundamental cultural forces. At the same time, the cultural commitment to equality is not expressed exclusively in political terms but in addition is expressed in the attitudes and behaviors of family members as well as of workers and employers in the labor market. We focus here on these extra-political effects of cultural change.

The cultural narrative is revealed in the diffusion of egalitarian beliefs across a wide range of work and family attitudes. There are four classes of attitudes that may be particularly susceptible to such egalitarianism:

1. *Increasing tastes for equality.* Employers may gradually shed their preferences for certain categories of labor and instead develop tastes for equality in hiring and promotion.

2. *Declining beliefs in pollution.* Male workers may become less likely to believe that an occupation is devalued or polluted when women enter it.[15]

3. *Declining beliefs in female domesticity.* Men and women may become less likely to support a division of labor in which women are responsible for domestic duties and men work in the external labor market.

4. *Decline in occupational essentialism.* Men and women may be viewed as less likely to have fundamentally different talents and abilities.

Whereas the economic, organizational, and political narratives are largely driven by demand-side mechanisms, the distinctive feature of cultural egalitarianism is that it partly operates on the supply side as well. In particular, weakening beliefs in "female domesticity" should orient women increasingly to the external labor market and motivate them to invest in *more* human capital, while the decline in "essentialist beliefs" should motivate them to invest increasingly in the *same types* of human capital as men.

We will discuss each of these four classes of effects. The first two demand-side effects need not be covered in great detail, as the mechanisms are straightforward and have already been discussed. We led off this section by noting that various forms of labor-market discrimination against women should become less prominent (see lines A1 to A3) as tastes for equality diffuse and employers become increasingly wed to egalitarianism, shed their preferences for certain classes of labor, and come to question institutionalized practices that privilege men in hiring and promotion. Likewise, when employers and managers become more egalitarian, they may wish to actualize this commitment through various workplace adaptations such as maternity leave, family leave, and child-care subsidies (line C2). The presumed polluting effect of women (discussed in chapter 3) should also be undermined by the diffusion of egalitarian views. When women are increasingly regarded as the status equals of men, their entry into an occupation no longer pollutes it and should therefore be met with less opposition on the part of male incumbents (line D1).

The supply-side aspects of the cultural account are more complicated and are best understood by reviewing the conventional wisdom on how cultural beliefs about gender differences have historically served to maintain gender inequality (see especially Marini and Brinton 1984). It has long been argued that stereotypes about natural male and female characteristics are disseminated and perpetuated through popular culture and the media, through social interaction in which significant others—parents, peers, and teachers—implicitly or explicitly support such stereotypes, and through cognitive processes in which individuals pursue and remember evidence that is consistent with their preexisting stereotypes and ignore, discount, or forget evidence that undermines them (Fiske 1998; Reskin 2000). As children grow up, they internalize the sex-typed expectations of others and convert these expectations into durable sex-typed aspirations and preferences, some of which operate at the subconscious level. For example, when girls internalize essentialist stereotypes that associate males with mathematical ability, they become less likely to prefer and aspire to work that utilizes such skills, to embark on the requisite training for such work, or to persist in such work in the face of difficulties. This line of argument presumes that gender-specific preferences become internalized in childhood, affect subsequent investment decisions and aspirations, and form a stable component of the adult personality (Parsons and Bales 1955; Chodorow 1978; Bourdieu 2001).

How does the diffusion of cultural egalitarianism break down such supply-side mechanisms? As cultural egalitarianism spreads, women and men are increasingly assumed to have the same rights, responsibilities, and abilities, thereby weakening conventional stereotypes about male-female difference. This new worldview affects individual cognition and ultimately is embodied in individual action. As a result, judgments about the proper balance between market labor and domestic labor become more similar across genders (line C1), and the types of occupations to which men and women aspire likewise become more similar (line B1).

The diffusion of egalitarianism may also affect how workers come to understand their skills and abilities (line B2). As Shelley J. Correll (2001) elegantly demonstrates, women tend to regard themselves as less competent than men at male-typed tasks, even when, objectively measured, they are just as competent (see also chapter 9, this volume). This implies that women will eschew male-typed work not only because they find it less desirable or appropriate but also because they believe that they are less competent at it. Even in the absence of sex-specific preferences, internalized beliefs about gender differences in ability can result in biased self-evaluations of performance, thereby contributing to segregation. The diffusion of egalitarian views implies that such gender-biased judgments about competence should gradually break down.[16]

The usual feedback effects should also be relevant here. Whether change is generated by the economic costs of discrimination (the economic narrative), the diffusion of bureaucratic organization (the organizational narrative), or the diffusion of egalitarian beliefs (the cultural narrative), women should come to anticipate less discrimination in the workplace. As women anticipate that the workplace will better reward their human capital, they are motivated to invest in more of it (line E1), thus diminishing the rationale for the traditional division of labor in the family (line C1).

Although this "discrimination-reduction" feedback effect pertains to all narratives, we have noted in table 1.1 that the cultural narrative generates an additional form of feedback distinctive to that narrative (line E2). When egalitarian views are embraced by parents, coworkers, and friends as well as by managers, this has far-reaching effects on the wider "cultural climate" within which women and men make decisions about the amount and type of human capital to acquire. This is important because workers who transgress norms about gender-appropriate labor have historically been subjected to informal sanctions (Goffman 1977; West and Zimmerman 1987; Fenstermaker and West 2002). For example, parents may disapprove of their son's wishes to become a nurse, or construction workers may harass a female entrant. These sanctions come to be anticipated and thus shape individual aspirations, preferences, and human-capital investments (see Kanter 1977). The historic staying power and perniciousness of gender essentialism can be attributed in part to such sanctions; indeed, even individuals who disavow conventional gender norms may find themselves taking them into account, given that they perceive that others still embrace them and may impose sanctions against "gender egalitarians" (see Fenstermaker and West 2002, 29–30). Insofar as cultural egalitarianism begins to take hold, such sanctions should occur less frequently, and individuals should be able to make decisions about their lives without taking sanctions as much into account.

The diffusion of egalitarianism may therefore have far-reaching effects that operate via all of the proximate mechanisms outlined in table 1.1. In evaluating this narrative, a crucial question is whether it comes packaged with a diffusion mechanism that is as plausible as those underlying other narratives, especially the economic one. The latter narrative rests on two assumptions: that at least some gender-egalitarian practices, such as a reduction in pure discrimination, are efficient, and that a competitive market will gradually select for such efficient practices. We have noted that one can reasonably question either of these assumptions, but the mechanism is at least well specified.

Does the cultural narrative have such an elegant mechanism of diffusion? This question becomes especially important if predictions about the future are sought. There is much evidence that overtly racist or sexist ideologies have been discredited over the last half-century, but this trend cannot be convincingly projected into the future without some mechanism suggesting a self-perpetuating dynamic. The conventional view in this regard is that a series of crucial historical events—the Enlightenment, the defeat of Nazism, the civil rights movement—have served to define equality as one of our core cultural commitments. Absent some revolutionary event that changes this cultural trajectory, the course of human history becomes the "working out" of this commitment, a task that involves shedding subsidiary values, such as the "freedom" to discriminate, that sometimes come into conflict with our deeper commitment to egalitarianism. This deepening of our core commitment to equality takes the form not merely of increasing the number of groups to which guarantees of equality are extended (gays, people with disabilities, AIDS patients) but also of devising reforms that better realize these guarantees. The core mechanism that drives cultural diffusion may therefore be understood as the gradual "reconciling" of competing values to a new value—equality—that has been elevated by one or more historical events to a position of prominence.

Limitations

Within the cultural domain, the diffusion of egalitarianism is an extremely important development, one that will likely continue apace unless some unforeseen catastrophic event induces us to rethink our core cultural commitments. Although the future of egalitarianism appears bright, it is well to consider the limits of the particular version of egalitarianism that has taken hold and that continues to diffuse. Among the many competing egalitarian visions, it is clear that "liberal egalitarian" strands remain dominant, implying that our collective commitment to gender equality mainly takes the form of developing procedural guarantees of equal opportunity. This commitment to liberal egalitarianism is quite compatible with the essentialist presumption that men and women have fundamentally different tastes, skills, and abilities (see Charles and Grusky 2004).[17] That is, liberal egalitarianism represents women and men as autonomous agents entitled to equal opportunities and treatment, not as socially or culturally constructed agents. The centrality of autonomy within this vision allows for the persistence of fundamentally gendered outlooks and identities. For a liberal egalitarian, it is enough to defend the right of women to fairly compete for any occupation to which they aspire, without questioning how those aspirations were formed or why they may differ from the aspirations of men. It follows that liberal egalitarians may embrace an "equal but (potentially) different" conceptualization of gender and social justice.

If this version of egalitarianism continues to diffuse, the push toward complete equality may be slowed. This suppressive effect occurs through proximate mechanisms on both the supply and demand sides. On the supply side, we cannot expect liberal egalitarians to attend much to individual aspirations (line B1) and self-assessments (line B2), meaning that the persistence of gender differences in these outlooks and identities will not be scrutinized or challenged to the extent that they would under more radical egalitarian commitments. On the demand side, the liberal egalitarian commitment delegitimates all forms of pure discrimination (lines A1, A3) but it does not as directly challenge statistical discrimination that rests on essentialist presumptions (line A2). In a world in which women have disproportionately "invested" in nurturance and service, essentialist presumptions about gender differences in capabilities have ample room to flourish and statistical discrimination may well continue.

The key question is whether competing strands of egalitarianism that do take issue with such essentialist presumptions will gradually call into question the processes by which women and men come to develop different tastes. Within some circles, parents clearly feel obliged to convey to their female children that they have every right, perhaps even an obligation, to pursue conventionally male-typed professions, such as scientist or mathematician.[18] Although less likely, it is also possible that grassroots reform efforts designed to counter the presumptions of essentialist ideologies will gain support. There is indeed some evidence of such efforts:

1. It is increasingly common for primary schools to adopt curricula that call essentialist assumptions into question. We are referring, for example, to primers that feature girls in conventionally male-typed roles.

2. Federal programs have been developed to encourage women to enter engineering, mathematics, and other stereotypically male pursuits. These programs include the NASA Federal Women's Program and the National Science Foundation Program for Gender Equity in Science, Mathematics, Engineering, and Technology.

3. The mass media depict an increasingly complicated world in which women are sometimes assigned roles that break the rules of essentialism (police detectives, surgeons, warriors), though of course they also continue to be conventionally cast as secretaries, nurses, and teachers.

These developments suggest that a new anti-essentialist logic may ultimately emerge to challenge or at least supplement liberal egalitarianism. For this reason, and no doubt many others, the gender gap in aspirations is clearly narrowing (see, for instance, Jacobs 2003). Despite these hints of change, it is still striking that essentialist ideologies appear to have a continuing appeal for many people, which may hamper further change in occupational segregation and in the gender pay gap. As we see it, gender inequality is not simply another form of ascription destined to wither away as cultural egalitarianism spreads (see Parsons 1970), but instead is a very special form distinguished by the durability of its essentialist legitimation.

CONCLUSION

We have sought to show that most analyses of gender inequality place emphasis on proximate mechanisms of change and stability and pay relatively little attention to the macro-level forces that generate change in the proximate mechanisms themselves. When macro-level forces are recognized or invoked, the tendency is to work within the context of a single narrative, thus privileging a limited set of proximate mechanisms. We have expanded the analysis of gender inequality by distinguishing among a number of narratives of change and showing how they rely upon different constellations of proximate mechanisms.

This approach generates a richer picture of the underlying sources of past change and the prospects for future progress. In particular, it suggests that the future of gender inequality rests on a struggle between egalitarian and essentialist forces that is not quite as one-sided as theorists focusing on a narrower set of mechanisms have sometimes claimed. To be sure, powerful macro-level forces have fueled a spectacular revolution over the last half-century, and these forces continue to work to undermine gender inequality. The importance of these forces cannot be overstated, yet further declines in gender inequality may be more difficult to secure and may play out more slowly. Almost by definition, the easier gains have now been achieved and the securing of additional gains may require more fundamental changes in essentialist practices and ideologies. Rather than viewing gender inequality as an ascriptive residual that withers away under egalitarian pressures, it is best regarded as an organic feature of modern economies that is in some respects ideologically consistent with egalitarianism, at least as the latter is understood and practiced today.

At minimum, we are suggesting that simple extrapolations of past trends should be avoided, since it is at least possible that the mechanisms underlying those trends will have a diminished role in the future. This perspective does not imply that future change is necessarily stalemated. If the pessimistic view is that easy reductions in equality have already been "creamed off," the optimistic view envisions self-reinforcing "feedback effects" in which early positive interventions gain momentum over time. In this benign circle, reduced discrimination is one of the main triggers that brings about initial labor-market gains for women, gains that then encourage further shifts in the amount and type of women's human-capital investments as well as continued reallocation of household responsibilities between partners. At the same time, cultural shifts promoting gender equality and an expansion of women's roles may impact the supply side, contributing to increases in women's human-capital acquisition and a reduction in gender specialization within the family. These changes would encourage further reductions in barriers to women in the labor market by eroding the rationale behind statistical discrimination. Are these types of triggers powerful enough to overcome the essentialist values that support the domestic division of labor and gender-specific human-capital investments? This question, which reemerges throughout the book, obviously remains an open one.

The future of gender inequality is further complicated because it is deeply affected by a variety of indirect forces that we have not emphasized. We have mainly focused on social change that operates relatively directly on gender inequality. Often, factors impacting women's outcomes may be indirect in the sense that change occurs as an unintended, latent consequence of changes in seemingly unrelated social domains (see chapters 2 and 7, this volume). For example, economic forces may disproportionately expand occupational sectors in which women happen to be concentrated, such as the service sector. This sectoral shift can generate an increased demand for female labor and corresponding changes in rates of female labor-force participation and pay (see especially Oppenheimer 1970/1976; Goldin 1990; chapter 2 in this volume). As another example, Francine D. Blau and Lawrence M. Kahn show in chapter 2 that the returns to labor-force experience increased over the 1980s, disadvantaging women because they have less experience on average than men. In each of the foregoing cases, the causal forces—labor demand shifts, changing returns to experience—are nominally gender-indifferent, yet they nonetheless have unintended effects on the rates of female labor-force participation and the pay gap between men and women.

The chapters in this book present a set of nuanced arguments addressing the issues we have reviewed in this introduction. The lines of evidence and debate presented in these pages are intended to stimulate readers to think more deeply and in new ways about the extent to which gender will or will not remain a major fault line of inequality in the decades to come. It is our hope that the book will contribute to informed and far-ranging discussions about how gender inequality is generated, sustained, and ultimately altered.

NOTES

1. See also Kenneth Arrow (1973). Although Becker's work dealt with race discrimination, the preceding discussion reflects what is usually viewed as a reasonable extension of his analysis to other groups, such as women, who might also encounter discrimination.
2. We can characterize an organizational practice as "efficient" when it maximizes profits, market share, or some other standard economic outcome.
3. The statistical discrimination model may be elaborated to allow for the possibility that productivity is less reliably predicted for women than for men. In the interest of simplicity, we do not consider that alternative here, though we note that Dennis J. Aigner

and Glen G. Cain (1977) do not regard it as a likely source of large and persistent discriminatory wage differentials.

4. In the presence of feedback effects, initial differences based on erroneous perceptions may become self-fulfilling and be perpetuated (Arrow 1973; Lundberg and Startz 1983). When women realize that employers would under-reward their human capital, their incentive to invest in it is diminished, even if that under-reward is based on erroneous perceptions. It follows that competitive forces may not eliminate even that form of statistical discrimination based on (initially) erroneous perceptions.

5. The term "family-friendly" should probably be understood as a code for "women-friendly" (see Glass 2004).

6. It is important to note that not all efficient workplace adaptations necessarily promote gender equality in the workplace or the family. For example, if it proves efficient to institute dead-end "mommy tracks," market forces will operate to produce greater inequality between men and women within the firms instituting such tracking practices.

7. Prior to the 1950s, "marriage bars" frequently excluded married women from employment in clerical and teaching positions, a practice that Goldin (1990) argues could be compatible with profit maximization to the extent that marriage reduced female productivity, and employers found it costly to alter employment practices and wages of individual workers on a discretionary basis.

8. This "embedding" of discrimination in a social context plays out in various ways. For example, Blau and Kahn (2000) present evidence that, in many European countries where unions and the government play a large role in wage setting, the gender pay gap may be reduced by the resulting overall wage compression.

9. For a summary of the evidence on gender, see Francine D. Blau, Marianne A. Ferber, and Anne E. Winkler (2002, 242–46). John J. Donohue and James J. Heckman (1991) make an especially powerful case for the dramatic impact of these laws and regulations on black-white differentials.

10. The rise of internal labor markets (ILMs) can of course have countervailing effects that deeply disadvantage women. We discuss these effects in the next section.

11. For a fuller elaboration of the model, see Goldin (2002).

12. There are two competing hypotheses about how segregation comes to be expressed at detailed occupational levels. Although we are arguing here that women tend to be drawn into "essentially female" specializations, the obvious competing argument is that they are sent into specializations that are less desirable in terms of income and other rewards, and then these specializations become typed as "essentially female" after the fact. We are not aware of research that convincingly adjudicates between these two interpretations.

13. It has been reported that eight states have fully implemented a pay-equity plan and all but five states have initiated some degree of pay-equity activity such as salary increases for female-dominated or minority-dominated job categories. For example, see Susan E. Gardner and Christopher Daniel (1998), as cited in Michael Baker and Nicole M. Fortin (2000).

14. Christopher J. Ruhm and Jacqueline L. Teague (1997) note, however, that mandated programs may be efficient if information about benefit usage is intrinsically asymmet-

ric. For example, firms that voluntarily provide a benefit such as parental leave will disproportionately attract workers who have a high probability of utilizing it, increasing costs to these firms. Because of this adverse selection problem, such policies may be underprovided when offered voluntarily, making government-mandated interventions attractive.

15. George A. Akerlof and Rachel E. Kranton (2000) present a model in which occupations are associated with societal notions of male and female, leading men to resist the entry of women into their area of work because of the loss in male identity or sense of self that this would entail. A growing cultural commitment to gender equality is also likely to weaken this motivation for the exclusion of women.

16. The experimental evidence of "stereotype threat" also suggests that negative perceptions of the abilities of women and minorities can adversely affect their performance (see, for example, Steven J. Spencer, Claude M. Steele, and Diane M. Quinn 1999). We obviously would not claim that gender-biased assessments of self-competence are so powerful as to *preclude* women from working in male-typed pursuits. Clearly, many women do work in male-typed occupations, although presumably fewer do so than would be the case if the processes identified by Correll (2001) and Spencer, Steele, and Quinn (1999) were not at work.

17. The standard version of such essentialism regards women as especially skilled in nurturing and interpersonal tasks and men as especially skilled in physical, analytical, and technical tasks.

18. It is rather less common, we suspect, for parents to instruct their male children that female-typed occupations are worth pursuing (see chapter 9, this volume, on the "asymmetry" of change).

REFERENCES

Aigner, Dennis J., and Glen G. Cain. 1977. "Statistical Theories of Discrimination in Labor Markets." *Industrial and Labor Relations Review* 30(2): 175–87.

Akerlof, George A., and Rachel E. Kranton. 2000. "Economics and Identity." *Quarterly Journal of Economics* 115(3): 715–53.

Arrow, Kenneth. 1973. "The Theory of Discrimination." In *Discrimination in Labor Markets*, edited by Orley Ashenfelter and Albert Rees. Princeton: Princeton University Press.

Baker, Michael, and Nicole M. Fortin. 2000. "Does Comparable Worth Work in a Decentralized Labor Market?" NBER Working Paper No. 7937. Washington, D.C.: National Bureau of Economic Research (October).

Barash, Susan Shapiro. 2004. *The New Wife: The Evolving Role of the American Wife*. Lenexa, Kans.: Nonetheless Press.

Baron, James N. 1984. "Organizational Perspectives on Stratification." *Annual Review of Sociology* 10: 37–69.

Becker, Gary S. 1957/1971. *The Economics of Discrimination*. 2nd edition. Chicago: University of Chicago Press.

Bergmann, Barbara R. 1974. "Occupational Segregation, Wages and Profits When Employers Discriminate by Race or Sex." *Eastern Economic Journal* 1(1 and 2): 103–10.

Black, Dan A. 1995. "Discrimination in an Equilibrium Search Model." *Journal of Labor Economics* 13(2): 309–34.

Blau, Francine D. 1977. *Equal Pay in the Office*. Lexington, Mass.: Lexington Books.

———. 1998. "Trends in the Well-being of American Women, 1970–1995." *Journal of Economic Literature* 36(1): 112–65.

Blau, Francine D., Marianne A. Ferber, and Anne E. Winkler. 2002. *The Economics of Women, Men, and Work*. 4th edition. Upper Saddle River, N.J.: Prentice-Hall.

Blau, Francine D., and Lawrence M. Kahn. 2000. "Gender Differences in Pay." *Journal of Economic Perspectives* 14(4): 75–99.

———. 2003. "Understanding International Differences in the Gender Pay Gap." *Journal of Labor Economics* 21(1): 106–44.

Blau, Francine D., Patricia Simpson, and Deborah Anderson. 1998. "Continuing Progress? Trends in Occupational Segregation over the 1970s and 1980s." *Feminist Economics* 4(3): 29–71.

Bourdieu, Pierre. 2001. *Masculine Domination*. Cambridge: Polity Press.

Bourguignon, François. 2006. "From Income to Endowments: The Difficult Task of Expanding the Income Poverty Paradigm." In *Conceptual Challenges in the Study of Poverty and Inequality*, edited by David B. Grusky and Ravi Kanbur. Palo Alto: Stanford University Press.

Charles, Maria, and David B. Grusky. 2004. *Occupational Ghettos: The Worldwide Segregation of Women and Men*. Palo Alto: Stanford University Press.

Chodorow, Nancy J. 1978. *The Reproduction of Mothering: Psychoanalysis and the Sociology of Gender*. Berkeley: University of California Press.

Correll, Shelley J. 2001. "Gender and the Career Choice Process: The Role of Biased Self-Assessments." *American Journal of Sociology* 106(6): 1691–1730.

DiMaggio, Paul, and Walter W. Powell. 1983. "The Iron Cage Revisited: Institutional Isomorphism and Collective Rationality in Organizational Fields." *American Sociological Review* 48(2): 147–60.

Dobbin, Frank, John R. Sutton, John W. Meyer, and W. Richard Scott. 1993. "Equal Opportunity Law and the Construction of Internal Labor Markets." *American Journal of Sociology* 99(2): 396–427.

Donohue, John J., and James J. Heckman. 1991. "Continuous versus Episodic Change: The Impact of Civil Rights Policy on the Economic Status of Blacks." *Journal of Economic Literature* 29(4): 1603–43.

England, Paula. 1992. *Comparable Worth: Theories and Evidence*. New York: Aldine de Gruyter.

Faludi, Susan. 1991. *Backlash: The Undeclared War Against American Women*. New York: Crown.

Fenstermaker, Sarah, and Candace West. 2002. *Doing Gender, Doing Difference: Inequality, Power, and Institutional Change*. New York: Routledge.

Fiske, Susan T. 1998. "Stereotyping, Prejudice, and Discrimination." In *Handbook of Social Psychology*, edited by D. T. Gilbert, Susan T. Fiske, and G. Lindzey. New York: McGraw-Hill.

Gardner, Susan E., and Christopher Daniel. 1998. "Implementing Comparable Worth/Pay Equity: Experiences of Cutting-Edge States." *Public Personnel Management* 27(4): 475–89.

Glass, Jennifer. 2004. "Blessing or Curse? Work-Family Policies and Mother's Wage Growth." *Work and Occupations* 31(4): 367–94.

Goffman, Erving. 1977. "The Arrangement Between the Sexes." *Theory and Society* 4: 301–31.

Goldin, Claudia. 1990. *Understanding the Gender Gap: An Economic History of American Women.* New York: Oxford University Press.

———. 2002. "A Pollution Theory of Discrimination: Male and Female Differences in Occupations and Earnings." NBER Working Paper No. 8985. Washington, D.C.: National Bureau of Economic Research (June).

Gornick, Janet C., Marcia K. Meyers, and Katherin E. Ross. 1997. "Supporting the Employment of Mothers: Policy Variation Across Fourteen Welfare States." *Journal of European Social Policy* 7(1): 45–70.

Holzer, Harry J., and David Neumark. 2000. "Assessing Affirmative Action." *Journal of Economic Literature* 38(3): 483–568.

Jackson, Robert Max. 1998. *Destined for Equality: The Inevitable Rise of Women's Status.* Cambridge, Mass.: Harvard University Press.

Jacobs, Jerry. 2003. "Detours on the Road to Equality: Women, Work and Higher Education." *Contexts* 2: 32–41.

Kanter, Rosabeth Moss. 1977. *Men and Women of the Corporation.* New York: Basic.

Lundberg, Shelly J., and Richard Startz. 1983. "Private Discrimination and Social Intervention in Competitive Labor Markets." *American Economic Review* 73(3): 340–47.

Macpherson, David A., and Barry T. Hirsch. 1995. "Wages and Gender Composition: Why Do Women's Jobs Pay Less?" *Journal of Labor Economics* 13(3): 426–71.

Marini, Margaret Mooney, and Mary C. Brinton. 1984. "Sex Typing and Occupational Socialization." In *Sex Segregation in the Workplace: Trends, Explanations, and Remedies*, edited by Barbara Reskin. Washington, D.C.: National Academy Press.

Meyer, John W. 2001. "The Evolution of Modern Stratification Systems." In *Social Stratification: Class, Race and Gender in Sociological Perspective*, edited by David B. Grusky. 2nd edition. Boulder, Colo.: Westview Press.

Meyer, John W., and Brian Rowan. 1977. "Institutionalized Organization: Formal Structure as Myth and Ceremony." *American Journal of Sociology* 83(2): 340–63.

Oppenheimer, Valerie Kincade. 1970/1976. *The Female Labor Force in the United States: Demographic and Economic Factors Governing Its Growth and Changing Composition.* Westport, Conn.: Greenwood Press.

Parsons, Talcott. 1970. "Equality and Inequality in Modern Society, or Social Stratification Revisited." In *Social Stratification: Research and Theory for the 1970s*, edited by Edward O. Laumann. Indianapolis: Bobbs-Merrill: 14–72.

Parsons, Talcott, and Robert F. Bales. 1955. *Family, Socialization, and Interaction Process.* Glencoe, Ill.: Free Press.

Polachek, Solomon W. 1981. "Occupational Self-Selection: A Human Capital Approach to Sex Differences in Occupational Structure." *Review of Economics and Statistics* 63(1): 60–69.

Reskin, Barbara F. 2000. "The Proximate Causes of Employment Discrimination." *Contemporary Sociology* 29(2): 319–28.

Reskin, Barbara F., and Debra Branch McBrier. 2000. "Why Not Ascription? Organizations' Employment of Male and Female Managers." *American Sociological Review* 65(2): 210–33.

Reskin, Barbara, and Patricia A. Roos. 1990. *Job Queues, Gender Queues: Explaining Women's Inroads into Male Occupations.* Philadelphia: Temple University Press.

Ruhm, Christopher J. 1998. "The Economic Consequences of Parental Leave Mandates: Lessons from Europe." *Quarterly Journal of Economics* 113(1): 285–317.

Ruhm, Christopher J., and Jacqueline L. Teague. 1997. "Parental Leave Policies in Europe and North America." In *Gender and Family Issues in the Workplace*, edited by Francine D. Blau and Ronald G. Ehrenberg. New York: Russell Sage Foundation.

Spencer, Steven J., Claude M. Steele, and Diane M. Quinn. 1999. "Stereotype Threat and Women's Math Performance." *Journal of Experimental Social Psychology* 35(1): 4–28.

Sunstein, Cass. 1991. "Why Markets Don't Stop Discrimination." *Social Philosophy and Policy* 8: 22–37.

West, Candace, and Don H. Zimmerman. 1987. "Doing Gender." *Gender and Society* 1(2): 125–51.

Part II

Making Sense of Change and Stability in Gender Inequality

Chapter 2

The Gender Pay Gap: Going, Going . . . but Not Gone

Francine D. Blau and Lawrence M. Kahn

A s the title of our chapter implies, the trends in the gender pay gap in the United States form a somewhat mixed picture. On the one hand, after nearly half a century of stability in the earnings of women relative to men, starting in 1930, there has been since the late seventies a substantial increase in women's relative earnings.[1] What makes this development especially dramatic and significant is that the recent changes contrast markedly with the relative stability of earlier years. Moreover, while not the focus of our attention here, it is worth mentioning that since the seventies there have also been major changes in the types of jobs in which women and men are employed, and a marked entry of women into jobs that had traditionally been overwhelmingly male.[2]

These post-1980 earnings changes are also interesting because women's gains in wage parity with comparable men have been prevalent across a wide spectrum. At first, a large portion of the female gains were centered on younger women, but now women of all ages have narrowed the pay gap with men, though younger women's gains may be somewhat greater. The same broad progress is visible when we look at the trends in the gender pay gap by education. Less-educated women have narrowed the pay gap with less-educated men and highly educated women have reduced the pay gap with highly educated men.

The earnings gains of women are particularly remarkable because they have occurred during a period when overall wage inequality was rising: over approximately the past quarter-century the difference in pay between workers with high wages and workers with low wages has widened considerably. Yet, women, a low-paid group, have nonetheless been able to narrow the pay gap with a relatively better-paid group, men.

These findings support our initial observations that women have made significant progress in narrowing the gender pay gap. Nonetheless, women continue to earn considerably less than men on average, and the convergence of men's and women's pay slowed noticeably in the 1990s. Although there were some gains for women in the early 2000s, the long-run significance of this recent experience is unclear. The evidence that convergence has slowed in recent years suggests the possibility that the narrowing of the gender pay gap will not continue into the future. Moreover, there is evidence that although discrimination against women in the labor market has declined, some discrimination does still exist.

A final point relating to the mixed labor-market progress of women is that although the gender pay gap has narrowed, we see a rising gap between how well highly skilled, highly educated women and less-skilled and less-educated women are faring. Precisely this pattern is also observed among men, but it has less often been recognized as occurring among women as well. Such rising returns to skill underlie the trend toward rising overall wage inequality that we alluded to above.

In this chapter, we first consider why there has been so much focus on the gender pay gap and why this disparity and its sources continue to garner considerable interest among social scientists in general and economists in particular. We then review the trends in detail. Following that, we consider explanations for the pay gap in general and for the convergence that we have seen so far. Next, we document the growing gaps between more- and less-educated women because this is a piece of the story that is generally less well known. Finally we attempt to gaze into our crystal ball and consider the future. However, it is important to realize that when social scientists or economists consider the future, they are probably wrong as often as they are right. And the mixed picture we have described here for trends in the gender pay gap makes the future especially difficult to predict. Thus it is difficult to say whether and when robust convergence in the gender pay gap will resume.

WHY WAGES ARE IMPORTANT

First and most obvious, wages are important because they affect people's economic well-being. It is of course important to recognize that there is not necessarily a one-to-one correlation between wages and well-being: a low-wage person could be part of a family in which there are many high-wage earners. Indeed, before the women's liberation movement and other social changes brought this issue of women's wages to the fore, the prevalent view was that the gender pay gap, although sizable, was not much source for concern. It was generally assumed that most adult women were married and adequately supported by their husbands. If this view was ever accurate, it is clearly much less so today. Most married-couple families have two earners who contribute significantly to family well-being. In addition, the number of female-headed families who are fully dependent on the female head's wages—or whatever other sources of income the family may have—is growing.

A second reason for interest in women's relative wages relates to issues of fairness and equity. To the extent that the aggregate gender pay gap reflects pay differentials between equally productive men and women, it may be considered inequitable, in the absence of compensating features of jobs such as safety or security, which will be discussed. In a market economy, worth is often measured by money. If women earn less, they are regarded as in some sense as having less worth. A gender pay gap among equally productive workers may also be considered inefficient if it causes employers and consumers to make production and consumption decisions that do not accurately reflect true social costs, and hence is likely to result in a misallocation of resources. In comparison to the nondiscriminatory situation, society produces "too little" of the outputs that use "overpriced" male labor, given that equally productive female labor is available to expand production at a lower price. Society produces "too much" of the outputs that use "underpriced" female labor, given that the contribution of equally productive labor is valued more highly in the male sector as measured by its price. The inefficiency caused by discrimination is even greater when we take into account feedback effects. If women are deterred from investing in their human capital because of discrimination, society is unable to fully utilize a valuable resource.

Third, wages tend to be correlated with other favorable job characteristics, meaning that high-wage workers are also more likely to have more extensive benefits, better working conditions, more status, and more career opportunities. This broad statement requires some qualification. Economic analysis predicts that there should be compensating wage differentials for negatives associated with certain jobs: for example, equally skilled workers receive a wage premium for doing unsafe work or for facing a particularly high risk of layoff.[3] But in the data, it is difficult to control for all aspects of skill. Thus, more-skilled workers are likely to have the option of both higher wages and better working conditions than less-skilled workers, producing the positive correlation we alluded to earlier. Moreover, discrimination could take the form of being placed in jobs with lower wages and worse working conditions. Furthermore, sociologists have found that women are disproportionately represented in relatively high-status white-collar occupations, and so by conventional measures, predominantly female jobs do not actually turn out to be, on average, lower in status than traditionally male jobs by conventional measures (England 1979). Nonetheless, wages are interesting and important because they tend, broadly speaking, to be correlated with positive job attributes, many of which are much more difficult to measure or readily summarize quantitatively than wages.

Finally, another important aspect of wages is their function as inputs into people's decision making. For example, economic models of labor-force participation and fertility include the wages available to the individual in the labor market as an important determinant. Historically, there has been a division of labor among married couples in which the husband was the breadwinner and the wife was the homemaker, or, if they both worked, the wife's career was secondary to the husband's. This traditional division of labor undoubtedly developed for a variety of reasons related to economic conditions at an earlier historical point in time, as well as most likely cultural factors. However, an interesting insight of the economic analysis is that the traditional division of labor is reinforced by lower wages for women in the labor market. If a couple has a child and they would like someone to stay out of the labor force for a while, it makes a lot of sense for the low-wage partner to do it. Or, if they are deciding where to locate, it makes economic sense for the opportunities of the high wage member of the couple to determine this decision. A recent literature in economics also points to the importance of the wages of each partner in influencing their bargaining power within the family (see, for example, Lundberg and Pollak 1996).

TRENDS IN THE GENDER PAY GAP

In this section we look in more detail at the trends in the relative wages of women. Figure 2.1 presents data drawn from published government statistics on female-to-male earnings ratios of full-time workers. We focus on full-time workers to adjust for gender differences in hours worked. This is important because women are more likely than men to work part-time. Ideally we would like a measure of wages or an hourly rate of pay. Unfortunately, we do not have a similar long data series for hourly wages. Thus, we focus here on the earnings of full-time workers.

Figure 2.1 gives the gender earnings ratio for two data series on the relative earnings of female and male full-time workers available from published government statistics: the annual earnings series show annual earnings data on workers who are employed year-round as well as full time; the weekly earnings series show the earnings of full-time workers over the survey week, regardless of how many weeks per year the individual works. The annual earnings series has been available for the longest time period, 1955 to 2003; the weekly earnings series has been available for the period 1967 to 2003.

Both series show similar trends. Until the late 1970s or early 1980s there was a remarkable constancy in the ratio of female to male earnings, as a percentage: around 60 percent, despite some year-to-year fluctuations. If there was any discernible trend, it was a decrease in the percentage between 1955 and 1960. Then, over the 1980s, we see a period of a strong rising trend in the ratio as female earnings started to catch up to males', a trend that prevailed through perhaps 1990 or 1993, depending on the series. During the 1990s, the pace of convergence in both the annual and the weekly earnings series slowed and both series behaved more erratically. Then the pace of change picked up again in the early 2000s.[4] It is unclear whether this recent uptick signals a resumption of a strong, long-run trend toward convergence in male and female earnings or will prove to be of only short duration.[5]

Abstracting from the differential trends over the various subperiods and focusing on the period since the late 1970s as a whole, the gains have been quite remarkable, especially viewed in terms of the long constancy in the ratio that preceded this time. So, for example, based on the weekly earnings series, the female-to-male ratio rose from 61.3 percent in 1978 to 79.4 percent in 2003, but much of this increase was accomplished in a relatively short period of time: the ratio reached 76.8 percent by 1993. Of course, this is still not earnings parity, so clearly all sources of the pay differential between men and women have not been eradicated.

FIGURE 2.1 / Earnings of Full-Time Female Workers as Percentage of Full-Time Male Workers' Earnings, 1955 to 2003

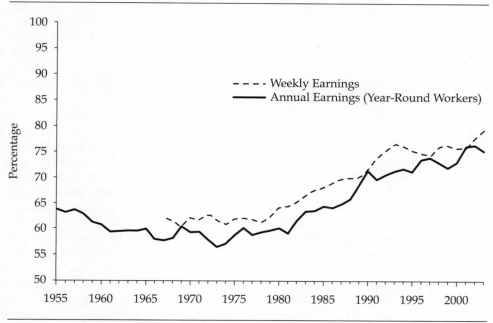

Source: U.S. Department of Labor (various issues).

How do we explain these earnings gains for women? To answer this question as well as the question of why women continue to earn less than men we need to first consider the basic factors behind the gender pay gap to begin with.

ECONOMISTS' EXPLANATIONS FOR THE GENDER PAY GAP: THE ROLE OF QUALIFICATIONS AND DISCRIMINATION

Economists point to a number of factors that could be important in explaining the lower earnings of women compared to men, but traditionally have focused on two primary factors: qualifications and discrimination. Following Chinhui Juhn, Kevin M. Murphy, and Brooks Pierce (1991), we call these "gender-specific" factors, because they relate specifically to differences between women and men, either in their qualifications or how they are treated. With regard to qualifications, the human-capital model has been especially important in pointing out the potential role played by education and experience.

The gender gap in educational attainment was never particularly large in the United States. The biggest difference historically was that, although women were more likely to graduate from high school than men, they were less likely to go on to college and graduate education. Moreover, men tended to concentrate in career-oriented fields of study such as engineering, law, medicine, and business, which led to relatively high earnings. These educational differences have decreased quite a bit in recent years, especially at the college level, where over half of college students are women; women have also greatly increased their representation in traditionally male professional fields. Thus gender differences in education levels have never explained a large portion of the overall gender pay gap; and some recent samples show women outpacing men in years of schooling.

The qualification that has proved to be quite important is work experience, because traditionally women moved in and out of the labor market as a result of family considerations. Before World War II, most women left the labor market permanently when they got married and had children. In the immediate postwar period, a pattern developed whereby older married women returned to the labor market after their children were in school or grown. An even bigger change has occurred in the past twenty to thirty years, as increasing numbers of women, including married women, started staying in the labor force fairly continuously even when they had small children.[6] Today, the majority of women, including those with children a year or less in age, are participating in the labor force. Nonetheless, on average, women have less work experience than men and that difference in qualifications is quantitatively important in explaining the gender pay gap.

Jacob Mincer and Solomon Polachek (1974) have done especially important work in highlighting the role of labor-market experience in explaining the gender pay gap. The traditional division of labor within the family leads women to accumulate less labor-market experience than men. Further, because women anticipate shorter and more discontinuous work lives, they have lower incentives to invest in market-oriented formal education and on-the-job training. Their resulting smaller human-capital investments lower their earnings relative to those of men. An additional way in which the traditional division of labor may disadvantage women is that the longer hours women spend on housework may also limit the effort they can put into their market jobs compared to men, controlling for hours worked, and hence also reduce their productivity and wages (Becker 1985).[7]

To the extent that women choose occupations for which on-the-job training is less important, gender differences in occupations are also expected. Women may especially avoid jobs requiring large investments in skills that are unique to a particular enterprise, because they will reap the returns to such investments only as long as they remain with that employer. At the same time, employers may be reluctant to hire women for such jobs because the firm bears some of the costs of such firm-specific training, and fears not getting a full return on that investment.[8]

Even controlling for experience and whatever other qualifications can readily be measured, there tends to be a pay difference between men and women that is not explained by qualifications differentials and may be due to discrimination. Gary Becker (1957/1971) has developed important analyses of labor-market discrimination. Although he was looking at racial differences, the idea of prejudice and its negative consequences are readily transferable to gender. Becker conceptualized discriminatory preferences as the desire to maintain social distance from the discriminated group—in his model, African Americans. In the case of gender, the issue may be related but slightly different: ideas of socially appropriate roles, rather than the desire to maintain social distance.[9]

Standard models in economics suggest discrimination can arise in a variety of ways. In Becker's model, discrimination is due to the discriminatory tastes of employers, coworkers, or customers. In models of "statistical discrimination," differences in the treatment of men and women arise from average differences between the two groups in the expected value of productivity (or in the reliability with which productivity may be predicted); employers may be led to discriminate on the basis of that average (see, for example, Aigner and Cain 1977). Finally, discriminatory exclusion of women from "male" jobs can result in an excess supply of labor in "female" occupations, depressing wages there for otherwise equally productive workers, as in Barbara Bergmann's (1974) "overcrowding" model.

The typical approach to analyzing the sources of the gender pay gap is to estimate wage regressions specifying the relationship between wages and productivity-related characteristics for men and women. The gender pay gap may then be statistically decomposed into two components: one due to gender differences in measured characteristics and the other "unexplained" and potentially due to discrimination. Such empirical studies provide evidence consistent with both human-capital differences and labor-market discrimination in explaining the gender pay gap.

However, any approach that relies on a statistical residual will be weakened by the possibility that not all the necessary explanatory variables were included in the regression. For example, even if measured human-capital characteristics can explain only a portion of the wage gap between men and women, it is possible that unmeasured group differences in qualifications may explain part of the residual. If men are more highly endowed with respect to these omitted variables, we would end up overestimating discrimination. Alternatively, if some of the factors controlled for in such regressions—such as occupation and tenure with the employer—themselves reflect the impact of discrimination, then discrimination will be underestimated. Moreover, if women face barriers to entry into certain occupations, they may have higher unmeasured productivity than men in the same jobs. This factor would also suggest an underestimate of discrimination if we controlled for occupation.[10]

Using the residual from a regression to estimate the effects of discrimination will also run into trouble if feedback effects are important. Even small initial discriminatory differences in wages may cumulate to large ones as men and women make decisions about human-capital investments and time allocation in the market and the home on the basis of these wage differentials.

Despite these caveats, results of statistical studies of the gender pay gap may nonetheless be instructive. Representative findings from analyses of this type may be illustrated by results from a recent paper by Francine D. Blau and Lawrence M. Kahn (2004). Using data from the Panel Study of Income Dynamics (PSID), which contains information on actual labor-market experience for a large, nationally representative sample, we found a wage differential between male and female full-time workers in 1998 of 20 percent. The restriction to full-time workers is designed to provide a pool of male and female workers who are as similar as possible.[11]

Table 2.1 shows the impact of various variables on the male-female wage differential, including indicators of "human capital" (those relating to education and experience) and occupation, industry, and union status. (Race is also included as a control variable, but its effect is small, since the proportion of each race group in the full-time sample is about the same for men and women.)

As would be expected, women's lesser amount of labor-market experience is found to explain a significant percentage of the gender wage differential, 10.5 percent. This reflects a three-and-a-half-year difference in full-time labor-market experience between men and women, which, though smaller than in previous years, is still a substantial factor explaining the wage gap. Interestingly, women in this subsample are found to have higher educational attainment than men, which works to *lower* the gender wage gap by 6.7 percent (as indicated by the negative sign in the table). In the population as a whole, men's educational attainment was still somewhat higher than women's, but when we focus on a subsample of the population that is employed full- time, women have a slight educational edge.

Finally, gender differences in occupation and industry are substantial and help to explain a considerable portion of the gender wage gap. Men are more likely to be in blue-collar jobs and to work in mining, construction, or durable manufacturing; they are also more likely to be in unionized employment. Women are more likely to be in clerical or professional jobs and to work in the service industry. Taken together, these variables explain 52.8 percent of the gender wage gap—27.4 percent for occupation, 21.9 percent for industry, and an additional 3.5 percent for union status.[12]

Although these findings suggest that gender differences in work-related characteristics are important, they also indicate that qualifications are only part of the story. The proportion of the wage differential that is *not* explained by these types of productivity-related characteristics includes the impact of labor-market discrimination, although, as previously mentioned, the residual may also include the effects of gender differences in unmeasured productivity levels or nonwage aspects of jobs. In this case, 41 percent of the gender gap cannot be explained even when gender differences in education, experience, industries, occupations, and union status are taken into account. We can consider the results of this study somewhat differently by looking at the gender wage ratio. The actual ("unadjusted") gender wage ratio is 80 percent; that is, women's wages are, on average, 80 percent of men's wages. If women had the same human-capital (education and experience) characteristics, industry and occupational distribution, and union membership as men, such an adjusted ratio would rise to 91 percent of men's wages. Thus, while measured characteristics are important, women still earn less than similar men even when all measured characteristics are taken into account. Furthermore, this adjustment for occupation, industry, and union status may be questionable to the extent that these variables are potentially influenced by discrimination.

There is also the possibility that the residual gap, however measured, reflects factors apart from discrimination. One that has received particular attention re-

TABLE 2.1 / Contribution to the Gender Wage Differential of Differences in Measured Characteristics (as a Percentage of the Total Differential), 1998

Characteristic	Percentage
Educational attainment	−6.7
Labor-force experience	10.5
Race	2.4
Occupational category	27.4
Industry category	21.9
Union status	3.5
Unexplained	41.1
Total	100.0
Wage differential (percentage)	20.3

Source: Calculated from data presented in Blau and Kahn (2004).
Note: Rows do not sum to exactly 100.0 because of rounding.

cently is the impact of children on women's wages, since evidence of children's negative effect on wages has been obtained, even in analyses that control for labor-market experience (Waldfogel 1998). The reason may be that in the past, having a child often meant that a woman withdrew from the labor force for a substantial period, breaking her tie to her employer and leading her to forgo the returns to any firm-specific training she might have acquired, as well as any rewards for having made an especially good job match. Given the sharp increase in the labor-force participation of women with young children that has occurred since the 1960s, this factor may have been of growing importance in influencing the aggregate gender gap.[13] However, the greater availability of parental leave, legally mandated in the United States since 1993, may well mitigate the effect of this factor on more recent cohorts. Indeed, Jane Waldfogel (1998) finds that the negative effect of children on wages is substantially reduced for mothers who have maternity-leave coverage.

Some studies on discrimination have taken different approaches to the question, thus avoiding some of the problems of traditional analyses. First are two studies that have applied traditional econometric techniques to especially homogeneous groups and employed extensive controls for qualifications, thus minimizing the effect of gender differences in unmeasured productivity characteristics. Robert G. Wood, Mary E. Corcoran, and Paul Courant (1993) studied graduates of the University of Michigan Law School in the classes of 1972 to 1975, fifteen years after graduation. The gap in pay between women and men was relatively small at the outset of their careers, but fifteen years later, women graduates' earnings were only 60 percent of men's. Some of this difference reflected choices that workers had made, including the propensity of women lawyers to work shorter hours. But even controlling for current hours worked as well as an extensive list of worker qualifications and other covariates—including family status, race, location, grades while in law school, and detailed work history data, such as years practiced law, months of part-time work, and type and size of employer—a male advantage of 13 percent remained. Catherine J. Weinberger (1998) examined wage differences among recent college graduates in 1985. Her controls included narrowly defined college major, college grade-point average, and specific educational institution attended. She found an unexplained pay gap of 10 to 15 percent between men and women one to two years after college graduation.

A second set of studies used an experimental approach to test for discrimination. David M. Neumark (1996) analyzed the results of a hiring "audit" in which people pretending to be job seekers were given similar résumés and sent to apply for jobs as wait staff at the same set of Philadelphia restaurants. In high-priced restaurants, a female applicant's probability of getting an interview was 40 percentage points lower than a male's and her probability of getting an offer was 50 percentage points lower. A second study examined the impact of the adoption of "blind" auditions by symphony orchestras in which a screen is used to conceal the identity of the candidate (Goldin and Rouse 2000). The presence of a screen substantially increased the probability that a woman would advance out of preliminary rounds and be the winner in the final round. The switch to blind auditions was found to explain 25 percent of the overall increase in the percentage of female musicians in the top five symphony orchestras in the United States, from less than 5 percent in 1970 to 25 percent in 1996.

In yet a third approach, several recent studies have examined predictions of Becker's (1957/1971) discrimination model. Becker and others have pointed out that competitive forces should reduce or eliminate discrimination in the long run because the least discriminatory firms, which hire more lower-priced female labor, would have lower costs of production and should drive the more discriminatory firms out of business. For this reason, Becker suggested that discrimination would be more severe in firms or sectors that are shielded to some extent from competitive pressures. In fact, Judith K. Hellerstein, David Neumark, and Kenneth Troske (2002) found that, among plants with high levels of product market power (in other words, who were shielded from competition), those employing relatively more women were more profitable. Working on similar premises, Sandra E. Black and Philip E. Strahan (2001) report that, with the deregulation of the banking industry that began in the mid-1970s, the gender pay gap in banking declined—as men's wages fell by considerably more, 12 percent, than women's, 3 percent. This suggests that during the period of regulation, banks shared the rents (that is, above-normal profits) fostered by regulation primarily with men, and so men lost the most in the shift to deregulation. Black and Elizabeth Brainerd (2004) find that increasing vulnerability to foreign competition reduced estimated gender wage discrimination in concentrated industries (that is, industries where firms have considerable market power). As in the case of the banking industry, increased competition was associated with a reduction in gender wage differentials, again as predicted by Becker's (1957/1971) model.

Finally, additional evidence on discrimination comes from court cases. A number of employment practices that explicitly discriminated against women used to be quite prevalent: including marriage bars that restricted the employment of married women (Goldin 1990), and the intentional segregation of men and women into separate job categories with associated separate and lower pay scales for women (for example, Bowe v. Colgate-Palmolive Co., 416 F.2d 711 {7th Cir. 1969}; IUE v. Westinghouse Electric Co., 631 F.2d 1094 {3rd Cir. 1980}). Although many such overt practices have receded, recent court cases suggest that employment practices still exist, which produce discriminatory outcomes for women.

For example, in 1994, Lucky Stores, a major grocery chain, agreed to a settlement of $107 million after the judge found that "sex discrimination was the standard operating procedure at Lucky with respect to placement, promotion, movement to full-time positions, and the allocation of additional hours" (Stender v. Lucky Stores, Inc., 803 F.supp.259 [N.D. Cal. 1992]; see also Ronette King, "Women Taking Action Against Many Companies," *Times-Picayune*, April 27, 1997). In 2000, the U.S. Information Agency agreed to pay $508 million to settle a case in which the Voice of America rejected women who applied for high-paying positions in the communications field. A lawyer representing the plaintiffs said that the women were told things like, "These jobs are only for men," or "We're looking for a male voice" (FEDHR 2000). Gender stereotyping and discrimination were revealed in the 1990 case against Price Waterhouse, a major accounting firm. The firm had denied partnership to the only woman considered, even though she had brought in more business than the other eighty-seven candidates for partner. Her colleagues criticized her for being "overbearing, 'macho' and abrasive and said she would have a better chance of making partner if she would wear makeup and jewelry, and walk, talk and dress 'more femininely.'" The Court found that Price Waterhouse maintained a partnership evaluation system that "permitted negative sexually stereotyped comments to influence partnership selection" (Bureau of National Affairs 1990; Tamar Lewin, "Partnership Awarded to Woman in Sex Bias Case," *New York Times*, May 16, 1990, A1).

Oftentimes, economists serve as expert witnesses in court cases alleging discrimination. Their analyses, when publicly available, provide a window into discriminatory practices that still exist to some extent in the labor market, although there is of course likely to be disagreement between experts employed by each side as to the type of evidence that is relevant or its interpretation. For example, the Lucky Stores case cited above generated an interesting exchange.

John Pencavel, a labor economist, testified for the plaintiffs. Analyzing company data, he discovered that women were paid 18 to 24 percent less than men. Interestingly, he also found that there was "little difference between male and female wage rates within job categories" (West 1993, 300); the overall pay gap was, then, logically due to women's placement in lower paying jobs. His finding that "the economic status of women at Lucky [was] inferior to that of men" was unaffected by adjustments for "seniority, store, marital status, age and ethnic background" (West 1993, 301). Joan Haworth, also a labor economist, but who testified for the defense, referred to company data on applications for different jobs (West 1993, 310–14). Based on these applications, she concluded that women had different work preferences from men (for example, men had a greater preference for night work). She further concluded, therefore, that the gender difference in representation across occupations was not due to company policy. Rather, it was due to gender differences in attitudes.

As noted, the judge decided the case in favor of the plaintiffs, writing: "The court finds the defendant's explanation that the statistical disparities between men and women at Lucky are caused by differences in the work interests of men and women to be unpersuasive." An interesting aspect of this case is that both sides agreed that male and female employees received equal pay for equal work and that the pay differential was associated with pay differences across occupations. They differed, however, as to whether the source of the occupational differences was the choices women made or discrimination. This disagreement mirrors the alternative explanations economists offer in general for wage and occupational differences between men and women: differences in qualifications based on the choices men and women make versus discrimination, which limits the opportunities and pay of women compared to men.

Some additional evidence supporting discrimination as a source of the type of occupational differences cited is provided by a recent study of eight years of data from an unidentified regional grocery chain on gender differences in job titles and wage rates. Like John Pencavel (2004), Michael Ransom and Ronald L. Oaxaca (2005) find a pattern of gender differences in initial job assignment and upward mobility within the firm that "generally penalized women, even when the analysis account[ed] for individuals' characteristics" (219). While one might again dispute the reason for these differences, the authors found that job segregation of women and men was dramatically lower in the period after 1984, when the company lost a discrimination suit, and 1986, when it reached a settlement that required it to initiate affirmative-action policies. This implies that it was possible to find women interested in higher-level jobs, leading one to doubt that the segregation was entirely due to women's choices.

These cases emphasize the role of occupational segregation by sex within firms in producing pay differences between men and women. Pencavel explicitly notes that there was little difference in pay between men and women in the same job. It is worth noting that economists and sociologists who have examined this issue across a wider range of firms have tended to come to a similar conclusion: pay differences between men and women in the same narrowly defined occupational categories within the same firm tend to be small (Blau 1977; Groshen 1991; Petersen and Morgan 1995; Bayard et al. 1999).[14] However, even when men and women are in the same occupation, they tend to be segregated by company, and such establishment segregation contributes substantially to the gender pay gap.

Economists' Explanations for the Gender Pay Gap: The Role of Wage Structure

In earlier work, building on a framework suggested by Juhn, Murphy, and Pierce (1991), we pointed out that there is another factor that needs to be considered when one is analyzing gender differences in pay, and that is wage structure (Blau and Kahn 1996, 1997). Wage structure is defined as the market returns to skills and the rewards for employment in particular sectors of the economy. Market returns to skills means the premiums the market determines for being a more experienced worker or a more highly educated worker. An example of rewards for employment in particular sectors of the economy is the fact that unionized workers tend to earn more than comparable nonunionized workers, or that workers in some industries, such as durable goods or manufacturing, may earn more than similarly qualified workers in other industries, say, services. In addition, considerable research suggests that predominantly female occupations pay less, even controlling for the measured personal characteristics of workers and a variety of characteristics of occupations, although the interpretation of such results remains in some dispute.[15]

We distinguish wage structure from gender-specific factors because the idea is that these are the returns to skills or the rewards for working in a particular industry or occupation regardless of whether you are male or female. That being so, why should wage structure affect the gender pay gap? To see how, let's think a bit more about the two factors we discussed earlier—gender differences in qualifications and labor-market discrimination. Suppose women do have less experience, on average, than men. Then, the higher the return to experience the larger the gender pay gap will be. Or, suppose that jobs staffed primarily by women pay less than jobs staffed primarily by men. Then, the higher the premium for being in a male occupation the larger the gender pay gap will be.

This is interesting because these market returns have in fact varied over time. In the last twenty-five years or so, the market returns to skills have increased. So this is a factor that, taken alone, would have worked to increase the gender pay gap, to the extent that women have lower skills than men, particularly labor-market experience. The rewards to being in male occupations and industries have increased as well, and that factor, taken alone, would have increased the pay gap as well. So, one question that we have raised in our research is: How have women been able to successfully swim against the tide of rising returns to skills and rising rewards to being in particular industries and occupations? That is, how have they managed to narrow the pay differential with men in the face of the adverse trends in wage structure that have worked against them?

Before looking at the results of our research on these questions, let's consider the issue of why the returns to skills have been increasing.[16] There is a fairly broad consensus among economists (though not complete unanimity) that within countries like the United States, one of the main reasons that the returns to skills have been rising is that the demand by employers for skilled workers has been rising relative to the demand for unskilled workers. Why has this occurred? There are at least two reasons. The one that that we would put the most weight on is technological change. So far the information and telecommunications revolution has worked to put more of a premium on skill (though other scenarios are possible). The other reason—on which we would put less weight, although it has also played a role—is international trade. Today, as a result of growing trade, less-skilled workers in the United States are to some extent competing against less-skilled workers from around the world, many of whom are available at much lower wages. Other factors in this development are a decline in the union movement (unions tend to push for more egalitarian pay structures); the falling real value of the minimum wage (adjusted for inflation, the minimum wage is actually lower today than it was in the late 1970s); an influx of unskilled immigrants; and a slowdown in the rate of growth of the number of college-educated workers.

Even though rising returns to skills may be hypothesized to widen the gender pay gap, all else equal, it is possible that the demand-side shifts discussed may have favored women relative to men in certain ways, and thus contributed to a decrease in the unexplained gender pay gap (Blau and Kahn 1997; Welch 2000). Technological change is believed to have caused within-industry demand-side shifts that favored white-collar workers in general (Berman, Bound, and Griliches 1994). Given the traditional male predominance in blue-collar jobs, this shift might be expected to benefit women relative to men. Similarly, to the extent that the spread of computer technology is an important source of recent technological change, the observation that women are more likely than men to use computers at work suggests that women as a group may have benefited from shifts in demand associated with computerization (Autor, Katz, and Krueger 1998; Weinberg 2000). Diffusion of computers likely also benefits women because computers restructure work in ways that de-emphasize physical strength (Weinberg 2000).

EXPLAINING THE TRENDS: THE 1980S

So how do we explain the trends in the gender pay gap? To answer this question, we summarize results from Blau and Kahn (1997, 2004; see also O'Neill and Polachek 1993; Welch 2000; Fortin and Lemieux 2000; and Mulligan and Rubenstein 2005). Using data from the PSID, we analyzed women's wage gains from 1979 to 1989, which, as we saw in figure 2.1, was a period of exceptionally rapid closing of the gender wage gap. We found that although higher rewards to skills did retard wage convergence during this period, this was more than offset by improvements in gender-specific factors.

Of particular importance was the decline in the experience difference between men and women: the gender gap in full-time experience fell from 6.6 to 4.3 years over this period. Shifts in major occupations played a significant role, too, as the employment of women as professionals and managers rose relative to men's and their relative employment in clerical and service jobs fell. Women's wages also increased relative to men's because of the decline of unions. Deunionization had a larger negative impact on male than female workers because men have traditionally been more likely than women to be unionized and thus experienced a larger decrease in unionization. Another factor that worked to encourage wage convergence substantially was a decrease in the "unexplained" portion of the gender differential—that is, a decline in the pay difference between men and women with the same measured characteristics (experience, education, occupation, industry, and union status).

Taken together, changes in qualifications and in the unexplained gap worked to increase the gender wage ratio substantially. Working in the opposite direction, however, were changes in wage structure that favored men over women during this period. An example of this, of particular importance, was a rise in the return to experience, since women have less of it, and increases in returns to employment in industries where men are more highly represented. These shifts in labor-market returns by themselves would have reduced the gender ratio substantially. Thus, in order for the gender ratio to increase, the factors favorably affecting women's wages had to be large enough to more than offset the impact of unfavorable shifts in returns. This was indeed the case, so that the gender pay gap did decline over the 1980s.

Can we say anything about the reasons for the decline in the unexplained gender wage gap that occurred over the 1980s? Such a shift may reflect a decline in labor-market discrimination against women, but it may also reflect an upgrading of women's unmeasured labor-market skills, a shift in labor-market demand favoring women over men, or changes in the composition of the labor force arising from the pattern of labor-force entries or exits. Indeed, all of these factors may well have played a role, and all appear credible during this period.

First, since women improved their relative level of measured skills, as shown by the narrowing of the gap in full-time job experience and in occupational differences between men and women, it is plausible that they also enhanced their relative level of unmeasured skills. For example, women's increasing labor-force attachment may have encouraged them to acquire more on-the-job training or encouraged their employers to offer them more training. Evidence also indicates that gender differences in college major, which have been strongly related to the gender wage gap among college graduates (Brown and Corcoran 1997), decreased over the 1970s and 1980s (Blau, Ferber, and Winkler 2002); thus the marketability of women's education has probably improved. The male-female difference in SAT math scores has also been declining, falling from 46 points in 1977 to 35 points in 1996 (Blau, Ferber, and Winkler 2002), which could be another sign of improved quality of women's education.

Second, the argument that discrimination against women declined in the 1980s may seem less credible than that women's unmeasured human-capital characteristics improved, for the federal government scaled back its antidiscrimination enforcement effort during the 1980s (Leonard 1989). However, as women increased their commitment to the labor force and improved their job skills, the rationale for statistical discrimination against them diminished; thus it is plausible that this type of discrimination decreased. Further, in the presence of feedback effects, employers' revised views can generate additional increases in women's wages by raising women's returns to investments in job qualifications and skills. To the extent that such qualifications are not fully controlled for in the statistical analysis used to explain the change in the gender wage gap, this may also help to account for the decline in the "unexplained" gap. Another possible reason for a decline in discrimination against women is that changes in social attitudes have made such discriminatory tastes increasingly less acceptable.

Third, the underlying labor-market demand-side shifts that widened wage inequality over the 1980s may have favored women relative to men in certain ways, and thus may have also contributed to a decrease in the unexplained gender gap. Overall, manufacturing employment declined. In addition, there is some evidence that technological change produced within-industry demand-side shifts that favored white-collar relative to blue-collar workers in general. Given the traditional male predominance in blue-collar jobs, this shift might be expected to benefit women relative to men, as would increased computer use.

Finally, another factor contributing to the considerable narrowing of the "unexplained" gender wage gap in the 1980s appears to be favorable shifts in the composition of the female labor force. Specifically, we found that, controlling for the measured characteristics mentioned earlier, the women who entered the labor force over this period tended to be those with relatively high (unmeasured) skills. This improved the quality of the female labor force and thus contributed to the narrowing the gender wage gap (Blau and Kahn 2004; see also Mulligan and Rubenstein 2005).

So far we have considered the effects of changes in wage structure and rising wage inequality on the gender pay gap. Such an approach assumes that estimates of changing labor-market returns are a useful indicator of the market rewards facing both men and women. Consistent with this assumption is evidence that widening wage inequality in the 1980s and 1990s was importantly affected by the economy-wide forces discussed: technological change, international trade, the decline in unionism, and the falling real value of the minimum wage (see, for example, Katz and Autor 1999). Moreover, increases in wage inequality during this period were similar for all workers, both men and women, suggesting that both groups were fairly similarly affected by these trends. However, it should be pointed out that under some circumstances, the gender pay gap could influence male inequality. For example, suppose there is a fixed overall hierarchy of jobs and that jobs determine wages. As women succeed in increasing the gender pay ratio by moving up in the overall distribution of jobs (and wages), men who are displaced move down, resulting in widening male wage inequality. It has been argued that recent trends in the gender pay gap and male wage inequality are consistent with such a model (Fortin and Lemieux 2000). In this view, women's gains have to some extent come at the expense of men's losses.

EXPLAINING THE TRENDS: THE 1990S

Why did convergence in female and male wages slow over the 1990s? Again, drawing on our previous work (Blau and Kahn 2000, 2004) we may suggest some tentative answers.[17] We found that human-capital trends cannot account for the slowdown: women improved their relative human capital by about the same amount in both the 1980s and the 1990s. In the 1980s this upgrading consisted of rising relative experience, whereas in the 1990s it consisted to a greater extent of increasing educational attainment of women relative to men. Nor did changes in wage structure in the 1990s have a more adverse effect on women than changes in the previous decade—in fact the impact of changing wage structure was actually more negative for women in the 1980s. Slowing convergence in men's and women's occupations and slowing deunionization in the 1990s was found to account for some of the slowdown, but only a small portion.

We found that the major reason for the slowdown in wage convergence in the 1990s was a slowdown in the narrowing of the "unexplained" gender pay gap in the 1990s compared to the 1980s. Our reasoning suggests that this could be due to slower improvement in women's unmeasured qualifications relative to men's in the 1990s than in the 1980s; a smaller decline in discrimination against women in the 1990s than in the 1980s; or less favorable demand-side shifts for women in the 1990s than in the 1980s. Each of these factors appears to have played a role in explaining the observed trends. In addition, controlling for measured characteristics, female labor-force entrants were less skilled during the 1990s, perhaps as a result of the entry of many relatively low-skilled, female single-family heads. Indeed, we found that differences between the two decades in such shifts in labor-force composition explained as much as 25 percent of the apparent slowdown in convergence in the unexplained gender pay gap in the 1990s.[18]

As noted earlier, women narrowed the experience gap at a slower pace in the 1990s than they did in the 1980s. Figure 2.2 shows the trends in male and female labor-force participation that underlie this development.

The most striking trend shown in the figure is that the difference in the participation rates of men and women has narrowed considerably since the starting year, 1965. This is due to a slow, steady decrease in male labor-force participation, combined with a much sharper and dramatic increase in female labor-force participation. The decrease in male participation primarily reflects the fact that men are retiring at earlier ages and are staying in school longer, rather than changes in gender roles. Another factor has been the weakening job market for less-skilled men (Juhn 1992).

Although the data in the figure begin in the mid-1960s, the large increases in female participation in fact date back to the 1940s. Interestingly, the trend toward rising female labor-force participation was strong and consistent until about 1990. After that, the line becomes noticeably flatter. Women's participation increased a bit through 1997, but there have been no further increases thereafter.

How do these participation trends relate to the average experience levels of women workers? Unfortunately, it is not possible to figure this out just by looking at participation rates, because the labor-force participation rate of women can increase for one of two reasons or for a combination of both. Participation may rise because a lot of new groups of women come into the labor market. This tends to lower the average experience of women workers because there are a lot of new entrants. Participation can also increase because women stay in the labor force more consistently over a period of time rather than moving in and out. This works to raise average experience levels of women workers.

Research has shown that during the 1970s the average experience of women did not increase because those two factors counterbalanced each other. There were a

FIGURE 2.2 / Trends in Female and Male Labor-Force Participation Rates, 1965 to 2003

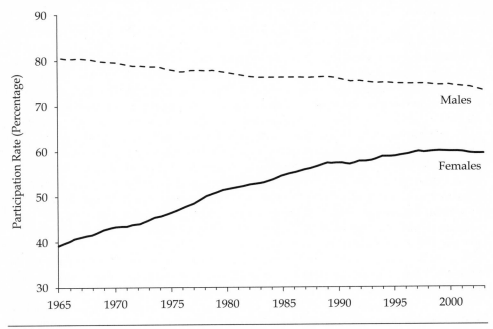

Source: U.S. Department of Labor (various issues).

lot of new entrants and there were a lot of women staying in the labor market more continuously; thus, average experience remained about the same (Goldin 1990). In the 1980s, the increase in the labor-force participation of women was due to more women remaining in the labor force more consistently, so that the average experience of women workers rose accordingly. This suggests that the flattening of the trend in female labor-force participation shown in the chart caused the gender gap in experience to decline more slowly in the 1990s than in the 1980s.

Before leaving the subject of the participation trends, it is interesting to consider their larger significance. Viewed more broadly, what the trends show is an enormous change in gender roles and a movement away from the traditional family of breadwinner husband and homemaker wife to a family where both husband and wife work outside the home, although not necessarily giving equal weight to each of their careers. The trends suggest that this "subtle revolution" (Smith 1979), having accomplished a great deal, may be slowing down now. Is it stopping? Not necessarily. Currently, more than three-quarters of women in the prime working-age range of twenty-five to fifty-four are in the labor force. This means that female labor-force participation rates in the United States are very high, although still below the male rates of around 90 percent in this age group. So it may not be surprising that, of necessity, future participation trends will be less dramatic than past trends.

GROWING INEQUALITY AMONG WOMEN

As noted earlier, in recent years women have succeeded in narrowing the pay gap between themselves and men in the face of an aggregate trend in the labor market toward rising wage inequality. There have also been increasing gaps between more- and less-skilled individuals in labor-force participation rates, which are a further indicator of adverse labor-market trends for the less-skilled. Much of the research on this issue has focused on males.[19] Thus in the interest of rounding out the picture of trends in women's economic status over the past twenty to thirty years, we will briefly review inequality trends among women. We find growing gaps between high- and low-skilled women that parallel the developments among men.

Table 2.2 shows the median earnings of year-round full-time workers by education group as a percentage of earnings of high school graduates for 1974 and 2003. It is clear that, relative to high school graduates, the earnings of both men and women who have not completed high school have fallen, whereas the relative earnings of the college-educated have increased considerably. For instance, in 1974, women and men who were high school dropouts earned 85.3 to 88.9 percent, respectively, of what high school graduates earned; by 2003, this percentage had sunk to 76.6 and 75.9. At the other end of the educational spectrum we see that women and men with college degrees earned about 50 percent more than high school graduates in 1974; by 2003, they earned 90 to 111 percent more. The ratios of each educational category's earnings relative to high school graduates are quite similar for men and women in both years, indicating that the extent of earnings differentials by education is about the same for both men and women, and that the increase in earnings inequality over this period, as measured by the widening disparities across educational groups, was also similar for both.

One difference in the earnings trends between men and women is worth noting however. The trends in real (inflation adjusted) earnings of women have been much more favorable than men's. Female real earnings have increased substantially over the past twenty-five years, while male median real earnings have stagnated (Blau, Ferber and Winkler 2002; Blau 1998). The divergence in the real-earnings experience of men and women was sharpest over the 1980s, which, as we have seen, was a period of the most significant narrowing of the gender pay gap. As noted, the earnings of both less-educated men and women are increasingly falling behind those of their more highly educated counterparts; for less-educated men this trend has been associated with substantial declines in real wages, whereas for less-educated women, real wages have either fallen only slightly (high school dropouts) or risen at a considerably slower rate (high school graduates).

Women and men who are more highly educated have also been increasing their labor-force participation relative to the less educated. This is illustrated in figures 2.3a, which shows labor-force participation by education for women aged twenty-five to sixty-four, and 2.3b, which shows men in the same age group, in 1970 and 2003. Figure 2.3a shows that although there was some positive relationship be-

TABLE 2.2 / Mean Earnings of Education Groups as Percentage of High School Graduates' Earnings, 1974 and 2003

	1974		2003	
Education	Men	Women	Men	Women
High school				
One to three years	88.9	85.3	75.9	76.6
Four years	100.0	100.0	100.0	100.0
College				
One to three years	113.6	112.6	122.8	119.5
Four or more years	155.0	147.2	211.3	190.4

Sources: For 2003—U.S. Census Bureau, Current Population Survey, 2004 Annual Social and Economic Supplement, available at http://ferret.bls.census.gov/macro/032004/perinc/new04_000.htm. For 1974—U.S. Census Bureau, "Historical Income Tables—People," table P-35, available at www.census.gov/hhes/income/histinc/p35.html.
Data refer to year-round, full-time workers eighteen years of age and older.
Median 2003 income for one to three years of college is computed as a weighted average of the medians for "some college, no degree" and "associate degree."

tween education and labor-force participation for women in 1970, it was not terribly strong. However, while participation rates of high school graduates and of college-educated women increased substantially over the period, with particularly large increases for those with some college, participation increases for high school dropouts were much smaller. This resulted in a stronger positive relationship between labor-force participation and education in 2003 than in 1970. Figure 2.3b shows a similar trend for men. Although men's labor-force participation fell for all education groups, it fell more for less-educated men. The fact that by 2003, women with some college were actually more likely to be in the labor force than male high school dropouts is illustrative of the substantial changes produced by these trends.

Thus the relative economic position of the less-educated has deteriorated across a number of dimensions for both women and men. In addition, there is a further dimension to these trends that uniquely affects women. The rising incidence of female-headed families and the consequent economic disabilities this entails for these women and their families have been heavily concentrated on less-educated women. This development has been particularly emphasized by Francine D. Blau (1998), who reports that the headship rate of women with less than a high school education (12.1 percent), fairly similar to that of all women (9.4 percent) in 1970, by 1995 had increased 12.2 percentage points, compared to an increase of 6.5 percentage points among all women and only 2 percentage points among college graduates.[20]

The trends discussed in this section come together to affect family well-being. Looking first at female-headed families, the heavy concentration of the rise in female family headship among less-educated women combined with the decrease in their labor-force participation and wages relative to that of other women has resulted in a decrease in the relative incomes of individuals in female-headed fami-

FIGURE 2.3a / Women's Labor-Force Participation by Education, 1970 and 2003, Aged Twenty-Five to Sixty-Four

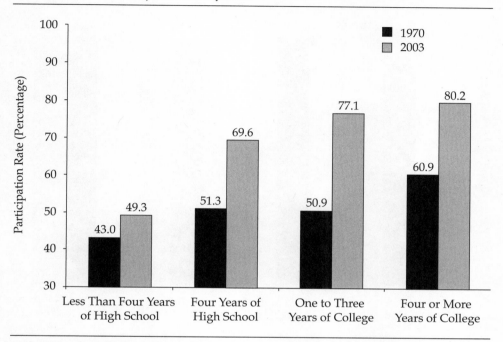

Source: U.S. Department of Labor (1989) and authors' calculations from the 2003 microdata file of the March Current Population Survey.

lies. Equivalence incomes for individuals are based on family income after adjusting for the number of family members and economies of scale. In 1989, the mean equivalence income of individuals in married-couple families was over double the income in female-headed families, up from 70 percent higher in 1969 (U.S. Department of Labor, Bureau of Labor Statistics 1995, 65). The consequences of being in a female-headed family are also more negative for less-educated women, and are becoming increasingly so. Fifty-nine percent of individuals in families headed by a single woman with a high school education or less were in the bottom quintile of the income distribution compared to 30 percent when the head had more than a high school education (U.S. Department of Labor, Bureau of Labor Statistics 1995).

There has also been a widening income gap between individuals in families headed by less-educated couples compared to more highly educated couples. People tend to marry individuals who are similar to themselves, so more highly educated people are more likely to be married to each other. Thus, married-couple families that are headed by individuals with college-level education are increasing

FIGURE 2.3b / Men's Labor-Force Participation by Education, 1970 and 2003, Aged Twenty-Five to Sixty-Four

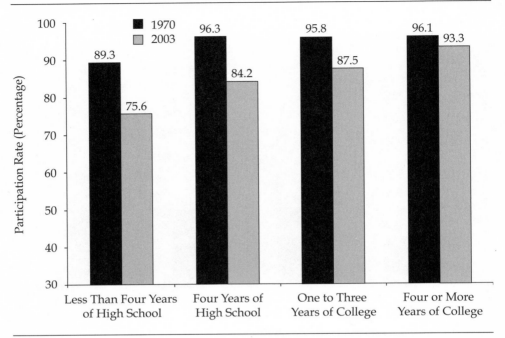

Source: U.S. Department of Labor (1989) and authors' calculations from the 2003 microdata file of the March Current Population Survey.

their family income relative to families headed by high school graduates or those with less than a high school education (Blau 1998).

The consequences of these developments for income inequality across married-couple families are unclear. Increases in labor-force participation of wives reduce earnings inequality across all persons or families, since there are fewer families in which the wife's earnings are zero. On the other hand, the increasing tendency of labor-force participation to be concentrated among high-education and thus high-income families and the increase in the correlation of husbands' and wives' earnings works to increase inequality (Karoly and Burtless 1995). Maria Cancian, Sheldon Danziger, and Peter Gottschalk (1993) found that, on net, wives' earnings have continued to equalize family income among married couples. Moreover, using a different methodology, Pencavel (2004) found that on net, rising female labor supply caused a reduction in family-earnings inequality of husband-wife families over the period from 1968 to 2001. However, Lynn A. Karoly and Gary Burtless (1995) found that the increasing employment of wives between 1979 and 1989 increased income inequality among all families, including married couples and those headed by single individuals.

PROSPECTS FOR THE FUTURE

Although we readily acknowledge that predicting the future is a tricky business, in line with the theme of this volume we cautiously offer some thoughts on the prospects for the future. What will happen to the gender pay gap in the coming years? Recent developments make the answer to this question particularly uncertain. As we have seen, after a period of consistent and sustained narrowing of the gender pay gap over the 1980s, convergence became more fitful in the 1990s. Perhaps what we saw in the 1990s was a mere pause; perhaps we were consolidating the really massive changes that had occurred over the preceding ten to twenty years—not just in the gender pay gap but also in women's labor-force participation and in the occupations in which they work; perhaps the next twenty years will show similar renewed gains on all these fronts. That could very well be. Or, after seeing big changes in the past, we may have reached a point where we will stay for quite a while and see less change in the future. It is even possible that under certain circumstances the gender pay gap could begin to widen, returning to levels of an earlier period. It may be instructive to consider the possible future course and likely impact of each of the factors that we have identified as influencing the gender pay gap.

Wage Inequality

Rising wage inequality for the workforce as a whole, to the extent that it results from increasing returns to skills like work experience that women have less of than men, on average, is expected to widen the gender pay gap, all else equal. It has been noted that wage inequality increased less during the 1990s than during the 1980s (Katz and Autor 1999). If this tapering off in the trend continues into the future, the negative effect of this factor on the pace of convergence in the gender pay gap will be small.

On the other hand, to the extent that rising wage inequality was due to demand-side shifts that favored women relative to men, it may be hypothesized that such shifts, and the relative advantage they may have given women relative to men, have also tapered off and are likely to be dampened in the future. This is suggested by the fact that the shedding of blue-collar manufacturing jobs was particularly pronounced in the 1980s. A closely related development, deunionization, which also disadvantaged men more than women, is likely to occur at a slower pace in the future, since unionization rates in the private sector have reached single digits, giving little scope for substantial future declines, and public-sector unionization remains relatively stable. Demand-side shifts favoring women may have slowed, but so too has the growth in the supply of women to the labor market. If this slower growth in supply continues into the future, it may mean that demand- and supply-side shifts will offset each other and taken together will not have much effect on convergence of pay.

Although overall female labor-force participation increased modestly in the 1990s, welfare reforms and other government policies spurred an increase in employment among single mothers (see, for example, Meyer and Rosenbaum 2001). The growth in participation among single heads of households, who tend on average to be less well educated than other women, could also have slowed wage convergence by shifting the composition of the female labor force toward low-wage women. We did indeed find some evidence consistent with this in our earlier work (Blau and Kahn 2004), though this factor does not appear to be the main reason for the slowing male-female wage convergence in the 1990s. Thus it seems unlikely that a further entry of single mothers into the labor force in the future will have a large impact on the aggregate gender pay gap.

Women's Qualifications

Moving toward the more traditional factors of women's relative qualifications and the possibility of labor-market discrimination against them, there is little reason to expect large changes here, either. The flattening of the growth in women's labor-force participation rates, if it continues, suggests that large increases in women's work experience and labor-force commitment are unlikely, although this statement must be qualified somewhat since, as we have explained, trends in the average experience of women cannot be inferred directly from changes in participation rates. Similarly, now that women constitute the majority of college students, further large gains in the relative educational attainment of women appear unlikely, though there is room for continued reductions in the gender differences in choice of college major and, at the graduate level, in entry into professional schools and Ph.D. programs in many fields.

Labor-Market Discrimination

Now that the most blatant forms of sex discrimination have been greatly reduced or eliminated and discrimination increasingly becomes more subtle and possibly even unconscious, future large declines in discrimination in the labor market may have become more difficult to attain. In addition, the decreases in statistical discrimination that we hypothesized as occurring in response to women's increasing labor-force attachment can be expected to slow as increases in women's attachment also slow. However, there seems to be room for some further decrease in statistical discrimination as the profound changes in gender roles that have already occurred continue to percolate through the labor market and the larger society and as additional changes continue to occur, albeit at a slower pace than in the past. It is possible that as women increasingly enter new areas and achieve success at higher levels even subtle barriers to change may be overcome. The glass ceiling may not have broken completely, but it is showing a lot of cracks and is likely to show more and more as time goes on.

Concluding Thoughts

Taking all these factors into account, our best guess is that we are going to have further changes in the direction of convergence, but most probably at a slower pace. We feel that is extremely unlikely that we will see a reversal of the gains in relative wages and labor-force participation women have experienced over the past twenty-five to thirty years. We do not expect to see a substantial widening of the male-female pay gap or labor-force participation gap. On the other hand, while precisely how much narrowing we will see in the future is an open question, the gender pay gap seems unlikely to vanish in the near term.

For one thing, women continue to experience discrimination in the labor market, and although its extent seems to be decreasing, it will not likely be completely eliminated soon. In addition, at least some of the remaining pay gap is surely tied to the gender division of labor in the home, both directly through its effect on women's labor-force attachment and indirectly through its impact on the strength of statistical discrimination against women. Women still retain primary responsibility for housework and child care in most American families. However, this pattern has been changing as families respond to rising labor-market opportunities for women that increase the opportunity cost of the conventional arrangements. Further, both voluntary and government-mandated policies that facilitate the integration of work and family responsibilities have become increasingly prevalent in recent years. Employers are likely to continue to expand such policies as they respond to the shifting composition of the workforce and a desire to retain employees in whom they have made substantial investments. In the longer run, the increasing availability of such policies will make it easier for women to combine work and family, and also for men to take on a greater share of household tasks.

Finally, our principal concern has been with the women's pay compared to men's, but we have also examined trends in inequality among women and found a deterioration in the relative economic status of less-educated women that is strikingly parallel to similar trends in the labor market for men. This development underscores the widening gap between more- and less-skilled Americans of both sexes, as well as its broad dimensions.

NOTES

1. Claudia Goldin's (1990) work indicates that there were earlier periods of substantial narrowing of the gender pay gap (58–63). She presents economy-wide data available only since 1890 that show a rise in the ratio of female to male earnings from 46 percent in 1890 to 56 percent in 1930. Goldin attributes these gains to an increase in the returns to schooling, an increase in the labor-market experience of women, and a decrease in the labor-market returns to physical strength. She also provides evidence of an increase in the relative pay of women in the manufacturing sector from 1815 to the turn of the twentieth century.

2. See, for example, Andrea H. Beller (1982) and Francine D. Blau, Patricia Simpson, and Deborah Anderson (1998).

3. Evidence for compensating differentials is particularly strong for occupational risk of death or injury (Rosen 1986). For evidence that a higher risk of unemployment leads to a compensating wage differential, see Robert H. Topel (1984).

4. Between 1980 and 1990, the average annual increase in the ratio was 1.14 percentage points for annual earnings and .74 percentage points for weekly earnings, whereas between 1990 and 2000 it was only .16 percentage points for annual earnings and .42 percentage points for weekly earnings. The growth in women's earnings relative to men's in the early 2000s was more robust: between 2000 and 2003, the average annual increase in the ratio was .75 percentage points for annual earnings and 1.14 percentage points for weekly earnings.

5. One short-term factor could be the recession of 2001 and the relatively high unemployment rates that lingered in its aftermath. The demand for male workers tends to be more cyclically sensitive than that for female workers owing to their greater concentration in blue-collar jobs and durable manufacturing industries.

6. For a summary of the trends in female labor-force participation, see Francine D. Blau, Marianne A. Ferber, and Anne E. Winkler (2002), chapter 4.

7. A number of studies have found that additional hours spent in housework by workers are associated with lower wages, all else equal (see, for example, Hersch and Stratton 1997). Other studies, using self-reports of effort levels, do not find that women put in less effort (see Bielby and Bielby 1988).

8. Firms may perceive that women are more likely to quit than men, but in fact the preponderance of the economic evidence on this question is that, controlling for qualifications and pay, women are no more likely to quit their jobs than men (Viscusi 1980; Blau and Kahn 1981; Ransom and Oaxaca 2005).

9. The notion of socially appropriate roles may also be a factor in racial discrimination, as when blacks have little difficulty in gaining access to menial jobs but encounter discrimination in obtaining higher-level positions.

10. If, as is likely, one is unable to completely control for nonwage job characteristics such as fringe benefits, safety, or job security, then the residual may again not give an accurate estimate of the extent of discrimination against women. We cannot say a priori what the effect of such omissions is. On the one hand, to the extent that men are likely to work in less safe or less secure jobs than women, such analyses may overestimate discrimination. On the other hand, to the extent that men have higher fringe-benefit levels, an analysis of wage residuals will understate discrimination. To some degree, these nonwage characteristics can be accounted for by controlling for industry and occupation, although, as mentioned, these controls may themselves reflect exclusionary hiring practices.

11. In addition to gender differences in qualifications and the extent of discrimination, the gender earnings differential may also be affected by the self-selection of women and men into full-time employment and, more generally, into the labor force. In other words, those choosing to participate and to work full-time may differ from those who do not participate or who work part-time, in terms of both their measured and unmeasured characteristics. One possibility, for example, is that labor-force participants are a positively selected group of those who have received higher wage offers. Similarly, full-

time workers may be more highly qualified and more committed to market work. In fact, we find that at a point in time, the gender pay gap is smaller if only full-time workers are considered than if part-timers and nonparticipants are included; we also examined the impact of changes in female and male selection into the labor force for trends in the gender pay gap (see next section). Other research that has examined the earnings differential for white and black women has found that if self-selection is not accounted for, the race differential is underestimated (see Neal 2004).

12. The study controls for twenty occupations and twenty-six industries.
13. For example, only 19 percent of married women with children under six years old worked outside the home in 1960, compared to 61 percent in 1999.
14. Kimberly Bayard et al. (1999) report larger within-firm pay differences than the other studies, but they used wider occupational categories than the other studies.
15. See, for example, Elaine Sorensen (1990), Barbara Stanek Kilbourne et al. (1994), and David A. MacPherson and Barry T. Hirsch (1995).
16. An excellent review and assessment of this literature is provided in Katz and Autor (1999).
17. See also references cited in previous section.
18. Casey B. Mulligan and Yona Rubenstein (2005) give a larger role to shifts in labor-force composition due to labor-force entry (selection) in explaining the trends.
19. For an exception see Blau (1998), which also examines these trends in considerably greater detail.
20. One question that might be raised about the apparent deterioration in the economic status of the less-educated charted here is the possibility that the observed trends reflect shifts in the composition of the least-educated category rather than changes in their opportunities or behavior. However, studies reporting similar findings for "within-cohort" and "across-cohort" comparisons suggest that compositional shifts do not account for the deteriorating economic position of less-educated Americans (Juhn, Murphy, and Pierce 1993; Blau 1998).

REFERENCES

Aigner, Dennis, and Glen Cain. 1977. "Statistical Theories of Discrimination in Labor Markets." *Industrial and Labor Relations Review* 30(2): 175–87.

Autor, David H., Lawrence F. Katz, and Alan B. Krueger. 1998. "Computing Inequality: Have Computers Changed the Labor Market?" *Quarterly Journal of Economics* 113(4): 1169–1214.

Bayard, Kimberly, Judith Hellerstein, David Neumark, and Kenneth Troske. 1999. "New Evidence on Sex Segregation and Sex Difference in Wages from Matched Employee-Employer Data." NBER Working Paper No. 7003. Washington, D.C.: National Bureau of Economic Research (March).

Becker, Gary S. 1957/1971. *The Economics of Discrimination.* 2nd edition. Chicago: University of Chicago Press.

———. 1985. "Human Capital, Effort, and the Sexual Division of Labor." *Journal of Labor Economics* 3(1 suppl.): S33–S58.

Beller, Andrea H. 1982. "Trends in Occupational Segregation by Sex: Determinants and Changes." *Journal of Human Resources* 17(3): 321–92.

Bergmann, Barbara. 1974. "Occupational Segregation, Wages, and Profits When Employers Discriminate by Race or Sex." *Eastern Economic Journal* 1(1–2): 103–10.

Berman, Eli, John Bound, and Zvi Griliches. 1994. "Changes in the Demand of Skilled Labor Within U.S. Manufacturing Industries: Evidence from the Annual Survey of Manufacturing." *Quarterly Journal of Economics* 109(2): 367–97.

Bielby, Denise D., and William T. Bielby. 1988. "She Works Hard for the Money: Household Responsibilities and the Allocation of Work Effort." *American Journal of Sociology* 93(5): 1031–59.

Black, Sandra E., and Elizabeth Brainerd. 2004. "The Impact of Globalization on Gender Discrimination." *Industrial & Labor Relations Review* 57(4): 540–59.

Black, Sandra E., and Philip E. Strahan. 2001. "The Division of Spoils: Rent-Sharing and Discrimination in a Regulated Industry." *American Economic Review* 91(4): 814–31.

Blau, Francine D. 1977. *Equal Pay in the Office.* Lexington, Mass.: Lexington Books.

———. 1998. "Trends in the Well-Being of American Women, 1970–1995." *Journal of Economic Literature* 36(1): 112–65.

Blau, Francine D., Marianne A. Ferber, and Anne E. Winkler. 2002. *The Economics of Women, Men, and Work.* 4th edition. Upper Saddle River, N.J.: Prentice-Hall.

Blau, Francine D., and Lawrence M. Kahn. 1981. "Race and Sex Differences in Quits by Young Workers." *Industrial and Labor Relations Review* 34(4): 563–77.

———. 1996. "Wage Structure and Gender Earnings Differentials: An International Comparison." *Economica* 63(250, suppl.): S29–S62.

———. 1997. "Swimming Upstream: Trends in the Gender Wage Differential in the 1980s." *Journal of Labor Economics* 15(1): 1–42.

———. 2000. "Gender Differences in Pay." *Journal of Economic Perspectives* 14(4): 75–99.

———. 2004. "The US Gender Pay Gap in the 1990s: Slowing Convergence." NBER Working Paper No. 10853. Cambridge, Mass.: National Bureau of Economic Research (October).

Blau, Francine D., Patricia Simpson, and Deborah Anderson. 1998. "Continuing Progress? Trends in Occupational Segregation over the 1970s and 1980s." *Feminist Economics* 4(3): 29–71.

Brown, Charles, and Mary Corcoran. 1997. "Sex-Based Differences in School Content and the Male/Female Wage Gap." *Journal of Labor Economics* 15(3): 431–65.

Bureau of National Affairs. 1990. "Appeals Court Orders Price Waterhouse to Award Partnership to Women in Sex Bias Case." *Daily Labor Report*, no. 235, December 6, A11–A13.

Cancian, Maria, Sheldon Danziger, and Peter Gottschalk. 1993. "Working Wives and Family Income Inequality Among Married Couples." In *Uneven Tides: Rising Inequality in America*, edited by Sheldon Danziger and Peter Gottschalk. New York: Russell Sage Foundation.

England, Paula. "Women and Occupational Prestige: A Case of Vacuous Sex Equality." 1979. *Signs: A Journal of Women in Culture and Society* 5(2): 252–65.

Federal Human Resources Week (FEDHR). 2000. April 5. 6: 47.

Fortin, Nicole M., and Thomas Lemieux. 2000. "Are Women's Wage Gains Men's Losses? A Distributional Test." *American Economic Review* 90(2): 456–60.

Goldin, Claudia. 1990. *Understanding the Gender Gap.* New York: Oxford University Press.

Goldin, Claudia, and Cecilia Rouse. 2000. "Orchestrating Impartiality: The Impact of 'Blind' Auditions on Female Musicians." *American Economic Review* 90(4): 715–41.

Groshen, Erica L. 1991. "The Structure of the Female/Male Wage Differential: Is It Who You Are, What You Do, or Where You Work?" *Journal of Human Resources* 26(3): 457–72.

Hellerstein, Judith K., David Neumark, and Kenneth Troske. 2002. "Market Forces and Sex Discrimination." *Journal of Human Resources* 37(2): 353–80.

Hersch, Joni, and Leslie Stratton. 1997. "Housework, Fixed Effects and Wages of Married Workers." *Journal of Human Resources* 32(2): 285–307.

Juhn, Chinhui. 1992. "Decline of Male Labor Market Participation: The Role of Declining Market Opportunities." *Quarterly Journal of Economics* 107(1): 79–121.

Juhn, Chinhui, Kevin M. Murphy, and Brooks Pierce. 1991. "Accounting for the Slowdown in Black-White Wage Convergence." In *Workers and Their Wages*, edited by Marvin Kosters. Washington, D.C.: American Enterprise Institute Press.

———. 1993. "Wage Inequality and the Rise in Returns to Skill." *Journal of Political Economy* 101(3): 410–42.

Karoly, Lynn A., and Gary Burtless. 1995. "Demographic Changes, Rising Earnings Inequality, and the Distribution of Personal Well-Being, 1959–1989." *Demography* 32(3): 379–406.

Katz, Lawrence F., and David H. Autor. 1999. "Changes in the Wage Structure and Earnings Inequality." In *Handbook of Labor Economics*, edited by Orley C. Ashenfelter and David Card. Volume 3A. Amsterdam: Elsevier.

Kilbourne, Barbara Stanek, Paula England, George Farkas, Kurt Beron, and Dorothea Weir. 1994. "Returns to Skill, Compensating Differentials, and Gender Bias: Effects of Occupational Characteristics on the Wages of White Women and Men." *American Journal of Sociology* 100(3): 689–719.

Leonard, Jonathan. 1989. "Women and Affirmative Action." *Journal of Economic Perspectives* 3(1): 61–75.

Lundberg, Shelly J., and Robert A. Pollak. 1996. "Bargaining and Distribution in Marriage." *Journal of Economic Perspectives* 10(4): 139–58.

MacPherson, David A., and Barry T. Hirsch. 1995. "Wages and Gender Composition: Why Do Women's Jobs Pay Less?" *Journal of Labor Economics* 13(3): 426–71.

Meyer, Bruce D., and Dan T. Rosenbaum. 2001. "Welfare, the Earned Income Tax Credit, and the Labor Supply of Single Mothers." *Quarterly Journal of Economics* 116(3): 1063–1114.

Mincer, Jacob, and Solomon Polachek. 1974. "Family Investments in Human Capital: Earnings of Women." Part 2. *Journal of Political Economy* 82(2): S76–S108.

Mulligan, Casey B., and Yona Rubenstein. 2005. "Selection, Investment, and Women's Relative Wages Since 1957." NBER Working Paper No. 11159. Cambridge, Mass.: National Bureau of Economic Research (February).

Neal, Derek. 2004. "The Measured Black-White Wage Gap Among Women Is Too Small." Part 2. *Journal of Political Economy* 112(1): S1-S28.

Neumark, David M. 1996. "Sex Discrimination in Restaurant Hiring: An Audit Study." *Quarterly Journal of Economics* 111(3): 915–41.

O'Neill, June, and Solomon Polachek. 1993. "Why the Gender Gap in Wages Narrowed in the 1980s." Part 1. *Journal of Labor Economics* 11(1): 205–28.

Pencavel, John. 2004. "The Association Between Earnings Inequality and Labor Supply in Husband-Wife Families." Working paper. Palo Alto: Stanford University.

Petersen, Trond, and Laurie A. Morgan. 1995. "Separate and Unequal: Occupation-Establishment Sex Segregation and the Gender Wage Gap." *American Journal of Sociology* 101(2): 329–61.

Ransom, Michael, and Ronald L. Oaxaca. 2005. "Intrafirm Mobility and Sex Differences in Pay." *Industrial and Labor Relations Review* 58(2): 219–37.

Rosen, Sherwin. 1986. "The Theory of Equalizing Differences." In *Handbook of Labor Economics*, edited by Orley C. Ashenfelter and Richard Layard. Volume 1. New York: North-Holland.

Smith, Ralph E. 1979. "The Movement of Women into the Labor Force." In *The Subtle Revolution: Women at Work*, edited by Ralph E. Smith. Washington, D.C.: Urban Institute.

Sorensen, Elaine. 1990. "The Crowding Hypothesis and Comparable Worth Issue." *Journal of Human Resources* 25(Winter): 55–89.

Topel, Robert H. 1984. "Equilibrium Earnings, Turnover, and Unemployment: New Evidence." *Journal of Labor Economics* 2(4): 500–22.

U.S. Department of Labor, Bureau of Labor Statistics. 1989. *Handbook of Labor Statistics*. Washington: U.S. Government Printing Office.

———. 1995. *Report on the American Workforce*. Washington: U.S. Government Printing Office.

———. Various years. *Employment Earnings* (various issues).

Viscusi, W. Kip. 1980. "Sex Differences in Worker Quitting." *Review of Economics and Statistics* 62(3): 388–98.

Waldfogel, Jane. 1998. "The Family Gap for Young Women in the United States and Britain: Can Maternity Leave Make a Difference?" *Journal of Labor Economics* 16(3): 505–45.

Weinberg, Bruce. 2000. "Computer Use and the Demand for Female Workers." *Industrial and Labor Relations Review* 53(January): 290–308.

Weinberger, Catherine J. 1998. "Race and Gender Wage Gaps in the Market for Recent College Graduates." *Industrial Relations* 37(2): 67–84.

Welch, Finis. 2000. "Growth in Women's Relative Wages and in Inequality Among Men: One Phenomenon or Two?" *American Economic Review* 90(2): 444–49.

West's Federal Supplement. 1993. Volume 803: 259–337.

Wood, Robert G., Mary E. Corcoran, and Paul Courant. 1993. "Pay Differences Among the Highly Paid: The Male-Female Earnings Gap in Lawyers' Salaries." *Journal of Labor Economics* 11(3): 417–41.

Chapter 3

The Rising (and then Declining) Significance of Gender

Claudia Goldin

Women now constitute almost half of the United States labor force. About 80 percent of women twenty-five to forty-four years old work for pay and 85 to 90 percent of female college graduates do. Looking across the full twentieth century the gender gap in labor-force participation has nearly closed (figure 3.1), and the gap in earnings has narrowed considerably, especially in the last twenty years (figure 3.2). One might be tempted to conclude that there has been a continual declining significance of gender in the labor market for the past hundred years or possibly longer.

But for some time before there was a declining significance of gender, there was a *rising* significance of gender in the paid labor market. Gender became a truly significant factor in the labor market in the first few decades of the twentieth century.[1] Ironically, gender differences emerged and were solidified at the very moment that women began to increase their labor-force participation after marriage and stream into white-collar work. The fraction of employed women in white-collar jobs climbed from 17.8 percent in 1900 to 44.2 percent in 1930 (see table 3.1).[2]

The notion that gender became significant in the labor market in the early twentieth century might well be greeted with skepticism. Gender, many will rightly claim, has always mattered in the labor market, and the sexual division of labor is ancient. Furthermore, labor-force participation rates and the ratio of female to male earnings *rose* during the mid-twentieth century. But I will try to convince you that gender distinctions in work, jobs, and promotion were extended and solidified in the early twentieth century and became long-lived. These gender distinctions emanated from the treatment of individuals as members of a group, rather than as separate individuals.[3]

The logic of this essay hinges on what I mean by the *significance of gender*. Various forces served to narrow gender roles and to increase women's economic status, such as their labor-force participation and their relative earnings. But—and

FIGURE 3.1   /   Labor-Force Participation Rates of Men and Women Twenty-Five to
Forty-Four Years Old, 1890 to 2000

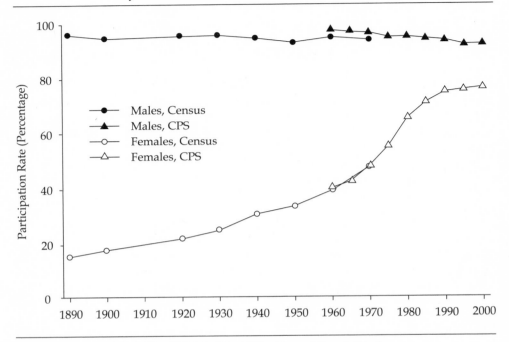

Sources: 1890 to 1960—Goldin (1990). 1960 to 2000—Current Population Surveys.

this is the important part—had gender not become as significant these positive
changes would have been even greater. Had women entered white-collar positions with a sense that they could advance, they would have invested more in their
training and education. Gender gaps would have shrunk even more. Another way
of making the point is that "wage discrimination," by which is meant the fraction
of the wage difference that cannot be explained by observables, increased from the
early part of the twentieth century to 1940 (see Goldin 1990, chapter 4). The increase moreover was large—from at most 20 percent of the gap to 55 percent of the
difference.

The early twentieth century could have been a major turning point in gender
distinctions in the labor market, education, training, and even the home. But it was
not. Even though the early twentieth century could have been a watershed in the
labor market, gender equality would not have miraculously emerged in the 1920s.
However, the history of women in the labor market could have been sufficiently
different to have hastened the advances of the past three decades by perhaps
twenty years. I conclude this essay with some reflections on the period of the declining significance of gender (1970 to the present), but my main concern here is
with its rising significance (1900 to 1940).

FIGURE 3.2 / Ratio of Female to Male Earnings for Full-Time, Year-Round Workers

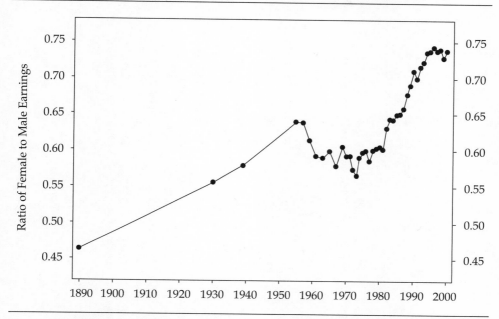

Sources: 1890 and 1930—Goldin (1990, table 3.2), 1955 to 1969—Goldin (1990, table 3.1), from Current Population Reports, series P-60. 1939—O'Neill and Polachek (1993, table 1), from published volumes of the 1940 federal population census. 1970 to 2000—U.S. Census Bureau, website, http://www.census.gov/hhec/income/histinc/p36.html, accessed March 23, 2002.
Notes: 1955 to 2000: Median, full-time, year-round workers (all races, all marital statuses) for fifteen years and older after 1980 and fourteen years and older before.
1890 and 1930: Weighted average of annual full-time earnings across all sectors. Earnings include wage and salary income before 1966 and total earnings subsequently.

My argument, in brief, is the following. Real equality between men and women in the paid labor force requires that women be employed after marriage and child-bearing. In the late nineteenth century, when most paid employment was in sectors such as manufacturing, agriculture, construction, and transportation, brawn was an important attribute, and many occupations were "sexed" rather than "gendered."[4] Employment for the bulk of adult, married women could not proceed until demand in the white-collar or "brain" sector increased relative to that in the blue-collar or "brawn" sector and until a large segment of women had at least some secondary schooling.

Because the brain and brawn distinctions are important to my argument, I want to clarify some potential objections. It should be understood that there were always brain jobs and that brawn jobs could be, and were often, performed by women. But even though it is a stretch to assume, as I will in the framework that follows, that jobs were once brawn and then became brain, it is undoubtedly the case that this was true for much of the economy. And even though it is also a

TABLE 3.1 / Distributions for Major Occupational Groups, by Sex, 1900 to 1970

	1900	1910	1920	1930	1940	1950	1960	1970
Males fourteen years old and older								
Total (in thousands)	23,711	29,847	33,569	37,993	39,168	42,554	43,531	46,970
White-collar workers	[0.176]	[0.202]	[0.214]	[0.252]	[0.266]	[0.305]	[0.354]	[0.398]
Professional, technical	0.034	0.035	0.038	0.048	0.058	0.072	0.104	0.141
Managers, officials	0.068	0.078	0.078	0.086	0.086	0.105	0.108	0.111
Clerical	0.028	0.044	0.053	0.055	0.058	0.064	0.072	0.076
Salesworkers	0.046	0.046	0.045	0.061	0.065	0.064	0.070	0.071
Manual and service workers	[0.408]	[0.451]	[0.482]	[0.500]	[0.517]	[0.546]	[0.561]	[0.557]
Manual workers	(0.376)	(0.413)	(0.445)	(0.452)	(0.456)	(0.484)	(0.497)	(0.475)
Craftsmen, foremen	0.126	0.141	0.160	0.162	0.155	0.190	0.206	0.211
Operatives	0.104	0.125	0.144	0.154	0.180	0.206	0.212	0.196
Laborers, excluding farm and mine	0.147	0.147	0.140	0.137	0.121	0.088	0.078	0.069
Service workers	(0.031)	(0.039)	(0.037)	(0.048)	(0.061)	(0.062)	(0.065)	(0.082)
Private household workers	0.002	0.002	0.002	0.002	0.004	0.002	0.002	0.001
Service, excluding private household	0.029	0.036	0.036	0.046	0.057	0.060	0.063	0.081
Farmworkers	[0.417]	[0.347]	[0.305]	[0.248]	[0.217]	[0.149]	[0.085]	[0.045]
Farmers and farm managers	0.230	0.197	0.184	0.152	0.133	0.100	0.055	0.027
Farm laborers and foremen	0.187	0.150	0.121	0.096	0.084	0.049	0.030	0.018

Females fourteen years old and older

Total (in thousands)	5,319	7,445	8,637	10,752	12,574	16,445	21,005	28,453
White-collar workers	[0.178]	[0.261]	[0.388]	[0.442]	[0.449]	[0.525]	[0.563]	[0.613]
Professional, technical	0.082	0.098	0.117	0.138	0.128	0.122	0.133	0.155
Managers, officials	0.014	0.020	0.022	0.027	0.033	0.043	0.038	0.036
Clerical	0.040	0.092	0.187	0.209	0.215	0.274	0.309	0.348
Salesworkers	0.043	0.051	0.063	0.069	0.074	0.086	0.083	0.074
Manual and service workers	[0.632]	[0.581]	[0.476]	[0.473]	[0.511]	[0.439]	[0.418]	[0.309]
Manual workers	(0.278)	(0.257)	(0.238)	(0.199)	(0.216)	(0.224)	(0.191)	(0.141)
Craftsmen, foremen	0.014	0.014	0.012	0.010	0.011	0.015	0.013	0.018
Operatives	0.238	0.229	0.202	0.174	0.195	0.200	0.172	0.148
Laborers, excluding farm and mine	0.026	0.014	0.023	0.015	0.011	0.009	0.006	0.010
Service workers	(0.355)	(0.324)	(0.239)	(0.275)	(0.294)	(0.215)	(0.228)	(0.202)
Private household workers	0.287	0.240	0.158	0.176	0.181	0.089	0.084	0.039
Service, excluding private household	0.068	0.085	0.081	0.097	0.113	0.126	0.144	0.163
Farmworkers	[0.190]	[0.158]	[0.135]	[0.084]	[0.040]	[0.037]	[0.019]	[0.014]
Farmers and farm managers	0.059	0.038	0.032	0.025	0.013	0.007	0.006	0.002
Farm laborers and foremen	0.131	0.120	0.103	0.060	0.028	0.029	0.013	0.006

Source: U.S. Bureau of the Census (1975), series D 182–232.
Notes: 1950 and 1960 use 1950 classification. Numbers in parentheses and brackets are the sum of their subcategories. Bracketed numbers for each column sum to one.

stretch to assume, as I will, that the bulk of brawn jobs actually required muscle that was beyond the physical capability or social capacity of women, there is much truth in that statement as well.

In the early twentieth century, the demand for white-collar workers increased, and the supply of women with secondary schooling did as well. Young women entered white-collar work straight out of high school; some even remained employed briefly after marriage. But the "reservation wage" for married women with young children was far higher than that for other women. Earnings would have to exceed the value of "home time" to entice them to remain employed while raising their children or to reenter the labor force after their children had grown up sufficiently. The new white-collar jobs offered the possibility of increased earnings with job market experience since many of these positions were "ladder" jobs. But jobs on the higher rungs of these ladders became closed to women in many office settings, as well as in other parts of the economy. Thus occupations in the white-collar or brain sector became gendered. Because gender became a more significant factor in the labor market, the increased labor-force participation of older married women was delayed by many decades.

LABOR-FORCE PARTICIPATION RATES

The rising significance of gender, as I have just noted, was accompanied by an increased labor-force participation of young, married women in the early twentieth century. The increase may seem odd and paradoxical, but it is an important part of the story. It demonstrates that young married women were poised to remain in the labor force if only the wage offered to them exceeded their reservation wage. But it did not for quite some time.

Consider the two lines in figure 3.3 giving the labor-force participation rates of younger married women (twenty-five to thirty-four years old) and older married women (forty-five to fifty-four years old). The graph covers the last hundred years and the two lines crisscross several times across the century, looking oddly like a double helix.

Labor-force rates for both groups began rather low, a point to which I will return in a moment. The lines then diverge. The rate for younger women increased far more than that for the older women. But around 1950 the lines cross. The labor-force rate for the older women greatly increased in the 1940s and 1950s, whereas the increase for the younger women was less steep. By the 1960s the labor-force participation rate for the older group was substantially higher than for the younger. But in the 1970s and early 1980s the younger group greatly increased its participation rates, and the two lines cross once again. By the end of the century the lines have come together, as they were at the start of the century but at a considerably higher level.

That is all very interesting. But what does it have to do with the rising significance of gender? The increased participation of the younger group in the first few decades of the century, I will contend, was a historic opportunity that could have

FIGURE 3.3 / Labor-Force Participation Rates of Two Age Groups of Currently Married Women

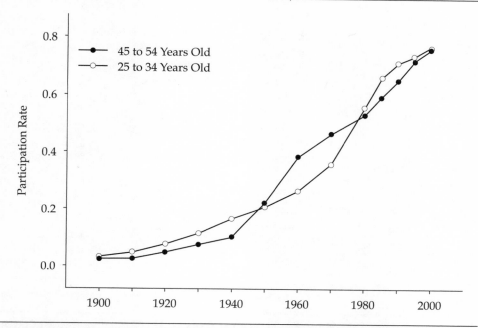

Source: 1900 to 1980—Goldin (1990). 1983 to 2000—Current Population Surveys.

provided an opening wedge. The greatly increased participation among the older group of women in the 1940s and 1950s consisted, in large measure, of women who in the 1920s had earlier expanded their paid market participation. The twenty-year-old in 1920 became the forty-year-old in 1940 and later the fifty-year-old in 1950. That is, the younger group of women not only entered the labor force in growing numbers in the 1920s and 1930s, but also expanded their participation when they were older.[5]

Even though figure 3.3 shows the participation rate of married women only, the rate for young single women (considering only those who were not currently attending school) also increased in the 1920s.[6] The vast majority of unmarried, employed women in the 1920s and 1930s dropped out of the labor force at the time of marriage, but the minority who remained employed after marriage stayed in the labor force for a considerable number of years. The female labor force, in other words, was rather "heterogeneous."[7]

Another revealing way of viewing the same labor force data is to array the rates by birth cohort and graph them by age (as opposed to arraying them by age and graphing by year as in figure 3.3). Labor-force participation rates arranged in this manner, by age and by cohort, are given in figure 3.4, for (white) married women.

FIGURE 3.4 / Labor-Force Participation Rates of Married White Women

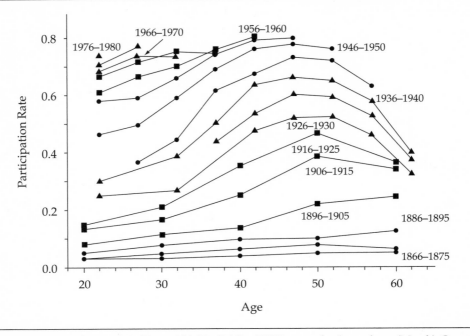

Sources: Birth cohorts 1866–75 to 1926–30, Goldin (1990); rest of cohorts from (March) Current Population Surveys.
Notes: Dates shown are birth-cohorts. Some dates are omitted when lines are close together, as in the cases of the 1876–1885, 1931–1935, 1941–1945, 1951–1955, and 1961–1965 cohorts.

They are given in figure 3.5 for all college graduate women independent of marital status.

Figure 3.4 gives labor-force participation rates by age for "synthetic" cohorts of married women born from 1866 to 1875 to 1976 to 1980. These are synthetic, not actual, cohorts because the graphs connect data across various federal decennial population censuses (or Current Population Surveys) by the birth year of the individuals and are not constructed from longitudinal data. These particular synthetic cohorts are only for currently married women. That is, a woman who marries at age twenty-one and remains married until age sixty-five will be correctly represented in these graphs. But a woman who marries at age thirty-two, divorces at age forty-five, and then remarries at age fifty-one will not be as accurately represented. She will enter the population at age thirty-two, leave at age forty-five, and reenter at age fifty-one. Some groups of individuals are better depicted than others. Despite that caveat, these graphs reveal an enormous amount about the synthetic and actual cohorts. Most important is that almost all cohorts of U.S. women had increased labor-force participation rates as they aged (within their married years).

FIGURE 3.5 / Labor-Force Participation Rates of College-Graduate Women, by Birth Cohort

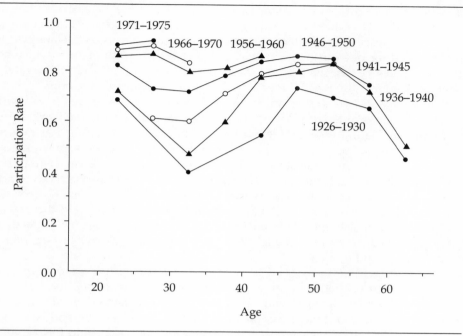

Source: Current Population Surveys (March).
Notes: Dates shown are birth cohorts.

The graph for college graduate women (figure 3.5) was constructed in a manner different from that for all education groups (figure 3.4). The former is for all marital statuses whereas the latter is only for married women. The caveat just mentioned about the synthetic cohorts does not apply to figure 3.5, although a different consideration is relevant. The composition by marital status in figure 3.5 changes as the cohort ages and, in consequence, participation rates decrease for the younger group many of whom married, had children, and left the labor force at least for a time.[8] Participation rates later increase with age, in a fashion similar to the data in figure 3.4 for married women across all educational groups. The participation rate levels are higher in figure 3.4 than in figure 3.3, as would be expected since the college group has a higher market wage.

The meaning of these cohort labor-force participation rates for the significance of gender in labor markets will be established in a moment. My more immediate point is simply that participation rates began to increase among young married women in the 1920s and 1930s. That observation leads me back to a clarification I earlier promised.

I noted before that the labor-force participation rates of married (white) women were rather low early in the twentieth century. These rates are so low that they would appear to be in error. They imply that married women contributed hardly at all to family income even when family income was quite meager.

One possibility is that the census question, which in the pre-1940 period asked occupation rather than employment, did not encourage women to state that they had worked for pay during some part of the year. Although that may have been the case, I believe that the reason for low participation rates is that these rates reflect market work, by which I mean paid employment outside the home.

Before the mid-twentieth century, married women often worked for pay within their own homes or those of friends or relatives as industrial home workers or as self-employed laundresses and seamstresses. They worked in family businesses as boardinghouse keepers or as shopkeepers in cities, and as agricultural workers on family farms. I have constructed estimates of shortfalls to the census data, and these shortfalls are substantial for the early decades of the twentieth century. But the shortfalls are mainly from work that was not directly remunerated (for example, from family businesses and family farms) and from work that did not take women out of their homes. The census data, while deficient in some respects, still provide a good measure of the labor-force participation of women outside their homes in the paid market.

Thus, the increase in married women's labor-force participation in the early decades of the twentieth century constituted a real change in their lives. Previous cohorts of married women may have labored in a manner hidden from the purview of the census takers. But they did not work at jobs that greatly expanded their social networks nor were they employed in firms that could have changed their lives by offering them job advancement.

TWO RELATED CHANGES IN THE EARLY TWENTIETH CENTURY

To understand the origins of the rising significance of gender I must recount two related changes of the early twentieth century. The first is the "high school movement."[9] The second is the emergence of ordinary white-collar work through the rise of the clerical, sales, and managerial sectors. Both changes are impressive in their magnitude and speed.

The High School Movement

The increase in high school attendance and graduation in the first few decades of the twentieth century created mass secondary schooling in America. Prior to 1900 secondary schooling was often directed at youths who were preparing for college entrance exams. A substantial fraction of high school graduates even as late as 1910 continued with some form of post-secondary-school training.

But around 1900 U.S. secondary schooling began a transformation that made it more useful for those entering work immediately after leaving high school. The changes were wide ranging and affected the high school curriculum. Language courses, for example, shifted from the dead tongues of Latin and Greek to the more immediately useful German and French. Bookkeeping, accounting, and various other commercial courses were added. In most cases, these changes made high school more relevant to youths who would not otherwise have attended, and thus served to increase their attendance and graduation rates. In other instances, however, these changes led children to be tracked into programs that prevented them from continuing with their education after high school. This is not the place to discuss the merits and demerits of early twentieth century educational reforms. The important point here is simply that the high school graduation rate of young people soared in the early twentieth century.

Less than 10 percent of all eighteen-year-olds graduated high school in 1910, but 35 percent did by 1930 outside the South. Attendance and graduation rates were considerably higher for girls than they were for boys, and they were higher for girls in every U.S. state before the Great Depression. The greater level of secondary school education for girls was sustained until unemployment rates soared in the 1930s, and teenage boys, who had previously worked in manufacturing and other sectors, were thrown out of work. But even though enrollment and graduation rates by sex narrowed in the 1930s, girls still went to school in greater numbers than boys.

The pull of manufacturing jobs for teenage boys, particularly those living in the industrial cities of the northeast and Midwest, was not the only reason for the difference in high school attendance and graduation rates by sex. The pecuniary return to a year of high school was greater for a young woman than for a young man in the industrial northeast given an equal lifetime of work.[10] But women labored considerably fewer years than did men. Unless young men had serious myopia concerning their future employment, one must find a more compelling reason for their lower high school graduation rates. The other reason for the higher enrollment and graduation rates of girls is that a high school degree and high school courses gave a young woman the ability to enter a white-collar job. Ordinary white-collar jobs, such as office positions, were nice, clean, and respectable. They paid relatively well and had shorter hours than manufacturing jobs. A woman who worked at a respectable job was well thought of and stood a greater chance of marrying a higher earning and more respectable husband. It should not be surprising that white-collar work was much preferred to manufacturing, even when the weekly pay was the same.

The "New" Economy of the Early Twentieth Century

The educational changes I summarized under the heading of the high school movement were not necessarily exogenous to structural changes in the economy. In the decades preceding these changes, parts of the U.S. economy began a grand transformation. Firms in manufacturing and in retail trade became larger, and the communications and public utilities sectors expanded significantly. The information sector of the economy grew as the cost of office equipment plummeted.[11] In consequence, more managerial and clerical workers—secretaries, stenographers, bookkeepers, and clerks of all types—were demanded.

In the 1890s these office positions were still the Dickensian black-coated variety. Secretaries were the guardians of the firm's secrets. Bookkeepers wore green shades and added long columns of numbers in their heads. The higher paid clerks had worked their way up from lowly office positions. Most of the office workers would have begun their employment with a belief that hard work, long tenure with the firm, and a pinch of good luck would get them a better position.

More relevant here is that, in 1890, most of these office workers were men. The secretary was not just a pretty face but, rather, the trusted employee of the company's president often in a direct line for his position. The bookkeeper was the company's accountant, not a girl working at a bookkeeping machine. Even the stenographer was often a man.

An aspect of these jobs that links educational and economic change is that most office jobs required a level of literacy and numeracy that could be achieved in secondary school. By the early twentieth century, the majority of firms hiring in these positions required some years of high school. By the 1930s the vast majority required a high school diploma.

The increase in high school education during the early 1900s was, in large part, caused by the increased demand for high school educated workers. But greater schooling must also have had an independent effect. The high school movement involved an enormous increase in public expenditures on education; schools were built and teachers were hired. Some youths were enticed to increase their education by the greater proximity of schools. But the majority of youths (or their parents) increased their demand for schooling to reap the greater rewards in the new economy.

THE OFFICE AND THE "NEW WOMAN"

The office jobs that initially expanded in number were of the skilled type—the Dickensian black-frocked clerks, the old-fashioned secretaries, and the green-shaded bookkeepers. Some of these positions were considered skilled because they were part of a job ladder within the firm. Ordinary clerks and secretaries and, possibly, even some stenographers and typists expected to be promoted one day. These jobs were soon replaced by newer positions that were not part of an internal job ladder.

Many of the new jobs were created by the mechanization of the office. Mechanization in the office began with the typewriter, later the calculator and comptometer (a form of adding machine). Duplicating, addressing, and billing machines, stenographic recorders, and filing systems rapidly followed. With electrification the industrial revolution of the office was in full swing and by the 1920s business magazines were filled with advertisements for office machinery.

The early twentieth century mechanization of the office was the white-collar counterpart of the industrial revolution in manufacturing that had swept America a century before. Their effects were similar. New work organization and machinery led to an intricate division of labor. Secretaries no longer kept the secrets of the office. Rather, they took dictation and typed letters. The functions of typist and stenographer became separate in most offices and were no longer bundled with those of a secretary. In large offices, such as those of the huge mail-order catalogue firms and the insurance companies, typists were assigned to different pools of varying skill and were paid commensurately with the group's typing speed and precision.

Similar changes occurred in other sectors of the economy. Retail stores, for example, greatly increased in size with the creation of department store chains. Owner-operators of small stores had manned the cash drawer, ordered the goods, took inventory, and stocked the shelves. But with increased scale, workers were hired to do separate tasks. Saleswomen and salesmen sold the goods, order-clerks placed the orders, stock-clerks handled inventory, and so on.

The growth of ordinary white-collar jobs in offices and retail stores and the increase of women in these positions led to an enormous shift in the occupational composition of working women between 1900 and 1930. In 1900 17.8 percent of all employed women (fourteen years and older) were white-collar workers in the professional, managerial, clerical, and sales categories; 8.3 percent were in the clerical and sales groups. But in 1930 44.2 percent of all employed women were in white-collar occupations; 27.8 percent were in the clerical and sales group—more than three times the percentage in 1900. The increase in white-collar employment in the subsequent three decades, from 1930 to 1960, was only 12 percentage points or less than half the increase in the previous three decades. (The occupational distribution data by sex, for 1900 to 1970, are given in table 3.1.)

Major ground for women's employment was broken in the early twentieth century, long before the immediate post–World War II years often credited with its change. One large difference between the two thirty-year periods, 1900 to 1930 and 1930 to 1960, is that the aggregate female labor-force participation rate did not increase by much from 1900 to 1930, whereas it increased substantially from 1930 to 1960.

Even though male workers in the white-collar occupational groups also increased their employment, the increase as a fraction of the labor force was far greater for women. About the same percentage of men and women were white-collar workers in 1900. But the increase for men was from 17.6 percent to 25.2 percent, one-third the change for women. For clerical and sales workers the increase was from 7.4 to 11.6 percent, or one-fifth the increase for women. Put another way, women were 18.5 percent of all white-collar workers in 1900 but were 33.2 percent in 1930. Whereas women were 20.2 percent of all clerical and sales personnel in 1900, they were 40.4 percent in 1930. However these data are expressed, the increase in white-collar and clerical work for women from 1900 to 1930 was truly spectacular.

By the 1920s workingwomen were no longer just domestic servants, manufacturing operatives, and piece-rate workers in factories and homes. They were white-collar workers and comprised almost half of all clerical and sales personnel. Young women, fresh out of high school, commercial institutes, and colleges and universities flocked to the new office jobs. More important for the discussion here is that they increasingly remained employed for brief periods after marriage.

In the early twentieth century the norm for workingwomen had been to leave paid work at the time of marriage, if not a bit before. But in the 1920s a new norm was forged. Women who had white-collar jobs did not necessarily quit work directly with marriage. Rather, some remained employed often until they decided to have a first child. The old norm had been formed when most jobs that women occupied were physically arduous, dirty, and not always respectable. The white-collar jobs of the office, in contrast, were clean, ladylike positions that used the mind more and muscle less. Husbands, families, and society, in general, rapidly discarded the old norm that a working wife brought shame to her family.

One complication is that "marriage bars"—policies that prohibited the hiring of married women and led to the dismissal of single women who married while employed—had been adopted by many school districts ever since the late nineteenth century. By the early twentieth century marriage bars began to appear in certain offices. The Great Depression accelerated the spread of marriage bars, introduced ostensibly to spread the work and give jobs to "breadwinners."[12] The economic downturn and these firm policies were major setbacks to the employment of married women. Yet the participation of young, married women continued to increase during the 1930s.

The 1920s was a time of social change in the lives of young women and the decade was aptly termed the era of the "new woman." The age at first marriage had increased before the 1920s and was fairly high by 1920; the birth rate had begun a long-run secular decline long before the 1920s and was low by 1920. The vote had been won; skirts were short; and so were hairdos. Much of the great American literature of the day reflected these changes and various authors, Sinclair Lewis and Theodore Dreiser among them, saw the potential for progress as well as the barriers to it. An example from the work of Sinclair Lewis, who was awarded the Nobel Prize in literature in 1930, will make my point.

The Job (1917) was the first novel in Sinclair Lewis's feminist trilogy.[13] The protagonist, Una Golden, was a young, cracker-jack stenographer in New York City who "could not imagine any future for . . . women in business." "The comfortable average men of the office," she observed with envy, "if they were but faithful and lived long enough, had opportunities, responsibility, forced upon them." Una eventually became a wealthy businesswoman and married a loving husband who admired her business acumen. But she was not content and mused at the end of the novel: "I will keep my job . . . But just the same . . . I want Walter, and I want his child." My point is not that a great American novelist wrote a modern story about career and family conflict, but that there were many stories and novels in the 1920s about independent-minded career women who had white-collar jobs.

BRAWN AND BRAIN JOBS

To understand the actual and potential role of the new office jobs, it will be convenient to divide occupations into brawn and brain jobs, even though many require a bit of both. For the early part of the twentieth century, however, this simplifying assumption is quite practical. Production jobs in manufacturing, as well as those in construction, transportation, and agriculture, were mainly of the brawn type. Office positions, however, required little brawn, but demanded thinking, literacy, numerical skill, and the like. They were brain jobs.

Many of the manufacturing positions that had substantial brawn requirements were limited to men, de facto. Entire industries in the late nineteenth and early twentieth centuries hired almost no women in production positions. Iron and steel in 1890, for example, employed 147,357 male production (craft and operative) workers but just two females across the entire United States. In that year, foundry and machine shops employed 205,530 male but only 1,040 female production workers. A similar sex composition existed in agricultural implements, carriages, cooperage, flouring and gristmill products, leather, liquors, lumber, timber products, and all of the building and construction trades. In fact, there were 23 industries (including the construction trades) in which men were at least 94 percent of all production workers across the entire United States. These industries accounted for 54 percent of all adult male production workers across all manufacturing employments.[14]

In some industries the brawn requirements that led to the virtual exclusion of female workers were actually vestigial and existed to protect jobs for male workers, often through union rules. The strength needed to perform the job could have been circumvented by the use of machinery, such as cranes and hoists, and was eliminated in some cases during the national crisis of World War I, and again during World War II when changes were made to factories that enabled the employment of women. In some factories machinery was added to render the work less physically demanding, whereas in others, work was divided so that the hauling and other physically demanding tasks were given to men. Examples in World War I are car and truck factories, foundries and machine tool shops. In World War II, the list is longer and includes aircraft, ammunition, gun, and tank production.[15]

Manufacturing firms occasionally hired women as replacement workers during strikes and they also hired women, contrary to union demands, to perform some of the lighter tasks in production. In the early 1900s, for example, a foundry union protested that the task of making small cores, which had lower strength requirements than the making of large cores, was offered to women. The position, it was claimed, was an integral part of an apprenticeship system in which male workers trained in the easier tasks, for example in the small cores, were then able to advance to the more arduous and skilled ones, for example to the larger cores. In a similar case involving slaughterhouses, there was no comparable claim and women were simply barred from the industry, possibly because it was feared they would lower wages or for other reasons. They were eventually hired, in some cases after a strike, but only in the sausage room.[16] In other cases, union demands were effectively nullified by changing supply conditions. The story of cigar makers is instructive. According to economist and social reformer Edith Abbott, the Cigar-Maker's International, established in 1851, adopted a constitution that excluded women (and blacks) but in 1867, after a large influx of Bohemian women who were skilled cigar makers, the union removed entry restrictions.[17]

EARNINGS FUNCTIONS IN BRAWN AND BRAIN JOBS IN THEORY AND IN FACT

Earnings Functions in Theory

A related aspect of the brawn and brain sectors concerns the earnings of workers across their employment histories. Consider the earnings of male workers in each of the two sectors, as depicted in figures 3.6a and 3.6b.

The brawn sector worker's wage at the beginning of his work experience is given by M_0 in figure 3.6a, and his wage does not increase much with time on the job.[18] Consider instead a male worker in the brain sector (figure 3.6b). He has a greater level of formal education than his brawn counterpart and, in consequence, earns more at the beginning of his job tenure and his earnings increase substantially with time on the job. The brain worker has greater slope to his earnings profile because he garners human capital and is advanced to more demanding positions. That is, the brain worker climbs an internal ladder, whereas the brawn worker does not or, when he does, the ladder is shorter.

Now consider adding women to each of these sectors. Women are at a considerable disadvantage in the brawn sector and begin with wages that are far below those of men. In figure 3.6a, for example, they begin at F_0. The disadvantage of women in the brawn sector comes about primarily because most women are not as strong as most men. That is not to say that the distribution of brawn by sex does not overlap, for it does. But the averages of the two distributions differ and substantial parts of the distributions are non-overlapping. Women have lower beginning wages, and even though their productivity increases with time on the job, their wages rise at the same rate as those of men whose initial wages are far higher. Thus, in figure 3.6a, a male worker at the start of his employment earns more than does a female worker, and he earns even more than a female worker with considerable job experience. But neither the male nor the female wage increases as much with time on the job as in the brain sector.

The brain sector should have evened out the playing field between men and women in the labor market. Women often obtained schooling of the same type as did men by attending public secondary schools, private business colleges, and academic colleges and universities.

In some sense, the brain sector did even the playing field. The initial wages of men and women were far closer in the brain sector than they were in the brawn sector. But "time on the job" did not yield the same return to women as it did to

FIGURE 3.6 / Schematic Diagrams of Male and Female Earnings Functions

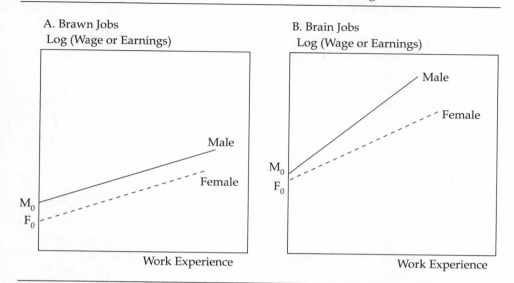

A. Brawn Jobs
Log (Wage or Earnings)

Male

Female

M_0
F_0

Work Experience

B. Brain Jobs
Log (Wage or Earnings)

Male

Female

M_0
F_0

Work Experience

Source: Author's depiction.

men. No level of work experience—with the firm or in all office work—led to much earnings growth for women, whereas it did for men. What this means is that the ratio of male to female earnings in the brain sector increased with greater levels of work experience. Rather staying relatively constant, as it did in brawn jobs, the ratio rose. In terms of a concept in labor economics, "wage discrimination" was actually *larger* in brain jobs than it was in the brawn jobs.

By wage discrimination is meant that part of the difference in wages by sex that is *not* explained by differences in observables that are related to productivity, such as work experience, education, and training. Rather, the wage difference is explained by a disparity by sex in the *returns* to these variables. Even if a man and a woman had the same levels of experience, education, and training, they would still have different wages because the return to each of the observables is different. Another possibility is that the constant term in the two equations (implicit in figure 3.6) is different. In the schematic representation of figure 3.6a, all wage discrimination is due to differences in initial earnings, that is, in the earnings of men and women at the start of their employment. In the case of jobs that only differ on the basis of strength requirements, the initial earnings difference would be primarily, but not entirely, due to differences in physical ability.[19]

Earnings Functions in Fact: Brawn Jobs

Figures 3.6a and 3.6b are schematic representations of longitudinal earnings patterns of men and women in the brain and brawn sectors. Longitudinal earnings data are not available for early-twentieth-century manufacturing workers but cross-section earnings do exist in data sets that contain many of the important co-variates. For office workers both retrospective and cross-section data exist for 1940, although I will discuss mainly the cross-section earnings data results.

The figure 3.6a representation, while schematic, is close to being correct. Table 3.2 reports the results from a survey of male and female workers in 1892 working primarily in manufacturing. Earnings functions for female manufacturing work-ers in the early 1900s give similar results.[20] The earnings functions for men and women are not as parallel as those depicted in figure 3.6a, but within the relevant range they are nearly so.[21]

In the survey that produced these data, workers were asked when they began paid employment, how many years they worked in their current occupation, and the number of years they were with their current employer. Thus work experience is measured three ways: total experience, years in an occupation, and years with a firm (usually called tenure). If an employee works for the same firm and in the same occupation since beginning paid employment, then the earnings function with respect to experience is given by the sum of the coefficients on total experi-ence, years in occupation, and years with firm.

As can be seen from the means of the cross-section sample, male workers re-mained in the same occupation for much of their work history but changed firms with some regularity.[22] Women had lower levels of total experience than men, but had more constancy with the current firm. In fact, the average woman had been with her current firm about the same time that she was in her current occupation. In the discussion that follows I will aggregate the three types of work experience.[23]

The male (log) earnings function, estimated as a quadratic in total work experi-ence, has a small squared term, whereas the female function, also estimated as a quadratic, has a much larger squared term and thus more curvature. Almost all women working in factories labored fewer than eight years. The mean of total work experience for women was five years and that for men was about fifteen years. Until about twelve years of work experience the earnings functions for men and women are virtually parallel. The female earnings function actually rises with work experience somewhat more than does that for males. Similar to the observation just made about the schematic representation in figure 3.6a, the most quantitatively important part of the difference in male and female earnings, given the observables, is due to the initial disparity in wages and *not* to differ-ences in the return to the observables. In fact, across the entire sample the inter-cept explains all of the difference in male and female earnings, conditional on the observables.[24]

One potentially complicating factor is that married men earned almost 17 per-cent more than unmarried men, conditional on the other observables, but that married women did not earn more (or less) than single women. But even if the in-tercept is computed for the unmarried, it explains almost the entire gap. I discuss the "marriage premium" in more detail in the section on office workers.

Thus wage discrimination in manufacturing existed primarily because of dif-ferences in the intercept terms. If anything, differences in the coefficients served to

TABLE 3.2 / Earnings Functions for Manufacturing Workers: Male and Female, 1892

	Males		Females	
Dependent Variable	Coefficient (T-Statistic)	Mean	Coefficient (T-Statistic)	Mean
Log (weekly earnings)		2.688		1.902
Constant	1.75		1.14	
	(24.06)		(10.87)	
Total experience	0.0524	15.02	0.0333	4.95
	(8.59)		(2.31)	
Total experience squared	−0.0009		−0.0011	
	(6.62)		(3.16)	
Years in occupation	0.0212	10.39	0.1077	3.76
	(3.30)		(5.44)	
Years in occupation squared	−0.0004		−0.0030	
	(2.51)		(4.43)	
Years with firm	0.0113	3.92	0.0236	2.57
	(1.20)		(1.06)	
Years with firm squared	−0.0001		−0.0014	
	(0.04)		(1.02)	
Never married	−0.1663	0.65	−0.0005	0.91
	(3.24)		(0.01)	
Maturity or schooling[a]	0.0247	8.47	0.0195	9.62
	(4.00)		(2.12)	
R^2	0.28		0.42	
Number of observations	833		228	

Source: Barry Eichengreen (1984).
Notes: "Total experience" is years since entering paid employment, "years in occupation" is the number of years the worker was employed in the current occupation, and "years with firm" is the number of years employed by the current firm. The data are primarily for manufacturing workers. Some male workers were in the construction industry and some female workers were in the service sector (for example, laundresses, waitresses, saleswomen).
[a]Variable is (age–age work began–6) and is, in consequence, a combination of years of education and "maturity" as measured by age conditional on total experience. Eichengreen (1984) terms this variable "schooling." See Goldin (1990, 102, n22) for a justification concerning why the variable is picking up maturity more than actual schooling.

decrease earnings differences between men and women. The earnings trajectory for work in offices was extremely different.

Earnings Functions in Fact: Brain Jobs

Clerical employments—the brain jobs—beginning sometime in the early twentieth century had earnings functions that can be far better represented by figure 3.6b than by figure 3.6a. In the schematic representation of figure 3.6b, initial earnings for men and women are nearly identical. But even though job tenure leads to increases in the earnings of men and women, the increases are considerably less for women.

Because brain jobs are obtained after education in high school, college, or at a commercial institute, the notion of the intercept is a bit more complicated than that given in figure 3.6a. One must also take into account the level of education achieved and the value of education to each sex. There are several methods of doing this in a regression context and fortunately the results for each are fairly similar for the data in question.[25] The method employed here estimates separate earnings functions by sex, adds the estimated value of education to the intercept term, and computes the difference.

The data set used is for 1939 and was collected from the archival records of a U.S. Department of Labor, Women's Bureau survey (see sources to table 3.3). The Women's Bureau surveyed firms in a wide range of industries that hired office workers in five U.S. cities (Houston, Kansas City, Los Angeles, Philadelphia, and Richmond).[26] The data for Philadelphia were coded from the original forms housed in Record Group no. 86 at the National Archives and the sample contains about 3,000 observations almost equally divided between men and women.[27]

Table 3.3 gives the estimated earnings functions where the explanatory variables are tenure, total office experience, years of high school, college or university, and business school.[28] Earnings at the start of office work were 7 percent higher for men than for women if both groups were unmarried and had four years of high school but no other education or training. The difference rises to 10 percent if both spent one year at a university or college, but declines to 6 percent if both had one year of business college (and no university or college training).[29]

As in the case of manufacturing workers, a complicating factor is that married male office workers earned, on average, 13 percent more than did unmarried male office workers but no difference existed by marital status for female office workers. During the Great Depression firms stated they had policies to pay married men more than single men and thus, presumably, more than married and single women with the same qualifications. A male marriage premium, of similar relative magnitude, has also been found in more recent data. Fixed effect estimation suggests that perhaps 80 percent of the premium is due to a "productivity" increase, rather than selection differences into marriage.[30] If the same held for the 1930s, then only a small part of the difference by sex would be due to different pay for similar characteristics. A more jaundiced view is that today, and in the past, married men are awarded a premium that is due neither to selection nor to productivity differences. Rather, the premium arises from a social dictum that firms should adequately provide for men's families.

Even though the intercept terms are similar by sex, the earnings function for men rises more steeply with work experience than it does for women. After five years in office work the average man earned 8 percent more than the average woman, after ten years the average man earned 14 percent more, and after fifteen years the difference widened to 21 percent.[31] Thus the earnings functions for office work in 1940 are rather different from those for manufacturing employments in 1890. Male and female earnings in office (brain) work were far more similar at the

TABLE 3.3 / Earnings Functions for Office Workers in 1940

Dependent Variable	Males			Females	
	Coefficient (T-Statistic)	Mean		Coefficient (T-Statistic)	Mean
Log (annual earnings)		7.339			6.951
Constant	6.54			6.46	
	(233.1)			(267.9)	
Years with firm	0.0106	10.21		0.0112	7.61
	(3.065)			(3.49)	
Years with firm squared	0.00010			0.00017	
	(0.967)			(1.49)	
Total office experience	0.0515	12.77		0.0363	10.39
	(14.25)			(11.86)	
Total office experience squared	−0.000872			−0.000711	
	(9.08)			(7.66)	
Married	0.132	0.484		−0.00481	0.197
	(7.84)			(0.327)	
Years of high school	0.0364	3.18		0.0395	3.22
	(6.09)			(7.86)	
Years of college or university	0.0827	0.724		0.0466	0.274
	(15.52)			(7.30)	
Years of business training	0.0307	0.184		0.0366	0.292
	(2.43)			(3.64)	
R^2	0.633			0.488	
Number of observations	1,492			1,395	

Source: "1940 Office Worker Survey" (1940), the National Archives, Record Group no. 86, boxes 472–486. See also Goldin (1990, data appendix).
Notes: Only those with greater than or equal to eight years of elementary school are included. This restriction excludes just 2.1 percent of the sample. "Years with the firm" is the number of years the worker was employed by the current firm. "Total office experience" is the number of years the worker was employed in any office job. Most workers in the survey were only employed in office positions and thus "total office experience" is almost always the same as all work experience.

start compared with their earnings in industrial (brawn) employment. But whereas the ratio of their earnings remained the same in industrial work, it widened with every year in office employment.

The Women's Bureau survey also asked retrospective information about the occupation that each worker had at the start of office work as well as their occupation at the time of the survey. At the beginning of their office employment men who had a high school diploma as their highest degree had starting positions as messenger, mail boy, mimeo-machine operator, and lower-skilled clerk, most of which were low-paying jobs. Most women with the same level of education had starting positions as stenographer, typist, switchboard operator, and secretary. Although some were lower-paying positions, most of these beginning positions paid a moderate amount. After an equivalent period of time in office work and with the same firm, men often advanced to positions such as those in the accounting group, manager, and supervisor, whereas most women remained in the positions they had at entry, be they stenographer, typist, or secretary. Some did advance from typist to secretary, but advancement rarely went further no matter how much experience they accumulated.

FIRM-LEVEL POLICIES IN OFFICES

Women were not advanced at the same rate that men were in most office settings and in the larger offices they were rarely advanced at all. Their lack of promotion is a mechanical explanation for why women's earnings fell behind men's with time on the job. There are many possible underlying reasons for the career stagnation of women and only some concern the bias of those who made promotion decisions. But some of the reasons are related to bias and can be discerned from firm-level policies that restricted certain jobs to men and other jobs to women.

The firm-level policies, which first appeared in the early 1900s, did *not* limit all the well-paying jobs to men and all the menial jobs to women. Rather, many menial starting jobs, as I just noted, were among the ones reserved for men and some that required a modicum of training were among the ones reserved for women. It might not seem odd that certain jobs were reserved for men. But it might at first glance appear curious that any jobs were barred to men and that many of the more menial positions were reserved for men.

Firm-level policies are difficult to track today and they are generally more difficult to track historically.[32] But because the Women's Bureau of the Department of Labor surveyed hundreds of firms we know a considerable amount about firm policies in the 1920s and the 1930s.

The Women's Bureau study that was the basis for the individual-level data set just used also contains a related set of questions inquired at the firm level.[33] Several hundred firms in each city, across virtually all sectors, were surveyed and a firm representative, generally a top ranking manager or human resource officer, answered questions about employment practices and policies.[34] According to the Women's Bureau the survey was designed to study the use of office machinery by firms. The survey did inquire about office machinery and asked many useful questions about the size and composition of the firm as well as other fairly innocuous questions about employment policies, such as centralized hiring, paid vacations, and sick days. These questions are among the first to have been asked in a large scale survey that can reveal the existence of modern labor market practices. But additional questions were requested that belie the stated reason for the survey. These questions are far less innocuous.

The survey inquired about practices and policies that *today* might reveal sex, age, marital status, race, and ethnic discrimination or employment bias. As can be seen in the facsimile of the survey, figure 3.7, the Women's Bureau asked the minimum and maximum ages for hiring, whether the firm had hiring restrictions with

FIGURE 3.7   /   Facsimile of 1940 Women's Bureau Firm-Level Survey

---

Department of Labor   Agent _____
Women's Bureau   Date _____
OFFICE WORKERS' STUDY 1940

1. Firm name _____   2. Business_____   3. Address_____
4. Persons interviewed and positions _____
5. Who are the executives? _____ administrators? _____ professional workers?_____

	Men	Women	Total
6. No. clerical workers regularly employed 1939	____	____	____
7. No. clerical workers employed as extras 1939	____	____	____
8. No. new clerical workers taken on in 1939	____	____	____

9. Hours of work: Daily ____ Saturday ____ Total weekly ____ Overtime ____
10. Office organization: list departments _____ types of machines used _____
11. Method of wage payment: monthly, semimonthly, weekly, daily, hourly, piece, bonuses

12. Employment requirements and practices (discuss by job where differences exist)
  a. Hiring: Who hires new employees? _____
     What are beginning rates of pay? _____ system of advancement? _____
  b. Source of applicants _____
  c. Age: Minimum ____ Maximum ____
  d. Marital status
     Are married women employed? _____
     Are women who marry in service allowed to remain? _____
  e. Sex
     Which jobs open to men only? _____
     To women only? _____
  f. Educational requirements
     1. General _____ 2. Special business training _____
  g. Policies with reference to race and color _____

13. General policies
  Vacations with pay _____ To whom? _____ Length? _____
  Sick leave _____ Dismissal wage and notice_____
  Promotional policy and salary increases _____ Retirement plans _____

Organization: Trade union or other _____

Other welfare activities _____

Source: "1940 Office Worker Survey" (1940), National Archives, Record Group no. 86, boxes 496–500. See also Goldin (1990, data appendix).
Note: Questions discussed in the text are in bold.

regard to race or color, whether married women were employed, and whether single women in the employ of the firm were dismissed if they married. It also requested a list of the jobs that were *by policy* open to men only and those that were open to women only.

Although these questions appear from our current litigious standpoint to provide unequivocal smoking gun evidence, there was apparently no hesitation on the part of the respondents to answer them. About one-third of the firms responded that they had a policy that discriminated by race or color and most of these stated that they did not hire African Americans in clerical positions. Many firms boasted that they engaged in no *race* discrimination, by which they meant ethnic discrimination, but stated they would not hire "Negroes" in office positions (although they prided themselves in hiring "Italians").[35] Other firms noted that they hired neither Jews nor blacks. Firms were equally at ease in admitting they had policies requiring the dismissal of single women when they married and that barred the hiring of married women. The survey was taken, after all, in the ninth year of the Great Depression. Many firms proudly added, although they were not directly prompted on the matter, that they paid married men more than single men.

As revealing as these questions are, the ones that interest me here are those that asked which jobs were restricted to women only and which to men only *by firm policy*. I will summarize the answers to these questions from several hundred of these records.[36]

Fully 72 percent of the surveyed firms (with ten or more female and ten or more male office employees) had policies that reserved some positions to men, and an equal percentage had policies regarding women's jobs. About 63 percent of all firms had policies that restricted *both* male and female jobs, reserving some for men and some for women. Interestingly, whereas 46 percent of the firms admitted they had employment restrictions based on race, 52 percent of the firms that limited some positions to "women only" had racial policies.[37]

The jobs that were restricted to women only were often those that required training *before* job entry (in stenography, comptometer operations, typing, and the use of bookkeeping machinery, to list a few) but did not lead to advanced positions except possibly to that of secretary.[38] The jobs restricted to men only were the advanced positions, such as auditor, cashier, supervisor, and most positions leading to them. Some of these ladder positions appear to have been rather menial, such as messenger, office boy ("source of future staff"), and certain bookkeeping jobs ("so men can learn the business").[39]

We have, historically, become so familiar with, and thus inured to, policies similar to these that we often do not question why firms restricted jobs by sex. What were firms gaining from the restrictions that kept women out of certain jobs (men only) and those that kept men out of other jobs (women only)?

The easier part of this question concerns why some positions were reserved for men. Such a restriction can be viewed as outright Becker-type discrimination (group A prefers not to associate with group B) with all of its segregation and wage consequences.[40] I will shortly discuss a framework, which I term a "pollution theory" of discrimination, that I believe can better address the question. It is one in which there is asymmetric information concerning women's productivity and in which both prestige and income from a job give utility to men.

The answer to the second question—why did firms restrict jobs to be female only—follows from the first. If women are barred from jobs that have an internal ladder and lead to the good jobs, then they will be hired into only those jobs that do not have advancement possibilities. These positions become quintessentially dead end jobs. If a man were in such a job, he would probably complain. According to an official at Leeds and Northrup, manufacturers of electrical instruments in Philadelphia, the firm had a policy of not hiring men as a bookkeeping machine operator, stenographer, or secretary since there was "no chance for advancement for men, hence they would be dissatisfied."[41] Therefore, firms barred men from those positions. The result was that the jobs offered to women were neither high in the wage distribution, nor were they the very lowest paying positions. We will see that this is an implication of the "pollution theory."

HOUSEHOLD PRODUCTION AND CHILD CARE BEFORE 1950

Before I describe the framework for understanding the rising significance of gender, I must settle a nagging issue. My reference to the possibility of real change in the 1920s may have stirred some doubts about its practicality. Child-care responsibilities were even greater in the 1920s than they are today. Household production, one might think, had not changed much for centuries. That is, it might appear that the labor supply function for married women would not have shifted out by much, if at all, by the 1920s and that it would have been rather inelastic with respect to women's wages. In some sense the characterization that household production had not changed much is correct. But in other ways it is not. There was change, some of it rather large.

Fertility in the 1920s was actually at an all time low in the United States, and it continued to decrease into the Great Depression. For the cohort of women born around 1905, the lifetime number of children ever born per married woman was as low as it would be for any cohort of American women until that born around 1945. Furthermore, for the cohort born around 1905 about 20 percent of ever-married (white) women had zero births over their lifetimes. Today the figure is 13.3 percent for all thirty-five- to forty-four-year-old ever-married women and 14.2 percent for thirty-five- to forty-four-year-old non-Hispanic whites. The conclusion is clear: the cohort born around 1905 had few children and a large fraction had no children.

The household, however, still involved considerable labor. But by 1924, 65 percent of urban households had electricity and 80 percent would by 1930. Electric irons and mechanical washing machines were diffusing rapidly; refrigerators and vacuum cleaners would come just a bit later. My point is that gender differences in the labor market would have mattered far less had economic and educational changes in the early part of the twentieth century been given the chance to flower. The question, then, is why they were not given a chance.

THE POLLUTION THEORY OF DISCRIMINATION

What were the forces behind the rising significance of gender? Those familiar with a Becker-type model of discrimination, in which one group has a preference not to work or interact with another group, might think that it will suffice.[42] But think again. Every man has a mother, most have wives, and some men have sisters. Men do not seem to be averse to being around women in the same way that Arabs and Jews are, Catholics and Protestants have been, and whites and non-whites still are in many parts of the nation. Discrimination against women is different. One has to find the *reason* why men are averse to having women in their job.

Perhaps a version of the "statistical discrimination" framework will be better for these purposes.[43] In a statistical discrimination model, group identity (for example, sex, race) provides additional information regarding an attribute such as productivity, criminality, or reliability. Even though the Becker model of discrimination and the statistical discrimination framework have important and insightful implications, neither fits the historical facts concerning occupational segregation by sex. I have, therefore, formulated another framework that I call the pollution theory model of discrimination.[44] It is a hybrid model: the tastes or preferences of employees matter, as in the Becker model, and there is asymmetric information, as in the statistical discrimination framework.[45]

The model is straightforward although the actual workings of it are less so. The simple intuition is that men want to keep women out of certain jobs because women "pollute" the prestige that men get from being in those jobs.[46] Women's entry into these jobs indicates or signals that the qualifications for the job have been reduced and this reduces the prestige that is accorded to men in these occupations.

The model has two periods. In period 1 all men, but no women at all, are employed and they are in occupations commensurate with their skill. The skill of both men and women is measured by a single-valued characteristic, C (for example, analytical ability, strength, creativity). Thus, if C were analytical ability, a high value of C would be required to be an engineer or a chemist and a low value would be required to be a laborer or a factory operative. There is one and only one occupation for which each level of C is the minimum level required. A competitive equilibrium in workers will result if each man is employed in the occupation for which his value of C is the minimum value required. In the version of the model summarized here, I assume that the demand for the output of each occupation is infinitely elastic (that is, output prices are given) and therefore that there is no "crowding" in any occupation. That is, even if women could enter an occupation, they would not depress the wages of men and therefore this is not the reason men will oppose the entry of women.

An important aspect of the model concerns asymmetries in information. The dis-

tribution of C for men, the median of C for women, and the value of C for each occupation in period 1 are known by all. But the value of C for any particular woman
is known only by her and by her prospective employer. Another informational
asymmetry concerns whether a technological shock to the occupational requirement has occurred. Only those currently in the occupation know whether the minimum level of C needed for an occupation in period 1 has changed by period 2.

In period 2 women apply to enter the occupations currently filled by men only.
In this sense, the model contains an important historical element. In 1900, for example, many occupations contained few or no women in part because the labor-
force participation of married women was extremely low.

Jobs confer both a wage, which is a function of C, and a level of "prestige,"
which is initially a function of the minimum level of C known to be required for
the job in period 1. When a woman tries to enter a currently all-male occupation
her skill level is assumed, by those *outside* the occupation, to be the *median* skill
level of all women rather than her actual skill level, which is not known by those
outside the occupation. The prestige a male worker receives from being in an occupation is conferred by those *outside* the occupation, for example by those in his
community or in the local bar or at the sports club. Thus the skill level that is *believed* to be required for the occupation is the only aspect of the occupation that
matters for the prestige level.

Because the initial level of C for each occupation is known, why should the prestige from an occupation change when a woman enters it? The reason is that technological shocks are randomly experienced by occupations and these shocks reduce the minimum level of skill required for the occupation.[47] (Recall that only
those in the occupation know the exact nature of the shock.) A woman who tries to
enter a (male) job having a skill requirement above the skill of the median woman
will encounter serious opposition from male workers. Her entry will *signal that the
occupation was hit by one of these random shocks*. Note that because demand is infinitely elastic, there are no wage effects. Men are not hostile to women because their
entry will depress wages.

As an example, consider the occupation of firefighting. Until recently there were
virtually no female firefighters in the United States. Even today there are many
municipalities that do not have any women firefighters on their force. Firefighter
recruits must pass a grueling physical test that involves carrying a heavy pack,
running up many flights of stairs, and performing various firefighting tasks. As
equipment became lighter due to technological advances, such as those in hose
construction, the physical tests were changed and more women were able to pass
them. Male firefighters in various parts of the United States challenged the hiring
of women by adding tasks to the new tests and by harassing women who passed
the tests and were hired into the force.[48] In the pollution framework, male firefighters were protecting the prestige of their occupation by changing the test
and harassing female firefighters. But even if the technology had not changed and
even if a woman could pass the original test, men might still want to prevent a
woman from entering. The reason is that no one would know that the occupation
had not been hit with a random technology shock that reduced the skill required

for the occupation. All they would see is that a woman was hired and they would infer that the occupation had been "deskilled."

An implication of the pollution theory model is that jobs will be segregated by sex above the median level of the productivity characteristic (C) for women, *even if men and women have the same distribution of productivity*. Jobs will be integrated by sex below the median level of C for women. Because of the asymmetric information setup of the framework, women cannot gain entry into jobs above the median of their productivity characteristic because they will be perceived as polluting the prestige of the men in those occupations.

But, if women can be credentialed, that is if they can prove to all that they are equal to the men already in the occupation, there will be no decrease in prestige with their entry. I contend that this credentialing was an important part of the declining significance of gender. Beginning in the late 1960s and early 1970s young women entered professional schools to train as managers, doctors, and lawyers, among other professions. Possible reasons that women increased their numbers in professional schools, especially those conferring credentials, include the resurgence of feminism in the 1960s, federal anti-discrimination legislation, and the diffusion of the oral contraceptives among young, unmarried women.[49]

IMPLICATIONS OF MALE AND FEMALE BRAIN JOBS

Unlike the brawn jobs that had true requirements that actually limited women's productivity in them, the new office jobs acquired an "aura of gender." Jobs became "female" and jobs became "male." One might say that jobs developed "secondary sex characteristics." The jobs that became female were made into dead-end jobs and white collars faded into pink. The lower positions, that were once the training ground for upper positions, now became benches rather than rungs on a ladder.

Because of these gender distinctions, the supply side movements from decreased birth rates and changes in household production technology never had a full chance to flower in the 1920s and beyond, and the demand side shifts in the white-collar sector affected primarily the employment of single and young married women. Perhaps of more importance is that labor market and job investment dynamics were altered. Women did not have as great an incentive to remain in the labor force.[50] Nor did they have as great an incentive to invest in various types of education and training.

The well-educated woman from the 1940s to the 1960s took a job that had a relatively flat earnings profile, such as teacher, librarian, social worker, or nurse.[51] These positions allowed for lifecycle interruptions with little earnings penalty. It is likely that many would have done the same even had the barriers just discussed not been in place. But there would have been another large group who would not have.

Reverberations of the barriers to women's advancement in ordinary white-collar work in the 1920s to the 1940s surfaced in the 1950s and 1960s. Even college graduate women who wanted to be on the fast track, who wanted more than the dead-end positions and more than the flat earnings profile jobs, were often asked one simple question when they applied for work: "Can you type?"

Rather than a continued increase in married women's labor-force participation among twenty- and thirty-year olds, there was stagnation. Rather than a continuation of the low birth rates, there was a resurgence of large families—the "baby boom." Young women in the 1950s and early 1960s were aware of the problems their immediate predecessors had encountered in the labor markets. Discouraged about their prospects, many had large families and remained at home.[52] The age at first marriage, even among college graduate women, was extremely low in the 1950s and 1960s. Half of all college graduate women married within two years of graduating from a four-year college and that trend continued until the cohort born around 1950 or in about 1973.

Was this because there was little else that women, particularly the college-educated, could do that was sustaining? A strong argument can be made to the effect that long-term gender change was slowed in the 1950s and 1960s by the forces that were put in place in the 1920s—by the origins of wage discrimination that produced the "rising significance of gender."

But then something changed.

THE DECLINING SIGNIFICANCE OF GENDER: SUMMARY AND CONCLUSION

How did we move from a rising to a declining significance of gender? Recall that there were new nice jobs and greater levels of education in the 1920s, both of which increased the participation of young women, even young married women, in the labor force. Policies arose at the firm level that created sex-segregated occupations. These, in turn, altered the incentives for education and training among women. A framework that can help us understand the origins of these policies is the "pollution theory" of discrimination, in which there is asymmetric information concerning the productivity characteristic of women. Men are averse to having women enter their occupation when women's productivity is not observable and verifiable by all.

One way to break out of the world of pollution is to have the credentialing of various occupations. In the 1970s women became more credentialed by acquiring advanced degrees. There are many factors that could have produced this result. Among them are social factors such as feminism, the Pill, and the social upheaval of the Vietnam war era. There is also government policy such as affirmative action, the Civil Rights Act, and Title IX. In my own work I have emphasized the role of the Pill, but there is much room for the complementary effects of these other factors. This is not the place to examine the declining significance of gender in the second half of the twentieth century. My purpose, rather, has been to expose the fact that long before there was a declining significance of gender in the labor market there was a rising significance of gender and that it delayed real change.

This chapter is a revised version of NBER Working Paper no. 8915 and was presented to the Cornell University Inequality Program Symposium on "The Declining Significance of Gender," October 2001, and was the first of the author's two Marshall Lectures at Cambridge University, April 30 and May 1, 2002. I thank Francine Blau, Mary Brinton, Robert Max Jackson, Larry Katz, and Michael Waldman for comments. Rebecca Kalmus provided exceptional research assistance and Bert Huang lent expert help with legal search engines.

NOTES

1. I should note at the outset that I do not mean to imply that "gender" was an unimportant distinction prior to the early twentieth century or that occupations were not extremely sex-segregated. I am, however, arguing that gender became more important in terms of income forgone from labor market restrictions placed on women by firms and other institutions.
2. The increase from 1900 to 1930 was more than two times that from 1930 to 1960 (26.4 percentage points versus 12.1 percentage points), often viewed as decades of greatly increased participation of women in white-collar jobs. In fact, the percentage point increase from 1900 to 1930 was about the same as that from 1930 to 2000, when about 73 percent were in white-collar jobs.
3. See Blau (1977) on this point.
4. That was not the case in all workplaces in which brawn apparently mattered, as I will later make clear.
5. Many of these young women were unmarried when they first entered the labor force and are not included in figure 3.3.
6. I exclude individuals in school because the fraction who were attending school greatly increased during the period considered. The labor-force participation rate of young women actually decreased, but the increase for those attending school more than offset it. The rate for fifteen- to twenty-four-year-old (white) single women decreased from 0.466 in 1920 to 0.426 in 1930. But the schooling rate for this age group increased from 0.316 in 1920 to 0.493 in 1930, and thus the rate excluding those at school increased from 0.682 to 0.841 (labor force data from Goldin 1990; schooling data from Goldin 1994 and U.S. Department of Education 1993; population data from U.S. Bureau of the Census 1975).
7. See Goldin (1989) and Heckman and Willis (1977) on "heterogeneous" female labor-force participation. Goldin (1989) shows that the female labor force was relatively heterogeneous in the 1920s to 1950s, and Heckman and Willis (1977) demonstrate that heterogeneity continued into the 1970s. If the labor force is "completely heterogeneous" and the participation rate is 20 percent, then 20 percent of the women are in the labor force all year and 80 percent are not in at all. Furthermore, those women who are in the labor force remain in for long periods and are joined by others, when the participation rate rises, who were not in the labor force recently. In contrast, a "completely homoge-

neous" female labor force is one for which all women are in the labor force for the same number of weeks per year and, as the participation rate rises, each increases the number of weeks she works. "Complete heterogeneity" and "complete homogeneity" are extremes of a spectrum.

8. Another caveat is that cohorts increase their education as they age either because they actually gain more education or because there is educational "creep" or "inflation."

9. By the "high school movement" I mean the rapid increase in enrollment and graduation from the nation's secondary schools from around 1910 to 1940 and also the building of secondary schools particularly in the less densely settled parts of the nation. See Goldin (1998).

10. Goldin and Katz (2000) use the 1915 Iowa State Census to estimate the pecuniary return to a year of high school in 1914 Iowa. Iowa did not have much manufacturing and, in particular, there were few industries that offered young men relatively high wages. Thus returns to education were fairly similar by sex, but the same was probably not the case in the more industrial parts of America where young men could find relatively high paying jobs even without a high school education.

11. A decline in the relative price of office equipment could lead to an increase or a decrease in the demand for office workers and will depend on the substitutability between labor and capital in the information sector and on the increased demand for information.

12. See Goldin (1991) on marriage bars before and during the Great Depression.

13. *Main Street* (1920), the best known of the trilogy, was second, and *Ann Vickers* (1933) was last.

14. U.S. Census Office (1895) and Goldin (1990, table 3.4).

15. On the use of machinery during World War I, see New York State, Department of Labor (1919).

16. See Goldin (1990, 104) on entry barriers to women in foundries and slaughterhouses. For one possible reason for these entry barriers, see the following "pollution theory" section and Goldin (2002).

17. See Abbott (1907).

18. "Experience" here can be thought of as total work experience, although I will later distinguish among total work experience, occupation experience, and tenure with a firm.

19. See Goldin (1990) on using piece-rate data to estimate the portion of the difference in the constant terms due to physical ability.

20. Although the 1892 survey is for California and includes women in various service occupations (for example, laundress, waitress, saleswoman), the earnings function estimated for the female observations is nearly identical to that from data covering a large number of cities and industries in 1888. See Goldin (1990, chapter 4), which also contains a discussion of earnings functions and historical data.

21. Thus, the rate of increase for a year of job experience in manufacturing circa 1890 was about the same for men and women during the first ten or so years of job experience. Earnings for women then leveled off whereas those for men continued to rise. At twenty or so years of experience, therefore, the differences in earnings between men and women were large. The similarity of returns to experience, therefore, holds only for the observable, and thus relevant, range of women's job experience.

22. These are not necessarily the means from longitudinal data.

23. If total work experience (Exp) is coterminous with that in an occupation and for an employer, the earnings function is: $\log w = K + 0.0849 \text{ Exp} - 0.0014 \text{ Exp}^2$ for males and $\log w = K + 0.1646 \text{ Exp} - 0.0055 \text{ Exp}^2$ for females, where K = all other factors.

24. The intercept difference for unmarried males and unmarried females using the table 3.2 results is 0.466, the difference for all males and all females is 0.524, and that for married males and females is 0.632. The log wage difference estimated at 4.95 years of total experience (the mean for females) is 0.521 and that at 15.02 years (the mean for males) is 0.512. Therefore, the intercept difference explains almost the entire difference in earnings for unmarried males and females given the observables and explains more than the entire difference when the intercept includes all or part of the "marriage premium" for men.

25. One method pools the data for men and women, adds a dummy variable for "female," and uses the coefficient on female as the difference in earnings by sex for beginning workers. An extension of this method is to interact the education and training variables (and any others that are predetermined) with female. The difference in the intercepts would be the coefficient on female plus those on the interaction terms multiplied by the means of the variables. Yet another way to compute the difference in the intercepts by sex is to estimate earnings functions for each sex, add the estimated value of education to the intercept term, and take the difference. I use the latter method.

26. The data were collected in 1940 but inquired of earnings and occupations in 1939. See U.S. Department of Labor, Women's Bureau (1942).

27. See Data Appendix in Goldin (1990). The original sample used in Goldin (1990) contained 1,206 observations. Additional data from the original surveys of Women's Bureau Bulletin no. 188 were collected at the National Archives bringing the total usable sample size to 2,948.

28. Business school means some type of business training in a proprietary institution generally called a "business college."

29. No information was given on college or university major. Far more of the men than the women must have done drafting, engineering, and accounting degrees that enabled them to be placed in more lucrative positions. Even though most college educated women advanced no further than secretary, it is not possible using these data to determine whether college preparation was the reason for the better placement of college men.

30. Korenman and Neumark (1991). The 80 percent figure given by these authors could be an overstatement if the reason that men married is that they had matured sufficiently. These men would then be more productive when married, but marriage would not be a "treatment."

31. These calculations assume that total office experience and that with the current firm are the same. That is, I assume that office experience for the worker began with the current employer. The assumption is not far from the facts given by the means in table 3.3.

32. See Blau (1977) on sex segregation by firms within occupational categories.

33. The Women's Bureau performed an earlier survey of firms, in 1931, that asked similar questions regarding discrimination on the basis of marital status and that was also taken to determine the effects of mechanization on employment. That survey reflected firm policies before the Great Depression, although it also revealed changes at the onset

of the economic downturn. Only the firm-level portion survives (in the National Archives) and is considerably smaller and less complete than is the survey for 1939. See U.S. Department of Labor, Women's Bureau (1934) and Goldin (1990, 1991).

34. The sectors include manufacturing, law, real estate, retail, service, education, government, public utilities, railroad, communications, insurance, banking, and advertising.

35. The category of "race" on the form appears to have meant the various European nationalities whereas "color" meant African American, white, and Asian.

36. The data set consists of 329 firms in Kansas City, Los Angeles, and Philadelphia that hired office workers. The data I summarize are for the 195 firms with 10 or more male employees and 10 or more female employees because the answers are meaningful only if the firms hired both sexes and were sufficiently large to have had positions that could have been reserved for one or the other sex. See also Goldin (1990, chapter 5).

37. There is no significant correlation between racial bias and employment restrictions for men's jobs.

38. A few surveys remarked that certain jobs were restricted to men because they entailed night work or heavy lifting. I am excluding these restrictions from this discussion since they concern differences in strength and involve positions that may have been covered by state regulations.

39. From the surveys for the insurance companies Metropolitan Life ("office boy") and General Accident ("bookkeeping") both in Philadelphia. National Archives, Record Group no. 86, Boxes 496-500.

40. On Gary Becker's theory of discrimination, see Becker (1957).

41. National Archives, Record Group no. 86, boxes 496–500.

42. See Becker (1957).

43. Phelps (1972) and Arrow (1973) began the literature on "statistical discrimination." See also Aigner and Cain (1977).

44. For a more complete discussion see Goldin (2002).

45. The "pollution theory" of discrimination is a statistical discrimination model in which there is employee discrimination. I thank Francine Blau for pointing out that it is probably the first such model of this type.

46. See Akerlof and Kranton (2000) on a related model of identity.

47. I consider only technological shocks that decrease the minimum skill needed for the job. The shocks are assumed to be random or else there would be information concerning where they occurred.

48. Among the various high-profile cases is Berkman v. City of New York (U.S. District Court, 626 F. Supp. 591, 1985), in which two New York City female firefighters were physically harassed and the physical test for advancement from the probationary position was altered. A harassment case in Florida was settled by three female firefighters against the Reedy Creek Improvement District and Walt Disney World (The Orlando Sentinel, October 29, 1996, p. D1).

49. See Goldin and Katz (2002) on the "pill," for example.

50. Of course, some women did remain in the labor force for long periods after marriage and many older women reentered the labor force in the 1950s and 1960s, as we saw in figure 3.1. My point is that the increase could have been greater and could have included more positions that were ladder jobs rather than dead end positions.

51. In 1960, 64 percent of college graduate, employed women were teachers (including music teachers), librarians, nurses, and social workers (Ruggles et al. 2004, IPUMS of the 1960 federal population census).

52. Another possibility is that the baby boom intervened, leading young mothers to remain at home. See Easterlin (1980), for example, on the topic. My point here is that some portion of the fertility increase may have been endogenous to the type of work routinely offered women.

REFERENCES

Abbott, Edith. 1907. "Employment of Women in Industries: Cigar-Making—Its History and Present Tendencies." *Journal of Political Economy* 15(January): 1–25.

Aigner, Dennis J., and Glen G. Cain. 1977. "Statistical Theories of Discrimination in Labor Markets." *Industrial Labor Relations Review* 30(January): 175–87.

Akerlof, George A., and Rachel E. Kranton. 2000. "Economics and Identity." *Quarterly Journal of Economics* 115(August): 715-53.

Arrow, Kenneth J. 1973. "The Theory of Discrimination." In *Discrimination in Labor Markets,* edited by Orley Ashenfelter and Albert Rees. Princeton, N.J.: Princeton University Press.

Becker, Gary S. 1957. *The Economics of Discrimination.* Chicago: University of Chicago Press.

Blau, Francine. 1977. *Equal Pay in the Office.* Lexington, Mass.: Lexington Books.

Easterlin, Richard A. 1980. *Birth and Fortune: The Impact of Numbers on Personal Welfare.* New York: Basic Books.

Eichengreen, Barry. 1984. "Experience and the Male-Female Earnings Gap in the 1890s." *Journal of Economic History* 44(September): 822–34.

Goldin, Claudia. 1989. "Life-Cycle Labor Force Participation of Married Women: Historical Evidence and Implications." *Journal of Labor Economics* 7(January): 20–47.

———. 1990. *Understanding the Gender Gap: An Economic History of American Women.* New York: Oxford University Press.

———. 1991. "Marriage Bars: Discrimination Against Married Women Workers, 1920 to 1950." In *Favorites of Fortune: Technology, Growth, and Economic Development Since the Industrial Revolution,* edited by Henry Rosovsky, David Landes, and Patrice Higonnet. Cambridge, Mass.: Harvard University Press.

———. 1994. "Appendix to: How America Graduated from High School: An Exploratory Study, 1910 to 1960." NBER-Historical Working Paper, No. 57 (June).

———. 1998. "America's Graduation from High School: The Evolution and Spread of Secondary Schooling in the Twentieth Century." *Journal of Economic History* 58(June): 345–74.

———. 2002. "A Pollution Theory of Discrimination: Male and Female Occupations and Earnings." NBER Working Paper no. 8985 (June).

Goldin, Claudia, and Lawrence F. Katz. 2000. "Education and Income in the Early Twentieth Century: Evidence from the Prairies." *Journal of Economic History* 60(September): 782–818.

———. 2002. "The Power of the Pill: Oral Contraceptives and Women's Career and Marriage Decisions." *Journal of Political Economy* 110(August): 730–70.

Heckman, James J., and Robert J. Willis. 1977. "A Beta-logistic Model for the Analysis of Sequential Labor Force Participation by Married Women." *Journal of Political Economy* 85(February): 27–58.

Korenman, Sanders, and David Neumark. 1991. "Does Marriage Really Make Men More Productive?" *Journal of Human Resources* 26(Spring): 282–307.

New York State, Department of Labor. 1919. *Special Bulletin: The Industrial Replacement of Men by Women in the State of New York.* Prepared by the Bureau of Women in Industry, No. 93 (March).

1940 Office Worker Survey." 1940. National Archives, Washington, D.C., Record Group no. 86, boxes 472 to 486 and 496 to 500.

O'Neill, June, and Solomon Polachek. 1993. "Why the Gender Gap in Wages Narrowed in the 1980s." *Journal of Labor Economics* 11(January): 205–28.

Phelps, Edmund S. 1972. "The Statistical Theory of Racism and Sexism," *American Economic Review* 62(September): 659–61.

Ruggles, Steven, Matthew Sobek, Trent Alexander, Catherine A. Fitch, Ronald Goeken, Patricia Kelly Hall, Miriam King, and Chad Ronnander. 2004. *Integrated Public Use Microdata Series* [IPUMS]: *Version 3.0* [Machine-readable database]. Minneapolis, Minn.: Minnesota Population Center. Available at: http://www.ipums.org.

U.S. Bureau of the Census. 1975. *Historical Statistics of the United States: Colonial Times to 1970.* Washington: Government Printing Office.

U.S. Census Office. 1895. *Report on Manufacturing Industries in the United States at the Eleventh Census: 1890. Part I. Totals for States and Industries.* Washington: Government Printing Office.

U.S. Department of Education, National Center for Education Statistics. 1993. *120 Years of American Education: A Statistical Portrait.* Washington: Government Printing Office.

U.S. Department of Labor, Women's Bureau. 1934. *The Employment of Women in Offices,* by Ethel Erickson. Bulletin of the Women's Bureau, No. 120. Washington: Government Printing Office.

———. 1942. *Office Work in [Houston, Los Angeles, Kansas City, Richmond, and Philadelphia].* Bulletin of the Women's Bureau, Nos. 188–1, 2, 3, 4, and 5. Washington: Government Printing Office.

Chapter 4

How the Life-Cycle Human-Capital Model Explains Why the Gender Wage Gap Narrowed

Solomon W. Polachek

Married women's labor-force participation rose dramatically from 4.6 percent in 1890 to 61.0 percent in 2003. This rapid rise in female labor-force participation constitutes the single most noteworthy labor-market trend in the United States over the last century. Women are now over fifteen times more likely to be in the labor force than they were a hundred years ago. At the same time, men's labor-force participation declined moderately, from 84.3 percent in 1890 to 73.5 percent in 2003.[1] Concomitant with these two labor-force participation trends, the female-to-male wage ratio rose (albeit more erratically), from 34 percent in 1890 to about 76 percent in 2003.[2] The papers in this volume explore a number of explanations for this trend in the female-male wage ratio. In this chapter, I concentrate on the life-cycle human-capital model, originally developed by Yoram Ben-Porath (1967), which has a long history in earnings-function research. I adopt this model here to explore how the two different male and female labor-force participation trends explain time-series changes in male and female earnings.

According to the life-cycle human-capital model, one's incentive to invest in training is directly proportional to the time one expects to work over one's lifetime. For this reason, a secularly rising women's labor-force participation relative to men's increases women's lifetime work expectations for each successive generation. In turn, these increased expectations imply that women's job-training investments should intensify, compared to men's. As a result, theory predicts the female-to-male earnings gap to narrow. For this reason, the life-cycle human-capital model implies that from 1890 to 2003 women's relative earnings should have grown.

Early research using the life-cycle human-capital model to explain women's relative wages was not convincing. All initial empirical analyses to test the theory concentrated on data from 1960 to 1980. In these two decades, women's wages

102 /

grew only slightly more quickly than men's, leading to no significant decline in the gender wage gap. In 1960 women earned 59 cents for each dollar earned by males, yet by 1980 women's earnings had barely budged, resting at 63 cents to the male dollar. Clearly, if the life-cycle human-capital model was to be applicable, the female wage ratio would have risen more. Instead, in virtually all these early studies that employed these two decades of data, female wages remained stable relative to male wages.

Not until the publication of Claudia Goldin's (1990) *Understanding the Gender Gap*, did empirical analysis go beyond the 1960-to-1980 time period.[3] But at the time, many believed that the 3:5 gender wage ratio that then prevailed was a perpetual constant. It didn't help that an often-mentioned passage from Leviticus 27: 2–4, first cited by Victor Fuchs (1971), mandated the same pay ratio: "Speak unto the children of Israel and say unto them: When a man shall clearly utter a vow in person unto the Lord, according to thy evaluation, then thy evaluation shall be for a male from 20 years old unto 60 years old, even thy evaluation shall be 50 shekels of silver, after the shekel of the sanctuary. And if the speaker be a female, then thy evaluation shall be 30 shekels." However, as it turns out, the decades from 1960 to 1980 are anomalous. Rather than being constant, the male-female earnings gap continually declined from 1890 to 1990, with the exception of at least the thirty-year period 1950 to 1980. So the two decades 1960 to 1980, which form the basis of all initial studies, are atypical. From 1890 to 1940 the wage gap narrowed by about 0.5 percent annually, and from 1981 to the mid-1990s, the hourly wage gap narrowed by over 0.6 percent per year. Because the decades from 1960 to 1980 were uncharacteristic, one can easily see how research results exploring trends over these two unusual decades could lead scholars to be skeptical of predictions based on the life-cycle human-capital model. Unfortunately, all the initial empirical studies that analyzed the wage gap focused on these years.

The narrowing of the gender wage gap is this chapter's main theme. But to understand this narrowing, one must examine why women earned less than men in the first place. A number of reasons have been given. These include corporate discrimination in hiring; pay and promotion practices; employer misperceptions regarding women's relative productivity (statistical discrimination); employee discrimination regarding tastes in dealing with female fellow workers; consumer discrimination regarding purchasing products made or sold by women; and more. As already mentioned, this paper concentrates on the life-cycle human-capital model—yet another reason, also well explored in the literature. (See Polachek 2003 for a recent literature survey.) The life-cycle human-capital model shows how expected lifetime labor-force participation explains the gender wage gap. Using this approach, I first explore cross-sectional male-female wage differences; then I look at how the life-cycle human-capital model predicts trends in the gender wage ratio. I find that husband-wife division of labor in the home is an important consideration explaining why men's and women's lifetime labor-force participation differs and that these labor-force participation differences cause men and women to invest differently in job skills.

This division of labor may come about because of "efficient" allocation in the home, but it can also result because of a wife's inferior bargaining power within a marriage (Ott 1995), high marginal tax rates on wives' earnings (Kumar 2005), the unavailability of day-care centers (Kreyenfeld and Hank 2000), or simply cultural norms (Coltrane 2000). In past work, I refer to these latter considerations as "societal" discrimination, which I claimed is distinct from "market" discrimination (Polachek 1995). Here, I argue that for whatever reason (most likely, declining fertility and an increased probability of divorce, but more generally decreasing societal discrimination), women have been devoting more time over their lives to paid work outside the home. I claim that greater lifetime work creates incentives to invest in more marketable schooling as well as more on-the-job training. Given that males exhibit decreases in lifetime labor-force participation, women's increased "human-capital" investments raise their wages relative to men's. As a result, I argue, the theory predicts a diminishing gender wage gap.

In this chapter I outline how the life-cycle human-capital model accounts for the gender wage gap; my conclusion is that the gender wage gap diminishes as male and female lifetime work expectations become more similar. I suspect that the gender wage gap will continue to narrow, perhaps even more quickly, as long as current BLS predictions are accurate that men's labor-force participation will continue to fall, and women's participation will continue to rise (Fullerton and Toossi 2001).

LINKING EXPECTED LIFETIME WORK AND WAGES: THE BEN-PORATH MODEL

The life-cycle human-capital model (Ben-Porath 1967) links expected lifetime labor-force participation to one's incentive to obtain marketable training. This training, acquired in school, on the job, through seniority, via networking, and from mobility, in turn determines earnings potential. According to the model, expected lifetime work expectations are a crucial motivating ingredient in one's ability to eventually achieve high earnings.

The theory is as follows: There are costs and benefits to acquiring marketable skills. The costs are direct (such as tuition and learning materials and cost of living while studying) and indirect (mostly forgone wages during training). The benefits are augmented lifetime earnings.[4] The more years one works, the greater one's opportunity to reap the benefits of higher earnings. If one were never to work, marketable human-capital benefits would be *zero*, independent of how many professional or Ph.D. degrees one acquired. In a similar vein, dropping out of the labor force reduces lifetime work years, which according to the theory should decrease the potential rewards from investment in marketable skills. In contrast, those who expect to work long hours and who foresee the greatest number of years at work should have the highest expected returns. Thus, all else constant, the life-cycle model postulates the less one's lifetime labor-force participation, the lower the benefits to investment, and hence the smaller one's incentives to invest in training. Since women on average work fewer hours throughout their lives, the life-cycle model predicts that women will purchase less marketable investments than men. Statistical-discrimination theory likewise predicts that firms would invest less to train women than men (Landes 1977). Women's lower rates of job training relative to men translate to lower per-hour wages, so that the male-female wage gap is predicted to widen.[5] On the other hand, as women's lifetime labor-force participation rises, and as men's lifetime labor-force participation falls, the theory predicts that the male-female wage gap will narrow. Indeed, as I shall show, these trends are what the data indicate. But first, I mention a couple other implications of the life-cycle human-capital model to bolster its credibility.

First, as one gets older, earnings rise each year. The rate at which earnings increase varies over the life cycle. Young workers below the age of thirty-five experience the most rapid per-year earnings increases. Workers in their fifties find earnings growth to be relatively meager. For them, earnings rise hardly at all. Here again, the human-capital model explains why earnings growth varies over the life cycle. Early in life (below age thirty-five), individuals have a whole work-life ahead, and investment in training pays off, since returns are reaped for numerous years to come. Later in life, the "present value" of training is smaller because there are fewer work years to accumulate the returns. Accordingly, older individuals typically purchase less training, and so earnings rise less quickly. Of course, there are exceptions, such as in top executive positions, where pay increases markedly. Economists often view this phenomenon as a rank-order tournament (Lazear and Rosen 1981) in which large prizes go to the "winner." For a number of reasons, including "old boy" networks, these tournaments can be disadvantageous to women, which might explain aspects of the glass ceiling.

Second, according to the life-cycle human-capital model as modified by Polachek (1975a) and Yoram Weis and Reuben Gronau (1981), a worker with anticipated discontinuous labor-force participation follows a life-cycle-training pattern different than the continuously employed worker. Rather than beginning her worklife with large but diminishing amounts of training, such workers initially make small training investments, which decrease further until the workers exhibit discontinuous labor-force participation. The investments then rise moderately when these workers permanently reenter the workforce, which for women is usually when childbearing is complete. As a result, women's earnings need not exhibit the usual concave age-earnings profiles characteristic of men. For this reason, women's life-cycle earnings profiles are flatter than men's and often exhibit a non-monotonic pattern (exhibit a midlife dip), depending on the amount of intermittent work behavior (Mincer and Polachek 1974).

Given the importance of lifetime labor-force participation, the obvious question is: Why do women have different lifetime work patterns than men?

DIVISION OF LABOR IN THE HOME

Catalyst is a research organization designed to generate knowledge that helps expand options for women in upper-level business jobs. Felice Schwartz, whose 1989

Harvard Business Review article, "Management Women and the New Facts of Life," prompted the debate on the "mommy track," founded Catalyst in 1962. It is one of the leading nonprofit organizations focused on women's issues. Catalyst's original board of directors consisted of the presidents of Smith College, Wellesley College, Lawrence College, Mills College, and Sarah Lawrence College. Part of the organization's research concentrates on preparing a number of surveys on women's attitudes. In one recent survey of 3,000 women in their mid-twenties to mid-thirties, Catalyst found that one of the biggest barriers to women's advancement was personal and family responsibilities. Sixty-eight percent named this to be their main problem (Betsy Morris, "The New Trophy Husband," *Fortune*, October 14, 2002, 80).

To illustrate division of labor, one need only examine lifetime labor-force participation patterns for married males, married females, single males, and single females. Figure 4.1 depicts labor-force participation patterns by marital status for the United States in 1970 and 2001. On the horizontal axis is age. On the vertical axis are labor-force participation rates. These rates indicate the proportion of each gender–marital status group in the labor force. Beginning with 1970, married men have the highest lifetime labor-force participation. Married women have the lowest participation; it peaks at about 48 percent between the ages of twenty and twenty-four, and then again at 46.8 percent between ages thirty-five and forty-four.[6] The drop between twenty-five and thirty-four reflects intermittent labor-force participation related to childbearing. The gap between single males and females is the narrowest. By 2001, the differences are appreciably smaller. The biggest change is the degree to which married female labor-force participation rose over the three decades. However, even in 2001, married women's participation was just 66 to 75 percent that of married men, as evidenced by married women's lower lifetime labor-force participation compared to men's. The gap for singles is minuscule.

Figure 4.2 highlights gender differences in work participation, by race. Interestingly, here there is a somewhat larger gender difference in labor-force participation rates for whites than for nonwhites. To see this, note that white women participate less over their lifetime than nonwhite women, whereas white men participate more than nonwhite men. As I shall show later in the chapter, the bigger labor-force participation gap between white males and females suggests larger male-female wage differences for whites than for nonwhites—again, as predicted by the human-capital model.

One can examine these patterns from a slightly different perspective. Retrospective work-history data (asking respondents about their past work) as well as panel data (following respondents through time) illustrate the same lifetime work behavior, but do not rely on cross-sectional synthetic cohort data from individual respondents across various age groups. Given that synthetic cohorts confound cohort (generational) and life-cycle (aging) effects, one can argue that retrospective and panel data are superior. Data from Jacob Mincer's and my own (1974) study (based on the National Longitudinal Survey of Mature Women described at www.bls.gov/nls/home.htm) contrasts work patterns for married-once-spouse-present and never-married women. Never-married white women thirty to forty-

FIGURE 4.1 / U.S. Labor-Force Participation by Gender, Marital Status, and Age

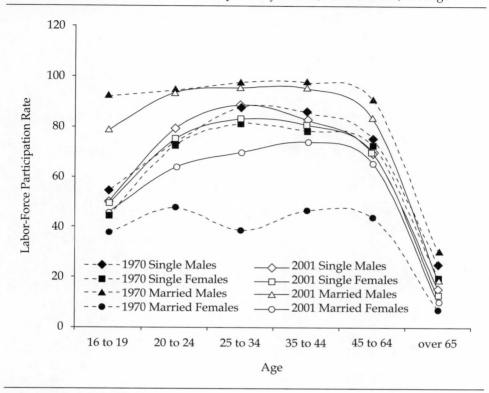

Source: U.S. Census Bureau (2002, table 568).

four years old in 1967 worked 14.5 years out of a possible 16.0 years. In contrast, married-once-spouse-present women worked only 6.4 out of about 16.8 years. As before, similar patterns emerge for black women, but again the differences are more muted, with never-married black women having slightly less lifetime work, and married-once-one-spouse-present black women having a bit more lifetime work (9.1 years) than whites. Thus, for blacks as well as whites, being married greatly diminishes lifetime work, slightly less for blacks than for whites.

These patterns emerge less starkly in more recent data. Using the 1980 Panel Study of Income Dynamics (PSID) data (described at: http://psidonline.isr.umich .edu/), Carole Miller (1993) finds that married women average 10.04 years spent outside the labor force. Similarly, using a panel of 2,659 individuals from the 1976-to-1987 PSID data, Polachek and Moon-Kak Kim (1994) find that women averaged 9.62 years out of the labor force, as compared to men's 2.22 years. Current data for foreign countries are comparable. For example, using Canadian data, Wayne Simpson (2000) finds that in 1993 married women with children averaged 7.6 years (or 36.4 percent of their work years) out of the labor force, whereas single

FIGURE 4.2 / Labor-Force Participation Rates by Gender, Race, and Age

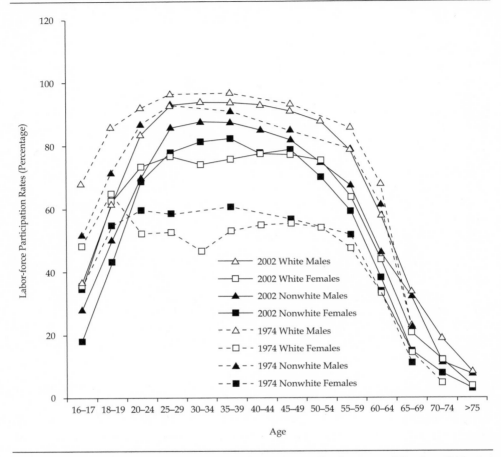

Source: U.S. Department of Labor, Bureau of Labor Statistics, *Employment and Earnings*. Table A-4 (October 1974) and table A-14 (October 2002).

women spent 1.5 (or 12.9 percent) of their work years out of the labor force. For men, this figure is .9 years (or 8.1 percent). Data within narrow professions yield similar results. Catalyst (2003) finds that only 29 percent of women MBA graduates work full-time continuously since graduation compared to 69 percent for men, and similarly only 35 percent of women law graduates worked continuously since graduation compared to 61 percent for men.

Although large marital status and gender differences in lifetime work still remain, these gender disparities are gradually diminishing. Female labor-force participation is rising secularly and male participation is falling. However, in the 1990s, the growth in female labor-force participation decelerated. Figure 4.3 shows this recent deceleration of the growth in women's labor-force participation during the 1990s. Women's lifetime labor-force participation in 1990 was dramatically

FIGURE 4.3 / Female Labor-Force Participation, by Age

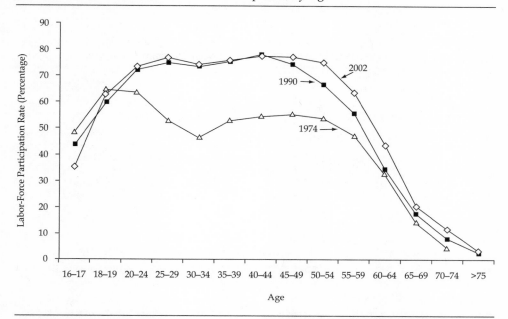

Source: U.S. Department of Labor, Bureau of Labor Statistics, *Employment and Earnings*. Table A-4 (October 1974), table A-4 (October 1990), and table A-14 (October 2002).

higher than 1974, but women's lifetime labor-force participation in 2002 was only marginally higher than in 1990. As shall be illustrated later, I believe this deceleration explains why the gender gap narrowed less quickly in the 1990s than in the 1980s.

Children exacerbate these differences. For example, as illustrated in table 4.1, Susan Harkness and Jane Waldfogel (2003) find significantly lower labor-force participation rates for women with children compared to women without. This is true not just in the United States, but in Australia, Canada, the United Kingdom, and Germany. The same result holds in Finland and Sweden, but the pattern is mitigated by Sweden's and Finland's social policies promoting women's work. In all cases except Finland, men's labor-force participation exceeds women's, but the gap is exceptionally wide between men, and women with children.

From the above evidence on lifetime labor-force participation rates (especially figure 4.1 and table 4.1), it can be seen that marital status and children play an important, but different, role when we consider men's and women's work behavior. For men, marriage and children are associated with more work, whereas for women, marriage and children are associated with less work—but these trends are changing. Marriage and children are slowly decreasing in importance. Again, as already stated, the reasons for the diverging work patterns are not well understood. They can come about because of efficient allocation of labor in the home, but

TABLE 4.1 / An International Comparison of the Full-Time Employment Status of Men and Women Aged Twenty-Four to Forty-Four

Full-Time Employment	Australia 1995	Canada 1994	United Kingdom 1995	United States 1994	Germany 1994	Finland 1991	Sweden 1991
All men	.830	.762	.790	.844	.830	.777	.771
Women without children	.731	.677	.763	.731	.722	.851	.745
Women with children	.258	.469	.256	.495	.352	.710	.611

Source: Harkness and Waldfogel (2003), based on the Luxembourg Income Study data.
Employment is defined as the share of individuals who have a job during the survey week. Full-time employment is defined as the share who have a job during the survey week and who work thirty or more hours per week.

they also can come about because of what I call "societal discrimination" (whereby women are "socialized" to sacrifice their career for their family), or they can come about for other reasons. Independent of the reason, according to the lifetime human-capital model, the division of labor within the family fosters very dissimilar lifetime work patterns for men and women. Less work over one's lifetime implies significantly smaller monetary gains from human-capital investments. Accordingly, the theory predicts men's investments to exceed women's, and as a result, male earnings to surpass women's earnings. In addition, the theory predicts that male earnings grow more quickly over the life cycle than women's earnings. I now examine these earnings configurations.

EVIDENCE IN SUPPORT OF THE LIFE-CYCLE HUMAN-CAPITAL MODEL

Age-earnings profiles differ for men and women. Throughout most of the life cycle, male profiles are higher and generally steeper, indicating not only greater earnings but also more rapid earnings growth. Initially, when men begin to work upon completion of school, male-female earnings differences are relatively small, then they widen in midlife, but decrease somewhat at older ages.[7] Particularly important are the reasons why the gender wage gap varies over the life cycle. But before discussing that, I describe the gender wage gap across marital status groups. Here a very curious pattern emerges. Wage profiles for single males and females are very similar. For singles, the wage gap is relatively small, and in many data sets actually diminishes with age. In contrast, the wage profiles differ dramatically for married men and women. Married men have higher and far steeper earnings profiles than married women.

Francine Blau and Lawrence Kahn (1992) illustrate these patterns using international data. Table 4.2 contains their results and table 4.3 contains comparable re-

TABLE 4.2 / Female-to-Male Earnings Ratios by Country, Corrected for Hours Worked

Country	Years	All Workers	Married Workers	Single Workers
Australia (annual)	1986	0.749	0.691	0.914
Austria (monthly)	1985–1987	0.723	0.656	0.970
Germany (monthly)	1985–1988	0.688	0.573	1.027
Norway (annual)	1982	0.731	0.716	0.916
Sweden (annual)	1980	0.767	0.724	0.935
Switzerland (monthly)	1987	0.617	0.578	0.945
United Kingdom (annual)	1985–1988	0.634	0.597	0.949
United States (annual)	1985–1988	0.685	0.594	0.955

Source: Blau and Kahn (1992).
The earnings ratios were evaluated at forty hours. The earnings ratios for married workers are for married workers with one person other than spouse in the household (for Sweden, Norway, and Austria, one child); those for single workers are for nonmarried people with no other persons in the household.

sults from the recently available Luxembourg Income Study (www.lisproject.org). For single men and women the wage gap is generally less than 10 percent. Single women on average earn over 90 percent what men earn. But married women earn far less than married men. Here the wage ratio is typically in the 60 to 70 percent range.

Further deconstruction illustrates that children play a major role in the gender wage gap. Married women with children earn less than married women without children (Harkness and Waldfogel 2003). Married women who space their births widely apart receive even lower wages (Polachek 1975b). Opposite patterns hold for men. Married men with children earn more, and spacing children at wide intervals is associated with even higher earnings (Polachek 1975b). Thus the wage

TABLE 4.3 / Female-to-Male Earnings Ratios by Country for Full-time Workers

Country	Year	All Workers	Married Workers	Single Workers
Germany	2000	0.691	0.662	0.852
United Kingdom	1995	0.757	0.690	0.996
United Kingdom	1999	0.783	0.736	0.977
United States	1997	0.713	0.635	0.972
United States	2000	0.716	0.635	0.966
Austria	1994	0.716	0.651	0.937
Austria	1997	0.771	0.754	0.911
Switzerland	1992	0.577	0.367	1.027
Sweden	1992	0.800	0.770	0.949
Australia	1989	0.738	0.696	0.906
Australia	1994	0.755	0.724	0.872

Source: Computed from Luxembourg Income Study (LIS) data available at: www.lisproject.org/.

gap varies by marital status, children, and spacing of children. As it turns out, these demographic variables are more important predictors of the gender wage gap than any other explanatory factors.

Recall that life-cycle human-capital theory provides a cogent elucidation of how training influences earnings. The more education and on-the-job training one obtains (in other words, the more human capital one gets), the more one earns. But also according to the theory, incentives for acquiring job skills depend on how much one *expects* to work, regardless of the reason for the differences in lifetime work behavior. Getting married, having children, and spacing children widely apart accentuate the division of labor within the family. For married men, this division of labor *raises* the amount of lifetime work, but reduces lifetime work for married women with children. As a result of this bifurcation, lifetime human-capital theory predicts married men's incentives to invest in marketable skills increase while married women's incentives decrease. According to the theory, these lifetime work differences should lead to higher married male wages and lower married female wages.

There is now ample evidence of the validity of these predictions. In addition to my study mentioned above (Polachek 1975b), the new "family pay gap" literature finds a so-called "motherhood" penalty. For example, Sanders Korenman and David Neumark (1992) ascertain that cross-sectional ordinary least squares and first-difference estimates understate the negative effect of children on wages. Jane Waldfogel (1998) shows that having children lowers a women's pay by about 10 percent, after controlling for age, education, experience, race, ethnicity, and marital status. Michelle Budig and Paula England (2001) detect about a 7 percent wage penalty per child. Using the National Longitudinal Survey Panel, Charles Baum (2002) confirms the finding that "interrupting work to give birth has a negative effect on wages" but that "this negative effect is at least partially eliminated when [controlling for] whether the mother returns to work at her pre-childbirth job" (Baum 2002, 2). Mark Berger et al. (2003) find evidence that "the forces towards specialization become stronger as the number of children increase, so that the spouse specializing in childcare [has] some combination of lower wages, hours worked and fringe benefits" (309). Similarly, looking at British data, Heather Joshi, Pierella Paci, and Waldfogel (1999, 543) show that "women who broke their employment at childbirth were subsequently paid less pay than childless women [whereas] mothers who maintained their employment continuously were as well paid as childless women," though it should be noted that neither were remunerated as well as men.[8]

It is interesting that gender differences are smaller among blacks than whites (table 4.4). In 2003 the gender earnings ratio for full-time wage and salary workers was .79 for whites and .88 for blacks. Recall that nonwhite women work more over their lifetime relative to nonwhite men, than white women compared to white men (see figure 4.2). Thus, the gender gap in labor-force participation for blacks is smaller than for whites. According to the life-cycle human-capital theory, a smaller lifetime labor-force participation difference implies a smaller difference in investment incentives. Accordingly, the gender wage gap for blacks should be smaller than the gender wage gap for whites. This is precisely what is observed.

Economists employ statistical decomposition techniques to measure the role of life-

TABLE 4.4 / Median Weekly Earnings of Full-Time Wage and Salary Workers

	1990	1995	2000	2001	2003
White male	494	566	669	694	715
White female	353	415	500	521	567
Female-to-male ratio	0.71	0.73	0.75	0.75	0.79
Black male	361	411	503	518	555
Black female	308	355	429	451	491
Female-to-male ratio	0.85	0.86	0.85	0.87	0.88

Sources: U.S. Census Bureau (2002, table 613; 2005, table 623).

time labor-force participation in explaining male-female wage differences.[9] Essentially they estimate how much women would earn if they were to work as much as men over their lifetimes. They define discrimination to be women's predicted earnings shortfalls in this computation. Thus, discrimination is the extent to which women earn less than men, holding other demographic attributes constant. A number of statistical biases mar this computation (see, for example, Polachek 1975b; Butler 1982; and Jones 1983). One particularly relevant bias is the failure to account for the amount of job skills women would have sought had they expected to work continuously. Typical implementation of the decomposition adjusts for training received given observed work experience, but not the training one would have received had one intended to work continuously. By not including this extra forgone training, these decompositions underestimate a discontinuous worker's potential wage. As such, discrimination is overestimated, given that discrimination is the difference between what the continuous worker actually earns and what one *projects* a discontinuous worker to earn were she to have participated continuously. Studies that appropriately incorporate the skills one would have obtained had one expected to work continuously explain between 63 and 95 percent of the gender wage gap (for example, Polachek 1975a; Goldin and Polachek 1987; Kao, Polachek, and Wunnava 1994).

SECULAR CHANGES IN THE WAGE GAP

If the life-cycle human-capital model carries weight, as I argue above, then the gender wage gap should narrow as women's lifetime labor-force participation increases. As I now show, this is exactly what one finds.

Figure 4.4 examines earnings ratio data for the United States compiled from Goldin (1990) and June O'Neill (2003). The vertical axis depicts the female-to-male earnings ratio and the horizontal axis represents the year. In all, five sets of data are plotted. Three cover the period from 1815 to just prior to 1940, one covers the period from 1955 to 1987, and the final one covers 1979 to 2001. The early data clearly trend upward. Similarly, the latter period, from the mid-1970s, do as well, with the possible exception of the years 1994 to 2000 (though the data again rebound in 2001).[10] Only the data from about 1935 to around the early 1980s are flat, showing

FIGURE 4.4   /   Female-to-Male Earnings Ratio

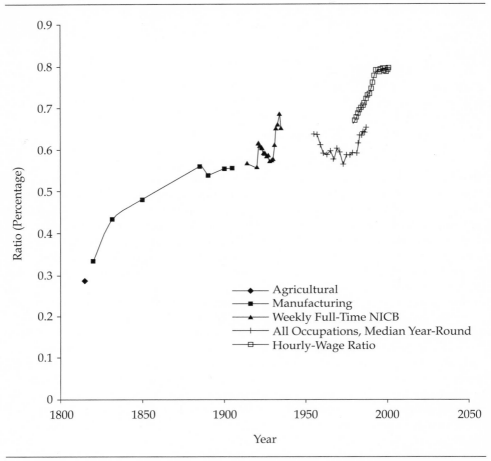

Sources: All series except hourly-wage ratio from Goldin (1990, table 3.1). For hourly-wage ratio computations, see O'Neill (2003).

virtually no increase in female compared to male economic success. But, as I mentioned, these decades are anomalous.

By comparing the 1970s and 1980s, my own research with John Robst offers an explanation as to why the 1970s (and probably the 1960s) might be anomalous (Polachek and J. Robst 2001). We show that beginning in 1980, the wage gap narrowed 1.7 percent more quickly than in the 1970s. In a sense this more rapid convergence is strange because female labor-force participation rose a bit faster in the 1970s than in the 1980s.[11] However, the reasons for these exceedingly paradoxical trends are consistent with the life-cycle human-capital model. The rapidly rising female labor-force participation in the 1960s and 1970s actually brought down female wages because the new inexperienced entrants earned less than the older, more senior employees, which made female wage growth appear less rapid. The decline diminished in importance during the 1980s as the relative increase in the numbers of new female entrants declined and as the proportion of years actually worked by women increased. If one were to adjust for labor-market joiners (and labor-market leavers), the male-female wage convergence is actually very similar for both decades (Polachek and Robst 2001). Indeed, the findings by Blau and Kahn (1997) suggest that the current research understates male-female wage convergence in the 1980s as well. Using statistical techniques that account for changes in the earnings structure, they find that women's progress was considerably greater than previously thought. O'Neill (2003) uses NLSY data to find that the adjusted female-to-male wage ratio in 2000 was over 95 percent. This certainly corroborates the convergence.

But similar trends are also observed for other nations. The Luxembourg Income Study is a collection of household data compiled from ongoing statistical surveys in twenty-six countries.[12] The database provides statistics on demographic, income, and expenditure variables on three levels: households, persons, and children. I concentrate on extracting education, age, and earnings data for white males and females from the person files of the countries, at least half of which contain information on hourly earnings.[13] Of those, I present plots of female-to-male wage ratios (figure 4.5) adjusted by education, potential labor-market experience and

FIGURE 4.5   /   Female-to-Male Wage Ratio Trends by Country, Adjusted for Education, Potential Experience, and Marital Status

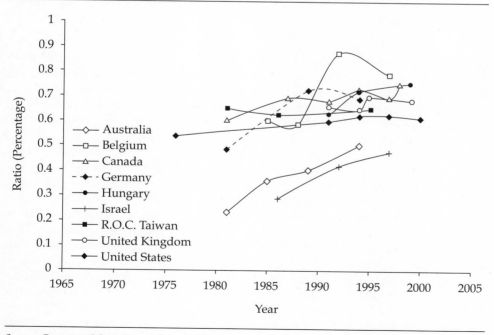

Source: Computed from Luxembourg Income Study (LIS) data (www.lisproject.org).

FIGURE 4.6 / Comparison of Female-to-Male Hourly Wage Ratios and Married
Female Labor-Force Participation

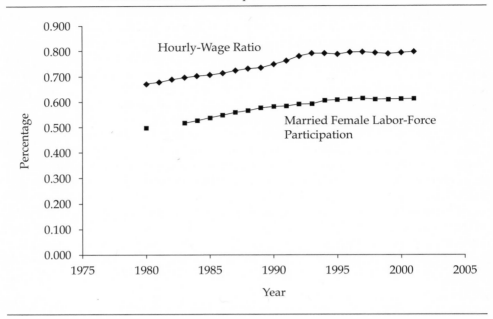

Sources: Hourly-wage ratios—see O'Neill (2003). Married female labor-force participation—see
U.S. Census Bureau (2002, table 569).

marital status (when available). For each country, the ratios were computed from
at least three cross-sectional wage regressions. Most countries exhibit increasing
female wage ratios. For example, Australia, Belgium, Canada, Germany, Hungary,
and Israel exhibit greater gender wage convergence than the United States. Given
rising female labor-market participation in these countries, this convergence is
consistent with the life-cycle human-capital model's predictions.

In the United States, gender wage convergence slowed down somewhat in the
1990s. This weakening of women's relative wage gains is apparent in figure 4.4.
The hourly wage series, which rose so precipitously from 1980, becomes relatively
flat from 1993 through 2001. During this seven-year period, women's wages rose
just .1 percent per year, compared to a 1.0 percent per year increase from 1980 to
1993. The obvious interesting question is: What brought about this reversal?

The latest research on this (Blau and Kahn 2004 and Mulligan and Rubenstein
2005) suggests that changes in the labor-force selectivity (the difference in unmeasured qualities between working and nonworking women), changes in discrimination, and shifts in supply and demand may have caused the narrowing of the
gender pay gap to wane. I take a simpler, more straightforward approach. Human-
capital theory argues that wages rise in conjunction with human-capital investments. But, as I have shown earlier in this chapter, the prime impetus for human-

capital investments is a strong lifetime work commitment. As already noted, women's (especially married women's) lifetime work expectations rose dramatically at least from 1890. (The trend from 1980 is given in figure 4.6.) But in the mid-1990s something different seems to have happened to married women's labor-force participation. The upward trend moderated radically. Whereas married women's labor-force participation rose almost 1 percent per year from 1970 to 1990, growth in women's participation nose-dived to .5 percent per year from 1990 to 1995. It declined even further, to just .1 percent, from 1995 to 2001.

The same logic that explains why a rising female labor-force participation rate boosts women's earnings can be employed to account for how a decreasing labor-force participation reduces women's earnings growth. Recall that earning power depends on human-capital training investments. In turn, training depends on expectation of lifetime labor-force participation. The more one works the greater one's incentive to get trained. And the more extensive one's training, the more one earns. Concomitantly, the less one works the smaller the incentive to acquire training. The less one trains, the smaller one's marketable skills, and the less one earns.

As female labor-force participation rose throughout the century, women undertook more schooling and other complementary on-the-job post-school training. On the other hand, incentives to continue investing more precipitously fell as labor activities began to hold steady, so that women's human-capital investments ceased to grow. Apparently, such is the case from 1993. The fervor of human-capital investment intensity ceased; hence wage growth dropped virtually to zero as women's labor-force participation growth dwindled. This relationship is evident in figure 4.6. The female-to-male wage ratio virtually parallels the married female labor-force participation rate. As this female participation rose from 1980 to 1993, so did relative female wages. As the growth in this female participation tapered off beginning in 1993, so did relative female wages. These are just the patterns the life-cycle human-capital model predicts.

What about the future? Is the slowing simply an aberration or will the gender gap again begin to narrow? Current projections indicate a slight acceleration of women's labor-force participation for all age groups, with the exception of those aged thirty-five to forty-four. If these projections are accurate, then the theory predicts that women's investments in marketable skills should again increase. In that case the wage gap should continue to narrow, perhaps even at an accelerated rate. Preliminary indications by the U.S. Department of Labor, Bureau of Labor Statistics (2003) indicate that this may be the case.

CONCLUDING THOUGHTS

One might argue that an article in the popular press is inappropriate in an academic context, but the October 14, 2002, issue of *Fortune* is a good (albeit atypical) illustration of the division of labor in the home. That particular issue features the fifty most powerful women in business. The author of cover story (Morris 2002) seeks to find out who is "behind every powerful woman," arguing that "increasingly it's a stay-at-home dad." The article depicts over a dozen successful women who attribute their accomplishments to an at-home husband managing the family (80):

> At Ford, Xerox, Sun, Schwab, Verizon, J. P. Morgan, Chase, Coca-Cola, almost every-where you look in the upper ranks of the Fortune 500, it could be the woman wearing the pants and the man minding hearth and home. Call him what you will, househus-band, stay-at-home-dad, domestic engineer, but credit him with setting aside his own career by dropping out, retiring early or going part-time so that his wife's career might flourish and their family might thrive. . . . Behind a great woman at work there is often a great man at home. He is the new trophy husband.

Granted, the families that the *Fortune* article portrays are unusual. For most families the division of labor is the opposite. At least in the past, husbands generally specialized in market work, not home activities. In contrast, wives as a rule dedicated themselves to home management, not employment for pay. I believe this household division of labor is of paramount importance in explaining social stratification and the resulting gender inequality. As illustrated by *Fortune* magazine, the opposite division of labor in the home is compatible with high-wage breadwinner women: the women go out to work and the men are stay-at-home husbands.

One other important point about the article: *Fortune* tried to write a "trophy husband" article five years earlier, but without success. Not because the editors couldn't find enough women at the top, but because the women at the top believed it too great a stigma to depict their spouses as house husbands. So in 1997 *Fortune* simply could not find enough executive women willing to talk about their husbands in that way, let alone get that kind of publicity.

I view this stigma to be one manifestation of what I call societal discrimination, which I define as processes instigated by the social order that lead to gender-role differentiation responsible for women's ultimate economic weakness. This role delineation may result from several factors. First, efficient behavior within the household (perhaps resulting from husbands being almost two years older and slightly more educated than their wives) makes it economically efficient for household members to specialize. Second, social norms inherent in the culture make it difficult for women to take on work responsibilities. This is especially true in a number of foreign cultures, particularly in the Middle East and Northern Africa, where female labor-force participation is as low as 12 percent of male labor-force participation.[14] But it also is present in the United States, where "women shoulder a major share of household and child-care responsibilities" (*Viewpoints* 2003, 1). Third, many past and present government labor-market and tax policies blatantly favor men. The fact that men tend to be very reluctant to share household responsibilities, the fact that women acquiesce to taking on most of the household burdens, the fact that high school guidance counselors frequently discourage women from certain male-dominated courses, the fact that the governments often impose hefty taxes on a wife's earnings (the marriage tax), and the fact that in the big scheme of things women got the right to vote only very recently are all symptoms of societal discrimination. I suggest that societal discrimination relates to the division of labor within the home.

I go as far as to argue that this detrimental division of labor is at the root of almost all the wage gap. One should note that early policy-relevant writings on the gender wage gap concentrated almost solely on discrimination by corporations and other employers. Yet many of the articles in this volume (and elsewhere) now acknowledge household responsibility and its effects on labor-market success as an important factor. Further, I make a case that decreases in societal discrimination diminish the divide between a husband's and wife's participation in the workforce, and that rising female lifetime labor-force participation coupled with decreasing male participation are causing movements in the direction of gender parity. I believe this is in part the reason why *Fortune* could do its story in 2002, but not in 1997. And I think that this societal discrimination is a topic worth exploring further and debating scientifically with evidence.

As has been seen, women's and men's roles have been changing over time. There is still a division of labor in the home, but it has been narrowing. Men's lifetime labor-force participation is diminishing and women's is rising. Human-capital theory predicts that this coming together implies that males are investing less in human-capital while females are investing more. As a result, according to the life-cycle human-capital theory, wage differences should have narrowed, and in fact they did. Throughout our history, the biggest economic change, in the United States and worldwide, has been the rise in women's for-pay labor-force activities, yet only recently have scholars compiled enough data to show a continually narrowing wage gap (except for of the period from about 1935 to 1980). But this is precisely what human-capital theory predicts: as lifetime work expectations rise, individuals' incentives to invest in human capital go up, and individual earnings rise. From 1890 through at least the mid-1990s, women's lifetime work and earnings rose, and from 1950 to 1980, women's labor-force participation growth accelerated to such an extent that new, inexperienced, low-wage women workers slowed down the convergence of the gender earnings gap.

Since the mid-1990s, a new trend may be emerging. The growing women's labor-force participation and wage growth waned from 1993 to 2001. A story in October 2005 in *The New York Times Magazine* (Belkin 2003) possibly demonstrates this trend. It portrayed a new breed of potentially high-powered women—women who are well educated, articulate, and on the fast track to success—but who decide to "opt out," rather than pursue their careers steadfastly.

According to Lisa Belkin, a recent survey by Catalyst found that "26 percent of women at the cusp of the most senior level of management don't want the promotion.[15] And it is why *Fortune* magazine found that of the 108 women who have appeared on its list of the top 50 most powerful women over the years, at least 20 have chosen to leave their high-powered jobs" (45). Belkin describes eight women (42):

> Each earned a degree from Princeton, which was a citadel of everything male until the first co-educated class entered in 1969. And after Princeton, the women . . . went on to do other things that women once were not expected to do. They received law

degrees from Harvard and Columbia. They chose husbands who could keep up with them, not simply support them. They waited to have children because work was too exciting. They put on power suits and marched off to take on the world.

And then, suddenly, they stopped. Katherine Brokaw left a prestigious law firm to stay home with three children. She maintained, "I don't want to be on the fast track leading to a partnership" (42). Similarly, Sarah McArthur Amsbary declared, "I don't want to be famous; I don't want to conquer the world; I don't want that kind of life" (44).

Whether the recent shrinking growth in women's labor-force participation prevails as a continuing trend remains to be seen. As explained, I doubt it will. But at least for now, one cannot help noting the relevance of life-cycle human-capital theory in explaining this recent new phenomenon. Just as the life-cycle human-capital model predicted rising relative female wages from 1890, it also explains the recent waning of trends in relative female wage growth.

My special thanks to Francine Blau and David Grusky for their stimulating discussions and valuable comments. Also, I thank Jeff Xiang for very able research assistance. Finally, I thank two anonymous referees for their comments.

NOTES

1. The 1890 data are from U.S. Bureau of the Census (1975) *Historical Statistics of the United States from Colonial Times Until 1970*, Series D49–62, p. 133. The 2003 data are from the 2004–5 *Statistical Abstract of the United States*, tables 570 (males) and 578 (females).
2. The 1830 figure is based on Claudia Goldin (1990, 60–61); the 2003 figure is based on June O'Neill and Dave O'Neill (2006).
3. There are at least three exceptions: Goldin (1984); O'Neill (1985); and Blau and Andrea Beller (1988). Also, see chapter 4 in Francesca Bettio (1988) for data on similar trends in Italy.
4. There are some other more intangible benefits to individuals—how one conducts him- or herself in everyday life—as well as social benefits such as reduced crime, lower unemployment, and greater economic growth. Some of these intangible benefits are discussed in Robert Michael (1973) and Dora Polachek and Polachek (1989). Such social and familial benefits might be one reason why some cultures value more highly educated wives, even though these cultures advocate wives' being in the home rather than the workplace.
5. This phenomenon is also true over the life cycle. Studies that examine life-cycle earnings within families show that the husband-wife wage gap is largest during the childbearing years (Polachek 1975b).
6. These figures are from U.S. Bureau of the Census (2003), table 568 (graphed in figure 4.1).

7. This pattern is prevalent in cross-sectional analysis (Polachek 1975b) as well as cohort-based analysis (Weinberger and Kuhn 2005).

8. Expecting to work less in the future could explain why currently childless women earn less than childless men. See Goldin and Polachek (1987).

9. The decomposition also "adjusts" for other factors such as race, occupation, industry, and additional socioeconomic and demographic factors.

10. Based on CPS Outgoing Rotation Groups (the CPS sample that contains information on usual weekly hours and earnings), O'Neill (2003) finds that the gender wage ratio is .792 in 1994, .788 in 1995, .795 in 1996, .796 in 1997, .793 in 1998, .789 in 1999, .793 in 2000, and .798 in 2001.

11. According to Blau, Marianne Ferber, and Anne Winkler (2002, chapter 4, n4), the average annual increase in labor-force participation was .7 percentage points for the 1980s and .8 percentage points for the 1970s, but fell to .3 percentage points in the 1990s.

12. An appendix containing a list of the countries contained in the LIS data is available from the author upon request. Also available is an appendix with the particular country surveys from which the data are drawn. Both are also available at: www.lisproject.org/.

13. Countries with no reported hourly wages have annual earnings. I could have used these data to compute earnings variance, but in order to be consistent with the computations done for the United States, I limited the analysis to countries reporting hourly earnings.

14. According to the United Nations Statistics Divison (2000), the 1997 female labor-force participation rate in Iraq was 9 percent, compared to a male rate of 77 percent. Similarly, in Pakistan the 2002 female labor-force participation rate was 16 percent compared to 83 percent for men, and in Oman it was 13 percent for women compared to 62 percent for men in 2000. In contrast, in the United States in 2003, the female labor-force participation rate is 60 percent, compared to 74 percent for men.

15. Belkin's statement is based on Catalyst's 2002 study "Women in Leadership: Comparing European and U.S. Executives." It is unfortunate that this study does not seek similar information for men. However, another Catalyst study (2003) of business school (MBAs) and law school graduates born between 1964 and 1975 indicates that 69 percent of the male law school graduates worked full-time continuously after graduation, whereas just 35 percent of women did this; and 61 percent of the male MBA graduates worked full-time continuously after graduation compared to 29 percent for women. Of the current MBAs, 15 percent of the women are working part-time, compared to 1 percent of the men, and 13 percent of the women are out of the workforce compared to 3 percent of the men. Further, this study states, "After accounting for leaves, gaps in employment, and part-time work, men and women MBA graduates who have worked full time continuously have similar promotion rates" (3).

REFERENCES

Baum, Charles. 2002. "The Effect of Work Interruptions on Women's Wages." *Labour* 16(1): 1–36.

Belkin, Lisa. 2003. "The Opt-Out Revolution." *The New York Times Magazine* October 26: 43–86.

Ben-Porath, Yoram. 1967. "The Production of Human Capital Over the Lifecycle." *Journal of Political Economy* 75(4, part 1): 352–65.

Berger, Mark, Dan Black, Amitabh Chandra, and Frank Scott. 2003. "Children, Non-Discriminatory Provision of Fringe Benefits, and Household Labor Market Decisions." In *Work Well-Being and Public* Policy, edited by Solomon Polachek. *Research in Labor Economics* 22: 309–49.

Bettio, Francesca. 1988. *The Sexual Division of Labour.* Oxford: Clarendon Press.

Blau, Francine, and Andrea Beller. 1988. "Trends in Earnings Differentials by Gender, 1971–1981. "*Industrial and Labor Relations Review* 41(4): 513–29.

Blau, Francine, Marianne Ferber, and Anne Winkler. 2002. *The Economics of Women, Men and Work.* Upper Saddle, N.J.: Prentice Hall.

Blau, Francine, and Lawrence Kahn. May 1992. "The Gender Earnings Gap: Learning from International Comparisons." *American Economic Review* 82(2): 533–38.

———. 1997. "Swimming Up Stream: Trends in the Gender Wage Differential in the 1980s." *Journal of Labor Economics* 15(1, part 1): 1–42.

———. 2004. "The U.S. Gender Pay Gap in the 1990s: Slowing Convergence." NBER Working Paper No. 10853. Washington, D.C.: National Bureau of Economic Research.

Budig, Michelle, and Paula England. 2001. "The Wage Penalty for Motherhood." *American Sociological Review* 66(2): 204–25.

Butler, Richard J. 1982. "Estimating Wage Discrimination in the Labor Market. "*Journal of Human Resources* 17(4): 606–21.

Catalyst. 2002. "Women in Leadership: Comparing European and U.S. Women Executives." Available at: http: //www.catalyst women.org/bookstore/files/fact/EU percent20and percent20US percent20WICL percent20comparison.pdf.

———. 2003. "Workplace Flexibility Is Still a Women's Advancement Issue." Available at: http://64.233.167.104/u/Catalyst?q=cache:3fGsh40s3UMJ:www.catalystwomen.org/knowledge/titles/files/view/Workplace%2520Flexibility%2520Is%2520Still%2520a%2520Women%27s%2520Advancement%2520Issue.pdf+viewpoints+august+2003&hl=en&ie=UTF-8.

Coltrane, Scott. 2000. "Research on Household Labor: Modeling and Measuring the Social Embeddedness of Routine Family Work." *Journal of Marriage and Family* 62(4): 1208–33.

Fuchs, Victor. 1971. "Differences in Hourly Earning Between Men and Women." *Monthly labor Review* 94(5): 9–15.

Fullerton, Howard, and Mitra Toossi. 2001. "Labor Force Projections to 2010: Steady Growth and Changing Composition." *Monthly Labor Review* November 124(11): 21–38.

Goldin, Claudia. 1984. "The Earnings Gap in Historical Perspective." In *Comparable Worth: Issue for the 80s.* Washington: U.S. Commission on Civil Rights.

———. 1990. *Understanding the Gender Gap: An Economic History of American Women.* Oxford: Oxford University Press.

Goldin, Claudia, and Solomon Polachek. 1987. "Residual Differences by Sex: Perspectives on the Gender Gap in Earnings." *American Economic Review* 77(2): 143–51.

Harkness, Susan, and Jane Waldfogel. 2003. "The Family Gap in Pay: Evidence from Seven Industrialized Countries." In *Worker Well-Being and Public Policy,* edited by Solomon Polachek. Amsterdam: JAI Press; Research in Labor Economics 22: 369–413.

Jones, F. L. 1983. "On Decomposing the Gender Wage Gap: A Critical Comment on Blinder's Decomposition." *Journal of Human Resources* 18(1): 126–30.

Joshi, Heather, Pierella Paci, and Jane Waldfogel. 1999. "The Wages of Motherhood: Better or Worse." *Cambridge Journal of Economics* 23(5): 543–64.

Kao, Charng, Solomon Polachek, and Phanindra Wunnava. 1994. "Male-Female Wage Differentials in Taiwan." *Economic Development and Cultural Change* 42(2): 351–74.

Korenman, Sanders, and David Neumark. 1992. "Marriage, Motherhood, and Wages." *Journal of Human Resources* 27(2): 233–55.

Kreyenfeld, Michaela, and Karsten Hank. 2000. "Does the Availability of Child Care Influence the Employment of Mothers? Findings from Western Germany." *Population Research and Policy Review* 19(4): 317–37.

Kumar, Anil. March 2005. "Lifecycle Consistent Estimation of Effect of Taxes on Female Labor Supply in the U.S: Evidence from Panel Data." Working paper. Dallas: Federal Reserve Bank of Dallas.

Landes, Elisabeth. 1977. "Sex-Differences in Wages and Employment: A Test of the Specific Capital Hypothesis." *Economic Inquiry* 15(4): 523–38.

Lazear, Edward, and Sherwin Rosen. 1981. "Rank-Order Tournaments as Optimum Labor Contracts." *Journal of Political Economy* 89(5): 841–64.

Michael, Robert. 1973. "Education on Non-Market Production." *Journal of Political Economy* 81(2, part 1): 306–27.

Miller, Carole. 1993. "Actual Experience, Potential Experience or Age, and Labor-force participation by Married Women." *Atlantic Economic Journal* 21(4): 60–66.

Mincer, Jacob, and Solomon Polachek. 1974. "Family Investments in Human Capital." *Journal of Political Economy* 82(2, part 2): S76–S108.

Morris, Betsy. 2002. "Trophy Husbands." *Fortune*. October 14: 79-98.

Mulligan, Casey, and Yona Rubenstein. 2005. "Selection, Investment, and Women's Relative Wages Since 1975." NBER Working Paper No. 11159. Cambridge, Mass.: National Bureau of Economic Research.

O'Neill, June. 1985. "The Trend in Male-Female Wage Gap in the United States." *Journal of Labor Economics* 3(1): S91–116.

———. 2003. "The Gender Gap in Wages, Circa 2000." Paper presented at the American Economic Association Meetings. Washington, D.C. (January).

O'Neill, June, and Dave O'Neill. 2006. "What Do Wage Differentials Tell Us About Labor Market Discrimination?" In *The Economics of Immigration and Social Policy*, edited by Soloman Polachek, Carmel Chiswick, and Hillel Rapoport. *Research in Labor Economics* 24: 293–357.

Ott, Notburga. 1995. "Fertility and the Division of Work Within the Family." In *Out of the Margin*, edited by Edith Kuiper and Jolande Sap. London and New York: Routledge.

Polachek, Dora, and Solomon Polachek. 1989. "An Indirect Test of Children's Influence on Efficiencies in Parental Consumer Behavior." *Journal of Consumer Affairs* 23(1): 91–110.

Polachek, Solomon. 1975a. "Differences in Expected Post-School Investment as a Determinant of Market Wage Differentials." *International Economic Review* 2: 451–70.

———. 1975b. "Potential Biases in Measuring Male-Female Discrimination." *Journal of Human Resources* 10(2): 205–30.

———. 1995. "Human Capital and the Gender Gap: A Response to Feminist Critiques."

In *Out of the Margin*, edited by Edith Kuiper and Jolande Sap. London and New York: Routledge.

———. 2003. "Mincer's Overtaking Point and the Lifecycle Earnings Distribution." *Review of Economics of the Household* 1(4): 273–304.

Polachek, Solomon, and Moon-Kak Kim. 1994. "Panel Estimates of the Gender Earnings Gap: Individual Specific Intercept and Individual Specific Slope Models." *Journal of Econometrics* 61(1): 23–42.

Polachek, Solomon, and John Robst. 2001. "Trends in the Male-Female Wage Gap: the 1980s Compared to the 1970s." *Southern Economic Journal* 67(4): 869–88.

Schwartz, Felice. 1989. "Management Women and the New Facts of Life." *Harvard Business Review* 67(1): 65–76.

Simpson, Wayne. 2000. "Intermittent Work Activities and Earnings." *Applied Economics* 32(14): 1777–86.

United Nations Statistics Division. 2000. *The World's Women 2000: Trends and Statistics.* Table 5d, "Statistics and Indicators on Women and Men." Available at http://unstats.un.org/unsd/ demographic.

U.S. Bureau of the Census. 1975. *Historical Statistics of the United States: colonial Times to 1970.* Washington: U.S. Department of Commerce, Bureau of the Census. Available at: http://www2.census.gov/prod2/statcomp/documents/CT197op1-01.pdf.

———. 2002. *Statistical Abstract of the United States 2002.* Washington: U.S. Government Printing Office. Available at: http://www.census.gov/statab/www/.

———. 2003. *Statistical Abstract of the United States, 2003.* Washington: U.S. Government Printing Office. Available at: http://www.census.gov/statab/www/.

———. 2005. *Statistical Abstract of the United States, 2004–5.* Washington: U.S. Government Printing Office. Available at: http://www.census.gov/statab/www/.

U.S. Department of Labor, Bureau of Labor Statistics. 1974. *Employment and Earnings.* Washington: U.S. Government Printing Office.

———. 1990. *Employment and Earnings.* Washington: U.S. Government Printing Office.

———. 2002. *Employment and Earnings.* Washington: U.S. Government Printing Office.

———. 2003. *Highlights of Women's Earnings 2002.* Report no. 972. Washington: U.S. Government Printing Office.

Viewpoints [a series based on Catalyst research]. 2003. "Workplace Flexibility is Still a Women's Advancement Issue." *Viewpoints* August: 1.

Waldfogel, Jane. 1998. "Understanding the 'Family Gap' in Pay for Women with Children." *Journal of Economic Perspectives* 12(1): 137–56.

Weinberger, Catherine, and Peter Kuhn. 2005. "The Narrowing of the U.S. Gender Earnings Gap, 1969–1999: A Cohort-Based Analysis." Working paper. Santa Barbara: University of California.

Weis, Yoram, and Reuben Gronau. 1981. "Expected Interruptions in Labor-force participation and Sex Related Differences in Earnings Growth." *Review of Economic Studies* 48(4): 607–19.

Chapter 5

How Much Progress in Closing the Long-Term Earnings Gap?

Heidi Hartmann, Stephen J. Rose, and Vicky Lovell

In this era of economic progress for women, when women are narrowing the wage gap with men, working more years and more hours per year, and entering previously male-dominated occupations, some argue that women now have all the equality they want—that any remaining differences between women and men in their economic behavior are a matter of personal preferences—some argue that further progress to achieve full equality is proceeding apace and is, indeed, inevitable, and some argue that women still have a long way to go, facing difficult barriers, with the timing or scale of the outcome by no means clear.

The goal of this chapter is to shed light on these issues, to map where we are in the achievement of economic equality for women, identify the barriers that remain, and assess what factors or forces help or hinder the goal of full equality. In our view, until full equality is reached, gender will remain significant in limiting women's opportunities and privileging men's.

In this chapter, we present findings from a new analysis of the Panel Study of Income Dynamics (PSID) on the hours of work, earnings, and occupations of men and women across a thirty-year period. Using a new measure of the "long-term earnings gap," we show that women still earn a very small proportion of what men earn. In essence, despite a substantially increased work effort by women, most women work substantially fewer years and hours per year than men, work in lower-paying occupations, earn less than men even when they get into male-dominated occupations, and remain financially dependent on men for income during the child-rearing years and indeed throughout much of their adult lives. The sweeping effects of the wage gap are largely unacknowledged because its typical measurement is limited to a single year and restricted to only the higher-earning portion of the workforce. When accumulated over many years for all men and women workers, the losses to women and their families due to the wage gap are large and can be devastating.

MEASURING THE LONG-TERM EARNINGS GAP

The most common way of measuring the wage gap restricts the comparison to women and men who work full-time on a weekly or annual basis in a single year. Especially when the comparison is restricted to full-time, full-year workers, such a wage gap calculation leaves out the approximately two-fifths of women workers who work less than full-time or full-year, most of whom earn much less than those who work full-time.[1] The wage gap has been narrowing for full-time workers, whether calculated on a weekly or annual basis, so that in 2003, the Census Bureau reported a ratio of women's to men's median earnings of 75.5 percent for full-time year-round workers, while the Bureau of Labor Statistics reported a ratio of 79.4 percent for the median weekly earnings of full-time female and male workers.[2] These ratios have moved up nearly 20 percentage points in the several decades since they were first calculated and give a pleasing, if somewhat slow, measure of the progress that women are making. The gap, by these measures, has fallen from about 40 percentage points to about 21 to 24 percentage points.

Such a small gap may actually overstate the progress women have made. Given that more women than men work part-time and that women take more time out of the labor market than men do, such comparisons leave out a large proportion of low-earning women who do not meet the full-time, full-year standard. Such comparisons also tacitly accept the constraints of current gender relationships. All of the women who make the constrained "choice" to work part-time or to take time off for family care are excluded from the comparisons, and their low- or zero-earnings years are excluded as well. The concept of the long-term earnings gap is designed to serve as a measure of women's relative economic self-sufficiency, in that it captures women's lifetime earnings relative to men's and averages all earnings across a given number of years. It is also a measure of the relative access women and men have to economic resources through working, given their family circumstances.[3] The long-term earnings gap developed in this study measures women's earnings relative to men's earnings for all prime-age adults (aged twenty-six to fifty-nine) who work at least one year across a fifteen-year period. Two fifteen-year periods are compared. The number of years chosen is arbitrary (and based on data availability) and could be lengthened to the full working life of thirty to forty-five years if data were available. The Women's Unit of the Cabinet Office in the United Kingdom (Rake 2000) has simulated lifetime earnings and earnings losses relative to men for women at different educational levels in different marital statuses with varying numbers of children; using this method, long-term earnings gaps are very large. Economists agree that permanent income (that is, earnings over many years, where unusual or transitory dips or gains are smoothed out) is the best measure of economic well-being. The fifteen-year earnings averages developed here are a good approximation of permanent income available to the individual from her or his own labor-market activity.

Women's total earnings, as they move in and out of the labor market, measure their ability to take income away from the labor market. These earnings are an important indicator of women's overall well-being and their ability to support themselves and their families and affect their health and retirement security in old age as well (Caiazza 2002; Caiazza and Hartmann, forthcoming; Lee and Shaw 2003; Mead et al. 2001). Although many women in their prime earning years live with higher-earning men, many others live on their own or are the primary earners in their marriages. Among these latter women especially, low earnings can make it difficult to provide for children's care and education and can retard asset accumulation, such as home ownership and pensions, that can provide security in old age. For the study sample, in the fifteen-year time period between 1983 and 1998, 50 percent of prime-age women (aged twenty-six to fifty-nine) were not married for all fifteen years. And, of married women who worked every year, 15 percent earned more than their husbands on average. Thus, nearly two-thirds of women were self-supporting or the primary earner in their families for at least some time during the study period. A recent Institute for Women's Policy Research (IWPR) study shows that if women were paid the same as comparable men, even if only for the hours women currently work, poverty rates would fall by half for both single mothers and married women (Hartmann, Allen, and Owens 1999). IWPR researchers have also found that approximately half of women enter retirement alone, no longer living with men even if they were once married (Shaw, Zuckerman, and Hartmann 1998). Elderly women who are widowed, divorced, or never married have a high poverty rate; more than 20 percent of this group is poor. Fewer than half of older women enter retirement with pensions, either their own or their husbands' (Lee and Shaw 2003). In a world in which marriage is becoming less pervasive, improving women's long-term earnings is key to improving their long-term economic security.

In stressing the long-term earnings of women as a primary indicator of their well-being, we do not intend to dismiss or diminish the value of family-care work done at home. There is no question that family-care work is essential to society. In a market-based economy, however, money earnings are the main determinant of one's long-term economic security because there is currently virtually no remuneration for care work within the family. Even though it is valuable and even *if* many women prefer it, the decision to spend time in family care nevertheless jeopardizes women's economic security, as labor-market and safety-net institutions are currently arranged. Women who exercise a preference for family-care work in the short term are vulnerable to sudden and serious disruption of their economic well-being over the long term.

In addition, the "choice" to perform care work is not an unconstrained one, since societal supports for family care are largely unavailable (especially in the United States) and the labor market is characterized by discrimination in pay and employment opportunities and a lack of accommodation of family-care needs. We tend to believe that in a world without discrimination and with adequate institutional support, women's and men's preferences for family care and paid work would be very similar, so that lifetime earnings ratios would approach 100 percent.

DATA SET

This study uses the Panel Study of Income Dynamics (PSID), conducted by the Institute for Survey Research at the University of Michigan since 1968 (see Hill 1992 for details).[4] This data set provides annual information on earnings, income, and changes in family structure for a sample that is roughly representative of the United States population. The survey is self-reproducing because it includes the adult children of the original panel members. We use data for two fifteen-year periods of the survey, from 1968 to 1982 and 1983 to 1998, and count as a worker any prime-age adult who has at least one year with some earnings in either period. The two time periods are analyzed separately. Many workers have earnings in each of the years in a study period, whereas others have breaks or interruptions in their careers. We measure the time spent on breaks or interruptions by the number of full calendar years without any earnings. Not surprisingly, women are much more likely than men to have a full calendar year out of the labor force. Only workers with reported labor-market information in all working years of each time period are included. Both self-employed and wage and salaried workers are included in the study sample. The age range of twenty-six to fifty-nine is chosen to avoid the changing circumstances at the beginning and end of careers. By age twenty-six, with few exceptions, people have finished their schooling and are well on their way to finding their best labor market match. Conversely, at age fifty-nine, most have not yet retired or cut back on their hours in anticipation of retirement. The resulting study sample has about 3,000 prime-age workers in the second period and approximately 2,300 in the first period. At the start of each time period studied, workers range from twenty-six to forty-four years, and at the end they range from forty-one to fifty-nine years. Approximately 73,000 person work-years are analyzed in the thirty-year study period. Despite some limitations,[5] data from the PSID are considered to be representative of the white and African American populations and closely match data taken from the U.S. Census Bureau's Current Population Survey, a much larger cross-sectional survey that is used to measure employment, earnings, and income (Fitzgerald, Gottschalk, and Moffitt 1998). Average earnings are adjusted for inflation and are presented in 1999 dollars; averages presented generally exclude zeros unless otherwise noted.[6]

LONG-TERM EARNINGS-GAP RESULTS

As women have made gains in the labor market, the reported gender earnings gap has narrowed and the level of concern about women's job opportunities and outcomes has declined. But the preponderance of the evidence suggests that discrimination has not been eliminated, that norms and institutional arrangements continue to reduce women's earnings, and that women's low earnings contribute to family poverty and reduce the overall well-being of women and their children (Hartmann, Allen, and Owens 1999).

TABLE 5.1 / The Long-Term Labor Market Experience of Men and Women

Panel A: Average Annual Earnings and the Long-Term Earnings Gap, 1983 to 1998

Population in Comparison (Aged 26 to 59)	Average Annual Earnings		Earnings Ratio[a]	Earnings Gap[b]
	Women	Men		
All workers with at least one year with earnings, counting zero-earnings years	$18,239	$48,178	37.9	62.1
All workers with at least one year with earnings, excluding zero-earnings years	$21,363	$49,068	43.5	56.5
All workers with earnings in every year	$29,507	$52,510	56.2	43.8

Panel B: Average Annual Earnings and the Long-Term Earnings Gap, 1968 to 1982

Population in Comparison (Aged 26 to 59)	Average Annual Earnings		Earnings Ratio[a]	Earnings Gap[b]
	Women	Men		
All workers with at least one year with earnings, counting zero-earnings years	$11,327	$46,575	24.3	75.7
All workers with at least one year with earnings, excluding zero-earnings years	$13,804	$47,268	29.2	70.8
All workers with earnings in every year	$22,273	$49,448	45.0	55.0

Source: Authors' calculations, based on the Panel Study of Income Dynamics.
[a]The earnings ratio is calculated as $100 \times$ women's average annual earnings ÷ men's average annual earnings.
[b]The earnings gap = 100.0 − the earnings ratio.

How should we measure the gender gap? If we focused just on those with the strongest labor-force attachment, we would overstate the earnings equality attained by the majority of women, who have less consistent labor-market participation. Therefore, in this study we calculate the gap in earnings in a variety of ways, from the most inclusive measure (all women and men with some work) to the most restrictive (most strongly attached to the labor market). All present a long-term perspective on the wage gap since they measure earnings differences accumulated and averaged across the fifteen years of the study. Table 5.1 presents a row with average earnings data for each fifteen-year period that includes zero earnings for all years in which workers had no earnings, to give the broadest view of long-term earnings differences between women and men. In the other tables, we focus on years in which earnings are positive, which gives another important perspective on how much women and men earn.

However the gap is calculated, it is important to note that women's and men's earnings differ for many reasons. Discriminatory treatment of women in the labor market (in hiring, working conditions, promotion, or pay) or in labor-market preparation (access to training and education, for example) is certainly important. Some of the difference is due to unequal social norms at home, school, and work, and some is due to preferential choices women and men make about career preparation, work, and family-care issues. Disentangling all these factors is difficult.

When women "choose" to spend more time out of the labor market taking care of children than their husbands do, how much of that choice is constrained by lack of affordable, good-quality alternative care, women's lower pay or inferior working conditions on the job, their expectations that they won't be promoted anyway, the lack of workplace flexibility, or social norms in their kinship network, religious group, or community? We do not attempt to analyze these factors separately here; rather, we present the aggregate differences that still remain in women's and men's long-term labor-market activity and the earnings outcomes that result.

The results are presented in table 5.1, panels A and B, for the two fifteen-year time periods analyzed. For the more recent period, 1983 to 1998, shown in panel A, the size of the gender gap in earnings ranges from 62 percent when all workers are included and even zero-earnings years are counted to 44 percent when the comparison is restricted to persistent workers with earnings every year. In the earlier fifteen-year period, the long-term earnings gaps were even larger, ranging from 76 percent when all workers are included to 55 percent when the comparison is limited to those with earnings every year. In the 1968-to-1982 period, the typical male worker earned 4.1 times what the typical female worker earned ($46,575 versus $11,327). By the later fifteen-year period, 1983 to 1998, the typical man out-earned the typical woman by only 2.1 times ($48,178 versus $18,239). While the long-term earnings-gap measure shows how large the gap is when comparing a typical working woman to a typical working man over a sizable portion of their careers, it also captures the dramatic changes that have occurred in women's work behavior in just thirty years. Using the Current Population Survey measure, the ratio of women's to men's earnings increased only 28 percent between 1960 and 2002. The long-term earnings ratio, in contrast, increased 56 percent between the two fifteen-year periods in this study.

A large part of this growth in women's relative earnings was undoubtedly due to their increase in hours worked; some was also due to women's gains in education and work experience, and some was likely due to a decline in discrimination against women. Among women and men who worked persistently every year, women's relative gains were smaller. In the earlier period, the steady male worker out-earned his female counterpart 2.2 to 1.0; in the later period, men's advantage was still 1.8 to 1.0.

In the following sections, we look in detail at the factors that contribute to the long-term earnings gap.

WORK HOURS, WORK INTERRUPTIONS, AND EARNINGS

Although women's and men's work careers have become more similar, important differences remain. In fact, these differences are amplified when one takes a fifteen-year perspective. Across fifteen years, women's total earnings are dramatically lower than men's. What accounts for this huge difference? As we shall see, several factors are important: women and men work different amounts of time, they work in different types of jobs, and they are paid differently even when they have similar levels of education.

Using the most recent available fifteen-year time frame (1983 to 1998) in the PSID, and including all earnings from low- and zero-earnings years due to time spent on family care or other activities, such as schooling, we find that the average woman, in her prime earning years, earns only 38 percent of what the average man earns. Across fifteen years, the average prime-age working woman earned only $273,592 while the average working man earned $722,693 (in 1999 dollars). This gap of 62 percent is more than twice as large as the 24 percent gap commonly reported. In the earlier fifteen-year period dating from the start of the PSID (1968 to 1982), the average prime-age working woman earned only $169,910, while the average working man earned $698,629 (in 1999 dollars). The gap in the earlier time period is even larger, at 76 percent. Between the two periods, women's earnings as a percent of men's increased from 24 percent to 38 percent, a substantial increase, but still far below parity for women. Using these measures, we see the progress of women in a more realistic light.

Let us consider work hours first and examine data from the second period, as more information is available for the later years. Table 5.2 shows that women and men spend considerably different amounts of time working over this fifteen-year study period. Approximately six of every seven men report earnings in every year while just fewer than half of women work every year. Across fifteen years, the majority (51 percent) of women but just 16 percent of men have at least one complete calendar year without any earnings. Almost three in ten women report four or more years without earnings, whereas fewer than one in twenty men report that many years without earnings.

Women also report working fewer hours each year they work than men report. For both women and men, those who report the most years out of the labor market also report the fewest hours of work in years with work, suggesting that low work attachment is reflected in both years of work and hours per year. As table 5.2 shows, annual work hours for women average 1,498 per year of work, more than 700 hours less than men's average of 2,219 hours. Even for men and women who report earnings in every year of the fifteen-year study period, women report nearly 500 fewer hours per year than men. In other words, persistent or strongly attached women workers work 22 percent fewer hours than persistent male workers.

Women also earn less per year and less per hour at every level of labor-force attachment shown in table 5.2. Even when the comparison is restricted to years in which both women and men have earnings (as it is in table 5.2), the average working man earns more than twice what the average working woman earns annually, for an annual female-to-male earnings ratio of 43.5. When the comparison is further restricted to those men and women with earnings in all fifteen years, the female-to-male ratio for annual earnings rises to 56.2. And, as many other studies also show, men out-earn women even controlling for hours worked. These data show that on average women earn about 60 percent of what men earn per hour. Finally, when comparing women and men who report earnings in all fifteen study years, women still earn only 69.6 percent on average of what men earn per hour.

Table 5.2 / The Long-Term Labor-Market Experience of Women and Men: Earnings, Work Hours, and Years Out of the Labor Force, 1983 to 1998

		Fifteen-Year Averages[a]				
Number of Years Out of Labor Force	Percentage	Annual Earnings	Annual Hours	Annual Earnings Ratio[b]	Hourly Wage[c]	Hourly-Wage Ratio[c]
Females						
All (aged 26 to 59)	100.0	$21,363	1,498	43.5	$12.82	60.0
None	48.5	$29,507	1,766	56.2	$15.72	69.6
One	10.2	$19,341	1,513	52.5	$12.25	72.3
Two or three	11.8	$14,868	1,376	51.7	$10.56	75.6
Four or more	29.5	$11,280	1,100	51.5	$9.25	63.8
Males						
All (aged 26 to 59)	100.0	$49,068	2,219		$21.38	
None	84.0	$52,510	2,260		$22.60	
One	7.5	$36,867	2,210		$16.94	
Two or three	4.8	$28,777	2,062		$13.97	
Four or more	3.7	$21,896	1,524		$14.50	

Source: Authors' calculations, based on the Panel Study of Income Dynamics.

[a]Zero-earnings years are not included; that is, averages for earnings and hours are calculated only for years when work is reported. Weighted data are used to calculate all figures.

[b]Earnings ratios are calculated as 100 × women's average annual earnings ÷ men's average annual earnings.

[c]Hourly wages are person-weighted rather than hour-weighted so that each person's wage counts equally in the calculation regardless of how few or many hours the person worked. The hourly-wage ratio is calculated as 100 × women's average hourly wages ÷ men's average hourly wages.

We can also compare the hours worked of the super-attached workforce—those who regularly work full-time, full-year (defined as working at least 1,750 hours for at least twelve of fifteen years; data not shown). Among prime-age workers from 1983 to 1998, 26 percent of women and 74 percent of men meet this standard of strongest labor-force participation. Even among this group, women report fewer work hours per year than men: 2,081 versus 2,312, or 10 percent less. The norm of working time for most men is thus considerably higher than the working-time norm of even the top quarter of women (those with the strongest labor-force attachment).

It is well established that women's participation in the labor market has increased dramatically over the last forty years. Table 5.3 reports on earnings levels and years without earnings for the first fifteen years of the PSID, 1968 to 1982. During these earlier years, 72 percent of prime-age women had at least one year with zero earnings compared with only 51 percent in the later years (see table 5.2); half had at least four years with no earnings compared with 30 percent in the later years. For male workers during these years, 87 percent had earnings every year (no years out of the labor force) compared with 84 percent in the later years.

TABLE 5.3 / The Long-Term Labor-Market Experience of Women and Men: Earnings and Years Out of the Labor Force, 1968 to 1982

Number of Years Out of Labor Force	Percentage	Average Annual Earnings[a]	Ratio of Women's Earnings to Men's[b]
Females			
All (aged 26 to 59)	100.0	$13,804	29.2
None	28.3	$22,273	45.0
One	8.3	$17,976	50.2
Two or three	13.5	$13,709	50.7
Four or more	49.9	$8,330	38.9
Males			
All (aged 26 to 59)	100.0	$47,268	
None	87.3	$49,448	
One	5.1	$35,809	
Two or three	4.2	$27,024	
Four or more	3.4	$21,418	

Source: Authors' calculations, based on the Panel Study of Income Dynamics.
[a]Zero-earnings years are not included; that is, annual averages for earnings are calculated only for years when work is reported.
[b]Earnings ratios are calculated as 100 × women's average annual earnings ÷ men's average annual earnings. Weighted data are used to calculate all figures.

Because of data limitations (working hours were not collected for all working wives in the early years of the PSID), comparisons of hours worked per year cannot be produced for this period. The ratios of annual female-to-male earnings during this earlier period (table 5.3) were substantially lower than those reported above (in table 5.2). Again counting only years with earnings (eliminating zero-earnings years) for all workers in the sample, table 5.3 shows that women earned just 29 percent of what men earned on average in the 1968-to-1982 period. Even among workers with strong labor-force attachment (those who worked all fifteen years), women earned just 45 cents for each dollar men earned.

WOMEN'S AND MEN'S LOCATIONS IN THE LABOR MARKET

If one major factor affecting women's total earnings is how much they work, another is where they work and what they are paid when they are working. The long-term perspective on occupational sex segregation is important because some have argued that there is considerable mobility between male- and female-typed jobs. If this were the case, over their careers many women could expect to move into "male" jobs and avoid the pay penalty frequently associated with female-dominated occupations. On the contrary, however, our long-term earnings measure shows that the majority of both men and women remain in a single one of six occupation-gender tiers for at least twelve of fifteen years, suggesting that sex segregation and the lack of comparable worth between the pay scales in male- and female-typed occupations is of considerable long-lasting consequence. Because of data availability issues, the analysis of women's and men's occupational distributions is limited to the second period studied, 1983 to 1998.

While fairness, especially in large, bureaucratic firms, would seem to dictate that workers in the same firm in the same position with the same seniority get paid the same amount (assuming similar performance levels), the reality of the labor market is that women and men are still often concentrated into occupations and job titles that they do not share with the opposite sex, and those traditionally held by men tend to pay more than those traditionally held by women. Although job segregation by sex has declined along with the pay gap, by most measures it is still substantial. According to Jerry Jacobs (2003), in 2000, 52 percent of all working women (in 1970 it was 67 percent) would have to change jobs in order for women and men to have the same distribution across occupations, based on analysis of the detailed census data on occupations.

The causes of sex segregation in the labor market and lower pay in jobs dominated by women are not all well understood, but involve such factors as social norms and cultural practices as well as prejudice and discrimination. Many of these practices begin to take shape as boys and girls progress through their schooling (American Association of University Women 1998). Xiaoling Shu and Margaret Mooney Marini (1998) show that even in high school, girls on average have different expectations than boys and take somewhat different courses (girls get better grades and have better attendance). Among those who go to college, female students tend to major in different fields than male students, and many of these majors lead them to different occupations than males, although this occurs less than in earlier years (Blau, Ferber, and Winkler 2002). Not surprisingly, research has shown that field of study has a strong effect on future earnings and that women-intensive majors have lower future earnings, yet even these differences are not enough to account for the large gender earnings differences observed (Weinberger 1998). A recent study of Wal-Mart's personnel practices shows that despite women's better performance evaluations and longer job tenure, they are less likely to be promoted than men, accounting for their lower representation among managers (Drogin 2003). Several additional examples of discriminatory practices are provided in chapter 2 in this volume, by Francine D. Blau and Lawrence M. Kahn. Another study shows that pay rates of jobs fall when more minorities and women enter the jobs, even though the job content (tasks and skills required) has not changed (Baron and Newman 1989). Gender differentiation in the labor market also seems to be self-reproducing. When nurses are mostly women and construction workers are mostly male, more young women say they want to be nurses than want to be construction workers (Reskin and Hartmann 1986). And worse yet, when women do express interest in nontraditional jobs, they are often not encouraged to pursue them by guidance counselors and others who believe women are unlikely to succeed in male-dominated work (Negrey et al. 2002).

Because very few people report being in the same detailed three-digit occupational code (as used by the Census Bureau) persistently for fifteen years, this study relies on a classification system developed by Stephen J. Rose and Anthony Carnevale (1998) to gauge sex segregation across workers' fifteen-year careers. This system groups occupations into eight broad categories, which are similar but not identical to the Census Bureau's broad categories (one-digit codes such as professionals, managers, craft workers, clerical workers, and so forth), adjusted to make the categories more internally consistent.[7] For the current study, the occupations are further grouped into three grand tiers on the basis of educational requirements (see Rose and Hartmann 2004, appendix, for more details):

1. Elite jobs—managers and professionals

2. Good jobs—supervisors (including nonprofessional self-employed workers and managers in food service and retail trade), blue-collar craft workers, technicians, police, firefighters, and clerical workers

3. Less-skilled jobs—sales clerks; personal, food, and related service workers; and unskilled blue-collar jobs

As will be seen, the use of level of education to define the tiers makes this occupational classification a unique tool for illustrating the impact of the lack of comparable worth (or the failure of jobs of equal value to be paid equally).[8]

Each tier is divided into two subgroupings of occupations, those that are held either disproportionately by men or disproportionately by women. Within each of these subgroups, at least 75 percent of the workers are of one gender. In the top tier, men are more likely to be business executives, scientists, lawyers, and doctors, whereas women are concentrated in the professions of teaching, nursing, and social work. In the middle tier, men work in construction crafts and other skilled blue-collar jobs and as police officers and fire-fighters, whereas women work as secretaries and medical technicians. In the bottom tier, the less-skilled jobs, men are disproportionately in unskilled factory jobs, whereas women are more likely to be retail sales clerks and personal-service workers.

Workers are assigned to one of these six groups if they work in that group for at least twelve of the fifteen years of the study period; only workers with earnings in all fifteen years are included in the analysis. Given the diversity of many people's careers, many workers do not spend twelve years in any of the six groups. People with mixed occupational histories make up the largest single category, encompassing about 42 percent of the strongly attached, or persistent, workers in the study sample (those with earnings in all fifteen years); the remaining 58 percent of strongly attached workers do have persistent employment in one of the six occupational clusters (see table 5.4).

Of those with mixed histories, workers who move between male and female professional and managerial jobs are identified separately because their earnings are much higher than those of other workers who move fairly regularly between occupations. The largest single group, about 38 percent for both women and men, move among less-skilled and good jobs. Of those who are persistently in one of the

TABLE 5.4 / Distribution of Continuously Employed Women and Men Across Career Occupational Groups, 1983 to 1998 (as a Percentage)

Tier	Male Sector	Female Sector	Mixed	Totals
Women[a]	Full-Time	Full-Time	Full-Time	Full-Time
All (aged 26 to 59)	21.3	36.7	41.6	99.9
Elite jobs	11.7	9.4	2.9	24.0
Good jobs	3.9	24.7	—	28.6
Less-skilled jobs	5.7	2.9	—	8.6
Mixed work histories[b]	—	—	38.7	38.7
Men[a]	All[c]	All[c]	All[c]	All[c]
All (aged 26 to 59)	50.1	7.7	42.2	100.0
Elite jobs	24.1	4.5	3.8	32.4
Good jobs	16.2	2.0	—	18.2
Less-skilled jobs	9.8	1.2	—	11.0
Mixed work histories[b]	—	—	38.4	38.4

Source: Authors' calculations, based on the Panel Study of Income Dynamics.
[a]Weighted data are used to calculate all figures.
[b]Workers with mixed work histories are those who move among jobs in the lower two tiers (good and less-skilled jobs).
[c]There is not much difference in the distribution across occupational groups between men who work full-time and all men (because most men work full-time).

six defined occupational groups, gender segregation is very pronounced especially for men: 92 percent of men are concentrated in the male jobs of each tier, whereas 63 percent of full-time women are found in the female jobs of each tier (for all persistent women workers, including part-timers with earnings every year, the proportion is 85 percent in the female jobs).

Few men are found in female career occupations. Among men who work in the elite tier of managerial and professional jobs, 74 percent are in male jobs and only 14 percent are in female jobs. Among men who work in both good and less-skilled jobs, 89 percent are in male jobs and 11 percent are in female jobs. This is a remarkable amount of sex segregation, given how aggregated these occupational classifications are.

Table 5.4 also shows that women are not as concentrated in the female sector as men are in the male sector. Since women's jobs have traditionally paid less, women may very well be seeking to branch out from these jobs. This is particularly true for women in the top occupational grouping: among women who work full-time, more women work in male elite jobs (12 percent) than work in female elite jobs (9 percent). Overall, women meeting the full-time work standard constitute just less than half of all female persistent workers (those with earnings every year).

Panel A of table 5.5 shows average pay for women and men in each of the six gender-tier sectors. In general, regardless of the tier or sector, women earn substantially less than men, even when only those women who work full-time are considered. For example, in the elite tier, women who work full-time in male jobs earn only 68 percent of men's earnings. It is quite interesting to note that, in the good and less-skilled job tiers, the relatively few men in female jobs have average pay that is almost comparable to those of men in male career jobs in the same tier. Thus, these men seem able to find or create a few higher-paying niches among female-dominated job groups that most often have lower pay. As panel B of table 5.5 shows, men in female jobs work substantially more hours on average than the full group of strongly attached women in female jobs, partially accounting for their higher earnings. Yet the men in these female jobs earn substantially more even than those women who work persistently full-time and have work hours comparable to men's.

In contrast, in the top tier, men in the predominantly female education and public service jobs have earnings that are significantly less than their counterparts who are in the male-dominated business and managerial jobs. The men in these female elite jobs (often called the intellectual and caring professions) have very high levels of education. Given that male elite jobs were probably open to these men, they may often have made their career choice on the basis of nonpecuniary reasons, and, like women, may suffer from the "comparable worth" problem—the devaluation of these jobs because they are identified with women.

While men who work in the female sectors in the middle and bottom tiers do nearly as well as men who work in the male sectors of those tiers, women workers in these two tiers do significantly better when they have the opportunity to get into male-dominated jobs, earning almost 50 percent more than women in female jobs earn in these tiers. The subgroup of these women who work persistently full-time earn even more in the male good jobs, earning on average only 8 percent less than the men in the same tier. Thus, enabling more women to enter the middle tier of male good jobs would raise women's wages significantly.

In contrast, full-time women workers in male jobs in the top tier earn only about 6 percent more on average than women in the top female jobs, and they earn about one-third less than the men in top male jobs. This result is surprising, since the women who enter these jobs in law, medicine, and high-level management have the specialized education and skills that command higher pay. Either women's entry into high-paying managerial and professional jobs is relatively new and women haven't acquired the same level of experience as men, or women are in lower-paying women's niches in these fields, or discrimination against women in pay and promotion in these occupations is more severe than in the other two tiers.[9]

It also should be noted that women in male jobs work much longer hours than women in female jobs in the same tier. In the top two tiers, this difference is particularly large, so that although women in male jobs may still work fewer hours than men in those jobs, the difference in hours is not nearly large enough to account for the difference in pay. The smaller group of full-time women workers works even more hours in these male jobs, yet they still have not reached earnings parity.

As table 5.5 shows, earnings for full-time women workers are higher than those for the full group of strongly attached women. Full-time women do best relative to

TABLE 5.5 / Earnings, Earnings Ratio, and Hours Worked of Continuously Employed Women and Men by Career Occupational Groups, 1983 to 1998

Panel A: Earnings

Tier	Male Sector			Female Sector			Earnings Ratio (Percentage), Full-Time Women to All Men	
	Women		Men	Women		Men	Male Sector	Female Sector
	All	Full-Time	All[a]	All	Full-Time	All[a]		
Elite jobs	$47,574	$51,085	$74,877	$38,842	$48,371	$52,405	68.2	92.3
Good jobs	$40,412	$46,309	$50,305	$27,262	$30,777	$47,768	92.1	64.4
Less-skilled jobs	$22,729	$25,319	$35,627	$15,143	$24,022	$32,313	71.1	74.3

Panel B: Hours Worked

Tier	Male Sector			Female Sector		
	Women		Men	Women		Men
	All	Full-Time	All[a]	All	Full-Time	All[a]
Elite jobs	2,154	2,264	2,332	1,705	2,117	2,158
Good jobs	2,247	2,469	2,221	1,860	1,989	2,156
Less-skilled jobs	1,871	2,018	2,199	1,670	2,279	2,016

Source: Authors' calculations, based on the Panel Study of Income Dynamics.
[a] There is not much difference in the distribution across occupational groups between men who work full-time and all men (because most men work full-time), so data are not reported separately for men who work full-time.

men in good male jobs, where the gender earnings ratio is 92 percent, and in elite female jobs, which also have a 92 percent earnings ratio. These ratios reflect a premium for women who work in good male jobs (compared to their pay elsewhere) and a penalty for men in elite female jobs. Women who work in the middle tier of female jobs are much less successful in raising their earnings by working full-time. Full-time working women who are clerical workers and medical technicians in the good-female-job sector earn just slightly more than full-time women in less-skilled jobs, even though they have much higher levels of education and skills. Yet women who hold jobs in the male sector of the middle tier earn 50 percent more than their counterparts in female jobs and 92 percent of what the men earn. These data suggest that women's work in female jobs in the middle tier may suffer especially from the lack of comparable pay for comparable work.

To sum up, in each tier, female-sector jobs pay significantly less than male-sector jobs, even though by definition both sets of occupations require the same level of educational preparation.

Women in the top tier of managerial and professional jobs have not yet made significant inroads into the highest-paid business jobs (the "glass-ceiling effect"), even when they do obtain jobs in the male sector. In the bottom two tiers, however, those women who are able to break free from women's jobs are able to realize large earnings gains.

For the preponderance of women who remain in the female sector of each tier, earnings are strikingly low. In general, even restricting the comparison to women who work full-time, women in women's jobs earn less than men in men's jobs one tier below: women in female elite jobs earn less than men in male good jobs, and women in female good jobs earn less than men in male less-skilled jobs. Finally, the analysis shows that although some of the earnings differences observed between women and men may arise partly from women's lower average work hours, hours differences alone do not account for all or even most of the earnings differences observed between strongly attached men and women workers.

WAGE GROWTH OVER TIME

One disadvantage of averaging data across fifteen-year study periods is that such an average hides any progress that might have been made during that time. We know that women in the 1983-to-1998 period work more years and have higher earnings relative to men than women did in the first fifteen years of the PSID, 1968 to 1982, suggesting that further changes likely occurred within the 1983-to-1998 period. To provide some insight on these likely changes, we focus on earnings growth. We determine which workers had earnings increases or decreases and compute an average annual growth rate in earnings for each continuously employed worker. Tracking average earnings over time as workers progress through their careers generally shows increases as workers gain seniority and more skills. As with any average, however, it is composed of a great variety of individual experiences and group experiences as well. Because of their different places in the labor market (women in services and men in manufacturing, for example), women's and men's earnings growth rates often differ. And because of changing economic conditions over time (boom and bust cycles, for example), different birth cohorts generally have different economic experiences. To simplify presentation of all these individual earnings histories, the results are divided into four groups: "declines" are defined as a computed yearly change of negative .5 percent per year or worse; "no change" is defined as the range within plus or minus .5 percent change per year; "small gains" are defined as .5 to 2.5 percent growth per year; and "gains" are defined as 2.5 percent per year growth or greater.

The results, shown in table 5.6, are disaggregated by gender and age of the worker at the beginning of the study period. Among men, only 58 percent were gainers over these years; 16 percent had steady earnings, and 26 percent had higher earnings at the beginning of these years than at the end. Indeed, the average gain for all men of 1.5 percent per year (not shown in this table) hides the fact that many men treaded water or lost ground. Younger men generally did better than older men, but even a third of young workers (aged between twenty-six and thirty-one years when the study began) did not have positive earnings trajectories. For women, the share of gainers was much higher (73 percent). Only about one in five (19 percent) had declining earnings paths. Just as for men, younger women did better than older women (78 percent with increases for the youngest cohort versus 56 percent for the oldest cohort).

These differing earnings trajectories for the men and women in this study are consistent with what we know from cross-sectional data observed each year. During the 1980s and through the mid-1990s, women's earnings rose relative to men's, and the earnings gap narrowed. Indeed, in much of the 1980s men's earnings stagnated as the manufacturing sector struggled. Women's earnings rose both because they were in a better place in the labor market than men and because they increased their education and accumulated more years of experience as they worked more hours. Barriers against them also may have eroded somewhat as civil rights laws continued to have effect and customs and expectations continued to change. Although the generally narrowing pay gap is encouraging, it is important to keep two caveats in mind: first, women started out at such a low level that it was relatively easy for them to move up; and second, women with work interruptions likely had to start over at a reduced level and then experienced large earnings gains.

MARRIAGE, CHILDREN, EARNINGS, AND FAMILY INCOME

Since it is widely acknowledged that women remain the primary caregivers of children, it is logical to ask how much of women's lower hours and earnings can be associated with their marital status and the presence of children. And, because many women spend much of their adult lives in families with men earners, women's own earnings are not the only important measure of their economic well-being. Of course, across fifteen years, individuals change their marital status and

TABLE 5.6 / Earnings Growth (Percentage) and Distribution Across Earnings Paths for Continuously Employed Women and Men by Age, 1983 to 1998

	Decreases or Negligible Growth			Increases		
	Subtotal	Decreases	No Change	Subtotal	Small Increases	Increases of More Than 2.5% per year
Women (weighted population = 16.3 million)						
All	28	19	9	73	26	47
26 to 31 years[a]	21	18	3	78	22	56
32 to 38 years[a]	28	15	13	71	28	43
39 to 45 years[a]	44	34	10	56	0	56
Men (weighted population = 28.1 million)						
All	42	26	16	58	28	30
26 to 31 years[a]	33	23	10	67	27	40
32 to 38 years[a]	40	24	16	60	29	31
39 to 45 years[a]	59	35	24	41	30	11

Source: Authors' calculations, based on the Panel Study of Income Dynamics.
[a]Age is respondent's age in 1983. Weighted data are used to calculate all figures.

children arrive in or leave their parents' home. During the period from 1983 to 1998, about one in seven adults in the study never had children in their household, while 30 percent of females and 24 percent of males had children present in all fifteen years. About 50 percent of the study adults were married in all fifteen years, and of this group about 40 percent had children present in all these years. To display data for families across a fifteen-year period, we present data by categories of years married and years with children.[10]

In this section we adjust family income for family size, to account for the economies of scale available to cohabiting individuals and to compare economic well-being across family size. Our adjusted family-income measure is calculated by multiplying real (inflation-adjusted) family income by the square root of three, and then dividing by the square root of the number of people in the family. This generates a standardized income measure as if all families had three members.[11]

Table 5.7 shows the relationship between marital status and family income, personal earnings, and working time.[12] For women, persistence in being married affects their economic well-being dramatically. Average annual family income is $71,455 for those who were always married but just $41,070 for those who were married two years or less. This higher standard of living for married women is attained even though they work in the labor market much less. Always-married women have just over five years of working full-time, full-year (more than 1,750 hours annually); by contrast seldom-married women have more than eight years of high yearly hours. Always-married women have more years out of the labor force and average just 1,161 hours in years when they are working. By contrast, the comparable annual work hours figure for women married two years or less is

TABLE 5.7 / Marital Status, Family Income, Earnings, and Working Time for Women and Men, 1983 to 1998

Marital Status[a]	Percentage[b]	Average Annual Family Income[c]	Average Annual Personal Earnings[d]	Average Annual Hours Worked[d]	Number of Years Not Working	Number of Years Working 1,750 Hours or More
Women (weighted population = 33.9 million)						
All (aged 26 to 59)	100	$61,319	$21,560	1,331	3.1	6.5
Always	50	$71,455	$19,372	1,161	3.6	5.3
Mostly	19	$60,624	$21,864	1,411	2.5	7.0
Some	14	$51,118	$24,594	1,567	2.8	8.0
Seldom	17	$41,070	$25,009	1,546	2.7	8.3
Men (weighted population = 32.7 million)						
All (aged 26 to 59)	100	$67,075	$45,952	2,120	0.9	12.3
Always	56	$68,201	$48,906	2,184	0.5	13.0
Mostly	25	$72,583	$47,513	2,203	0.6	12.5
Some	14	$60,221	$38,722	1,909	2.5	10.4
Seldom	6	$55,811	$32,550	1,796	2.2	9.6

Source: Authors' calculations, based on the Panel Study of Income Dynamics.
[a] "Always" refers to fifteen or more years married; "mostly" refers to nine to fourteen years; "some" refers to three to eight years; and "seldom" refers to zero to two years.
[b] May not sum exactly to 100 due to rounding.
[c] Family income has been adjusted to reflect family size.
[d] Zero-earnings years are not included; that is, annual averages for personal earnings and hours worked are calculated only for years when work is reported. Weighted data are used to calculate all figures.

1,546. Average annual personal earnings of always-married women are just 75 percent of seldom-married women's. This difference is entirely the result of differences in hours worked, since average hourly earnings are about the same for all women independent of their fifteen-year marital histories.

Table 5.7 also shows that being married at least nine years is an especially important factor for men. Always- and mostly-married men earn approximately the same amount, working about the same number of hours per year.[13] In contrast, for men who are only sometimes or seldom married, personal earnings are much lower, and they spend many more years out of the labor force, work fewer hours per year, and earn lower hourly wages when working.[14]

Comparing men and women reveals that their average annual adjusted family incomes across fifteen years are only slightly different—$67,075 for men versus $61,319 for women—despite men's earning more than twice as much as women. This pattern suggests that there is a joint husband-wife decision about working time and family care.[15] Since women's hourly wages are so much lower than their male counterparts', women likely often reduce their time in the paid labor force to provide family care. Thus, women's low labor-market earnings reinforce the gendered division of labor at home. Another way to put this is that for married women, their husbands' earnings often insulate them from the effects of their own low earnings. Low family incomes occur primarily in two situations—where the husbands are low earners or have multiple years out of the labor force and where women are single parents.

For the 31 percent of women who are married less than nine of fifteen years, this arrangement fails and they have a much lower living standard than women who are more consistently married.[16] Interestingly, men and women married two years or less look pretty similar to each other in terms of their years out of the labor market, years with low work hours, and personal earnings. Among men, however, the least-married group has the least work effort and the lowest earnings, while among women, the least-married group has the highest earnings and the second highest work effort.[17]

Tabulations for personal earnings, family income, and working time by years with children also reveal a number of interesting patterns for men and women (table 5.8). For women, slightly more than half had children present for at least ten of fifteen years. These women had the lowest individual earnings ($19,093) in the years when they worked. Women who had children present two years or less earned nearly $9,000 more per working year on average. Compared with women who seldom had children present, women who mostly have children present across fifteen years spend more years out of the paid labor market, work fewer hours, and earn less per hour. Both women's adjusted family incomes and their own earnings rise as years with children fall. Not only do women's higher earnings contribute to higher family income, but that income stretches further as the number of years children are present falls.[18]

Men, by contrast, have exactly the opposite pattern: those with children present for ten or more years have the highest individual earnings. Their adjusted family incomes also rise as years with children fall, but not as much as in the case for women. Men with children mostly present also tend to put in the most working hours to achieve their higher individual earnings.[19] Lower adjusted family incomes for this group stem from both wives' lower work hours and earnings and the larger number of children.

Just as with marriage (see note 16), the presence of children affects women's earnings less for women who work in all fifteen years. Family incomes are also higher overall for this group of strongly attached women workers, partly because of their own higher earnings and partly because they have fewer years with children overall. For these continuously employed women, personal earnings and work hours vary little across the number of years with children (12 percent for personal earnings and 4 percent for work hours versus 32 percent for personal earnings and 25 percent for work hours for all women workers shown in table 5.8).

Further analysis of the relationship between personal earnings and family income for all continuously employed women and men (regardless of marital status or presence of children) shows that there is a more direct relationship between personal earnings and family income for men than women, most likely because men are more often the larger earner in the marriage. The relatively few men with earnings below $25,000 were in families with average adjusted incomes below $40,000 (data not shown). In contrast, women with these low earnings were in households that averaged approximately $50,000 in adjusted family income. Of the 1 percent of men with average personal earnings below $15,000 annually, 40 percent had average family incomes below $25,000, whereas for the 18 percent of women with such low personal earnings, only 16 percent had family incomes below $25,000. Again, married women are generally insulated from their own low earnings by their husbands' earnings.

WIVES WHO EARN MORE THAN THEIR HUSBANDS

Although men are generally higher earners and contribute more to family income than women do, there are some wives who out-earn their husbands. In 2001, one wife in every four in dual-earner families had higher earnings than her husband; among all married couples, the wife's earnings exceeded the husband's in one out of every seven families (U.S. Census Bureau 2004b). In a given year, 10 percent of wives in dual-earner couples out-earn their husbands by 50 percent or more (Winkler 1998).

Our study offers some insight into the extent to which wives' higher earning is a short- or long-term family income strategy. Table 5.9 shows the group of men and women who work continuously over all fifteen years in the 1983-to-1998 period and are also married all fifteen years. Of this group (about one-third of the total sample in these years), 15 percent of wives earn more than their husbands on average across fifteen years. For the approximately 8 percent of continuously working and continuously married women who earn more than $50,000 per year, nearly half earn more than their husbands on average across the fifteen years. And of the approximately 12 percent of continuously working and married husbands who earn less than $25,000 per year, about half have wives who earn more than they do.

TABLE 5.8 / Presence of Children, Family Income, Earnings, and Working Time for Women and Men, 1983 to 1998

Presence of Children[a]	Percentage[b]	Average Annual Family Income[c]	Average Annual Personal Earnings[d]	Average Annual Hours Worked[d]	Number of Years Not Working	Number of Years Working More than 1,750 Hours
Women						
All	100	$61,319	$21,560	1,331	3.1	6.5
Mostly	53	$54,378	$19,093	1,215	3.3	5.8
Some	30	$63,302	$21,635	1,345	3.6	6.6
Seldom	17	$76,982	$28,016	1,619	1.9	8.2
Men						
All	100	$67,075	$45,952	2,120	0.9	12.3
Mostly	45	$61,701	$48,351	2,202	0.5	13.0
Some	27	$71,390	$46,112	2,101	1.1	12.0
Seldom	28	$73,920	$39,562	1,941	1.6	10.8

Source: Authors' calculations, based on the Panel Study of Income Dynamics.

[a] "Mostly" means ten to fifteen years with children; "some" means three to nine years; and "seldom" means zero to two years.

[b] May not sum exactly to 100 due to rounding.

[c] Family income has been adjusted to reflect family size.

[d] Zero-earnings years not included; that is, annual averages for personal earnings and hours worked are calculated only for years when work is reported.

TABLE 5.9 / Wives Who Earn More Than Their Husbands, 1983 to 1998 (Continuously Employed and Married Women and Men)

	Percentage[a]	Percentage of Wives Who Earn More Than Their Husbands
Wives' earnings		
All (aged 26 to 59)	100.0	15
Less than $15,000	23.0	0
$15,000 to $24,999	26.0	11
$25,000 to $49,999	43.0	19
$50,000 to $75,000	6.3	46
$75,000 and above	1.5	45
Husbands' earnings		
All (aged 26 to 59)	100.0	15
Less than $15,000	0.6	82
$15,000 to $24,999	11.0	40
$25,000 to $49,999	52.0	15
$50,000 to $75,000	27.0	3
$75,000 and above	10.0	6

Source: Authors' calculations, based on the Panel Study of Income Dynamics.
[a]May not sum exactly to 100 due to rounding.

The fifteen percent of women who earn more than their husbands do not necessarily earn very much more; many of them are "dual earners" rather than "primary" earners. About 4 percent earn less than 10 percent more than their husbands. Eleven percent earn at least 10 percent more, but only half of those (about 5 percent) earn 25 percent or more than their husbands do across the fifteen-year study period (data not shown). In terms of hourly wages, 24 percent of continuously working and continuously married wives earn more than their husbands on average across the fifteen years (data not shown). Since only fifteen percent out-earn their husbands during the average year, many of the wives with higher hourly wages are working less than their husbands on average, suggesting that many couples may be choosing not to maximize their joint income.[20] About one-third of continuously employed and married women have one or more years when they out-earn their husbands by at least 25 percent (data not shown). And for wives with college or graduate degrees, more than 85 percent had at least one year when they out-earned their husbands in terms of hourly wages (data not shown).[21]

WHAT IS TO BE DONE?

Experts disagree about the significance that should be attributed to the remaining differences found in women's and men's work experiences in and out of the labor market. In this chapter we argue that they are significant for many reasons.

First, the gender gap in earnings has a major influence on families' life choices and poverty rates, on older women's retirement security, and on single mothers' ability to provide for their children. All families with women earners or would-be earners would have a higher standard of living if women's wages and lifetime earnings were higher. Second, women face discrimination in the labor market and in pre–labor market preparation as well. The degree of sex segregation in the labor market is striking, and women's jobs at all educational levels pay less than men's jobs at the same level. Women's access to better-paying jobs and occupations is evidently still constrained. Third, although many women spend more time on family care than many men, the choices women and men make in allocating their time between work and family are heavily constrained. The lack of workplace flexibility and such societal provisions for family care as subsidized child and elder care means that most families have to fend for themselves. Women's typically lower wages, of course, make it more practical for the family to sacrifice the woman's rather than the man's earnings, and then, to compensate for the loss of the woman's earnings, the man often works even more hours.

Thus, a kind of perverse internal logic perpetuates a system with a rigid division of labor both in the workplace and in the home. Employers may feel justified in discriminating against women workers if they think they will be less devoted to their jobs because of family responsibilities. They may structure some jobs as part-time and dead-end for this reason and many women may accept this kind of employment because they cannot find better-paying jobs. Labor-market discrimination means lower earnings for women; women's low earnings mean women spend more time in family care; women's commitments to family care contribute to discrimination against them. Single mothers especially suffer as they must attempt to support their families on women's lower wage levels. Such a system surely fails to use human talent productively. How much total output is lost to society because the skills of women are not developed and put to work in the most productive way? To what extent are economic resources misallocated because of the constraints noted above? To what extent are both men and women denied the opportunity to allocate their time between home and work as they would most prefer?

In assessing the likelihood of future changes in women's working time and earnings, several trends favor continued gains in women's economic achievement. On the education front, women are now closing the graduate school gap with men. Women have begun to outnumber men in law and medical schools and have increased their numbers substantially in business schools (Conlin 2003). Yet, since women now outnumber men as graduates of four-year colleges, it seems likely that overall the rate at which women increase their years of education relative to men will slow.

Antidiscrimination and equal opportunity laws continue to open many jobs to women, and women are even beginning to break into the major corporate CEO ranks (eight of the Fortune 500 companies are now headed by women [Amy Joyce, "It's Lonely at the Top, Especially for Women," *Washington Post*, April 16, 2005, SP10]) and congressional and statewide elective offices (15.1 percent of the U.S. Congress is now female, and women hold eight governors' seats [Center for American Women and Politics 2005a, 2005b]). Although women's rate of achieving such highly visible leadership spots as these seems slow, and lags behind that in other countries (Inter-Parliamentary Union 2003), nevertheless progress is being made. Then, too, women may have an advantage in their location in the economy. As the economy continues its transition from agriculture and manufacturing to a new service economy based in offices, men lose their "natural" physical advantages, and the sectors where women's jobs or gender-integrated jobs predominate grow the most. Thus, overall, there are many reasons why women's economic gains are likely to continue.

But there are also reasons for concern. Primary among them is the dramatically lower life-time earnings of women relative to men described here. With women earning only 38 percent of what men do across a fifteen-year period, it is clear that it is still women who perform the majority of family care and take time out of the paid labor market to do so. More than ever, this research convinces us that family care must be more equitably shared between women and men as well as better subsidized by society as a whole if women are going to achieve equality with men. Like Paula England (see chapter 8, this volume), we fail to see an inexorable force pushing society in this direction, though we wish there were one. We do note, however, that states are beginning to make progress in providing more family-care benefits. Several states have instituted all-day kindergarten and a variety of pre-kindergarten programs. California has expanded its Temporary Disability Insurance program to include six weeks of paid family-care leave.

Despite these measures, there are many forces working in the opposite direction. We wonder whether a backlash may be leading toward a possible reestablishment of the "feminine mystique," a term coined by Betty Friedan in her 1963 book of the same name for the notion that women's ultimate fulfillment could come only through devotion to, and sacrifice for, family. Such a development could set women's progress back a decade or more. Both the *New York Times* (October 26, 2003) and *Time* magazine (March 22, 2004) ran cover stories on high-income mothers who "choose" to stay home with their children in the face of lack of family-friendly arrangements at work. The impact of such prominently placed stories is surely to endorse such choices and make more mothers comfortable with their lack of equal opportunity in the workplace as they devote themselves to the socially validated task of raising their children. The labor-force participation of mothers of infants fell in 1998, 2000, and 2002, so that it equalled approximately the 1996 rate (U.S. Census Bureau 2003, figure 2). While this may reflect reduced demand for workers associated with the economic recession of 2001, it may also be a response by the current generation of child-bearing-age women to the generation of women who came of age in the late 1960s and early 1970s, a generation whose college-educated women had a very high rate of childlessness; 28 percent remained childless at age forty (see Goldin 2004). A reinvigorated feminine mystique would encourage this generation to accept rather than challenge the remaining barriers women face in achieving equity in the family, the workplace, and other important domains such as political leadership.

The backlash against women's rights also takes the form, in the United States, of one of the two major national political parties having antiwomen planks in its platform. The Republican party takes stands against women's reproductive freedoms and the inclusion of the Equal Rights Amendment in the U.S. Constitution. A rise of fundamentalist religions, seeking to keep women in their place within marriage and the home, is common around the world. In 2004, the Vatican issued a special statement to criticize feminism for its "lethal effects" in undermining the "natural two-parent structure" and making "heterosexuality and homosexuality virtually equivalent" (Daniel Williams and Alan Cooperman, "Vatican Letter Denounces 'Lethal Effects' of Feminism," *Washington Post*, August 1, 2004, A-16). The Roman Catholic church also opposes abortion.

The last time the United States experienced a backlash against women's rights, after the Second World War, age at first-marriage fell, the birth rate rose, men soared ahead of women in college graduation, and women's share of Ph.D.s fell dramatically. Women's share of Ph.D.s did not recover to its 1930 proportion until 1971 (U.S. Department of Education, National Center for Education Statistics 2003). Clearly, women's march toward equality does not proceed smoothly, but rather experiences fits and starts and even backward movement occasionally.

Despite the building backlash and copious commentary blaming the women's movement for everything from falling test scores to the push for gay marriage, many factors are likely to continue to lead toward increasing women's equality. Women, even those with young children, are working for significant portions of their lives, and, as the analysis of the two time-periods in this study shows, are devoting more and more hours to work and fewer to family care. They are voting with their feet. The long-run trend in the labor-force participation of mothers has been one of tremendous increase. While many married women are partially insulated from the effects of their own lower earnings by living with higher-earning men, overall women are acting to reduce their economic dependence on husbands and to protect themselves from the vulnerabilities of divorce. Women are choosing the path to greater independence, arranging child care, balancing their work and care-giving tasks as best they can, and trying to get their partners to put in their fair share of housework and caregiving. Women are spending less of their adult lives in marriage, marrying later, and having fewer children; many will have at least one year as a single parent. Women's needs for equal earnings increase as they spend less time living with men.

What can be done to advance women's progress toward equality? In both increasing their educational preparation and their labor-force participation, women as individuals have made enormous changes in their lives. Further progress will require that men, employers, institutions, and governments change. Anything further that can be done to strengthen the bonds between women and their employers long-term will increase women's job tenure, raise their wages, and lead to further reductions in women's time out of the labor market. Encouraging men to take on their fair share of family-care responsibilities would also have positive effects on women's long-term earnings.

Greater emphasis on equal employment opportunity laws, including developing new remedies to achieve comparable worth and avoid resegregation, will also work to increase women's wages and their time in the labor market. Renewed attempts to enable women to enter resistant male-dominated jobs, especially those at the middle level (construction, police, firefighting) that pay women well when they do get in, are especially important in equalizing employment opportunities between men and women, as are programs to encourage women's representation in science, math, and engineering occupations.

Policies that bring up the bottom of the labor market help women disproportionately—increasing the minimum wage, requiring all employers to provide a minimum of paid sick leave days, encouraging collective bargaining—and will contribute to increasing women's labor-market attachment and long-term earnings.

Encouraging or requiring employers to make work more family-friendly, by offering flexible schedules, career-oriented part-time jobs, and so on, would make it easier for both women and men to combine family care with good-quality reduced-time jobs.

More public support of family-care benefits, such as paid family leave and child care, would also enable parents to combine paid work and family care better, enabling women especially to increase their attachment to the labor market.

Encouraging men to be full participants in family care, through the media as well as employer and public policies (such as requiring that any parental leave be shared by the mother and the father), would help women increase their commitment to paid work. A public education campaign against the double standard in parenting, in which mothers seem to be expected to meet a higher standard of care than fathers, is also needed.

Achieving equality in the workplace will likely require several more decades. In our view, the important thing is to keep the momentum going and prevent backsliding toward the reestablishment of the feminine mystique and 1950s family values. Instead, we must continue the progress our society has been making toward equal opportunity and fair compensation for women in the labor market and the more equitable sharing of family care between women and men.

The data analysis presented here was conducted by Stephen Rose while he was senior economist at Educational Testing Services, Inc. Heidi Hartmann's and Vicky Lovell's work on the project was supported by several funders of the Institute for Women's Policy Research (IWPR), including the Annie E. Casey and Ford Foundations. Jared Bernstein, Economic Policy Institute; Rebecca Blank, University of Michigan; William Dickens, the Brookings Institution; Paula England, Stanford University; Deborah Figart, Richard Stockton College; William Rodgers, Rutgers University; Barbara Gault, director of research at IWPR; and the editors of this volume provided helpful comments on earlier versions. The authors would also like to acknowledge excellent research assistance provided by Jeffrey Strohl, ETS, and Misha Werschkul, the former Mariam K. Chamberlain Fellow at IWPR. This chapter draws upon the IWPR report, *Still a Man's Labor Market: The Long-Term Earnings Gap* (2004), and presents additional data analyses not included there.

NOTES

1. The Census Bureau reports that 58.7 percent of women workers (employed and unemployed) worked 35 or more hours per week for 50 or more weeks in 2003 (U.S. Census Bureau 2004a).

2. These two federal data series are the most common source of wage-gap data; both are based on the Current Population Survey, a monthly survey of approximately 60,000 households. The U.S. Census Bureau bases its yearly wage-gap estimates on annual earnings reported in the Current Population Survey Annual Social and Economic Supplement (ASEC), which is fielded in March and asks respondents about the previous calendar year and includes the self-employed as well as wage and salaried workers; it covers all non-institutionalized civilians aged fifteen and older (U.S. Census Bureau 2004a). The Bureau of Labor Statistics bases its wage gap comparison on the annual average of median weekly earnings of full-time wage and salaried workers collected every month in the Current Population Survey (U.S. Department of Labor, Bureau of Labor Statistics 2004). Hourly wages are not commonly available but can be calculated using either data set.

3. A married woman's decision about her hours of work is clearly made jointly with her husband, though not necessarily made equitably (Lundberg and Pollak 1996), and a woman whose marriage dissolves may well increase her work hours; thus her access to economic resources through working could increase if her time spent married decreases.

4. The PSID is the only longitudinal data set that has been continuously maintained since 1968 and that covers all age groups.

5. Because the PSID began in 1968 and tracks the same individuals over time, the numbers of Hispanics and Asian Americans surveyed are considerably smaller than are warranted by current demographic conditions. Further, a reduction in funding in the 1990s reduced the processing ability of the sponsor of the PSID. The latest final release data was the survey conducted in 1993 in which questions were asked about earnings and employment in 1992. Only "early release" data are available through 1999 (concerning employment in 1998). In addition, starting in 1997, surveys were conducted every other year rather than every year. In this study, the missing year is simply ignored, and the second fifteen-year time window runs from 1983 to 1998 with one missing year. The first fifteen-year time window runs from 1968 to 1982. Note that because the early release data do not have all the imputations and consistency checks that are part of the final release, analyses through 1998 include only people with positive earnings in all fifteen years, the continuously employed, for whom any biases are expected to be minimal. Fifteen-year data for those with zero-earnings years are estimated using data from 1983 to 1992. Fifteen-year data regarding family income and marital and parental status are estimated using data from 1983 to 1996.

6. In order to minimize the effects of very high earners, earnings are top-coded at $200,000 when averages are computed.

7. The one-digit census categories are generally hierarchically based on pay and skill level—but they contain several anomalies that make the major groupings less consis-

tent than desirable, such as including both restaurant managers and corporate executives in the managerial category; including stock brokers and real estate agents with sales clerks in the sales category; and including police and firefighters with building guards. This phenomenon has been noted by other researchers and adjusting the categories to improve consistency is common (see Gittelman and Howell 1995 for an example).

8. As Donald Treiman (1979) shows, the vast majority of the variation in job evaluation scores between jobs is due to the skill component, which is relatively well measured by years of education.

9. For this study sample, women in these traditionally men's professions are older, not younger, than their male counterparts, casting doubt on the often-used explanation that women are simply less-experienced workers than men.

10. The full distributions are available from the authors.

11. This adjustment uses the same principle employed by the Census Bureau in setting poverty thresholds for families of different sizes, although the specific adjustment formula is different.

12. Personal earnings have been top-coded at $200,000 to reduce the effect of very high earnings on average earnings, and family income has been top-coded at $200,000, for a family size of three, to reduce the effect of very high family incomes on average family income. It is possible for a worker in this study to have personal earnings that are higher than adjusted family income, since personal earnings are not adjusted for family size.

13. The average family income for men married for nine to fourteen years is slightly higher than for those married all fifteen years because men married nine to fourteen years have some years in smaller households.

14. These differences were not the result of the relative youth of men with fewer married years, as always-married men were only slightly older than men who were married only some of the time or rarely. It is not clear whether men with less intense work effort are less attractive as marriage partners or if the lack of financial responsibility for a wife and children lead men to work less.

15. This decision is not necessarily one in which women and men have equal power. It may be best to think of one spouse's behavior as contingent upon the other's. Early economic models, based on Gary S. Becker (1974, 1981), use a unitary, altruistic model of household decision making, where decisions are made in an unexamined "black box." More recent research (including Blumstein and Schwartz 1983; Lazear and Michael 1988; England and Kilbourne 1990; Lundberg and Pollak 1996; and Agarwal 1997) challenge the unitary decision-making model and have explored the factors, such as class and position, that shape household decisions.

16. These data are based on all prime-age men and women in the 1983-to-1998 period. We also developed data for men and women who were in the labor force for all fifteen years. With this restriction, the effect of years married drops significantly. Among women, average family income is $77,500 for the always-married and $53,400 for the seldom-married; the difference in earnings is just 10 percent—$27,400 for the always married and $30,700 for the seldom married. Among men, there is no significant effect of the different lengths of marriage on family income, whereas the earnings level of the

always married is $52,301 versus a seldom-married level of $40,560, again reflecting a smaller impact of marriage for the continuously employed.

17. Selection likely plays a large role here. It is likely that women who spend less time in marriage have chosen to devote more time to their work careers, whereas men who spend less time in marriage may be those less willing, or able, to support a family (for men, those devoted to careers likely include having a family in their definition of success, something that is apparently more difficult for successful women to do). Gary N. Powell (1993) finds that a majority of women managers are not married and have no children; Ellen Galinsky et al. (2003) find that women executives are more likely to have delayed marriage and having children than are other women or men.

18. Tables 5.7 and 5.8 provide an interesting contrast. For women, the more years married, the lower their own earnings but the higher their family income, owing to higher male earnings. Additional years with children, however, lower both own earnings and family income. The many women who raise children outside marriage lack the income boost provided by male earnings.

19. They also were a bit younger than men with children present less often, which may be a reason why their hourly wage rates were not yet at a higher level.

20. Maximizing joint income would generally suggest that the higher-waged partner would specialize in wage work while the lower earning one would specialize in family care and home work; for approximately half of the wives who earn more than their husbands per hour this does not happen across the fifteen-year study.

21. These figures were recalculated by presence of children with little change in the results, most likely because continuously working women are among the most committed women, and marriage and children affect them less. Relaxing the requirement of continuous work to working for at least eight years also had little effect on the results.

REFERENCES

Agarwal, Bina. 1997. "'Bargaining' and Gender Relations: Within and Beyond the Household." *Feminist Economics* 3(1): 1–51.

American Association of University Women. 1998. *Gender Gaps. Where Schools Shortchange Our Children.* Washington, D.C.: American Association of University Women Educational Foundation.

Baron, James N., and Andrew E. Newman. 1989. "Pay the Man: Effects of Demographic Composition on Prescribed Wage Rates in the California Civil Service." In *Pay Equity: Empirical Inquiries*, edited by Robert T. Michael, Heidi I. Hartmann, and Brigid O'Farrell. Washington, D.C.: National Academy Press.

Becker, Gary S. 1974. "A Theory of Social Interactions." *Journal of Political Economy* 82(6): 1063–94.

———. 1981. *A Treatise on the Family.* Cambridge, Mass.: Harvard University Press.

Blau, Francine D., Marianne A. Ferber, and Anne E. Winkler. 2002. *The Economics of Women, Men, and Work.* Upper Saddle River, N.J.: Prentice-Hall.

Blumstein, Philip, and Pepper Schwartz. 1983. *American Couples.* New York: William Morrow.

Caiazza, Amy B., ed. 2002. *The Status of Women in the States*. Washington, D.C.: Institute for Women's Policy Research.

Caiazza, Amy B., and Heidi I. Hartmann, eds. Forthcoming. *Improving Social Indicators of Women's Status: Report on Recommendations from IWPR's Working Group on Social Indicators of Women's Status.* Washington, D.C.: Institute for Women's Policy Research.

Center for American Women and Politics. 2005a. *Statewide Elective Executive Women 2005.* New Brunswick, N.J.: Rutgers University, Center for American Women and Politics.

———. 2005b. *Women in the U.S. Congress 2005.* New Brunswick, N.J.: Rutgers University, Center for American Women and Politics.

Conlin, Michelle. 2003. "The New Gender Gap: From Kindergarten to Grad School, Boys are Becoming the Second Sex." *Business Week*, May 26.

Drogin, Richard. 2003. "Statistical Analysis of Gender Patterns in Wal-Mart Workforce." Available at http: //www.walmartclass. com/walmartclass94.pl?wsi=0&websys_screen =all reports, accessed October 3, 2003.

England, Paula, and Barbara Stanek Kilbourne. 1990. "Markets, Marriages and Other Mates: The Problem of Power." In *Beyond the Marketplace: Rethinking Economy and Society*, edited by Roger Friedland and A. F. Robertson. New York: Aldine de Gruyter.

Fitzgerald, John, Peter Gottschalk, and Robert Moffitt. 1998. *An Analysis of Sample Attrition in Panel Data: The Michigan Panel Study of Income Dynamics*. NBER Technical Working Paper No. 220. New York: National Bureau of Economic Research.

Galinsky, Ellen, Kimberlee Salmond, James T. Bond, Marcia Brumit Kropf, Meredith Moore, and Brad Harrington. 2003. *Leaders in a Global Economy: A Study of Executive Men and Women.* Boston: Families and Work Institute, Catalyst, and Boston College Center for Work and Family.

Gittelman, Maury B., and David R. Howell. 1995. "Changes in the Structure and Quality of Jobs in the United States." *Industrial and Labor Relations Review* 48(3): 420–41.

Goldin, Claudia. 2004. "The Long Road to the Fast Track: Career and Family." NBER Working Paper No. 10331. Cambridge, Mass.: National Bureau of Economic Research.

Hartmann, Heidi, Katherine Allen, and Christine Owens. 1999. *Equal Pay for Working Families.* Washington, D.C.: AFL-CIO and Institute for Women's Policy Research.

Hill, Martha S. 1992. *The Panel Study of Income Dynamics: A User's Guide.* Newbury Park, Calif.: Sage.

Inter-Parliamentary Union. 2003. "Women in National Parliaments: Situation as of 31 August 2003." Available at: http: //www.ipu.org/wmn-e/arc/world310803.htm.

Jacobs, Jerry A. 2003. "Detours on the Road to Equality: Women, Work and Higher Education." *Contexts*, Winter, 32–40.

Lazear, Edward P., and Robert T. Michael. 1988. *Allocation of Income Within the Household.* Chicago and London: University of Chicago Press.

Lee, Sunhwa, and Lois Shaw. 2003. *Gender and Economic Security in Retirement*. Washington, D.C.: Institute for Women's Policy Research.

Lundberg, Shelly, and Robert A. Pollak. 1996. "Bargaining and Distribution in Marriage." *Journal of Economic Perspectives* 10(4): 139–58.

Mead, Holly, Kristine Witkowski, Barbara Gault, and Heidi Hartmann. 2001. "The Influence of Income, Education, and Work Status on Women's Well-Being." *Women's Health Issues* 11(3): 160–72.

Negrey, Cynthia, Stacie Golin, Sunhwa Lee, Holly Mead, and Barbara Gault. 2002. *Working First but Working Poor: The Need for Education and Training Following Welfare Reform.* Washington, D.C.: Institute for Women's Policy Research.

Panel Study of Income Dynamics. 1968–1998. Survey Research Center, Institute for Social Research, University of Michigan. Available at: http: //psidonline.isr.umich.edu.

Powell, Gary N. 1993. *Women and Men in Management.* Newbury Park, Calif.: Sage.

Rake, Katherine. 2000. *Women's Incomes over a Lifetime.* London: Cabinet Office, Women's Unit.

Reskin, Barbara F., and Heidi I. Hartmann, eds. 1986. *Women's Work, Men's Work, Sex Segregation on the Job.* Washington, D.C.: National Academy Press.

Rose, Stephen J., and Anthony Carnevale. 1998. *Education for What? The New Office Economy.* Princeton: Educational Testing Service.

Rose, Stephen J., and Heidi I. Hartmann. 2004. *Still a Man's Labor Market: The Long-Term Earnings Gap.* Washington, D.C.: Institute for Women's Policy Research.

Shaw, Lois, Diana Zuckerman, and Heidi Hartmann. 1998. *The Impact of Social Security Reform on Women.* Washington, D.C.: Institute for Women's Policy Research.

Shu, Xiaoling, and Margaret Mooney Marini. 1998. "Gender-Related Change in the Occupational Aspirations of Youth." *Sociology of Education* 71(1): 43–67.

Treiman, Donald. 1979. *Job Evaluation: An Analytic Review.* Interim report to the Equal Employment Opportunity Commission, Committee on Occupational Classification and Analysis, National Research Council. Washington, D.C.: National Academy of Sciences.

U.S. Census Bureau. 2003. *Fertility of American Women: June 2002.* Current Population Reports, series P20, report no. 548. Washington: U.S. Government Printing Office.

———. 2004a. *Income, Poverty, and Health Insurance Coverage in the United States: 2003.* Current Population Reports, series P60, report no. 226. Washington: U.S. Government Printing Office (August).

———. 2004b. "Married-Couple Families with Wives' Earnings Greater Than Husbands' Earnings: 1981 to 2001 (selected years)." Current Population Survey Tables, "Families," table F-22, available at http: //www.census.gov/hhes/income/histinc/ f22.html.

U.S. Department of Education, National Center for Education Statistics. 2003. *Digest of Education Statistics, 2002.* Washington, D.C.: National Center for Education Statistics.

U.S. Department of Labor, Bureau of Labor Statistics. 2004. *Employment and Earnings.* Washington: U.S. Department of Labor (January).

Weinberger, Catherine J. 1998. "Race and Gender Wage Gaps in the Market for Recent College Graduates." *Industrial Relations* 37(1): 67–84.

Winkler, Anne E. 1998. "Earnings of Husbands and Wives in Dual-Earner Families." *Monthly Labor Review* 121(4): 42–48.

Chapter 6

The Glass Ceiling in the United States and Sweden: Lessons from the Family-Friendly Corner of the World, 1970 to 1990

Eva M. Meyersson Milgrom and Trond Petersen

T here is a dearth of women in top ranks within the professions and management, and the barriers to women's attaining these top ranks are often referred to as the glass ceiling. In this chapter we shall analyze and compare
the glass-ceiling phenomenon in the United States and Sweden. To quantify and
analyze this gender rank gap and explain the existence of this glass ceiling, we
consider the following questions: What is the effect of gender on the job rank
reached? To what extent do other individual factors, such as age, education, work
hours, and part- or full-time status, explain the rank reached? And how much of
the gender rank gap can be explained by differences between men and women
with reference to these other factors? Did the circumstances of women change over
the time period studied and, if so, in what way?

INTRODUCTION

When men and women today do the same work for the same employer, they are,
for all practical purposes, paid the same wages, at least in the United States, Sweden, and Norway. This source of the overall wage gap has thus probably been
close to eradicated. There is nevertheless still a substantial pay gap that needs to be
explained, and the main explanation no longer lies in the phenomenon of unequal
pay for equal for work for the same employer. The explanation must be sought
elsewhere, namely, in the segregation of men and women by occupations and establishments: women work in low-paid jobs and in establishments that pay low
wages, and men work in well-paid jobs and in workplaces where pay is high.[1]
    One particular form of sex segregation that has been much noted during the last

twenty years is the dearth of women in relatively higher positions in the professions and management. In 1986, two U.S. reporters writing in the *Wall Street Journal* coined the term "glass ceiling" for the rank or level within organizations beyond which women typically are not promoted.[2]

The glass-ceiling problem might in fact be represented as the characteristic segregation problem of the contemporary period. Although women have now entered upper nonmanual positions in substantial numbers (this has been called the "first gender revolution"), the upper nonmanual sector still remains highly segregated, with women facing a glass ceiling that prevents them from assuming high-level positions. One question that needs to be answered in gauging the future of gender inequality is whether there will be a "second revolution"—a withering-away of the glass ceiling.

The literature on this topic is extensive, yet very little systematic knowledge is available.[3] An apparently solid finding is that the magnitude of the glass-ceiling problem depends not only on potential employer discrimination but also on broad institutional factors in a society, such as the relationship between family and work, leave policies, the relative pay in managerial positions, and more. Cross-national comparisons have documented significant variations across Western nations in the extent of the glass ceiling. Perhaps surprisingly, it appears to be more severe in the Scandinavian countries, which have generous family policies, than in the United Kingdom, the United States, and other comparable countries.[4]

This study undertakes an empirical investigation with a comparative angle of the glass-ceiling problem, defined as the lack of women in top positions as a result of an intangible barrier within the hierarchy of a company that prevents women or minorities from obtaining upper-level positions.

We begin by illustrating the issue in the U.S. context, providing an overview using firm-level data on the glass ceiling, with data from the period the phrase was coined, showing its clear existence. This analysis is followed by an organizational case study illustrating some of the mechanisms that can generate a glass ceiling. We then turn to an analysis of the Swedish case, which we shortly will argue perhaps is the central test case in the Western world for many of the questions arising in connection with the glass ceiling. Beyond being a test case, for Sweden we also have access to unique data allowing us to look at the topic in novel and careful ways. The data set covers all establishments in major industries in the Swedish economy, covering about 40 percent of employees in the private sector, and all employees of these establishments over the period 1970 to 1990. We focus on the white-collar employees in the data.

For the Swedish case, we address several questions. What is the effect of gender on the job rank reached? How much of the gender rank effect can be explained by individual factors such as age, education, hours worked, and part- or full-time status? Did the circumstances of women change over the time period studied and, if so, in what way?

Why is Sweden in many respects a central case for studying the glass ceiling, one that can provide lessons for the United States? The central reason, by now well understood, is that work-family conflicts may be a large if not the largest impediment to women's success in management and the upper echelons of the professions (Waldfogel 1998). An unequal division of labor in the home along with high divorce rates leaving women in the majority of cases as the primary parent may explain why it is more difficult for women than men to succeed at high levels. But Sweden has done more to alleviate work-family conflicts than almost any other country. It has extensive family policies and is often considered a model for family legislation. Over the 1970-to-1990 period several key legislative changes were enacted in parental-leave policies and child-care provisions.

For example, the total leave period after childbirth was seven months at 90 percent pay in 1975, and this was increased to nine months in 1978, with fathers being able to share leave periods since 1974. Fathers accounted for 7 percent of leaves taken in 1988 (OECD 1995; see also Haas 1991), as compared to much lower numbers in other European countries. As Paula England (chapter 8, this volume) writes, noting that this must have an impact on gender equality: "[In] Sweden, the state replaces a portion of a parent's pay after the birth of a child, and recently instituted a policy so that couples who have the entire leave taken by one parent receive less paid leave." Nothing comparable is available in the United States. Prior to the 1993 Family and Medical Leave Act (FMLA) period, there was in many states only voluntary provision of maternity leave. As of 1991, only 37 percent of full-time employees in medium and large establishments and 18 percent of those in small establishments had maternity leave, of usually up to thirteen weeks, just over three months.

Perhaps equally important, public provision of child-care services is limited in the United States, whereas Sweden has extensive policies (see Kamerman 1991). In 1973, 11 percent of preschoolers had access to public child care, 38 percent in 1983, and 49 percent in 1988, at a subsidized rate (see Rønsen and Sundström 1996). Single parents pay lower fees.

Such policies should help parents combine work and family, and may contribute toward gender equality also at the top of organizational hierarchies. On this there is, however, some disagreement. What family policies undoubtedly do is make life easier for children and parents. Whether they also are good for achieving gender equality is less clear. For example, Catherine Hakim concludes (2000, 240), "In sum, Nordic women have not achieved any significant degree of equality with men in market work, in terms of access to the top jobs, occupations with authority, or higher pay." She continues (243), "Some scholars are now concluding that Nordic egalitarian policies have failed" and that "national policies that offer mothers substantial periods of paid and unpaid maternity leave, the right to work shorter hours, and other benefits to help reconcile work with family do have unintended side-effects."

In this chapter we elaborate on explanations for why there are so few women in top positions in management and the professions; present data that illustrate the issues in the U.S. context; describe the unique Swedish data set on all privately employed white-collar workers in the domain of the Swedish Employer Federation for the period 1970-1990; and show that the top-ranked positions still are predominantly held by men.

We then discuss aspects of the so-called pipeline problem: sex differences in age, in hours worked, and in education. We document the characteristics of employees in the top positions, and how these characteristics are distributed among women and men. Finally, we propose four different sources for the sex gap in rank: discrimination, educational choice, life cycle, and cohort effects.

WOMEN AND MEN IN TOP MANAGEMENT AND THE PROFESSIONS

An understanding of the future of the glass ceiling is best attained by gaining an understanding of how it arises. Several mechanisms operate, and each implies a distinctive future for the glass ceiling.

One mechanism is employer discrimination, what employers do to keep women out of top positions—or to include them, as when affirmative-action programs became important. Another mechanism is the choices made by employees or prospective employees in education, occupation, and family behavior. A third mechanism stems from institutional features of a given society, such as the provision of child care, maternity-leave policies, the relative size of managerial pay, and more.

In order to understand the lack of women in top management positions and the professions it is useful to explore the role of these three mechanisms that may hinder or facilitate female success, here referred to as supply-side, demand-side, and institutional processes. If, for example, it can be shown that employer discrimination plays a small role in the lack of women in top positions, then our attention should focus elsewhere, especially on what employees and job seekers do, in their educational choices, occupational choices, and family behavior. Equally important is providing an assessment of the institutional regimes that make the glass-ceiling less of a problem. For instance, do Swedish employers, given the family-friendly policies in their country, behave differently than U.S. employers? Swedish employers know that women can take generous maternity and sick leaves. Will they be less prone to promote women they know are likely to take time off for family care and part-time work? A substantial proportion of Swedish women take advantage of such policies as working part-time, knowing that such a choice may result in fewer promotions. In the United States, employers know that women tend to get married, have children, and then leave the workforce, or stay and work full-time, given the more limited access to part-time employment. U.S. women, on the other hand, may signal to an American employer her commitment to the job by not getting married and having children, hoping that the signal will be read and rewarded with promotions. An alternative interpretation of this form of female behavior is simply that in order to have a successful professional career, which can put big demands on time input, it is often very difficult at the same time to have children. There is not enough time for both. Abstaining from having children is then not a signaling behavior. It is entirely about time allocation.

Demand-Side Factors: Employers

The typical explanation for the lack of women in upper management and the professions is the classic employer-discrimination hypothesis: they simply are kept out of those jobs, usually by men higher up (see Hultin and Szulkin 1999). A variety of reasons for this hypothesis have been suggested. One argument could be purely psychological, like that of Rosabeth M. Kanter (1977, chapter 8), that male managers prefer men because managers prefer people who are like those who are already in similar positions. Another reason could be pure prejudice: men are thought to fit better into a leadership team, perhaps because women are considered to be too emotional (Kanter 1977; Reskin and Hartmann 1986). Or perhaps men prefer to preserve their power and privileges (Reskin 1988; Acker 1990). (Hultin and Szulkin 1999 present empirical support for the difference in female and male manager recruitment strategies.) Finally, there may be statistical discrimination, if women as a group are thought to be less qualified than men to be in positions of leadership, and such reasoning is applied to individual cases without heeding the candidates' specific qualifications (Phelps 1972; Arrow 1973; Bielby and Baron 1986).

These forms of discrimination are often referred to as demand-side factors: They result from actions of employers when they hire, promote, and fire. But even in the absence of discrimination from the demand side, inequalities in careers could arise for other reasons—from what employees and potential employees do.

Supply-Side Factors: Employees

If women invest less in education (overall they do not), or undertake different kinds of education (they typically do), or have less stable careers because of withdrawals from employment in order to meet family responsibilities, or invest fewer hours at work, then an attainment gap in wages, careers, and work responsibilities will develop, given the way organizations currently operate. These sources of inequality in outcomes are referred to as supply-side factors: they result from the actions taken by current and prospective employees, particularly from the way men and women divide their efforts between employment and family responsibilities (see, for example, Fuchs 1988; Waldfogel 1998; Henrekson 1999). These actions could arise from rational adaptation within the family, gender-specific socialization, or differences in preferences. In the context of the glass ceiling, these behaviors result in a so-called "frozen pipeline," a lack of qualified women whom employers can appoint to positions of leadership (see U.S. Department of Labor 1991).

According to the frozen-pipeline hypothesis, the glass ceiling appears to be largely attributable to supply-side differences in how men and women behave. To explore this further, it is useful to distinguish at least three separate frozen pipelines.

A first frozen pipeline comes from the domestic division of labor. The unequal division of labor in the family may for women affect the amount of education they acquire and the amount of effort subsequently allocated to market work. Many women just don't work the hours required for reaching positions of leadership.

A second frozen pipeline comes from potential sex segregation in educational choice. When organizations are about to appoint employees to positions of leadership, they are to a large extent constrained by the pool of entrants into the labor market as the situation stood ten to twenty years ago. This in turn depended on the supply of men and women coming out of universities and professional schools at the time. As late as 1975 to 1980, for every female graduate in civil engineering in Sweden, there were about eleven male graduates, and there was similar educational sex segregation in the U.S. (Jacobs 1996). When organizations made their choices in the 1990s, they had an unbalanced labor supply to draw on for managerial positions.[5] This pipeline problem is not primarily attributable to the amount of human capital that women accumulate, but rather to the type of human capital. That is, insofar as women do not invest in the type of training, such as engineering, that is favored in recruiting managers, they will later be promoted at a lower rate.

A third frozen pipeline may be generated by anticipated discrimination. In this scenario, the first and second pipeline problems arise primarily from decisions that women make as adaptations to expected employer discrimination. Expecting to be discriminated against, women may invest in different types of education, seek different occupations, and work fewer hours. This can occur even if in principle there are no problems of unequal division of labor in the home, even if there are no gender differences in preferences for staying home to care for children, for hours worked, or for various educational specialties. Women and men just adapt to how they perceive employers will differentially reward the sexes for a given choice. There has clearly been a decline over time in actual discrimination and probably one in perceived discrimination as well, but this mechanism may still operate for some groups of women.

The relevance of this mechanism is easily seen in a short historical perspective. Women in age groups from which top managers typically have been recruited during the last ten years, say ages forty-five to sixty, started their careers in labor-market environments more hostile to women. For example, Candice Krugman Beinecke, fifty-two, one of the few female CEOs in a U.S. law firm, reports that when she applied for a job at a New York law firm in 1970, she received a letter regretting to inform her that "we already have our woman lawyer" (*New York Times*, May 15, 1999). Such treatment could in the past, and also today, have influenced women to invest in different types of or in less human capital. And while probably uncommon today, remnants of these behaviors are still present in pockets of modern economies. In a recent U.S. sex discrimination case brought forward and settled by the Equal Employment and Opportunity Commission against a Wall Street firm, a female manager commented, "There are a lot of women I know who have left the street with four, five, six million in their pockets who say, I'm never going to reach the top, so I'll go do something else. That's a brain drain, so to speak" (Patrick McGeehan, "Discrimination on Wall Street; Run the Numbers and Weep,"

New York Times, July 14, 2004, C7). Younger cohorts of women, confronting a less hostile environment, do acquire human capital, but solving the problem of anticipated discrimination does require time and patience. The actual discrimination must first disappear, then women must react to it by making the relevant educational and work-effort choices, and finally there is a wait while currently younger women acquire experience to become qualified for higher positions.

As is clear from the third frozen pipeline, the various mechanisms may also interact. For example, the mechanism of anticipated discrimination, coupled with the mechanism of diminished employer discrimination over time, should lead to a particular pattern of cohort differences. Diminished employer discrimination should by itself over time lead to a declining sex gap in each age group, say among forty-to-fifty-year-olds, with a decrease from 1970 to 1990. But then, if women correctly perceive the reduced discrimination, one should also observe a change in educational choices, work hours, and the extent of part-time work among women as one gets closer to the present, if indeed those adaptations are caused by anticipated discrimination. Thus, for each birth cohort, at each given age, the sex gap in workplace achievement, in hours worked, and in education should decline with historical time.

Institutional Factors

A number of institutional factors could also explain the lack of women in management and the professions. Of major importance are the broader structural features of societies, such as its wage and income distribution, the provision of child-care services, and the educational system.

One institutional feature is associated with wage, income, and wealth distribution. To reach the top of the career ladder often requires exceptional amounts of effort and time. People make these investments for a variety of reasons related to the pure enjoyment of the work, power, prestige, and more, but the economic incentives are also important. Household chores, including cleaning the house, looking after children and bringing them to and from school, preparing meals, shopping, and so on, can consume a considerable amount of time and effort.[6] When women bear the primary burden of these chores, the economic return to pursuing a top-level job depends on the premium between the prospective wage and the cost of hiring others to do the household chores. Wage compression, that is, less wage inequality, then discourages the pursuit of careers more for women than for men.

In this respect, the greater wage compression in Sweden compared to Britain and especially the United States (see, for instance, Fritzell 1991) could be a significant factor in women's choices. We suggest that women in Sweden have less incentive than women in the United States to pursue high-level careers because the net-return to the top jobs, translated into the difference between take-home wages and child-care costs, is smaller in Sweden. Francine D. Blau and Lawrence Kahn (1996) show that although the overall gender wage gap is considerably lower in Sweden and Norway than in the United States, the percentage of women at the very bottom of the wage distribution is higher in Sweden and Norway than in the United States. Blau and Kahn (1997) further document that even though there was a large increase in income inequality in the U.S. in the 1980s, which, ceteris paribus, may be detrimental to the gender wage gap, women nevertheless gained income relative to men in this period. The reason is simply that women made heavy inroads into the professions, management, and jobs requiring high skills.

A second institutional feature important for women's choices is availability of child-care services, particularly in the earlier stages of a career, when women often have young children. The effects of this institution are not straightforward, however, because reducing the costs of raising children may lead to increased fertility, which in turn may be detrimental to female careers. This may have happened in Sweden in the 1980s, when it had the highest fertility rate in Europe (Hoem 1993; international comparisons of child-care policies can be found in Kamerman 1991; see also Rønsen and Sundström 1996).

A third institutional feature is the relationship between the educational system and the labor market and especially industry structure. Employers often seek employees with specific educational credentials, and the type of credentials that matter may change over time. In Sweden and other Scandinavian countries, but less so in the United States, the tradition in the manufacturing industry was to recruit primarily civil engineers. Not until relatively recently have people with master's degrees in economics or business administration become CEOs in publicly traded firms (see Meyerson 1992 for the case of Sweden). Women are better represented in business administration than in civil engineering. The organization of the educational system and the demand from the business sector can consequently influence occupational sex segregation.

Implications for the Future of the Glass Ceiling

What do these various factors imply for the future of the glass ceiling?

With respect to employer discrimination, it is difficult to assess whether it currently is important or not. It is, however, unquestionably less important in both absolute and relative terms than it was thirty years ago. There has been nothing short of a massive cultural change here, from a situation where it used to be fully acceptable to keep women out of certain positions in the professions and management to one where this is considered illegitimate and where intentional attempts to put up barriers to women's advancing will be met with opposition from coworkers, the media, and the legal system. There is every reason to expect that the role of employer discrimination will continue to diminish and that it will perhaps even disappear in the future.

On the supply side, the domestic division of labor suggests a less optimistic assessment of the future. Although much has changed over the last thirty years (see chapter 8, this volume), the division of labor in the home is likely to continue to be unequal, a circumstance due in part to men's and women's preference, in part to rational adaptation, and especially to high divorce rates, which leave women with child custody and restricts their careers further and at the same time puts pressures on divorced men to be economically successful in order to meet child and alimony payments. In contrast to England's cautiously pessimistic assessment, derived from the still unequal distribution of labor in the family, we find Robert Max Jackson's (chapter 7, this volume) more optimistic view: the logic and structure of modern bureaucratic organizations will lead to a continuation of past progress and the inevitable rise of women in modern business, political, and educational arenas.

As for the choices women make in the types of education they acquire, the future consequences are difficult to assess. Women's decisions may be a function of internalized stereotypes about the skills and aptitudes that women (nurturing, service-oriented) and men (technical) have or ought to have. It is difficult to root out stereotypes that are deeply embedded in primary and secondary socialization. Others have speculated that some of the differences in occupational choice have their source in innate biological differences (Pinker 2002, chapter 18), which are even less amenable to change. And recent social-psychological experiments have offered yet another explanation for the lack of women in some fields: men and women may behave rather differently in competitive situations, with women shying away from competition (Niederle and Vesterlund 2005; see also Gneezy, Niederle, and Rustichini 2003).

Nevertheless, much change has already occurred, and will continue to occur. We predict that the role of educational sex segregation will diminish over time. It is, nevertheless, a slow-moving process, as the lag between acquiring an educational credential and becoming ready for major managerial positions is usually twenty to thirty years. Educational choices also interact with changes in industrial structure. Service-type occupations have become more important while manufacturing positions have declined. This shift favors women. It increases the number of occupations that require the type of skills that women are more likely to have such as nurturing and service-oriented skills. This will in turn increase employers' access to a larger pool of female skill. Ceteris paribus, demand-side factors can then play a role in dissolving the glass ceiling and gender inequality will decrease.

As for anticipated discrimination, if the supply-side differences in the amount and type of education and training that men and women accumulate and the effort they invest at the workplace are driven mainly by expectations of employer discrimination among women, then the frozen pipeline should melt as the decline in such discrimination becomes widely known and women accordingly have a greater incentive to invest in human capital and to work long hours. It is not clear that there is yet widespread appreciation of diminished discrimination among women who are making investment decisions. If so, anticipated discrimination will still generate pipeline problems, but presumably good information will gradually alleviate the problem.

While it seems that in recent times supply-side and institutional factors may be more critical than demand-side factors in maintaining the glass ceiling, we may wonder and speculate about the differences in their likely impacts on its future. The domestic division of labor is most entrenched and least amenable to change, especially given high divorce rates where women in the vast majority of cases get child custody. By contrast, women are entering traditionally male educational paths in greater numbers and anticipated discrimination is also likely to diminish as women face less discrimination from employers. Thus, the domestic division of labor seems to be a factor favoring keeping the glass ceiling in place, whereas diminished discrimination and greater human-capital investments will put further pressure on the glass ceiling.

The effects of the broader institutional features—the societal wage distribution, the provision of child care, and the relationship between the educational system and the labor market—will, at a given point in time, show up in cross-national comparisons. Over time, as these features perhaps improve in the favor of women, they should help extinguish the glass ceiling. But as already discussed, there may be both first and secondary effects of these social institutions, such as in the case of family-friendly policies. Providing ample and reasonable child care also gives incentives for having children, which may be detrimental to female careers. A highly unequal wage distribution, such as in the United States, with very high wages at the top and very low at the bottom, is beneficial for those women who break through the glass ceiling. But more limited provision of child care and more limited leave policies may work in the opposite direction for American women, restricting their ability to take advantage of high salaries at the top.

THE GLASS CEILING IN THE UNITED STATES

We here discuss U.S. across-firm data on sex segregation in professional and managerial jobs, followed with data on such employees from a single large firm, then discuss whether the findings from this company may be typical of other U.S. firms, and what the future may entail.

U.S. Across-Firm Data

Our across-firm data comes from the National Survey of Professional, Administrative, Technical, and Clerical (PATC) Employees in 1981, collected by the Bureau of Labor Statistics (U.S. Department of Labor 1981), described in Petersen and Morgan (1995). We use data for seven professional and three administrative occupations. Each occupation is further divided into a set of ranks, corresponding to a hierarchy in terms of authority, responsibility, and required qualifications. This yields fifty-one occupation-by-rank groups for the professional and administrative occupations, where managerial positions are included among the higher ranks. For example, chemists—rank 1 is an entry-level job requiring a bachelor's degree in chemistry and no job experience, whereas rank 8 is a job where the incumbent "makes decisions and recommendations that are authoritative and have far-reaching impact on extensive chemical and related activities of the company" (U.S. Department of Labor 1981, 54). The data were collected from broadly defined industries: mining, construction, manufacturing, transportation, communications, electric utilities, gas, sanitary services, retail trade, finance, insurance, and selected services (31). Information about 740,000 employees in about 2,162 establishments was collected (see U.S. Department of Labor 1981, table 11, 11).

We give segregation measures at the occupation-establishment level, separately by occupation and rank for the professional and managerial employees (from Petersen and Morgan 1995, table 7). An occupation-establishment pair is defined as a particular occupation and rank within an occupation in a specific establishment, such as chemist—rank 7, working at Chiron in Emeryville, California. We have information on 16,433 occupation-establishment pairs, of which 4,036 are sex-integrated. Table 6.1 gives a distribution of occupation-establishment pairs among professional and managerial employees in ten occupations, showing whether they employ only men, only women, or are sex-integrated. These percentages are given separately by rank in each occupation. There are eight ranks, from 1 (lowest rank) to 8, the highest rank, corresponding to positions where the employee has considerable influence over management, strategy, and budgetary issues, within the company or a division of the company.

Going from lowest to highest rank, the percent of occupation-establishment pairs employing only men increases strongly in all the occupations. In the last line in the table, which summarizes the situation across the ten occupations, the percent of occupation-establishment units employing only men increases from 43.9 percent in rank 1 to 99.3 in rank 8. The percent of sex-integrated units drops from 24.6 in rank 1 to 8.8, 5.9, and 0.0 in ranks 6 to 8.

The amount of vertical sex segregation is thus very strong. At the very top rank, 8, less than 1 percent of the occupation-establishment pairs employ women, and less than 10 percent of the occupation-establishment pairs do so in ranks 6 and 7.

Organizational Case Study

How did this situation of segregation come about? Is it due to lower promotion rates for women, possibly resulting from employer discrimination? Is it due to a frozen pipeline, with too few women with the required amounts of experience and educational backgrounds? Our broad data do not allow us to explore these questions. Instead we examine an organizational case study from the same period where similar amounts of gender segregation are exhibited.

We use data from the personnel records on all external hires into managerial, administrative, and professional ranks in a large regulated firm engaged in producing and delivering services. It is a highly visible firm (for details, see Petersen and Saporta 2004). Its organizational structures and employment systems are similar to those in other large U.S. organizations across a wide array of industries (see Spilerman 1986). The data come from the period 1978 to 1986, when annual employment ranged from 26,000 to 31,000. Employees are assigned to four broad occupational groups: blue-collar (44 percent), clerical (20 percent), technical (8 percent), and managerial, administrative, and professional employees (28 percent).

We focus on the managerial, administrative, and professional employees. These are hired into a hierarchy of thirteen job levels, from 1 (low) to 13. Few make it to the top. In 1986, with 7,329 such employees, only 42, or about .5 percent, were placed in level 11 or higher. A promotion occurs when a higher job level is reached, from say rank 5 to 6.

Table 6.2 gives the effect of being male on the promotion rate (from Petersen and Saporta 2004, table 8). The analysis pertains to entrants into the organization in this period, and furthermore to entrants into professional, administrative, and managerial positions. This way we can compare employees who belong to roughly the same cohorts and have similar career ladders.

The evidence is clear. Overall, from column 1, men are promoted at about a 15 percent lower rate than women. This means that if 20 percent of the women were promoted in a given year, 17 percent of the men were. Controlling for the variables in columns 2 to 6, there is no sex difference in the promotion rate: the sex coefficient is close to and not significantly different from zero, except in column 2. Considering the evidence in columns 7 and 8, where interaction terms between sex and the currently occupied job level are included, we get a more subtle result. In the lowest level, 1, men are promoted at a slightly higher rate than women. But then in levels 2 and above, with the exception of level 3 in column 7, women are promoted at a higher rate than men, and in levels 4 and above significantly so (at the .05 level). Moreover, in levels 5 and above the promotion rate is considerably higher for women than men. This corresponds to results found in other organizations (Spilerman and Petersen 1999).[7]

In conclusion, if individual characteristics are not taken into account, women are promoted at a higher rate than men. Taking such variables into account, there is no difference between men and women in promotion rates. Finally, taking into account the possibility that the promotion rates for men and women may depend on the job level, the contention put forth by the glass-ceiling hypothesis, women are promoted at a lower rate in the lowest level and at a higher rate in the higher levels, exactly opposite of what we would expect.

There is no evidence for the employer-discrimination hypothesis when it comes to promotions in this particular case study. Note that in these analyses we have not included elaborate controls for occupational group or career ladder, distinguishing only six broad occupational groups. So even in the absence of extensive controls for particular career ladders, there are few or no differences between men and women in promotion rates.

But even with equal promotion rates, there may be discrimination at the point of hire, which may lead to a subsequent attainment gap. As Francine Blau and Marianne A. Ferber (1987, 51) write, "Once men and women are channeled into different types of entry jobs, the normal everyday operation of the firm will virtually ensure sex differences in productivity, promotion opportunities, and pay." Observed differences in wages may thus largely be a result of differential hiring and initial placement. An overall gender wage gap will remain even with fair promotion and wage-setting policies within firms, as long as there is differential treatment in the hiring process (see also Stinchcombe 1990, 259).

Table 6.1 / Distribution in the United States of Occupation-Establishment Pairs That Are Segregated (Men Only and Women Only) and Integrated, by Occupation, by Occupation and Rank, and Overall, for Professional and Administrative Employees

Occupation		Occupation-Establishment	Occupation-by-Rank-Establishment	By Rank in Occupation-Establishment Pair							
1		2	3	1	2	3	4	5	6	7	8
				4	5	6	7	8	9	10	11
Accountants	M	45.4	59.9	33.3	41.8	59.5	73.5	82.9	91.9		
	F	4.4	9.7	21.6	15.2	8.8	4.0	3.5	1.5		
	I	50.2	30.4	45.2	42.9	31.7	22.5	13.7	6.7		
	N	(1,633)	(4,342)	(575)	(787)	(1,317)	(979)	(549)	(135)		
Chief accountants	M	97.5	83.4	97.8	95.9	98.9	44.7				
	F	2.1	16.3	2.2	2.7	1.1	55.3				
	I	0.4	0.4	0.0	1.4	0.0	0.0				
	N	(237)	(283)	(46)	(74)	(87)	(76)				
Auditors	M	42.5	55.0	34.7	41.3	56.1	77.4				
	F	4.9	10.2	16.1	14.9	9.3	3.7				
	I	52.7	34.8	49.2	43.8	34.6	18.9				
	N	(391)	(844)	(118)	(208)	(301)	(217)				
Public accountant	M	6.1	22.7	12.5	16.3	22.9	42.5				
	F	0.0	0.5	0.0	0.0	0.0	2.5				
	I	93.9	76.8	87.5	83.7	77.1	55.0				
	N	(49)	(185)	(48)	(49)	(48)	(40)				
Attorneys	M	52.6	68.4	45.0	51.7	67.1	77.9	88.4	92.2		
	F	3.4	7.2	15.3	15.6	6.6	1.8	0.7	0.0		
	I	44.0	24.5	39.6	32.7	26.4	20.3	10.9	7.8		
	N	(416)	(993)	(111)	(205)	(258)	(217)	(138)	(64)		
Chemists	M	52.2	66.2	39.3	44.6	66.0	71.0	79.2	86.5	93.3	
	F	2.2	4.8	18.9	9.9	3.3	2.6	0.5	0.0	0.0	
	I	45.5	29.0	41.8	45.5	30.7	26.4	20.3	13.5	6.7	
	N	(404)	(1,262)	(122)	(202)	(303)	(269)	(202)	(104)	(60)	

		(2)	(3)	(4)	(5)	(6)	(7)	(8)	(9)	(10)	(11)
Engineers	M	65.4	80.4	59.5	63.9	76.3	84.5	88.5	91.4	94.3	99.3
	F	0.2	0.5	2.2	0.9	0.5	0.2	0.0	0.0	0.0	0.7
	I	34.4	19.2	38.3	35.2	23.3	15.3	11.5	8.6	5.7	0.7
	N	(1,249)	(5,252)	(501)	(659)	(1,045)	(1,091)	(904)	(579)	(332)	(141)
Job analysts	M	23.2	33.0	19.2	15.4	28.4	57.5				
	F	40.8	48.6	65.4	75.8	53.2	15.1				
	I	36.0	18.4	15.4	8.8	18.4	27.4				
	N	(250)	(364)	(26)	(91)	(141)	(106)				
Directors of personnel	M	86.8	87.3	78.8	83.4	94.2	93.8				
	F	10.9	11.0	17.5	14.3	5.1	6.3				
	I	2.3	1.8	3.8	2.3	0.7	0.0				
	N	(433)	(456)	(80)	(175)	(137)	(64)				
Buyers	M	50.1	61.9	36.7	57.0	74.2	85.3				
	F	9.4	14.1	40.6	14.7	2.4	1.1				
	I	40.5	24.0	22.7	28.3	23.3	13.7				
	N	(1,354)	(2,452)	(458)	(932)	(784)	(278)				
All occupations	M	54.6	67.6	43.9	53.3	67.2	77.3	85.7	90.9	94.1	99.3
	F	6.2	7.8	19.8	13.1	6.3	3.8	1.2	0.2	0.0	0.7
	I	39.2	24.6	36.4	33.6	26.5	18.9	13.1	8.8	5.9	0.0
	N	(6,416)	(16,433)	(2,085)	(3,382)	(4,421)	(3,337)	(1,793)	(882)	(392)	(141)

Source: Petersen and Morgan (1995, table 7), reprinted with permission. © The University of Chicago Press.

Note: For description of data see "The Glass Ceiling in the United States." Column 1 gives the three segregation statuses for each occupation, where "M" stands for male only, "F" for female only, "I" for integrated, and "N" gives the number of occupation-establishment or occupation-rank-establishment pairs for which the statistics is computed. Column 2 gives, separately by occupation, the percentages of the establishments that in the given occupation, not taking into account the rank of employees within an occupation, employ only women ("M"), employ only men ("F"), and employ both men and women ("I"). Here, an occupation-establishment pair is integrated when there is at least one woman and one man in the pair, even though they may be employed at different ranks in the pair. Columns 3 to 10 give the same percentages for occupation-by-rank-establishment pairs, first across all ranks (column 3, "O-R-E") and second separately for each rank (columns 4 to 11) within an occupation. The bottom of the table, "All Occupations," gives the corresponding percentages across the ten occupations.

TABLE 6.2 / Estimates in the United States of the Effect of Sex on the Promotion Rate Within the Organization

	1	2	3	4	5	6	7	8
Male (= 1)	−.158	−.081	−.066*	−.053*	−.014*	−.009*	.116	.114
	(.038)	(.036)	(.037)	(.037)	(.038)	(.037)	(.055)	(.052)
Level × male[a]								
2							−.311*	−.127*
							(.219)	(.086)
3							−.072*	−.237
							(.088)	(.108)
4							−.212	−.551
							(.111)	(.156)
5							−.523	−.631
							(.158)	(.226)
6+							−.646	−.741
							(.230)	(.243)

Source: Petersen and Saporta (2004, table 8), reprinted with permission. © The University of Chicago Press.

Note: For description of data and results see "The Glass Ceiling in the United States." In the analyses we include only employees who entered the organization from 1978 to 1986 in managerial, administrative, and professional positions. The hazard-rate models predict promotions within the organization. In column 1 the exponential model is used, while in columns 2 to 8 the proportional hazards version of the log-logistic model is used (see Petersen 1995, section 7). The role of seniority in predicting promotions is taken into account as a time-dependent covariate, updated every twelve months. The explanatory variables are as follows. In column 1, only sex and a constant term enter. Column 2 adds to the variables in column 1 education (as four dummy variables), age (as one continuous variable), and seniority (as one continuous variable). Column 3 adds to the variables in column 2 occupational group (five dummy variables). Column 4 adds to the variables in column 3 the job level at hire (one continuous variable). Column 5 adds to the variables in column 4 the current job level (as five dummy variables), but does not include as in column 4 the job level at hire. Column 6 adds to the variables in column 3 both the job level at hire and the current level. Column 7 adds to the variables in column 5 interaction terms between the currently occupied job level and sex, thus excluding the job level at hire. Column 8 adds to the variables in column 6 the same interaction terms as in column 7, thus including also the job level at hire. Except for the variables sex and job level at hire, all variables may change over time.

[a]This gives, in columns 7 and 8, the interaction term between sex and the currently occupied job level. The reference group is job level 1, captured by the main effect of sex in line 1, with estimates of .116 and .114. The top group is job level 6 and higher, denoted by "6 + ," capturing the differential effect of being female in job level 6 and above.

*Not significantly different from zero at the five-percentage level (two-tailed tests).

Exploring differences at the point of hire requires paying attention to potential differences in prior work experience. Men and women may differ in the amount of experience they bring to the company. This will induce a gap at the time of hire. But as women gain experience in the company and prove to be valuable employees, the organization may compensate for the initially lower placement by higher promotion rates and higher salary increases. We have no measure of prior experience. But it clearly is correlated with age. Among younger hires, the sex differential in experience should be small, holding education constant. But among older

TABLE 6.3 / Estimates in the United States of the Effect of Sex (Male = 1) on the Job
Level Among Full-Time Employees at Time of Hire (Seniority = 0),
Separately for Each of Seven Age Groups (Estimated Standard Errors in
Parentheses)

Age Group	1	2	3
18 to 24	−.024*(.026)	−.017*(.026)	.000*(.026)
25 to 29	.195 (.058)	.225 (.054)	.200 (.056)
30 to 34	.340 (.107)	.391 (.104)	.271 (.102)
35 to 39	.876 (.183)	.883 (.178)	.795 (.179)
40 to 44	1.515 (.356)	1.635 (.346)	1.518 (.364)
45 to 49	1.746 (.640)	2.260 (.585)	2.296 (.623)
50 +	1.986 (.699)	1.568 (.662)	1.406 (.862)

Source: Petersen and Saporta (2004, table 10), reprinted with permission. © The University of
Chicago Press.
Note: For description of data see "The Glass Ceiling in the United States." The dependent variable
in the three regression equations in columns 1 to 3 is the job level at time of hire (that is, seniority =
0 years). Each regression is estimated using ordinary least squares. An ordinary probit analysis
yielded for all practical purposes the same substantive results. The regression in column 1 contains
in addition to the sex effect (male = 1) and the interaction terms between sex and the six dummy
variables for age, a constant term, main effects for age (six dummy variables), and the effects of hire
year (as eight dummy variables). The reference group for age is eighteen to twenty-four years old
at time of hire. In line 1 of column 1 the number −.024 means that among eighteen-to-twenty-four-
year-olds, men on average are hired at a job level about a fortieth below that of women, that is, at
the same level. In line 4, for age thirty-five to thirty-nine, the number .876 means that among those
thirty-five to thirty-nine years old, men are hired at almost a full job level above women. The next
two regressions sequentially add more variables. The regression in column 2 adds, to those in column 1, variables for education group (four dummy variables). The regression in column 3 adds, to
those in column 2, variables for occupational group (five dummy variables).
*Not significantly different from zero at the 5-percent level (two-tailed tests).
†Significantly different from zero at the 10-percent but not at the 5-percent level (two-tailed tests).

entrants, the experience differential likely increases with age; most men will have
worked continuously whereas most women will have taken more time off to care
for children.

To explore this experience differential we report separate regression models for
job rank at time of hire, here including interaction terms between being male and
age (from Petersen and Saporta 2004, table 10). The results are given in table 6.3.

Again, the results are clear. For job rank at time of hire, the sex differential is
strongly age-dependent: there is no or only a small sex difference in rank up until
age thirty-four, and then there is a sharply growing sex gap in rank from age
thirty-five to fifty, to about 2.0 ranks. For salary at hire, the results are similar (results not shown). The gap increases from about 5 to 50 percent as age goes from the
eighteen-to-twenty-four range to fifty-plus.

This pattern of job-rank and salary differentials may clearly reflect differences in
experience. Younger men and women will have about the same experience, but
with age, men on average accumulate more experience than women. This yields a
payoff in placement at initial hire at higher ages.

What about the frozen pipeline? Table 6.4 gives the distribution of men and

TABLE 6.4 / Percentage of all 1986 Managerial, Administrative, and Professional Employees on Job Level, by Seniority and Gender

Years of Seniority	Sex	Job Level						Sum	N
		1	2 to 3	4 to 5	6 to 8	9 to 10	11 to 13		
0 to 4	Men	19.1	60.5	15.9	3.7	0.5	0.4	100.0	1,312
	Women	36.8	51.7	9.9	1.4	0.2	0.0	100.0	573
5 to 8	Men	11.6	47.5	33.6	6.5	0.8	0.1	100.0	1,064
	Women	33.0	40.8	20.5	4.9	0.8	0.0	100.0	370
9 to 10	Men	6.6	37.8	39.0	12.0	2.9	1.7	100.0	241
	Women	35.0	45.0	13.3	5.0	1.7	0.0	100.0	60
11 to 15	Men	9.6	45.7	29.3	12.4	2.5	0.6	100.1	670
	Women	35.9	42.3	18.3	2.1	1.4	0.0	100.0	142
16 to 20	Men	7.0	44.8	30.7	14.4	2.7	0.5	100.0	848
	Women	40.7	46.5	11.6	1.2	0.0	0.0	100.0	86
21 to 25	Men	6.7	52.4	27.8	10.4	2.2	0.5	100.0	822
	Women	32.4	51.4	13.5	2.7	0.0	0.0	100.0	37
26 to 30	Men	7.6	48.9	28.0	13.2	0.9	1.4	100.0	536
	Women	18.7	49.2	24.6	6.4	1.1	0.0	100.0	18
31 to 35	Men	6.8	44.0	32.1	14.8	1.0	1.3	100.0	293
	Women	18.7	49.2	24.6	6.4	1.1	0.0	100.0	8
36 +	Men	7.5	39.0	39.0	15.8	5.0	3.7	100.0	241
	Women	62.5	37.5	0.0	0.0	0.0	0.0	100.0	8

Source: Petersen and Saporta (2004, table 13), reprinted with permission. © The University of Chicago Press.

Note: For description of data see "The Glass Ceiling in the United States." For discussion of results see "Conclusions and Discussion." Not all the percentages sum to 100 due to rounding errors. The job-level structure among managerial, administrative, and professional employees goes from level 1 (low) to 13. The table pertains to everyone present in managerial, administrative, and professional positions in 1986, irrespective of when they entered the organization. There were 7,329 such employees in 1986, 1,302 women and 6,027 men. The table also includes employees internally promoted to managerial, administrative, and professional positions, for example, from blue-collar jobs.

women in terms of rank in the organization, by years of seniority (from Petersen and Saporta 2004, table 13). These are given for all the managerial, administrative, and professional employees present in 1986, not only the entrants as in tables 6.2 and 6.3.

The story is very simple. There is no question that there is a glass ceiling at job rank 11: not a single woman is employed above rank 10. Furthermore, to a large extent this is due to the very small number of women with high seniority. To see why, note first that only about .5 percent of the 7,329 employees are placed in job ranks 11 to 13. Of the 42 men in those ranks, 7 have seniority of 11 to 20 years, and 25 have seniority of 21 years or more. Of the 3,410 men with seniority of 11 years or more, .93 percent are placed in job ranks 11 to 13. The number of women with seniority of 11 years or more is 299. But 70 percent of them started their careers in the organization at its very lowest level, the entry-level clerical position, whereas only 14 percent, 43 women, entered the organization in managerial, administrative, and professional ranks. Very few men in the top managerial job ranks, 11 to 13, started their careers in nonmanagerial ranks, and of the seven (17 percent) who did, 6 have 26 years or more seniority in the organization.

Taking the longer time frame, then, shows that the main problem is that the pool of women with high seniority is very small. The ratio of women to men with seniority of eleven years or more is 1:11; with seniority of twenty-one years or more, it is 1:27 men. Had the same percentage of women with these levels of seniority reached the top job ranks as men do, we should find exactly one woman in job ranks 11 to 13. That we find zero women is within the realm of what to expect from chance. Additionally, as already mentioned, most of the pool of females with high levels of seniority entered the organization in positions from which top-level managers rarely are recruited. For the forty-three women with eleven years' or more seniority who started their careers in the organization in managerial, administrative, and professional positions, the average number of years spent in each job rank was 9.4, whereas for the same group of 763 men it was 13.5. So there is no evidence of a slower rate of promotion for these women.

This case study thus shows no evidence of lower promotion rates for women among the managerial, administrative, and professional employees; it actually shows a small advantage to being female, especially above rank 6. The glass ceiling in this organization appears not to arise from differential promotion rates, at least not in the 1988-to-1996 period. There is, however, clearly a frozen pipeline in the organization. There are very few women with high levels of seniority who qualify for promotion to the highest rank.

How Representative Is the Case Study?

It is not easy to know how representative our study is, as the evidence is not extensive. Some studies show that women suffer a net promotion disadvantage in lower levels of organizational hierarchies while enjoying a net advantage at higher levels (see DiPrete 1989, chapter 9; Spilerman and Petersen 1999; see also Rosenfeld 1992). Similar results are found in the federal bureaucracy (Lewis 1986) and for a large corporation (Tsui and Gutek 1984), the latter study using less appropriate data. Other studies, such as those of Barry A. Gerhart and George T. Milkovich (1989) and Heidi I. Hartmann (1987), find little evidence of differential promotion rates between men and women, once one takes into account their jobs within an organizational hierarchy, while Elisabeth A. Paulin and Jennifer M. Mellor (1996) report some nonsignificant negative effects for white females in a financial services firm. D. Anthony Butterfield and Gary N. Powell (1997) find a nonsignificant female advantage in promotion to top management in a federal bureaucracy department in the period from 1987 to 1994. William S. Barnett, James N. Baron, and Toby E. Stuart (2000) report higher promotion rates for women in the California Civil Service system from 1978 to 1986. Some studies that are not based on firm-level data, such as Linda K. Stroh, Jeanne M. Brett, and Anne H. Reilly (1996), find no sex differences in promotion rates. But these are less decisive. As for salary increases within organizations, much the same has been documented: there are few differences, or if there are, women are at an advantage (see Gerhart and Milkovich 1989; Tsui and Gutek 1984). Barnett, Baron, and Stuart (2000) find that at time of promotion men receive the higher increases. But since women are promoted at a higher rate, average monthly salary increases end up being identical.

Although the present case study perhaps goes into more detail than other studies, the results are similar. There is little evidence of differential promotion rates once comparisons are done at the establishment level, which indicates a limited impact of employer discrimination but big impact from employee choices. There is clear evidence of a frozen pipeline.

Changes over Time

The data presented pertain to the first half of the 1980s. But what are the changes over time?

It is difficult to assemble relevant over-time data on women in upper management. The Equal Employment Opportunity Commission (EEOC) routinely reports data, but on a much broader set of management positions than only those at the top. In the period 1978 to 1988, the percentage in management occupations who were female increased from 26.5 to 39.4, a remarkable change in a short period (U.S. Department of Labor 1989). Between 1990 and 2003, for a different definition of management positions, the percentage of officials and managers who were females increased from 29.3 to 35.9, also a notable increase (Equal Employment Opportunity Commission 2003, 17). The increase over time is more important here than the actual percentages. At the very top, the change has been slower. In part that is due to a frozen pipeline, in that a person often needs an MBA degree and twenty to twenty-five years of experience to reach the very highest levels. For appointments in 2000, one needs to look at the pools of females coming out of MBA and similar programs in the period from 1975 to 1985, when these pools were much smaller than today. Progress may have been slow, but there has been progress nevertheless. Still to be thoroughly investigated is the question of whether it has been slower than what one would expect, given the pools of women with the relevant backgrounds.

There has been more significant progress in the sciences, engineering, and academia. At each rank, including full professor, the percentage that is female in Research I academic institutions went up from 1979 to 1995 (National Research Council 2001, 183). Women made up 7.7 percent of the faculty in 1979, 13.1 in 1989, and 16.2 in 1995. Among full professors the percentage that is female went from 2.8 in 1979 to 6.3 in 1989 to 9.5 in 1995 (295). And while the percentage of the male faculty employed at the full professor level was stable at 56 to 58 percent, it went up from 19.4 to 30.3 among women. There is clearly a long distance to numerical parity, but there is also significant progress here.

These developments would lead one to predict that over time, the glass ceiling will diminish in importance. Given the persistence of educational segregation, the continued unequal distribution of work in the family, and high divorce rates, it is perhaps unlikely that women will reach numerical parity, but it is likely that women's access to upper-management positions will continue to improve, given the significant emphasis in many organizations on recruiting and retaining women at those levels.

SWEDISH DATA

We can look more closely at the question of whether there is a glass ceiling and how it is constructed when we examine for the same period the case of Sweden. We have access to detailed and comprehensive data covering almost all industries. In addition to assessing the extent of the ceiling and the importance of supply-side factors, we also gain understanding of how it operates in an entirely different institutional setting.

The data were collected and compiled by the Central Confederation of Employers (Svenska Arbetsgivare Föreningen, or SAF) from their database on wage statistics, assembled from individual firms' personnel records and data for each firm establishment (plant). The data are extensive and detailed. They contain information for all white-collar workers in every industry (except the insurance and banking industries) in the private sector within the SAF domain. Member firms provided information to the database once or twice a year from 1970 to 1990. The data were used for inputs in the annual wage negotiations, were monitored not only by SAF but also by the labor unions, and are of exceptionally high quality. They should be very reliable compared to the information from standard sample surveys or personal reports of pay rates, hours worked, and occupational titles.

The firm (establishment) company characteristics recorded include detailed industry code, size (number of employees), region, and area within the region. For every employee, information was obtained on sex, age, occupation, wages, hours worked, and level and type of education.

The data on occupation contain a relatively detailed description of job content, and the coding system makes it possible to compare establishments and industries. We shall refer to this job content information as occupational codes, although the data might also be described as job titles, in 1990 covering 276-285 positions altogether. The occupational code system, BNT, consists of fifty-one broad occupational groups.[8] Within each occupational group a further distinction is made with respect to rank, with seven ranks altogether. The rank is defined by the job's level of difficulty, of responsibility, and so forth, and run from a low of 1 to a high of 7 (in the original data 2 is high and 8 is low). Not all occupations have the entire seven ranks; some do not have rank 1 and some do not have the top ranks 5, 6, and

7. In 1990, fifty-one occupational groups with four to seven ranks each yields 283 separate job titles.

The data cover practically the entire occupational spectrum, including managers and professionals. Company CEOs are excluded, as are the chief executive officers on the executive team. The amount of employment among white-collar employees increased substantially, from 299,154 in 1970 to 391,997 in 1990. The percentage female also increased, from 24.8 to 34.6 percent.

The number of job titles (all occupations and ranks) observed each year ranged from 256 to 345. The number of broader occupation categories varied between forty-nine and seventy-one. Table 6.5 lists the occupations for the year 1990. The data presented here cover only white-collar workers, in 1990 about 392,000 employees. But in addition these organizations in 1990 also employed about 612,000 blue-collar workers. Employment in the organizations studied is thus about one million workers, roughly 24.5 percent of all employees in Sweden and 41.2 percent of employees in the private sector of the Swedish labor market.[9]

Over time there was a striking widening of the opportunity structure at both ends of the occupational ranks. Between 1970 and 1990 the percentage of occupations where the lowest rank (1) is available increased from 18.0 to 43.1 percent and, at the other end, the percentage of occupations where the highest rank (7) is available increased from 42.6 to 52.9 percent. These changes in lowest and highest ranks available are a result of both changes within existing occupations and the addition of new occupations. For example, of the thirty-six occupations common to 1970 and 1990, five had a higher maximum rank in 1990 than 1970, while the remaining 31 had the same maximum rank in both years. Most of the occupations offer long career ladders with many ranks available. In the period 1970 to 1975, 80 percent of the occupations had four or more ranks available; from 1978 on, 94 to 98 percent of the occupations had four or more and 59 percent had as many as six or seven ranks available.

THE GLASS CEILING: DISTRIBUTION OF MEN AND WOMEN BY RANK

We now document the distribution of men and women on occupational rank and how it has changed over time. Table 6.6 shows that the mean rank for men remained constant over the twenty-year period, at slightly under 4. The mean rank for women increased every year throughout the period, from about 2 in 1970 to about 3 in 1990. This is an increase of an entire rank, on a scale where the lowest and highest ranks are 1 and 7. Thus the initial overall gap of about two ranks, or women at half the rank of men, has been closed by one rank. In 1990, women on average were only one rank below men.

The distribution rank shows several noteworthy patterns. There is a concentration of women in the lower ranks and a relative lack of women in the top ranks. Over time, the percentage of the women who are in the lower ranks has declined strongly, but they are still decidedly overrepresented. At the two top ranks the rep-

(*Text continues on p. 181.*)

TABLE 6.5 / Distribution in Sweden of Employees on Occupations, Percentage Women, and Distribution on Rank Within Occupation, in 1990

			On Rank Within Occupation (1 to 7)							
	Overall	Percentage Women	1	2	3	4	5	6	7	
Occupation	1	2	3	4	5	6	7	8	9	10
Administrative work										
01 General analytical work	0.7	33.8	0.3	6.1	14.1	26.3	34.99	16.35	1.9	100.0
02 Secretarial work	5.8	99.1	4.1	29.5	46.0	18.8	1.5	0.1		100.0
03 Administrative efficiency improvement and development	0.2	21.6	1.0	11.8	37.3	38.2	10.9	0.9		100.0
04 Applied data processing, systems analysis and programming	3.7	20.5		1.4	12.4	41.2	36.3	7.8	0.9	100.0
05 Applied data processing operation	1.1	35.5	3.4	19.5	42.9	26.1	6.8	1.2	0.1	100.0
06 Key punching	0.7	96.0	14.1	73.6	10.7	1.4				100.0
Production management										
07 Administration of local plants and branches	0.3	2.7				26.2	40.4	23.0	10.4	100.0
08 Management of production, transportation and maintenance	2.9	2.2			8.8	31.9	38.1	17.0	4.1	100.0
09 Work supervision within production, repairs	7.5	5.8		4.6	47.3	43.6	4.2	0.3		100.0
10 Work supervision within building and construction	3.0	2.0		11.7	35.7	39.4	13.1	0.3		100.0
11 Administration, production, supervision in forestry	0.3	3.4			27.4	59.0	9.9	3.5	0.2	100.0
Research and development										
12 Mathematical work and calculation methodology	0.5	10.6	0.2	6.6	14.0	32.0	37.1	9.3	0.8	100.0
13 Laboratory work	3.8	36.2	0.7	7.5	21.8	33.5	26.5	8.7	1.3	100.0

(Table continues on p. 178.)

Construction and design									
14 Mechanical and electrical design engineering	7.6	9.5	0.4	3.3	14.0	43.1	31.8	7.4	1.0	100.0
15 Construction and construction programming	2.5	16.0		7.5	23.7	33.6	25.9	6.9	1.0	100.0
16 Architectural work	0.9	39.4		6.8	16.6	35.6	31.8	8.8	0.4	100.0
17 Design, drawing, and decoration	0.3	49.5		16.4	38.2	33.7	10.9	0.7		100.0
18 Photography	0.1	26.0		13.2	36.4	43.0	7.4			100.0
19 Sound technology	0.0	3.8		11.5	46.2	34.6	7.7			100.0
Technical methodology, planning, control, service, and industrial preventive health care									
20 Production engineering	2.3	8.7		7.0	16.2	50.7	22.4	3.5	0.3	100.0
21 Production planning	2.0	23.1	0.7	9.6	34.2	40.9	11.8	2.7	0.2	100.0
22 Traffic and transportation planning	1.5	43.7	1.2	39.5	38.8	14.9	4.9	0.6	0.6	100.0
23 Quality control	1.6	9.2	0.3	7.3	26.6	38.9	20.9	5.4	0.6	100.0
24 Technical service	3.3	2.6		8.1	36.1	38.5	14.4	2.5	0.3	100.0
25 Industrial preventive health care	0.5	11.2		13.1	20.9	33.4	27.0	5.4	0.2	100.0
Communications, library, and archival work									
26 Information work	0.3	49.7			13.9	41.8	33.3	9.8	1.1	100.0
27 Editorial work, publishing	0.2	60.1		5.9	26.0	33.9	27.9	6.1	0.2	100.0
28 Editorial work, technical information	0.2	23.8			13.9	50.2	31.9	3.9	0.1	100.0
29 Libraries, archives and documentation	0.2	69.4	3.3	18.3	35.9	26.3	13.3	2.8		100.0

Personnel work										
30 Personnel service	2.2	69.4	0.9	15.9	37.5	23.7	13.8	6.7	1.5	100.0
31 Planning of education, training, and teaching	1.0	50.8		11.3	31.0	40.2	14.4	2.8	0.3	100.0
32 Medical care within industries	0.7	88.3		1.4	12.8	80.4	5.3			100.0
General services										
33 Restaurant work	0.2	79.4		54.0	31.3	14.7				100.0
Business and trade										
34 Marketing and sales	15.5	19.9	0.9	11.7	30.8	34.0	16.5	5.2	0.8	100.0
35 Sales within stores and department stores	0.6	38.4			46.8	40.1	10.8	2.3		100.0
36 Travel agency work	0.9	77.6		28.8	57.2	11.1	2.9			100.0
37 Sales at exhibitions, spare part depots	0.4	38.3	6.1	72.7	16.3	4.8				100.0
38 Customer service	0.0	76.1	3.7	46.0	36.2	12.9	0.6	0.6		100.0
39 Tender calculation	0.7	12.6		6.9	33.9	41.0	16.2	2.0		100.0
40 Order processing	2.2	61.7		29.0	43.6	21.5	5.3	0.6		100.0
41 Internal processing of customer requests	0.0	25.0			25.0	37.5	12.5	25.0		100.0
42 Advertising	0.4	50.8		8.9	24.3	40.8	22.9	2.9	0.2	100.0
43 Buying	2.7	38.1	0.5	16.0	28.0	34.1	17.0	4.0	0.5	100.0
44 Management of inventory and sales	2.2	16.9	8.1	40.0	35.4	12.1	3.5	0.8		100.0
45 Shipping and freight services	2.1	52.3	2.4	31.6	39.9	18.8	6.2	1.1		100.0

(Table continues on p. 180.)

Financial work and office
services

	Overall	Percentage Women	1	2	3	4	5	6	7	All
46 Financial administration	10.3	70.3	2.9	25.0	36.6	19.9	10.8	4.0	0.8	100.0
47 Management of housing and real estate	0.3	29.3	2.4	19.8	33.7	25.7	13.7	4.7		100.0
48 Auditing	0.7	47.2		27.2	28.6	23.1	18.1	2.8	0.2	100.0
49 Telephone work	1.4	99.3	3.4	57.2	38.5	0.9				100.0
50 Office services	1.6	55.7	23.0	55.7	14.8	4.9	1.4	0.2		100.0
51 Chauffeuring	0.0	4.3		100.0						100.0
All	100.0	34.6	1.6	15.7	30.5	31.4	15.8	4.3	0.7	100.0

Source: Reprinted from Petersen and Meyerson (1999, table 2), with permission from Elsevier.

Note: For description of data and procedures see "The Glass Ceiling in the United States." The first column, "Overall," gives the distribution of employees on the fifty-one occupational groups. In column 1, four occupations are listed as having 0.0 percent of the employees. This occurred when less than 0.05 percent of the employees were in an occupation, namely in sound technology, customer services, internal processing of customer requests, and chauffeuring, with 26, 163, 8, and 161 employees respectively. The second column, "Percentage Women," gives the percentage of the employees in the occupation who are women. Columns 3 to 9 give separately for each occupation the distribution of employees within the occupation on rank. Column 10 gives the sum of the percentages in columns 2 to 8. The rank variable goes from a low of 1 to a high of 7, indicating roughly the level of difficulty of the position within the broader occupational group. The empty cells in the table correspond to cases where the specific combination of occupation-by-rank does not exist. The last line in the table gives in column 1 the sum of the percentages for the fifty-one occupations in column 1, column 2 gives the percent of all employees who are women, while columns 3 to 9 give the distribution of all employees on rank, regardless of their occupation.

resentation of women is negligible, but has increased. In 1970, there were hardly any women in those ranks. For each woman in rank 6 there were about one hundred fifty men, and for each woman in rank 7 there were about seven hundred men. In 1990, the situation had improved: At rank 6, for each woman there were about twenty men; at rank 7, for each woman there were about forty men. In 1990, the probability of being in rank 6 was about ten times higher for men than women, and in rank 7 it was an entire twenty-five times higher for men. The table thus gives clear evidence of a glass ceiling.

FROZEN PIPELINES

We turn now to the questions: Why Are There So Few Women at Top Ranks? What are the sources of the lack of qualified women whom employers can appoint to positions of leadership? Recall the frozen-pipeline hypothesis: that the glass ceiling is to some extent a result of supply-side differences in how men and women behave. That women on average are placed lower than men may be due to several factors other than employer discrimination, including differences in age, seniority, hours worked, part-time status, and educational backgrounds. We discuss these issues in terms of "pipeline problems," of which there are three: a first frozen pipeline comes from the domestic division of labor; the second frozen pipeline comes from potential sex segregation in educational choice; a third frozen pipeline may be generated by anticipated discrimination. To explore the effects of some of these factors we present descriptive statistics separately by age, part-time status, hours, and education. We compare the characteristics of employees in all jobs with those in the highest-ranked jobs. These statistics suggest that part of the explanation for the glass ceiling may be that so few women acquire the qualifications needed for the top jobs. The next section elaborates these results, presenting multivariate analyses with rank as the dependent variable.

Pipeline Problem 1: Few Women with the Relevant Experience, Age, and Part-Time Status

The first pipeline problem is the unequal domestic division of labor in the home. One of its manifestations is that women often withdraw from careers for shorter or longer periods. In our data, this may show up as lower average age for women than men at each occupational rank, as some proportion of the older women withdraw from careers as they progress through the occupational system and have children. In, say, rank 4, the vast majority of men remain employed, but some proportion of the women withdraw to take care of children, and then are potentially replaced with younger women. Thus, age can function as a proxy for work experience.

The average age by job rank increases with occupational rank for both sexes, in all years (with two minor exceptions). Furthermore, for men and women average

TABLE 6.6 / Distribution (Percentages) by Rank by Year and Sex and Percentage in Each Rank That Are Women

	1970			1975			1978		
	Men	Women	Percentage Women	Men	Women	Percentage Women	Men	Women	Percentage Women
Rank	1	2	3	4	5	6	7	8	9
1	2.39	38.24	84.05	1.72	21.80	83.39	1.52	16.33	82.16
2	14.28	34.97	44.63	10.90	46.51	62.84	9.68	46.32	67.29
3	34.74	19.58	15.64	31.69	23.02	22.35	30.25	26.61	27.44
4	28.99	6.10	6.48	33.72	7.25	7.85	35.14	8.91	9.83
5	13.48	1.00	2.38	15.50	1.28	3.17	16.63	1.66	4.11
6	4.93	0.11	0.71	5.27	0.13	0.99	5.60	0.17	1.29
7	1.20	0.01	0.15	1.20	0.00	0.16	1.17	0.01	0.26
Sum	100.01	100.01		100.00	99.99		99.99	100.01	
Average	3.56	1.97	24.76	3.71	2.20	28.38	3.77	2.34	30.07

Source: Reprinted from Petersen and Meyerson (1999, table 4), with permission from Elsevier; Meyerson and Petersen (1997a, table 4.3).
Note: The first column within each year gives the distribution of men on the ranks, while the second column gives the distribution of the women on the ranks. The third column within each year gives the percentage of employees in

age is more similar at the lower than higher ranks. At the highest ranks, 6 and 7, the average age is two to seven years lower for women throughout the entire period (except for 1970). In 1990 the average age at rank 7 was forty-four for women and forty-nine for men.

This sex difference in age by rank may reflect a number of factors. Perhaps it is due to younger women being on average somewhat better educated than older women. To the extent that organizations want women in positions of leadership, they would need to appoint those who are younger than their male counterparts in order to find women with the right educational qualifications. It can also reflect the increasing labor-force participation rates for women, as the pool of younger women from which to draw leaders is much larger than the pool of older women. In 1970, the average age of the white-collar workers in the sample was forty for men, and thirty-three for women, a gap of seven years. Thirty-eight percent of the men were thirty-five or younger, whereas an entire 62 percent of the women were. By 1990, the age gap had shrunk dramatically, from seven years to three: the average age was forty-two for men and thirty-nine for women; 30 percent of men were thirty-five or younger, against 39 percent of the women. Thus, between 1970 and 1990, the average age of workers increased 1.5 years for men and 6.5 years for women. This increase in female age documents the increased attachment of women to the labor force: not only did they enter it, they also to a large degree stayed in it.

In summary, treating age as a proxy for experience, it is clear that as one moves up the career ladder, the experience gap between men and women increases. In the

TABLE 6.6 / *Continued*

	1980			1985			1990	
Men	Women	Percentage Women	Men	Women	Percentage Women	Men	Women	Percentage Women
10	11	12	13	14	15	16	17	18
1.31	13.28	81.94	0.91	6.73	78.30	0.64	3.52	74.34
8.97	44.94	69.09	7.46	39.74	72.13	6.88	32.33	71.29
29.29	29.09	30.71	27.02	35.45	38.93	25.81	39.50	44.72
35.58	10.46	11.60	37.02	14.55	16.03	37.89	19.16	21.01
17.75	1.99	4.77	20.14	3.12	7.01	21.61	4.82	10.56
5.89	0.23	1.69	6.31	0.39	2.88	6.18	0.63	5.08
1.22	0.01	0.31	1.14	0.02	0.98	0.97	0.04	2.35
100.01	100.00		100.00	100.00		99.98	100.00	
3.82	2.44	30.85	3.92	2.69	32.70	3.95	2.91	34.59

the given rank that were women. The last line gives, for the two first columns within each year, the average rank for men and women, respectively, in that year. The third column, in the last line, gives the percentage of employees in that year who were women.

higher occupational ranks, employers will face relatively smaller pools of females with long experience from which to recruit into even higher positions.

Another manifestation of the unequal division of labor in the home should be higher rates of part-time employment among women and fewer hours worked. Table 6.7 shows that the percentage of full-time employed increases with occupational rank. At the highest occupational rank, only 0 to 10 percent of women and 0 to 3 percent of men worked part-time. This pattern is the same throughout the period (1970 is excluded from the description, because for that year no reliable information on part-time status was available). At the two lowest ranks, 1 and 2, 40 to 50 percent of women worked part-time, whereas only 0 to 5 percent of men did so.

What is then the sex composition of full-time employees, the potential recruitment pools for managerial positions. The last line in Table 6.7 shows that 27 percent of all women worked part-time in 1975. During the 1980s the figure rose dramatically, to 40 percent, and in 1990 it was 32 percent. Very few men worked part-time; less than half a percent in 1975, to about 3 percent in the decade from 1980 to 1990. At each level women work part-time more often than men. Reduced hours at work may result in lower access to top positions.

Another way to look at work input is to study the hours worked instead of only distinguishing between part-time and full-time status. The number of hours worked is much higher at the top ranks than at lower ones. On average we find that women work fewer hours than men. In 1990 men worked on average 39.1 hours per week and women 35.5 hours; in 1975 men worked 39 hours while women worked 33.2.

TABLE 6.7 / Percentage of Swedish Workers Working Part-Time, by Year, Sex, and Rank, 1975 to 1990

| | 1975 | | 1978 | | 1980 | | 1985 | | 1990 | |
	Men	Women	Men	Women	Men	Women	Men	Women	Men	Women
Rank	1	2	3	4	5	6	7	8	9	10
1	2.0	31.4	5.4	41.5	7.4	45.8	7.5	46.1	6.6	38.6
2	0.7	29.4	3.6	40.0	4.9	45.0	4.9	44.9	4.5	37.6
3	0.3	23.1	1.9	32.5	3.3	37.7	2.9	37.7	3.2	32.3
4	0.3	19.2	1.7	27.2	3.0	31.9	2.7	30.7	2.9	25.7
5	0.3	13.3	1.5	17.3	2.9	22.2	2.6	21.4	3.0	19.5
6	0.2	7.4	1.4	13.8	2.5	12.3	3.1	14.0	2.9	8.8
7	0.2	0.0	1.5	0.0	3.1	10.0	3.3	0.0	3.0	3.3
Total	0.4	27.4	2.0	36.7	3.3	41.1	3.0	39.5	3.1	32.2

Source: Reprinted from Petersen and Meyerson (1999, table 10), with permission from Elsevier; Meyerson and Petersen (1997a, table 4.5).
Note: There are no statistics for 1970 in this table because the part-time data were deemed to be unreliable for that year.

It is striking that at the lower ranks women on average work many fewer hours than men; at ranks 1 to 3, they work four to five hours less per week. In contrast, at the two top ranks, 6 and 7, men and women work at about the same number of hours per week, in each of the six years shown in table 6.7. This shows that to the extent women succeed in reaching the top levels, they put in as much work effort as the men, but at lower ranks they put in fewer hours. Working fewer hours probably diminishes their chances of being promoted to higher ranks. We have not investigated whether the women who made it to ranks 6 and 7 worked as many hours as the men before the promotion, but it is a good guess that they did.

In an earlier section, "Women and Men in Top Management and the Professions," we discussed how decreased discrimination from employers, and the realization among men and women that this has occurred, could lead to a decline in the percentage of women working part-time. Instead we see that the percentage of women who worked part-time increased between 1975 and 1985. Broader institutional factors offer likely explanations. Part-time work was made more universally available in Sweden and Scandinavia during this period. At the same time, combining family and work was made easier through an increase in the provision of child care. These two processes may have helped to recruit women into the labor force who previously would have elected not to work. With increased availability of part-time employment and expanded child care options, they chose to enter the labor force. The net effect is higher rates of part-time employment. In Sweden, part-time work has been supply-driven and a majority of the women working part-time do so because it suits them best (Båvner 2001; Sundström 1982, 1991; Albrecht et al. 1999).

Pipeline Problem 2: Education

Education is a central determinant for allocation of employees to various positions, especially to higher ranks within professions and management. We have access to some information on both the level and type of education at different ranks, but not all. Especially at lower occupational ranks there is no information on education mainly because establishments did not provide the information on employees who worked in positions and establishments where educational type and level were not relevant.

Educational level per se is rarely central for explaining success in reaching managerial ranks. It is the type of education that matters. University degrees in medieval literature and accounting may well yield the same level of education but they qualify the holder for very different careers. It is probably rare for employers to be primarily interested in the number of years spent in school. Instead they may demand specific qualifications in well-defined fields such as computer science, engineering, accounting, business administration, and law.[10] This may especially be the case for entry-level jobs, when applicants are recently out of school, and it will definitely be the case for core tasks within an organization. But the subsequent experience an employee can expect to acquire depends strongly on the initial placement, which in turn is determined in large measure by educational qualifications. For recruitment to higher positions, the experience acquired becomes crucial. Psychologists are not hired to build bridges and classicists are not given complex programming jobs. Even though one's specific educational background may be of limited relevance in higher managerial positions, as these rarely involve operational activities, the relevant prior experience in operations and core organizational areas may be crucial. The ascent of general managers with MBA degrees—who presumably can manage anything—does not make those with specific experience superfluous.

Table 6.8 gives a distribution by type of education, first for all employees and then for those in ranks 6 and 7, with special focus on some of the most important higher-educational groups from which managers were drawn: the social sciences, including economics, business, and law, and technical fields such as engineering.

Information on education was missing for about 50 percent of employees, both men and women. As mentioned above, these are mostly employees with low levels of education or people working in establishments and occupations where education is of little consequence for the tasks performed. This is also borne out by the fact that among those in ranks 6 and 7, the percentage with missing education lies between 16.6 and 23.3 rather than between 52.5 and 62.6, as among all employees. Education is important and usually high for managers, so fewer of them lack education data.

The largest group, aside from those for whom education level was not available, is in the technical fields, such as engineering and civil engineering. But more important, the percentage of employees in the top ranks from one of those fields is remarkably high. For 1970 and 1990, among employees in ranks 6 and 7, 36 percent and 31.6 percent, respectively, had backgrounds in engineering or civil engineer-

TABLE 6.8 / Distribution (Percentages) of Employees in Sweden by Type of Education

	1970		1975		1978		1980		1985		1990	
	All[a]	Top[b]	All	Top	All	Top	All	Top	All	Top	All	Top
Type of Education	1	2	3	4	5	6	7	8	9	10	11	12
Missing	62.6	19.8	54.9	16.6	55.0	17.0	54.1	16.8	52.7	19.7	52.5	23.3
Basic	4.9	2.1	7.3	2.4	7.1	2.2	7.2	2.4	7.3	2.5	7.0	2.9
Humanities	0.2	0.4	0.3	0.4	0.3	0.4	0.2	0.3	0.3	0.4	0.3	0.3
Pedagogical	0.1	0.1	0.1	0.1	0.1	0.2	0.1	0.2	0.1	0.2	0.1	0.2
Social sciences, law												
Miscellaneous fields	5.9	7.2	8.0	6.8	8.5	6.5	8.8	6.4	9.2	5.7	9.5	5.2
Business, lower level	0.7	2.9	0.9	3.6	0.9	3.5	0.9	3.3	0.8	2.7	0.7	2.2
Civil economists	0.6	5.5	0.8	5.5	0.8	5.6	0.9	5.7	1.3	5.8	1.5	5.5
Law, social sciences, B.A., M.A.	0.3	1.5	0.9	2.6	0.9	3.1	0.9	3.5	0.9	3.9	0.8	3.9
Law, social sciences, license, Ph.D.	0.0	0.1	0.0	0.1	0.0	0.2	0.0	0.1	0.0	0.2	0.0	0.2
Technical fields												
Miscellaneous fields	11.5	18.1	13.1	19.3	13.0	18.9	13.3	18.4	14.4	17.2	15.6	16.8
Engineering	9.8	16.9	9.0	15.5	8.1	14.5	7.6	14.0	6.0	11.8	4.4	8.8
Civil engineering	2.4	19.2	3.1	20.1	3.4	21.3	3.8	21.3	4.6	22.3	5.1	22.6
Natural sciences, B.A., M.A.	0.2	0.6	0.4	0.8	0.4	0.8	0.5	1.2	0.5	1.6	0.5	2.0
Natural sciences, license, Ph.D.	0.2	2.4	0.2	2.9	0.2	3.0	0.3	3.1	0.3	3.2	0.3	3.3
Transportation	0.1	0.1	0.2	0.3	0.2	0.3	0.2	0.4	0.2	0.2	0.1	0.2
Health	0.2	1.5	0.2	0.9	0.3	0.9	0.3	0.9	0.6	1.0	0.8	1.3
Agriculture	0.2	1.3	0.4	1.4	0.4	1.4	0.5	1.5	0.5	1.1	0.4	0.8
Service	0.2	0.3	0.3	0.6	0.2	0.5	0.2	0.7	0.2	0.6	0.2	0.6
Unclassifiable	0.1	0.0	0.1	0.0	0.1	0.0	0.1	0.0	0.2	0.0	0.2	0.1
Sum	100.0	100.0	100.0	100.0	100.0	100.0	100.0	100.0	100.0	100.0	100.0	100.0

Source: Reprinted from Petersen and Meyerson (1999, table 18), with permission from Elsevier; Meyerson and Petersen (1997a, table 4.6).

[a] "All" stands for all employees.

[b] "Top" for employees in ranks 6 to 7. Within each year, the first column gives the distribution of all employees on the type of education while the second column gives the distribution of employees in rank 6 to 7 on the type of education.

ing, while only 8.4 percent and 7.7 percent had backgrounds in lower-level business or civil economics. In 1990, 53.5 percent of the employees in ranks 6 and 7 were drawn from technical fields, whereas only 25.9 percent of all employees had educations in those fields. Engineering and technical educations were very important job requirements for managerial careers in Sweden in the period considered.

Table 6.9 gives the distribution of men and women by the types of education and the percentage of the graduates who were female in each type of education. We see here the concentration of women with education in the social sciences, law, and administration and their relative absence in technical fields. In 1970, for each female engineer there were about ninety-nine men, and for each female civil engineer there were about eighty-two men. In 1990, the corresponding numbers were forty-two and eight, a tremendous improvement but still a very uneven distribution. Consider the situation for employers in 1990: for each potential female employee with an engineering background there will be forty-two men. The gender segregation in higher education in technical fields is extreme. These are precisely the fields from which many managers were drawn. In business, economics, and social science fields, the situation has improved markedly over the twenty-year period. For example, in 1970, for each female civil economist there were twenty men, whereas in 1990 there were only two.

One may therefore conjecture that a principal reason for the lack of women in upper management is their choice of education. We have yet to investigate the joint operation of age, part-time status, hours worked, educational level, and type of education for the discrepancies between men and women in occupational rank. Women and men may ultimately achieve an equal distribution on educational types, but the women may on average be younger, which in turn typically will yield a lower placement in organizational hierarchies.

PIPELINE PROBLEM 3: DISCRIMINATION, LIFE CYCLE, OR COHORT EFFECTS?

In the preceding section we looked at the relationship between rank and four variables: age, part-time status, hours worked, and educational attainment. We found clear differences between men and women on those dimensions. In this section we explore the impact of the differences, asking the question: Do men and women with similar attributes, such as education, age, part-time status, and hours worked, occupy the same ranks? We perform a multivariate analysis of rank on age, hours worked, part-time status, and education. The estimated impact of sex on the rank occupied can be interpreted as the average difference in rank between men and women with the same age, part-time status, hours worked, and education.[11] Beyond reporting the regression coefficients we here also discuss some conceptually more complex goals, which can be difficult to keep distinct. A brief explanation is in order.

In part we investigate aspects of the pipeline problem: (1) How the gender gap varies with educational choice and specialization, and (2) how the gender gap, in

TABLE 6.9 / Distribution (Percentages) in Sweden of Men and Women in Types of Education and Percentage of Women Employees in Each Type of Education by Year

	1970			1975			1978		
	M[a]	W[b]	W[c]	M	W	W	M	W	W
Type of Education	1	2	3	4	5	6	7	8	9
Missing	57.7	77.5	30.7	49.4	68.7	35.6	49.7	67.5	36.9
Basic	4.0	7.6	38.8	5.9	11.0	42.7	5.4	10.9	46.3
Humanities	0.1	0.3	38.0	0.2	0.5	49.6	0.2	0.5	51.0
Pedagogy	0.1	0.1	23.1	0.1	0.1	27.6	0.1	0.1	26.0
Social sciences, law									
Miscellaneous fields	4.0	11.4	48.4	5.0	15.3	54.7	5.2	16.1	57.3
Business, lower level	1.0	0.1	3.8	1.2	0.2	6.8	1.2	0.3	9.4
Civil economists	0.7	0.1	4.7	1.0	0.2	6.8	1.1	0.2	8.7
Law, social sciences,									
B.A., M.A.	0.4	0.1	8.7	1.0	0.5	14.9	1.1	0.5	15.8
Law, social sciences,									
license, Ph.D.	0.0	0.0	14.3	0.0	0.0	17.4	0.0	0.0	18.3
Technical fields									
Miscellaneous fields	14.8	1.5	3.1	17.6	1.7	3.6	17.8	1.8	4.2
Engineer	12.9	0.4	1.0	12.4	0.4	1.1	11.5	0.3	1.3
Civil engineer	3.1	0.1	1.2	4.2	0.3	2.6	4.7	0.5	4.0
National sciences,									
B.A., M.A.	0.2	0.2	19.3	0.4	0.3	20.8	0.5	0.3	20.5
National sciences,									
license, Ph.D.	0.2	0.0	2.8	0.3	0.0	3.0	0.3	0.0	3.7
Transportation	0.1	0.0	11.2	0.2	0.1	7.8	0.3	0.1	8.1
Health fields	0.2	0.4	46.3	0.1	0.5	66.5	0.1	0.6	67.2
Agriculture	0.3	0.0	1.7	0.5	0.0	1.7	0.6	0.0	2.3
Service	0.2	0.1	15.7	0.3	0.1	13.6	0.3	0.1	18.1
Unclassifiable	0.1	0.1	22.4	0.1	0.2	36.3	0.1	0.1	39.1
Sum	100.0	100.0	24.8[d]	100.0	100.0	28.4	100.0	100.0	30.1

Source: Reprinted from Petersen and Meyerson (1999, table 19), with permission from Elsevier; Meyerson and Petersen (1997a, table 4.7).

[a]The first column within each year gives the distribution of men in the types of education.

[b]The second column within each year gives the distribution of the women in the types of education.

the cross-section, varies with age—whether the gap is bigger in child-rearing years than before or after.

In part we investigate whether there is evidence of employer discrimination and changing employer discrimination over time: (3) whether the gender gap disappears once controls have been made for education, part-time status, hours worked, and occupation; (4) how the gender gap varies with birth cohort, holding age constant, exploring whether there is evidence of decreased discrimination over time;

TABLE 6.9 / *Continued*

	1980			1985			1990	
M	W	W	M	W	W	M	W	W
10	11	12	13	14	15	16	17	18
48.7	66.2	37.7	48.0	62.5	38.8	48.6	60.0	39.5
5.6	10.9	46.7	5.6	10.9	48.9	5.3	10.3	50.4
0.2	0.4	55.5	0.2	0.5	58.8	0.1	0.5	65.6
0.1	0.1	23.2	0.1	0.1	34.0	0.1	0.1	36.2
5.2	16.8	49.1	4.9	18.0	64.1	4.8	18.3	67.0
1.2	0.3	11.4	1.0	0.5	18.4	0.8	0.5	26.7
1.2	0.3	10.7	1.5	0.8	20.3	1.6	1.3	30.2
1.1	0.5	16.3	1.1	0.6	21.7	0.9	0.6	26.8
0.0	0.0	13.6	0.0	0.0	14.0	0.0	0.0	18.2
18.4	1.9	4.5	20.2	2.5	5.6	22.0	3.5	7.7
10.9	0.3	1.4	8.8	0.3	1.8	6.5	0.3	2.3
5.3	0.7	5.2	6.4	1.1	7.4	6.9	1.7	11.5
0.5	0.4	22.2	0.6	0.4	25.3	0.6	0.4	29.2
0.4	0.0	5.4	0.4	0.1	7.6	0.4	0.1	10.6
0.2	0.1	8.5	0.2	0.0	8.8	0.2	0.0	10.1
0.1	0.7	70.5	0.2	1.5	79.0	0.3	1.8	79.5
0.7	0.1	4.4	0.7	0.1	6.9	0.5	0.2	15.2
0.3	0.1	18.9	0.2	0.2	24.4	0.2	0.2	31.9
0.1	0.1	39.0	0.2	0.2	30.9	0.2	0.2	36.6
100.0	100.0	30.9	100.0	100.0	32.7	100.0	100.0	34.6

[c]The third column within each year gives the percentage of employees in the given type of education that were women.

[d]In the last line the third column gives the percentage of employees in that year who were women.

In the table, "M" and "W" stand for men and women, respectively.

and (5) how the gender gap, for a given birth cohort, evolves with age. This is a pipeline 1 problem, the impact of the unequal distribution of work in the family, but now it is investigated over the life cycle of a cohort rather than across age groups in the cross-section, as in (2).

The objectives in (2), (4), and (5) are thus interrelated. In the cross-section, the gender gap may increase with age, as has been widely documented for wages, and as explored for rank in (2). This may be due to discrimination. But it may also be due to cohort differences, where older women entered the labor market in less hospitable periods, and continue to suffer the disadvantages they faced at career entry. This then is explored in (4). But then, within each cohort, with its given set of disadvantages at the time of career entry, there may be a specific pattern by age as it grows older, where the pattern may reflect discrimination, resulting in an increasing gap, or it may reflect life-cycle adaptations to family circumstances with an increasing gap in at least ages thirty to fifty. This we explore in (5).

Overall Gender Effects

The results are given in table 6.10. The first column within each year, denoted "Short," gives the gender effect when we control for educational level, part-time status, and hours worked, for all ages in the first line; in the consecutive lines the gender effect is estimated separately by age group. The second column, denoted "Full," also takes into account that men and women may be in different occupations. The first line shows that in each year, the gender effect is smaller when one controls for occupation, the "short" versus the "full" regressions.

Without control for occupation, the gender effect in 1970 was –.927, that is, women were on average placed almost one rank below that of comparable men, but then the effect declined every year, except in 1975, to a difference in ranks of –.703 in 1990. Adding the control for occupation, the gender effect in 1990 was –.589, and women were positioned on average half a rank below men.

Taking into account the variables in the regression equations reduces the differences in rank between men and women. In 1970 the variables age, hours worked, and education explain about a third of the average difference of 1.5 ranks found in table 6.6: if women and men had had the same distributions on age, part-time status, hours worked, and education, the difference in ranks would in 1970 be reduced from 1.5 to 1. In 1990, the average difference in ranks between men and women was 1. When the variables are taken into account, this difference gets reduced to about .703, or even to .589, of a rank, with controls for occupation. So age, part-time status, hours worked, and education reduce the difference in ranks by 30 to 40 percent, not by as much as in 1970, but still by a considerable amount, in particular when one keeps in mind that in 1990 there was a smaller difference to reduce in the first place. Controlling additionally for occupation reduces the rank gap another 30 to 40 percent.

More on Pipeline Problem 2: Gender Effects in Three Educational Groups

Table 6.11 further explores the relationships between rank and sex among those with degrees in one of three educational fields: economics and business administration, technical fields such as engineering, and social sciences and the law. These three broad educational fields are important in management. Within each year, the

TABLE 6.10 / Effect in Sweden of Being Female on Job Rank, from Short and Full Regressions

Age Group	1970 Short[b]	1970 Full[c]	1975 Short	1975 Full	1978 Short	1978 Full	1980 Short	1980 Full	1985 Short	1985 Full	1990 Short	1990 Full
	1	2	3	4	5	6	7	8	9	10	11	12
All ages[d]	-.927	-.468	-.953	-.862	-.926	-.830	-.892	-.798	-.810	-.706	-.703	-.589
20 to 25[ae]	-.539	-.111	-.506	-.434	-.441	-.367	-.264	-.209	-.308	-.216	-.176	-.101
26 to 30	-.599	-.180	-.625	-.556	-.520	-.450	-.448	-.388	-.387	-.314	-.299	-.227
31 to 35	-.952	-.471	-.860	-.771	-.753	-.674	-.707	-.639	-.609	-.541	-.488	-.412
36 to 40	-1.249	-.719	-1.172	-1.066	-1.045	-.948	-.977	-.886	-.820	-.742	-.689	-.614
41 to 45	-1.395	-.831	-1.312	-1.195	-1.225	-1.120	-1.197	-1.096	-.983	-.890	-.838	-.744
46 to 50	-1.368	-.839	-1.385	-1.264	-1.320	-1.206	-1.283	-1.185	-1.112	-.999	-.960	-.844
51 to 55	-1.485	-.905	-1.354	-1.247	-1.315	-1.205	-1.294	-1.180	-1.153	-1.054	-1.032	-.905
56 to 60	-1.349	-.830	-1.339	-1.227	-1.324	-1.221	-1.262	-1.161	-1.168	-1.051	-1.023	-.907
61 and over	-1.139	-.783	-1.270	-1.164	-1.231	-1.126	-1.303	-1.195	-1.157	-1.045	-1.072	-.937

Source: Reprinted from Petersen and Meyerson (1999, table 22), with permission from Elsevier; Meyerson and Petersen (1997a, table 4.10).
All coefficients are significantly different from 0 at better than the 1 percent level; in fact all of them better than at the 0.1 percent level.
[a] Those younger than twenty are excluded from the analysis. There were very few of them and they can legitimately be considered as yet not having started a career among the white-collar workers.
[b] The short regression includes the variables sex, dummy variables for age (nine age groups), part-time status (except in 1970), hours worked, and level of education (1 to 7).
[c] The full regression adds dummy variables for occupation to those variables.
[d] "All ages," a common sex effect is estimated for all age groups and age itself is controlled by a set of dummy variables.
[e] In the regressions by age group, separate age effects are estimated for each age group. In these, the effects of the other variables in the regression equations do not vary across age groups, thus do not include interaction terms between age group and the other variables.

TABLE 6.11 / Effect of Being Female on Job Rank, by Education, in Sweden, from Short and Full Regressions

| | 1970 | | 1975 | | 1978 | | 1980 | | 1985 | | 1990 | |
| | Short[c] | Full[d] | Short | Full | Short | Full | Short | Full | Short | Full | Short | Full |
Type of Education	1	2	3	4	5	6	7	8	9	10	11	12
Social sciences, law												
All ages[e]	-.318	-.142*	-.524	-.380	-.535	-.440	-.582	-.502	-.506	-.446	-.510	-.452
26 to 30[bf]	-.114*	-.005*	-.464	-.296	-.387	-.226	-.231	-.168*	-.003*	-.003*	.003*	-.001*
31 to 35	-.321*	-.408	-.447	-.335	-.426	-.353	-.564	-.521	-.241	-.284	-.103*	-.103*
36 to 40	-1.266	-.727	-.885	-.885	-.883	-.825	-.606	-.520	-.594	-.534	-.416	-.422
41 to 45	-.867	-.598*	-1.172	-.928	-.924	-.830	-1.004	-.851	-.530	-.485	-.606	-.552
46 to 50	-.691*	-.406*	-1.701	-1.488	-1.142	-1.054	-.885	-.814	-1.018	-.832	-.590	-.534
51 to 55	-.247*	.096*	-.784*	-.402*	-2.829	-2.347	-1.873	-1.241	-.918	-.842	-1.109	-.902
56 to 60	.288*	.329*	-.834	-.622*	-1.265	-.824	-1.669	-1.315	-1.760	-1.172	-.903	-.824
61 and over[a]	.705*	.916*					-.588*	-.402*	-1.521	-1.289	-2.275	-1.738
Economics, business administration												
All ages	-.787	-.432	-.775	-.693	-.617	-.586	-.614	-.562	-.534	-.463	-.426	-.352
26 to 30	-.536	-.270	-.437	-.320	-.260	-.211	-.265	-.165	-.175	-.126	-.040*	-.010*
31 to 35	-.899	-.420	-.676	-.636	-.536	-.500	-.466	-.447	-.433	-.352	-.322	-.254
36 to 40	-1.088	-.593	-1.204	-1.182	-.867	-.847	-.831	-.773	-.636	-.577	-.567	-.485
41 to 45	-.989	-.605	-1.297	-1.205	-.968	-.986	-.984	-.963	-.939	-.886	-.714	-.638
46 to 50	-1.098	-.770	-.897	-.743	-1.150	-1.075	-1.161	-1.136	-.905	-.788	-.833	-.720
51 to 55	-.750	-.425*	-.767	-.761	-.734	-.734	-.856	-.757	-.957	-.908	-.893	-.773
56 to 60	-.674	-.249*	-1.273	-1.184	-.801	-.824	-.845	-.816	-1.099	-.905	-.989	-.912
61 and over	.535*	.053*	-1.480	-1.185	-1.082	-.957	-.915	-.835	-.804	-.732	-.827	-.690

Technical fields

All ages	-.462	-.356	-.418	-.386	-.381	-.358	-.325	-.310	-.303	-.277	-.212	-.199
26 to 30	-.143	-.109*	-.225	-.218	-.134	-.136	-.003*	-.002*	-.005*	-.004*	-.003*	-.002*
31 to 35	-.530	-.402	-.413	-.386	-.316	-.296	-.301	-.296	-.149	-.136	-.101	-.100
36 to 40	-.541	-.478	-.602	-.549	-.487	-.466	-.405	-.387	-.416	-.398	-.232	-.228
41 to 45	-.937	-.791	-.692	-.645	-.660	-.606	-.661	-.635	-.480	-.443	-.427	-.410
46 to 50	-1.012	-.791	-.955	-.892	-1.047	-.969	-.965	-.919	-.695	-.635	-.443	-.430
51 to 55	-.757	-.550	-.892	-.775	-.721	-.672	-.872	-.809	-.848	-.763	-.541	-.514
56 to 60	-.927	-.538	-.501	-.412	-.802	-.742	-.658	-.613	-.775	-.732	-.720	-.689
61 and over	.379*	.526*	.516*	.488*	-.346*	-.276*	-.537	-.438	-.765	-.703	-.483	-.402

Source: Reprinted from Petersen and Meyerson (1999, table 23), with permission from Elsevier; Meyerson and Petersen (1997a, table 4.11).

aAmong employees in the social sciences and law there were in 1975 and 1978 not a sufficient number of women aged sixty-one and over to allow an estimate of the sex effect for that age group.

bThose younger than twenty-five are excluded from the analysis. There were very few of them and they can legitimately be considered as yet not having started a career among the white-collar workers, given the kinds of educational fields they are in.

cThe short regression includes the variables sex, dummy variables for age (eight age groups), part-time status (except in 1970), hours worked, and type of education within educational field.

dThe full regression adds dummy variables for occupation to those variables.

e"All ages," a common sex effect is estimated for all age groups and age itself is controlled by a set of dummy variables.

fIn the regressions by age group, separate age effects are estimated for each age group. In these, the effects of the other variables in the regression equations do not vary across age groups, thus do not include interaction terms between age group and the other variables.

*Not significantly different from 0 at the 5 percent level. The other coefficients are, and in the vast majority of cases even at the 0.1 percent level.

first column gives the effect of being female on the rank reached, controlling for the same variables as in table 6.10. The second column adds dummy variables for the occupation. Within each broad educational field, the first line gives the gender effect when all age groups are considered at the same time. The following lines give the gender effects separately by age group. The analysis has been restricted to those aged twenty-five and older, as most of the employees with these educations are older.

When we focus on more homogeneous educational groups it is clear that the effect of being female is smaller. Those with technical backgrounds make up the single most important educational group among managers, in 1990 supplying 53.5 percent of employees in ranks 6 and 7. The gender effect on rank in this group, controlling for occupation, was very low: in the −.3 to −.4 range in the 1970-to-1980 period, dropped to −.277 in 1985, and finally to −.199 in 1990. These coefficients were all significantly different from zero at the .05 level, but by 1990 the size was negligible. The average difference in ranks between men and women was a fifth of a rank (out of seven ranks). It is still a difference, but a small one.

Among those with backgrounds in economics and business administration, the gender effect also declined over the years, with some exceptions, to a level of −.352 in 1990, when occupation is taken into account. This is also a small difference of a third of a rank.

In 1990, the gender effect was largest among employees with higher education in social sciences and law but it was still not very large, less than −.5, or half a rank. (It was surprisingly low in 1970, for reasons unknown to us.) One may speculate that the gender effect is smaller in technical fields because job tasks are easier to measure and performance, evaluated in a less subjective way, is less vulnerable to subjective management impressions and self-presentation.

In summary, when we study educational groups that are somewhat homogeneous and that are important for recruitment of managers, the gender effect on rank becomes much smaller—and that has been the case over the entire period. With a more equal distribution of men and women over these educational categories, women's representation in managerial ranks would also have been much closer to parity with men.

This demonstrates the role of sex segregation in educational choice. Had women had the same distribution on education as men, the sex gap in rank would presumably have been close to zero.

More on Pipeline Problem 1: Gender Effects by Age Group

Family obligations are often cited as one reason for the relative lack of women in management. Women with the right kinds of education and experience either do not put in the required effort in order to be promoted or are reluctant to take a promotion if offered one, because they invest a large effort in the family sphere. Our data provide no information on family obligations, but there is nevertheless a way to approach the difficulty of measurement in this area. As women progress in their careers and also in age, they also generally acquire more family responsibilities, especially because of young children. This fact may lead to a higher total effort of women across work and home, but a decrease in the amount put in at work. This may in turn have a negative effect on career progression or at least put women at a disadvantage relative to men. The difference in job investment will show up as higher gaps as age increases, especially at ages thirty-five and up, the age groups where the pressure from children among highly educated women becomes strong at the same time as men's careers tend to take off.

This is why, in the regression analysis depicted in table 6.10, separate effects of being female were estimated for several age groups defined by five-year intervals. The results are quite straightforward. The gap is very small for the younger age groups but then increases. Controlling for occupation, the estimated differences are about a tenth of a rank for those twenty to twenty-four years old and a fifth for those twenty-five to twenty-nine years old, but then doubles to two-fifths of a rank among those thirty to thirty-four years old. This jump probably reflects the increased family obligations in those age groups. Then at higher ages, the gap no longer increases with age, probably reflecting the fact that family obligations do not become more burdensome or even taper off. In both the short and full regression the gender effects peak in four of six years in the age groups forty-five to forty-nine and fifty to fifty-four, reaching an average difference of about a whole rank. Some permanent damage was thus done to women's careers at ages thirty-five to fifty, from which it was hard to recover fully.

For the three education groups considered in table 6.11, the gender effects are considerably smaller in the younger age groups. For example, in 1990 in technical fields it is less than a tenth of a rank among those thirty-five and younger, and only a fifth of a rank among those thirty-six to forty years old. The pattern is similar among those in economics and business, as well as among those in the social sciences and law, but with slightly bigger gender effects. The gender effect peaks at different ages across the years and educational fields. In technical fields it peaks at ages forty-six to fifty, after which it declines.

Interpreting Discrimination, Life Cycle, and Cohort

How are the results in tables 6.10 and 6.11 to be interpreted? There are several possibilities. A first interpretation is that employers systematically discriminate: when women reach a certain age and a career stage they also reach a career plateau beyond which they do not rise. Under this interpretation there should be a widening of the gender gap with age. This is the glass-ceiling hypothesis.

A second interpretation, stemming from the pipeline 1 problem discussed earlier, is that life-cycle effects are operating. Women may have the right kinds of education and experiences but either they do not put in the required effort to be promoted or they are reluctant to take a promotion if offered one. The reason for refusing promotion might be the larger effort they invest in the family sphere, the area where an unequal division of labor persists. As women progress in their careers and also in age, they on average acquire more family responsibilities. If they decrease the effort put into work, they are likely to be at a disadvantage relative to men. This will again show up as higher gaps as age increases, especially in women's early and late thirties. According to this argument, we should expect to find a widening of the gap in the age groups thirty to fifty. Above age fifty the gap should decrease slightly, as many of these women can increase their work effort and perhaps partially recoup some of what they lost earlier. Under this interpretation the gap should increase with age, then flatten out, and perhaps subsequently decline.

A third interpretation is that we here see the operation of reduced discrimination over time, which shows up as distinct cohort effects. Older women entered the labor market during periods when there was more sex discrimination. Those women were then placed at lower ranks within their chosen occupation and workplace. They could also have experienced more limited opportunities for choosing occupations and firms. Initial placement, especially in occupation and firm, may have long-lasting effects. And this may be the case even though more opportunities opened up for women over the twenty-year period. Having been denied the opportunity early in their career to run in a race that lasts for many years, women might find it difficult to reenter at a later stage, and it is too late to start over again. Thus the pattern of gender effects that we observe in the cross-section may reflect the differences that existed when an age group entered the labor market.

Under this interpretation, there should in the cross-section be an increase in the gap with age but within a given birth cohort the gap should remain more or less constant as its members get older. This pattern would then reflect diminished discrimination over time. Such a trend could also be reinforced by differential adaptations to anticipated discrimination, whereby the younger cohorts to a larger degree make more investment in education and work than older cohorts because they observed the decline in discrimination and hence the increased rewards to such investments.

These three interpretations—discrimination, life-cycle, and cohort effects—may all hold to some degree. To explore these, we need to report the age pattern for sex differences separately by birth cohort rather than for each cross-section, as in tables 6.10 and 6.11. At the top of table 6.12, which is a rearrangement of table 6.10, eleven birth cohorts are distinguished, from the birth cohort 1910 to 1914, who were fifty-six to sixty years old in 1970, to the birth cohort 1960 to 1964, who were twenty-one to twenty-five years old in 1985. In each column, for each cohort, we report the gender effect for each five-year interval from 1970 to 1990, dropping the "off" year, 1978, from the table. This shows the evolution of the sex differential in a given cohort as its members get older. For some cohorts we get only two points of data, because they were either too young or too old to contribute more data points in the period covered, whereas we can follow other cohorts over the entire twenty-year period.

Within a given year, say 1980, we see the clear pattern of gender effects by age in the cross-section, as already shown in table 6.10: the gap increases with age, from a quarter of a rank to slightly above one and a quarter ranks. Within cohorts, as

TABLE 6.12 / Effect in Sweden of Being Female on Job Rank, from Short and Full Regressions, by Birth Cohort, in 1970 and Later

	Birth Cohort										
	1910–1914	1915–1919	1920–1924	1925–1929	1930–1934	1935–1939	1940–1944	1945–1949	1950–1955	1955–1959	1960–1964
	1	2	3	4	5	6	7	8	9	10	11
Short											
1970	-1.349	-1.485	-1.368	-1.395	-1.249	-0.952	-0.599	-0.539			
1975	-1.270	-1.339	-1.354	-1.385	-1.312	-1.172	-0.860	-0.625	-0.506		
1980		-1.303	-1.262	-1.294	-1.283	-1.197	-0.977	-0.707	-0.418	-0.264	
1985			-1.157	-1.168	-1.153	-1.112	-0.983	-0.820	-0.609	-0.387	-0.308
1990				-1.072	-1.023	-1.032	-0.960	-0.838	-0.689	-0.488	-0.299
Full											
1970	-0.830	-0.905	-0.839	-0.831	-0.719	-0.471	-0.180	-0.111			
1975	-1.164	-1.227	-1.247	-1.264	-1.195	-1.066	-0.771	-0.556	-0.434		
1980		-1.195	-1.161	-1.180	-1.185	-1.096	-0.886	-0.639	-0.388	-0.209	
1985			-1.045	-1.051	-1.054	-0.999	-0.890	-0.742	-0.541	-0.314	-0.216
1990				-0.937	-0.907	-0.905	-0.844	-0.744	-0.614	-0.412	-0.227

Source: Reprinted from Petersen and Meyerson (1999, table 24), with permission from Elsevier.

Note: These numbers are all taken from table 10. They have here been reorganized so that in each column we follow a given birth cohort as they get older with five years from one period to the next, where periods are defined by 1970, 1975, 1980, 1985, and 1990. In the case of the 1910 to 1914 cohort we follow them from 1970 to 1975, when they were 56 to 60 and 61 years old or more. In the case of the 1940 to 1944 cohort we follow them every five years for the entire twenty-year period, from 1970, when they were 26 to 30, to 1990, when they were 46 to 50 years old.

All coefficients are significantly different from 0 at better than the 1 percent level; in fact all of them are better than at the 0.1 percent level.

one reads down a column across five-year intervals, the gap stays relatively constant as a cohort grows older, but there are very big differences between cohorts. This empirical finding points to the cohort interpretation of the age effect on the gender rank gap, a pattern that probably stems from reduced discrimination over time. For most of the cohorts there is a slight increase in the gap in the early part of the career, but then a comparable slight decrease in the later part. This additional pattern, occurring within the broader pattern of large cohort effects, is consistent with a life-cycle interpretation. We see a variation in impact of age consistent with variations in family obligations. But the cohort effects on the sex gap are more substantial than the within-cohort effects of age.

In figure 6.1 we visually present the patterns in table 6.12. The year 1970 is dropped, as it deviates from later years for reasons not known to us. We see the clear, flat pattern of the gap in rank as a cohort grows older, in both the short and full regressions. We also see the marked cohort differences, with much larger gaps in older cohorts. This is exactly the same pattern shown for U.S. engineers by Laurie Morgan (1998, figure 1).

In conclusion, there is no question that very strong cohort effects are seen in the glass ceiling. The year of birth had a strong effect on how women did relative to men, and this impact remains more or less constant over the life cycle. This is strong evidence for a decline in the extent of discrimination over the period. To distinguish between discrimination and the life-cycle effects is challenging, but on balance, to the extent that there are effects in addition to those of cohort, the life-cycle effects seem to be prevalent. This is so because within a cohort the gender effects by age seem to follow a U-shape pattern, initially increasing slightly, then slightly decreasing. Such a pattern is what one would expect if adaptation to family circumstances is more important in female than male careers.

These considerations are essential to concerns about the glass ceiling. For further elaboration, we therefore present in table 6.13 the same compilation of numbers for the three educational subfields, assembled from table 6.11. Here, too, there are strong cohort effects. We see precisely the same pattern of age effects within a cohort. A plausible interpretation is again that the older cohorts entered more hostile labor markets, and the effects remain with them. Another is that the older cohorts of women differed in certain attributes such as experience or lifestyle, perhaps devoting more time to family relative to paid labor than women in younger cohorts do.

Beyond initial placement in occupation and firms, which certainly affects subsequent attainment, what can account for the fact that the older women remained so disadvantaged throughout their careers even as the labor market became friendlier to women? We can only speculate. One possible reason is that the promotion decisions for these women were made mostly by older men who grew up in labor-market environments hostile to women. Perhaps these men continued to act according to norms thought perfectly legitimate twenty to thirty years ago. Each generation may have its own set of norms and worldviews. And when the older employees tend to make many of the important decisions about younger employ-

FIGURE 6.1   /   Effect in Sweden of Being Female on Rank, by Birth Cohort for Each Year

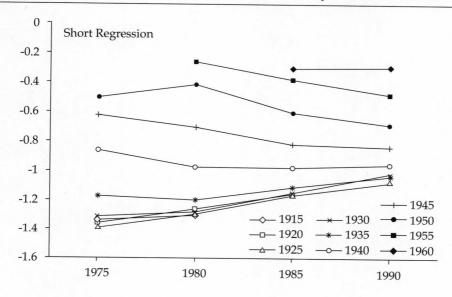

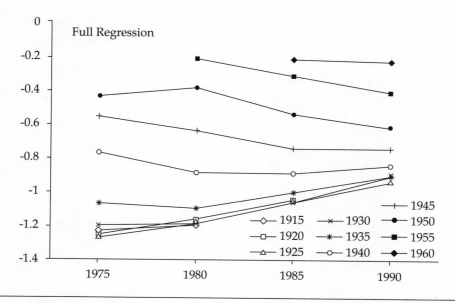

Sources: Reprinted from Petersen and Meyerson (1999, figure 1) with permission from Elsevier.

TABLE 6.13 / Effect in Sweden of Being Female on Job Rank from Short and Full Regressions, by Birth Cohort and Type of Education, 1970 to 1990

		Birth Cohort								
	1910–1914	1915–1919	1920–1924	1925–1929	1930–1934	1935–1939	1940–1944	1945–1949	1950–1954	1955–1959
	1	2	3	4	5	6	7	8	9	10
Social sciences, law										
Short										
1970		−0.247*	−0.691*	−0.867	−1.266	−0.321*	−0.114*			
1975		−0.834	−0.784*	−1.701	−1.172	−0.885	−0.447	−0.464		
1980		−0.588*	−1.669	−1.873	−0.885	−1.004	−0.606	−0.564	−0.231	
1985			−1.521	−1.760	−0.918	−1.018	−0.530	−0.594	−0.241	−0.003*
1990				−2.275	−0.903	−1.109	−0.590	−0.606	−0.416	−0.103*
Full										
1970		0.096*	−0.406*	−0.598*	−0.724	−0.408	−0.005*			
1975		−0.622*	−0.402*	−1.488	−0.928	−0.885	−0.335	−0.296		
1980		−0.402*	−1.315	−1.241	−0.814	−0.851	−0.520	−0.521	−0.168*	
1985			−1.289	−1.171	−0.842	−0.832	−0.485	−0.534	−0.284	−0.003*
1990				−1.738	−0.824	−0.902	−0.534	−0.552	−0.422	−0.103*
Economics, business administration										
Short										
1970	−0.674	−0.750	−1.098	−0.989	−1.088	−0.899	−0.536			
1975	−1.480	−1.273	−0.767	−0.897	−1.297	−1.204	−0.676	−0.437		
1980		−0.915	−0.845	−0.856	−1.161	−0.984	−0.831	−0.466	−0.265	
1985			−0.804	−1.099	−0.957	−0.905	−0.939	−0.636	−0.433	−0.175
1990				−0.827	−0.989	−0.893	−0.833	−0.714	−0.567	−0.322

	1	2	3	4	5	6	7	8	9	10
Full										
1970	−0.249	−0.425	−0.770	−0.605	−0.593	−0.420	−0.270			
1975	−1.185	−1.184	−0.761	−0.743	−1.205	−1.182	−0.636	−0.320		
1980		−0.835	−0.816	−0.757	−1.136	−0.963	−0.773	−0.447	−0.165	
1985			−0.732	−0.905	−0.908	−0.788	−0.886	−0.577	−0.352	−0.126
1990				−0.690	−0.912	−0.773	−0.720	−0.638	−0.485	−0.254
Technical fields										
Short										
1970	−0.927	−0.757	−1.012	−0.937	−0.541	−0.530	−0.143			
1975	0.516	−0.501	−0.892	−0.955	−0.692	−0.602	−0.413	−0.225		
1980		−0.537	−0.658	−0.872	−0.965	−0.661	−0.405	−0.301	−0.003	
1985			−0.765	−0.775	−0.848	−0.695	−0.480	−0.416	−0.149	−0.005
1990				−0.483	−0.720	−0.541	−0.443	−0.427	−0.232	−0.101
Full										
1970	−0.538	−0.550	−0.791	−0.791	−0.478	−0.402	−0.109			
1975	0.488	−0.412	−0.775	−0.892	−0.645	−0.549	−0.386	−0.218		
1980		−0.438	−0.613	−0.809	−0.919	−0.635	−0.387	−0.296	−0.002	
1985			−0.703	−0.732	−0.763	−0.635	−0.443	−0.398	−0.136	−0.004
1990				−0.402	−0.689	−0.514	−0.430	−0.410	−0.228	−0.100

Source: Reprinted from Petersen and Meyerson (1999, table 25), with permission from Elsevier.

Note: These numbers are all taken from table 11. They have here been reorganized so that in each column we follow a given birth cohort as they get older with five years from one period to the next, where periods are defined by 1970, 1975, 1980, 1985, 1990. In the case of the 1910 to 1914 cohort we follow them from 1970 to 1975, when they were 56 to 60 and 61 and above. In the case of the 1940 to 1944 cohort we follow them every five years for the entire twenty-year period, from 1970, when they were 26 to 30, to 1990, when they were 46 to 50 years old.

*Not significantly different from 0 at the 5 percent level.

ees, those decisions easily come to reflect the values the older employees were socialized into.

SUMMARY

Data from the United States in the 1980s show that there are few women at the top ranks in the professions and management, both in absolute terms and relative to women's numerical presence in organizations. A case study of a large visible U.S. firm from the same period showed that this glass ceiling is not due to differential promotion rates. Men and women are promoted at about the same rate. It is due rather to a "frozen pipeline" of qualified female candidates. There were very few women with both the education and experience required for reaching the top positions in the firm. There were twenty-seven men with twenty-one years or more seniority in the company for each woman with the same tenure.

Sweden provides an important test case for investigating the issues in connection with the glass ceiling, due primarily to its extensive family policies, which mandate generous and universal provision of child care, maternity-leave policies, and more, which may facilitate combining family and career and thus aid women in achieving professional success. We thus turned to an investigation of the glass ceiling in Sweden, using data for a twenty-one-year period, 1970 to 1990.

There is a glass ceiling also in Sweden: there are very few women in the top two ranks within organizations, in absolute terms and relative to women's numerical presence in the organizations. Over the last twenty years, however, the position of women has improved markedly relative to men. More women are in the next-to-top ranks within their chosen occupations.

There are several sources of this glass ceiling, stemming not only from potential employer discrimination but also from at least three distinct supply-side, or "frozen-pipeline," problems.

As for employer discrimination, its existence and magnitude are difficult to assess. What is clear, however, is that it has declined sharply over the twenty-one-year period from 1970 to 1990: from a total of seven ranks, the gender gap dropped from an average of two ranks to one, and these gaps shrank more after controlling for relevant personal-level characteristics.

Looking at the evolution of the gap in rank by following birth cohorts over time gives even more striking results. In the cross-section, when the gender gap in rank is investigated separately by age group, there is a consistent increase in gap with age. This could be—and often is—interpreted as being due to employer discrimination: at a certain age and career stage, women reach a glass ceiling beyond which they cannot progress, whereas male careers continue to improve. However, when seen from the viewpoint of a birth cohort, as each cohort progresses in age, the gender gap in rank remains fairly stable. There are however large differences between birth cohorts. The gap is much smaller, at each given age, among younger cohorts. Those who were fifty years old in 1990 experienced a clearly lower gap than those who were fifty in 1970. This points to diminished discrimination over time as each cohort enters the labor market. The finding is consistent with a cohort interpretation of the glass ceiling (see Morgan 1998): the time of entry into the labor market matters more than specific barriers that arise during a career.

As for pipeline problems, the glass ceiling clearly results in large part from the different educational choices of men and women. In the Swedish case, managers in the manufacturing firms that dominate its economy are recruited from a limited cluster of educational backgrounds, mostly technical fields such as engineering and to a lesser degree economics and business administration. Women still lack strong presence in these fields. As late as 1990, among the white-collar employees studied here, for each female civil engineer there were eight men and for each female MBA there were two men. Those numbers were dramatically more skewed in earlier years.[12] Within each of three broad educational fields, the gender gap in rank is quite small, especially in the important technical field, which includes engineering, which evidenced a gap of less than a fifth of a rank in 1990. It is thus not disparate treatment of men and women within a given educational field that is the principal problem but rather the unequal distribution of men and women in educational fields. Had this distribution been equal, the gender gap in rank would also have dropped strongly, with 80 percent to about a fifth of a rank among the important group of engineers and civil engineers.

Another pipeline problem comes from the domestic division of labor, whereby women do most of the work to maintain the household and care for children. This career withdrawal results in women's accumulating less experience and doing a lot of part-time work, both of which limit their likelihood of future promotion. In the top two ranks, the women's average age is five to seven lower than men's, indicating that employers face pools of women who on average have less experience than men, but also that employers perhaps are willing to appoint to top positions women who are younger than men.

There is some suggestive evidence in our analysis of the impact of the domestic division of labor. It shows up in the age pattern of the gender gap in rank. As summarized earlier, within each birth cohort there is a small increase in the gender gap as one goes from the twenty-to-twenty-five age group to the thirty-to-fifty age group. But above age fifty, when many women are able to increase their labor-force participation again, the gap stabilizes and sometimes even declines. Family obligations, which may peak for those aged thirty to fifty, make their impact felt through more part-time work, fewer hours, and more withdrawals from careers (see, for example, Shauman and Xie 1996).

The obvious conclusion is that the scarcity of women in the higher ranks results in large part from the dearth of women with appropriate educational backgrounds, full-time status, age, and experience. They were not necessarily selected out by men higher up, but in large measure selected themselves out through educational choices and work adaptations made at earlier stages of their lives.

THE DECLINING SIGNIFICANCE OF GENDER AND THE FUTURE OF THE GLASS CEILING

Is there then evidence for positing a declining significance of gender? To this question our data speak unambiguously. There is in Sweden a very clear declining effect of being female on the average rank reached over the twenty-one-year period studied. Even more important, when we follow birth cohorts, the gap stays relatively constant with age. But the gap is much smaller, at each given age, among younger cohorts. As new cohorts enter the labor market, there is a gradual closing of the gap. There is no question that the significance of gender has declined.

As for forecasting trends, it is significant that the data reveal large cohort effects, with smaller gaps in more recent birth cohorts. This is likely to continue. The role of potential employer discrimination will in all likelihood decline further. Some pipeline problems will also be alleviated. If one extends current trends, one can predict that gender parity in years of education is about to occur, although gender segregation by educational field still is a problem. Men will probably continue to increase their share of household tasks, but high divorce rates and their consequence of women getting child custody will counteract such changes. Family-friendly policies may or may not help dismantle the glass ceiling. The highly unequal wage distribution in the United States is certainly an advantage for professionals and especially for female professionals. In part it gives incentives for being professionally successful and the availability of cheap labor enables women to outsource many domestic tasks. Women in the Scandinavian countries face larger obstacles in this regard.

The important role of women's own choices in explaining the gender gap in rank calls for more attention to the factors that influence those choices. As Richard Breen and Cecilia García-Peñalosa (2002) emphasize, women's choices may be made in anticipation of future discrimination in a male-dominated labor market. These authors posit that even high-ability women may base their choices regarding education, occupation, and hours worked on the expectation that they will be the primary caregivers of their families, as their mothers and grandmothers were.

Policies aimed at easing women's participation in the labor market can, as already mentioned, have mixed effects. Breen and García-Peñalosa point out the paradoxical empirical fact that even though the Swedish and other Scandinavian welfare states have tried to make the combination of parenting and labor-market participation less burdensome for both men and women, occupational sex segregation is still higher in Sweden than in many other Western countries (see Meyersson Milgrom, Petersen, and Snartland 2001; Breen and García-Peñalosa 2002, table 1). This suggests that alleviating the gender gap in rank may not be a matter solely of letting time pass and letting younger cohorts enter managerial ranks. Child-care and maternity-leave policies that make part- and reduced-time employment more attractive, especially for women, are helpful for the women they assist, but they may nevertheless contribute to the maintenance of glass ceiling, because women who choose reduced hours typically disqualify themselves from the highest-ranked jobs.

As long as women bear the primary burden of home and family, a gender gap in rank is likely to persist. The top jobs in industry are largely filled by people who invest heavily in their careers, and such investments are diminished by home-care responsibilities. If this analysis is correct, then the gender gap, although already grown smaller, is unlikely to disappear as long as women bear a disproportionate share of home-care obligations. Differences in educational choice have the same effects. As our analysis showed, within homogeneous educational groups, the gender gap in rank has practically vanished in Sweden, but with sex segregation in education a gap will persist.

In light of the results from Sweden, it seems clear that the family-friendly policies of recent years may not overcome the effects of the domestic division of labor (and indeed may possibly exacerbate them). New measures are needed to break the glass ceiling.

This chapter is based on individual-level wage data made available by the main employers' association in Sweden, the Swedish Employers' Confederation (Svenska Arbetsgivare Föreningen, SAF). We are grateful to Ari Hietasalo and Åke Kempe of SAF for their extensive and exceptionally expert cooperation in preparing these data for analysis. We thank Michael Salabasis and John Ekberg at the Stockholm School of Economics for excellent research assistance and Milena Hileman for editorial assistance. We also thank Heather Haveman, Laurie Morgan, and the editors for comments.

An early version of this study was presented at the Industrial Institute for Economic and Social Research (IUI), Stockholm, and Ekonomiska Rådet, Stockholm. We are grateful for financial support from the Swedish Ministry of Labor, the Swedish Council for Research in the Humanities and Social Sciences (HSFR), and the Council for Work Life Research. The tables and some of the text in this paper are taken from Trond Petersen and Laurie Morgan (1995), Eva M. Meyerson and Petersen (1997a), Petersen and Meyerson (1999), and Petersen and Ishak Saporta (2004).

NOTES

1. See, for example, Eva M. Meyersson Milgrom, Trond Petersen, and Vemund Snartland (2001), Meyerson and Petersen (1997b), Petersen et al. (1997), and Petersen and Laurie Morgan (1995). One unusually careful study has challenged this conclusion (Bayard et al. 2003), claiming that the within-job wage gap is on the order of 10 to 15 percent, but this study used less-than-ideal data. Hourly wages are imputed from annual earnings, and reported weeks and usual hours worked per week, possibly from several different

jobs held at same and different times during the year. The earnings data pertain to the year prior to the measures of occupation and establishment, 1989 versus 1990.

2. See, for example, Ann M. Morrison and Mary Ann Von Glinow (1990), U.S. Department of Labor (1991), Yvonne B. Due (1991), Marilyn J. Davidson and Cary L. Cooper (1992), and Irmelin Drage and Anne G. Solberg (1995). According to "A Report on the Glass Ceiling Initiative" (U.S. Department of Labor 1991, 6): "Minorities and women have made significant gains at the entry level of employment into the first levels of management. Yet they have not experienced similar gains into the mid- and senior levels of management notwithstanding increased experience, credentials, overall qualifications, and a greater attachment to the work force."

3. For Sweden specifically, the main focus of the present study, see the empirical studies by James Albrecht, Anders Björklund, and Susan Vroman (2003), Martha Blomquist (1994), Mia Hultin (1996), and Cecilia Jonung (1996), as well as the summaries of some current knowledge and what needs to be done in Statens Offentliga Utredningar SOU (1998). See also the early and perceptive discussion concerning conditions in the 1920s to 1930s in Karin Kock (1938, see especially 443–44).

4. A large-scale international comparison, which includes Norway and Sweden and several other countries, is found in Erik Olin Wright, Janeen Baxter, and Gunn E. Birkelund (1995), elaborated in Wright (1997, chapter 12), and also summarized by Birkelund ("Kvinner og Ledelse-Norge en Sinke," *Dagbladet*, June 24, 1995). Wright, Baxter, and Birkelund (1995) describe the broad patterns of cross-national variations in gender inequality at the higher levels of organizations.

5. Although attained education levels for young men and women are about the same today, there are still large differences in choices of education types (Jonsson 1997a). Janne O. Jonsson (1997b, figure 1.2, 20) shows how segregation in education choices in Sweden decreased from early cohorts to later ones.

6. Despite the fact that productivity in household tasks has increased, household-work hours have not changed over the last hundred years in Sweden. A household spends between fifty and fifty-seven hours per week on household work. The composition of household tasks has changed (see Nyberg 1989). Having both parents working full-time in addition to fifty hours of household work creates problems for men and women, whether they are both career-oriented or not. For a discussion, see Magnus Henrekson (1999). For a discussion of time-use and the division of labor see also Ragni H. Kitterød (1995).

7. Among all managerial, administrative, and professional employees, entrants and existing ones, the annual promotion rate over the 1978-to-1986 period is fairly stable, ranging from 15.9 to 20.4 percent. It appears not to be affected by fluctuations in departures and net growth. The departure rate hovers around 4 to 7 percent, reaching an entire 8.5 percent in 1981. The net growth rate in employment is mostly between 5 and 7 percent, but reached 13.5 percent in 1980 and a low of –.3 percent in 1986.

8. The BNT code was developed first in 1955 and has been revised several times since (Statens Offentliga Utredningar 1993, 204; Svenska Arbetsgivareföreningen 1982). Its main purpose was to aid in the collection of wage statistics. It was initially not intended for setting wages for jobs and individuals. The system of BNT codes is not very different from the salary-grade ranks in use in many large U.S. organizations. A salary grade level indicates the level of responsibility and qualifications of the incumbent in the po-

sition, but without there being a strong tie between the grade level and the actual salary itself, though a clear correlation exists (Spilerman 1986).

9. In 1990, there were 4.5 million economically active persons in Sweden; 4.1 million of them were employees, 2.4 in the private sector and 1.7 million in the public sector.

10. Studies of job advertisements in newspapers confirm this conjecture. When employers advertise jobs, they typically demand quite specific qualifications—not only engineers, but, more specifically, say, chemical engineers. Even different kinds of economic education have their separate niches (see Larsen 1995).

11. We also did a subset of these analyses using an ordered probit model. The substantive results were similar. The interpretation of quantities in that model is cumbersome and it requires presentation of considerably more information with no obvious gain in insight.

12. A study of U.S. engineers in the period 1982 to 1989 found very small gender earnings differences of 1 to 4 percent among younger cohorts, who graduated in 1972 to 1989 (Morgan 1998). The differences stayed constant or became smaller over the seven-year period, even thirteen to sixteen years after graduation. Karin Vangsnes (1992) reports, in Norway, similar small differences among engineers forty or younger.

REFERENCES

Acker, John. 1990. "Hierarchies, Jobs, Bodies: A Theory of Gendered Organization." *Gender and Society* 4(June): 139–58.

Albrecht, James, Anders Björklund, and Susan Vroman. 2003. "Is There a Glass Ceiling in Sweden?" *Journal of Labor Economics* 21(1): 145–77.

Albrecht, James W., Per-Anders Edin, Susan B. Vroman, and Marianne Sundström. 1999. "Career Interruptions and Subsequent Earnings: A Reexamination Using Swedish Data." *Journal of Human Resources* 34(2): 294–311.

Arrow, Kenneth J. 1973. "The Theory of Discrimination." In *Discrimination in Labor Markets*, edited by Orley Aschenfelter and Albert Rees. Princeton: Princeton University Press.

Barnett, William S., James N. Baron, and Toby E. Stuart. 2000. "Avenues of Attainment: Occupational Demography and Organizational Careers in the California Civil Service." *American Journal of Sociology* 106(1): 88–144.

Båvner, Per. 2001. *Half-Full or Half Empty? Part-Time Work and Well–Being Among Swedish Women*. Stockholm: Swedish Institute for Social Research, working paper no. 49/2001.

Bayard, Kimberly, Judith Hellerstein, David Neumark, and Kenneth Troske. 2003. "New Evidence on Sex Segregation and Sex Differences in Wages from Matched Employee-Employer Data." *Journal of Labor Economics* 21(4): 887–922.

Bielby, William T., and James N. Baron. 1986. "Men and Women at Work: Sex Segregation and Statistical Discrimination." *American Journal of Sociology* 91(4): 759–99.

Blau Francine D., and Marianne A. Ferber. 1987. "Discrimination: Empirical Evidence from the United States." *American Economic Review* 77(2): 316–20.

Blau, Francine D., and Lawrence Kahn. 1996. "Wage Structure and Gender Earnings Differentials: An International Comparison." *Economica* 63(supplement): S29–62.

———. 1997. "Swimming Upstream: Trends in the Wage Gender Wage Differentials in the 1980s." *Journal of Labor Economics* 15(1): 1–42.

Blomquist, Martha. 1994. *Könshierarkier i Gungning: Kvinnor i Kunskapsföretag. Studia Sociologica Upsaliensia*, no. 39. Uppsala, Sweden. Acta Universitatis Upsaliensis.

Breen, Richard, and Cecilia García-Peñalosa. 2002. "Bayesian Learning and Gender Segregation." *Journal of Labor Economics* 20(4): 899–922.

Butterfield, D. Anthony, and Gary N. Powell. 1997. "Effect of Race on Promotion to Top Management in a Federal Department." *Academy of Management Journal* 40(1): 112–28.

Davidson, Marilyn J., and Cary L. Cooper. 1992. *Shattering the Glass Ceiling: The Woman Manager*. London: Paul Chapman.

DiPrete, Thomas. 1989. *The Bureaucratic Labor Market*. New York: Plenum Press.

Drage, Irmelin, and Anne G. Solberg. 1995. *Gjennom Glasstaket* [Through the Glass Ceiling]. Oslo: TANO AS.

Due, Yvonne B. 1991. *Køn, Karriere, Familie*. Denmark: Jurist-og Økonomiförbundets Forlag.

Equal Employment Opportunity Commission. 2003. *Characteristics of Private Sector Employment*. Washington, D.C.

Fritzell, Johan. 1991. *Icke av Marknaden Allena: Inkomstfördelningen i Sverige*. Stockholm: Almqvist & Wiksell International.

Fuchs, Victor. 1988. *Women's Quest for Economic Equality*. Cambridge, Mass.: Harvard University Press.

Gerhart, Barry A., and George T. Milkovich. 1989. "Salaries, Salary Growth, and Promotions of Men and Women in a Large Private Firm." In *Pay Equity: Empirical Inquiries*, edited by Robert T. Michael, Heidi I. Hartmann, and Brigid O'Farrell. Washington, D.C.: National Academy Press.

Gneezy, Uri, Muriel Niederle, and Aldo Rustichini. 2003. "Performance in Competitive Environments: Gender Differences." *Quarterly Journal of Economics* 118: 1049–74.

Haas, Linda. 1991. "Equal Parenthood and Social Policy: Lessons from a Study of Parental Leave in Sweden." In *Parental Leave and Child Care: Setting a Research and Policy Agenda*, edited by Janet S. Hyde and Marilyn J. Essex. Philadelphia, Pa.: Temple University Press.

Hakim, Catherine. 2000. *Work-Lifestyle Choices in the 21st Century*. New York: Oxford University Press.

Hartmann, Heidi I. 1987. "Internal Labor Markets and Gender: A Case Study of Promotion." In *Gender in the Workplace*, edited by Clair Brown and Joseph A. Pechman. Washington, D.C.: Brookings Institution.

Henrekson, Magnus. 1999. " Tjänstesektorn och jämställdheten bland näringslivets högre chefer [The Service Sector and Gender Equality Among Executives in Swedish Industry]." *Kvinnovetenskaplig Tidskrift* 20(3).

Hoem, Jan. 1993. "Public Policy as the Fuel of Fertility: Effects of Policy Reform on the Pace of Childbearing in Sweden in the 1980s." *Acta Sociologica* 36(1): 19–31.

Hultin, Mia. 1996. "Gender Differences in Authority Attainment—The Swedish Case." Unpublished manuscript. Sofi: University of Stockholm.

Hultin, Mia, and Ryszard Szulkin. 1999. "Wages and Unequal Access to Organizational Power: An Empirical Test of Gender Discrimination." *Administrative Science Quarterly* 44: 453–72.

Jacobs, Jerry A. 1996. "Gender Inequality and Higher Education." *Annual Review of Sociology* 22: 153–85.

Jonsson, Janne O. 1997a. "Utbildningsskillnader mellan män och kvinnor." In *Vilka är de och hur kan de förklaras?*, edited by Egon Hemlin. Stockholm: Riksbankens Jubileumsfond & Gidlunds Förlag.

————. 1997b. "Hur skall vi förklara könsskillnader I utbildningsval?" In *Glastak och glasväggar? Den könssegregerade arbetsmarknaden*, edited by Inga Persson and Eskil Wadensjö. SOU publication 137. Arbetsmarknadsdepartementet.

Jonung, Cecilia. 1996. "Economic Theories of Occupational Segregation by Sex—Implications for Change over Time." In *Gender Specific Occupational Segregation*, edited by P. Bergman. Nuremberg, Germany: Institut für Arbeitsmarkt-Und Berufsforschung der Bundesanstalt für Arbeit.

Kamerman, Sheila B. 1991. "Child Care Policies and Programs: An International Overview." *Journal of Social Issues* 47(2): 179–96.

Kanter, Rosabeth M. 1977. *Men and Women of the Corporation*. New York: Basic Books.

Kitterød, Ragni H. 1995. "Time Use and Division of Labour Among Norwegian and Swedish Parents." In *Building Family Welfare*, edited by Birgit Arves-Pares. Stockholm: Nordstedts Tryckeri, AB.

Kock, Karin. 1938. *Kvinnoarbetet i Sverige*. Ur betankandet, Angående gifta kvinnors förvärvsarbete. Avgivet av Kvinnoarbetskommittén. SOU 1938: 47.

Larsen, Knut Arlid. 1995. *Søking og rekryttering til ledige stillinger*. Report no. 1996:2. Oslo: Arbeidsdirektoratet, Kontor for statistikk og planlegging.

Lewis, Gregory B. 1986. "Gender and Promotion." *Journal of Human Resources* 21(3): 406–19.

Meyerson, Eva M. 1992. *The Impact of Ownership Structure and Team Composition on Firm Performance*. Report prepared for the Industrial Institute for Economic and Social Research. Stockholm: Almqvist & Wiksell.

Meyerson, Eva M., and Trond Petersen. 1997a. "Finns det ett Glastak för Kvinnor? En Studie av Svenska Arbetsplatser i Privat Näringsliv 1970–1990." In *Glastak och Glasväggar? Den Könssegregerade Arbetsmarknaden*, edited by Inga Persson and Eskil Wadensjö. SOU 1997:137. Stockholm: Fritzes.

————. 1997b. "Lika Lön för Lika Arbete: En Studie av Svenska Förhållanden i Internationell Belysning." In *Kvinnors och Mäns Löner. Varför Så Olika?*, edited by E. Wadensjö and I. Persson. SOU publication 1997:136. Stockholm: Fritzes.

Meyersson Milgrom, Eva M., Trond Petersen, and Vemund Snartland. 2001. "Equal Pay for Equal Work? Evidence from Sweden, Norway and the U.S." *Scandinavian Journal of Economics* 4: 559–83.

Morgan, Laurie. 1998. "Glass-Ceiling Effect or Cohort Effect? A Longitudinal Study of the Gender Earnings Gap for Engineers, 1982 to 1989." *American Sociological Review* 63(4): 479–93.

Morrison, Ann M., and Mary Ann Von Glinow. 1990. "Women and Minorities in Management." *American Psychologist* 45(2): 200–8.

National Research Council. 2001. *From Scarcity to Visibility. Gender Differences in the Careers of Doctoral Scientists and Engineers*, edited by J. Scott Long. Washington, D.C.: National Academy Press.

Niederle, Muriel, and Lise Vesterlund. 2005. "Do Women Shy Away from Competition? Do Men Compete Too Much?" NBER Working Paper No. 11464. Cambridge, Mass.: National Bureau of Economic Research.

Nyberg, Anita. 1989. "Hushållsteknik—mödrars möda och mäns makt?" In *Teknokrati, Arbete och Makt*, edited by S. Beckman. Stockholm: Carlsson.

OECD. 1995. "Long-Term Leave for Parents in OECD Countries." *Employment Outlook* (July): 171–202. Paris: Organisation for Economic Co-operation and Development, Department of Economics and Statistics.

Paulin, Elisabeth A., and Jennifer M. Mellor. 1996. "Gender, Race, Promotion Within a Private Sector Firm." *Industrial Relations* 135(2): 375–92.

Petersen, Trond. 1995. "Analysis of Event Histories." In *Handbook of Statistical Modeling for the Social and Behavioral Sciences*, edited by Gerard Arminger, Clifford C. Clogg, and Michael E. Sobel. New York: Plenum Press.

Petersen Trond, and Eva M. Meyerson. 1999. "More Glory and Less Injustice: The Glass Ceiling in Sweden, 1970–1990." In *Research in Social Stratification and Mobility*, edited by Kevin T. Leicht. Greenwood, Conn.: JAI Press.

Petersen, Trond, and Laurie A. Morgan. 1995. "Separate and Unequal: Occupation-Establishment Segregation and the Gender Wage Gap." *American Journal of Sociology* 101(2): 329–65.

Petersen, Trond, and Ishak Saporta. 2004. "The Opportunity Structure for Discrimination." *American Journal of Sociology* 108(4): 852–901.

Petersen, Trond, Vemund Snartland, Lars-Erik Becken, and Karen M. Olsen. 1997. "Within-Job Wage Discrimination and the Gender Wage Gap: The Case of Norway." *European Sociological Review* 13(2): 199–214.

Phelps, Edwin S. 1972. "The Statistical Theory of Racism and Sexism." *American Economic Review* 62: 659–61.

Pinker, Steven. 2002. *The Blank Slate*. New York: Penguin Books.

Reskin, Barbara F. 1988. "Bringing the Men Back In: Sex Differentiation and the Devaluation of Women's Work." *Gender and Society* 2(1): 58–81.

Reskin, Barbara F., and Heidi I. Hartmann, eds. 1986. *Women's Work, Men's Work: Sex Segregation on the Job*. Washington, D.C.: National Academy Press.

Rønsen, Marit, and Marianne Sundström. 1996. "Maternal Employment in Scandinavia: A Comparison of the After-Birth Employment Activity of Norwegian and Swedish Women." *Journal of Population Economics* 9(3): 267–85.

Rosenfeld, Rachel A. 1992. "Job Mobility and Career Processes." *Annual Review of Sociology* 18: 39–61.

Shauman, Kimberly A., and Yue A. Xie. 1996. "Geographic Mobility of Scientists: Sex Differences and Family Constraints." *Demography* 33(4): 455–68.

Spilerman, Seymour. 1986. "Organizational Rules and the Features of Work Careers." *Research in Social Stratification and Mobility* 5: 41–102.

Spilerman, Seymour, and Trond Petersen. 1999. "Organizational Structure, Determinants of Promotion, and Gender Differences in Attainment." *Social Science Research* 28: 203–27.

Statens Offentliga Utredningar (SOU). 1993. *Löneskillnader och lönediskriminering? Om Kvinnor och Män i Arbetsmarknaden*. SOU 1993:7. Stockholm: Allmänna Förlaget.

———. 1998. *Ty Makten Är Din...* SOU 1998:6. Stockholm: Allmänna Förlaget.

Stinchcombe, Arthur L. 1990. *Information and Organization*. Berkeley: University of California Press.

Stroh, Linda K., Jeanne M. Brett, and Anne H. Reilly. 1996. "Family Structure, Glass Ceiling, and Traditional Explanations for the Differential Rate of Turnover of Female and Male Managers." *Journal of Vocational Behavior* 49: 99–118.

Sundström, Marianne. 1982. "Part-time Work and Trade-Union Activities Among Women." *Economic and Industrial Democracy* 3: 561–67.

———. 1991. "Part-time Work in Sweden: Trends and Equality Effects." *Journal of Economic Issues* 25: 167–78.

Svenska Arbetsgivareföreningen. 1982. *Befattningsnomenklatur. Tjänstemän*. Stockholm: SAF Förlag.

Tsui, Anne S., and Barbara Gutek. 1984. "A Role Set Analysis of Gender Differences in Performance, Affective Relationships and Career Success of Industrial Middle Managers." *Academy of Management Journal* 27(3): 619–35.

U.S. Department of Labor. 1981. "National Survey of Professional, Administrative, Technical, and Clerical Pay, March 1981." *BLS*, Bulletin 2108. Washington: U.S. Government Printing Office.

———. 1989. *Facts on Working Women*. Women's Bureau, no. 89-4. Washington: U.S. Government Printing Office.

———. 1991. *A Report on the Glass Ceiling Initiative*. Washington: U.S. Government Printing Office.

Vangsnes, Karin. 1992. *Kvinner med høyere teknisk og økonomisk utdanning i næringslivet*. Oslo: Likestillingsrådet.

Waldfogel, Jane. 1998. "The Family Gap for Young Women in the United States and Britain: Can Maternity Leave Make a Difference?" *Journal of Labor Economics* 16(3): 505–45.

Wright, Erik Olin. 1997. *Class Counts*. New York: Cambridge University Press.

Wright, Erik Olin, Janeen Baxter, and Gunn Elisabeth Birkelund. 1995. "The Gender Gap in Workplace Authority: A Cross-National Study." *American Sociological Review* 60(3): 407–35.

Part III

Possible Futures of Gender Inequality

Chapter 7

Opposing Forces: How, Why, and When Will Gender Inequality Disappear?

Robert Max Jackson

What does the future hold for gender inequality? In the United States and many other countries, women's status has improved remarkably over the past two centuries. Will we continue to move ever closer to full gender equality? Or could gender relations stagnate where they are or even move backward?

That gender remains a crucial aspect of social organization is not in question. In all too many parts of the world women are exposed to humiliations ranging from mockery to rape, from small rituals curtailing their freedom to absolute limitations in what they can do, what they can wear, whom they can marry, and where they can go. Gender is a ruling idea in people's lives—even where egalitarian ideology is common, as among young, affluent, educated Americans—that defines different expectations for behavior, dress, orientation to children, sexuality, and obligations to provide income.

To pose meaningful questions about the possible declining significance of gender is not, therefore, to ask whether gender still matters or even how much it matters. Rather, we want to inquire how the implications of gender for social life have changed. In my work I have sought to show how and why gender inequality has declined over the past two centuries. Here I extend that analysis forward: If the past is a guide to the future, what can we reasonably expect will happen to gender inequality in the future?

For millennia, women everywhere were subordinate to men under the most diverse economic, political, and cultural conditions. But in recent centuries, an extraordinary process has emerged, developed, and diffused across the world, eroding gender inequality, elevating women's status, and transforming modern society.

If a young woman from the early nineteenth century could be whisked into our own time, she would surely be stunned by the improvements in women's status.

Women voting, holding political office, attending college, taking jobs, owning businesses, living on their own, traveling by themselves. Extraordinary! How these images contrast with the society described by Alexis de Tocqueville in the 1830s (1835/1966, 601): "In America, more than anywhere else in the world, care has been taken constantly to trace clearly distinct spheres of action for the two sexes. . . . You will never find American women in charge of the external relations of the family, managing a business, or interfering in politics. "

Contemporary young women often see present conditions differently. Why are so few women in positions of power, they ask? Why are women expected to bear the burden of caring for children or others needing care? Why do women earn less money than men? Why should women have to live with the anxiety about sexual harassment in their offices and still fear attack as they walk down the street?

We have two contrasting visions of women's status. Compared to the restrictions that faced women two centuries ago, the degree to which gender inequality has declined seems remarkable. When weighed against an imagined state of full and unimpeded equality, the continued shortcomings in women's status seem inexplicable and remarkably frustrating. These visions are complementary, not inconsistent. The degree of current gender inequality can only be assessed by means of comparison, to the past or to an imagined future. Therefore, before asking if, how, or to what degree the significance of gender inequality will continue to decline, we need to choose a perspective from which we will make our assessments.

The historical perspective I use focuses on long-term social processes that have determined and will continue to determine the trajectory of gender inequality. I argue that the driving force behind gender inequality's decline over the past two centuries—the *why*—is a redistribution of power and interests that has come about as a result of modern economic and political organization interacting with women's continuous resentment of and resistance to subordination. Thus, the why is not a shift in moral sentiments or a series of disconnected historical developments (although these were part of the historical unfolding) but a series of structural shifts. The actions that drove gender inequality's decline—the *how*—were widely dispersed, involved both women and men, were executed by both ordinary and powerful people, represented both individual and organizational efforts, and were largely motivated by immediate self-interests, not concerns about gender inequality. *When* women will gain equality is indeterminate. I argue that the eventual eradication of gender inequality is an inevitable outcome of these long-term causal forces, which will not be stopped by countervailing forces. However, the pace of inequality's decline can be speeded or slowed by collective action, political maneuvering, or unforeseeable historical upheaval.

While my theoretical analysis of women's rising status suggests a powerful dynamic of change that will extend into the future, some other theorists have argued that countervailing forces threaten to halt continued movement toward gender equality. I contend that these arguments have serious empirical and theoretical flaws.

While theorists have proposed a variety of countervailing forces could threaten continued improvements in women's status, the logical form of their arguments is similar. First, the past improvement in women's status is generally recognized as considerable, although significant inequities remain. Second, the reasons for inequality's past decline are usually left relatively undefined but are commonly assumed to involve a group of historically specific and somewhat contingent events and processes, such as women's movements, wars and other crises, and changes in labor needs of business. Third, some facet of gender inequality, such as childcare, is highlighted as being apparently resistant to change. That a condition resists change is usually inferred from the empirical observation that changes in the condition have not kept pace with women's rising status. The conditions that concern theorists are ones that seem to prevent women competing equally with men. Fourth, it is suggested that the resistance to change characterizing these problematic aspects of inequality may be strong enough to withstand the social and historical forces that might otherwise produce greater equality. Fifth, apparently preferring to err on the safe side, theorists conclude that continued progress toward equality is in jeopardy.

In contrast to this chain of logic, which I consider flawed, I argue that we cannot understand and explain the persistence of gender inequality today until we have an adequate theory explaining inequality's dramatic decline over the past two centuries. By posing a causal theoretical-historical argument and stressing the role of dispersed and structurally induced processes in gender inequality's decline, my theory generally discounts the relevance of short-term changes in the explanation of long-term transitions.

Furthermore, my analysis stresses theoretical concerns over empirical ones. Debates over the trajectory of gender inequality have sometimes been hampered by efforts to declare one empirical finding more accurate or important than another and by reliance on simple projections of past trends. The how, why, and when of gender inequality's decline are better understood as theoretical problems. Like most meaningful theoretical problems, they have an empirical basis and empirical implications. To be sure, the facts of the past and present are the material from which we can fashion images of possible futures, yet only through theories showing how those past facts were produced can we accurately imagine what facts can be expected from the future.

Thus, I suggest that an alternative logic is analytically superior to the reasoning commonly used by those who argue that countervailing forces threaten to stop movement toward equality. First, I contend that gender inequality's decline over the past two centuries has resulted from a complex process that is linked to fundamental elements of modern economic and political structures. The movement of power outside families has made women and men equivalent objects of exploitation and control for economic and political organizations while simultaneously making women's enduring resistance to inequality effective and expandable for the first time. These effects are an unavoidable result of multiple characteristics of the modern order and will continue to be operative as long as the economic and political orders retain their general form. Moreover, the breakdown of inequality has its own secondary capacity to become self-propelling, accelerating and institutionalizing the movement toward equality as has occurred over the past several decades.

I argue, further, that to formulate a plausible argument that this complex process will not continue to move us toward equality would require a theory of countervailing processes with sufficient power to obstruct the engine of change. Such a model must pass both empirical and theoretical tests of sufficiency and plausibility. While some aspects of gender inequality—such as women's child-rearing responsibilities or the sex segregation of occupations—have changed at a disappointing pace, neither their empirical history nor theoretical models of their impact suggest they have the capacity to block the path to equality.

HOW AND WHY HAS GENDER INEQUALITY DECLINED?

Why has male dominance, after persisting stably through many millennia and enduring varied and dramatic economic, political, and cultural upheavals, undergone a steady, progressive decline for the past two centuries? Answering this question is one of the greatest theoretical challenges facing contemporary social science.

In its most general sense, gender inequality refers to the broad range of conditions by which women have been disadvantaged, including their economic opportunities, political standing, legal status, personal freedom, familial obligations, access to education, and cultural representation. Over the past few decades, we have accumulated innumerable studies of gender inequality's experience and causes in every walk of life; studies that document the improvements in women's political, legal, economic, educational, and cultural status; and studies that seek to explain particular aspects of gender inequality's decline, such as women's increased employment, the improvement in women's education, the winning of the vote, or the rise of the modern feminist movement. This research notwithstanding, efforts to discover a general theoretical explanation of the relatively recent broad decline in gender inequality are uncommon.

In my study of gender inequality's two-century decline in the United States, *Destined for Equality* (Jackson 1998), I sought to meet this challenge. In that book I analyzed diverse changes in gender inequality as they accumulated over two hundred years, to develop a theory explaining why this extraordinary transformation has occurred. This theoretical analysis aims to show that a fundamental, comprehensible process has driven gender inequality's decline. This process encompasses and clarifies the many specific changes contributing to gender inequality's decline and the theory incorporates and builds on the existing scholarship about them. Here I will summarize some of the essential points of that theory, provide some illustrative historical contexts that show the theory's intent, and explain the logic behind the theory.[1]

Key Historical Characteristics of Gender Inequality's Decline

When viewed from a distance, the history of women's rising status in the United States appears steady and orderly over the past two centuries, across varied realms of social life. When examined closely, however, this history seems to be woven from an endless variety of broken threads, a multitude of independent events that represent a potpourri of circumstances, actors, motives, strategies, and effects.

The challenge is to connect the continuity of change seen from a distance with the discontinuity seen from close up, to connect the seemingly disparate strands of change and discontinuous events to an enduring set of underlying ultimate causes (see Lieberson and Lynn 2002; Reskin 2003). These enduring causal processes create conditions that induce the proximate causes and outcomes, shaping predispositions, calculations, responses, opportunities, and effects without directly producing or requiring any specific actions or sequence of events. Over time, they create conditions under which diverse actors will pursue strategies consistent with improving the relative status of women although these actors' intentions are to further their self-interests or cope with unavoidable exigencies.

Table 7.1 summarizes the rise in women's status during the past two centuries and some of the areas where inequality still persists. The most important areas of past positive change are legal and political status and economic opportunities, because standings in these arenas largely decide people's opportunities for personal achievements and social status. The legal, political, and economic arenas are also the main loci of power in this society, so that a group's status in these arenas largely decides its treatment. The other categories—higher education, accessibility of divorce, sexuality, and cultural imagery—have a lesser, secondary role in the preservation or erosion of inequality, but they are equally important to the experience of it. Dividing the past two centuries into three broad periods, the table shows how conditions in each of the social arenas became progressively more favorable to women; the final column suggests key remaining unequal conditions that still need considerable change to approach equality.

In the first of the three periods, during the nineteenth century, the state extended to married women legal rights to control income and property. Businesses began hiring young, single women, first from the working class and, later, some from the middle class. Women gained access to secondary education and then some colleges began to admit them. Divorce, while difficult to obtain, became available as an escape from marriage. The ideological denial of women's sexuality was belied by women's increasing interest in obtaining effective contraception. Similarly, women's increasing participation in suffrage activities from the mid-century onward suggests an emergent conception of their identity that was at odds with the idea that men and women should keep to their "separate spheres."

In the first half of the twentieth century, the second period, women gained political status through suffrage. The number of employed women continued to rise, as some white-collar jobs emerged for middle-class, educated women and employers began to hire married women. Women's access to a college education rose steadily throughout the period. Contraception became widely available and middle-class advice manuals gave expression to the increasingly widespread expectation that women could enjoy sex within marriage. While divorce retained considerable stigma, it became much more available and accepted. Depictions of women

TABLE 7.1 / Women's Changing Status in American Society

	Nineteenth Century	Late-Nineteenth to Mid-Twentieth Century	Mid-Twentieth Century to Present	Future Changes Needed for Equality
Legal and political status	Formal legal equality instituted	Formal political equality instituted	Formal economic equality instituted	Equity in high political offices
Economic opportunity	Working-class jobs appear for single women only	Some jobs for married women and for educated women	All kinds of jobs available to all kinds of women	Equity in high-status jobs
Higher education	A few women enter public universities and new women's colleges	Increasing college; little graduate or professional	Full access at all levels	Equal presence in prestigious fields
Divorce	Almost none; made available for dire circumstances	Increasingly available, but difficult	Freely available and accepted	Equity after divorce
Sexuality and reproductive control	Repressive sexuality; little reproductive control	Positive sexuality but double standard; increasing reproductive control	High sexual freedom and reproductive control	End sexual harassment and fear of rape
Cultural image	Virtuous domesticity and subordination	Educated motherhood, capable for employment and public service	Careers, marital equality	End perception of sexes as inherently different

Source: Author's compilation.

as glamorous, smart, and ambitious emerged in popular culture, particularly the movies.

Since the middle of the twentieth century, women's status has risen significantly as women gained positions in all levels of political life and the government formulated varied policies against discrimination. Women's employment levels, the range of jobs they held, and their wages have continued to converge with those of men. Women's college enrollment surpassed men's and women gained full access to advanced degree and professional programs. The emergence of both divorce and women's sexual freedom knocked down more barriers. Although both men's and women's cultural images remained complex and inconsistent, they continued to become more similar, and women were increasingly portrayed as powerful, independent, equal participants in all facets of life.

This brief depiction gives a sense of the breadth of changes contributing to gender inequality's decline and the continuity of that decline over the long term. Continuity is crucial to the theoretical argument: gender inequality has decreased gradually over many generations, and under a wide range of changing political, economic, and cultural conditions. This historical continuity suggests the action of enduring processes or conditions, not specific catalyzing events nor even historical periods. Yet many people sense that even though a lot has changed in the past few decades, improvements in women's status before then were sporadic and relatively isolated in their significance. This is not true. What is true is that the changes' overall impact on people's lives was limited in the beginning—in a context of overwhelming inequality, only so much relief was possible. Nevertheless, during each period, significant changes occurred in each of the areas of social life summarized in table 7.1. The consistently broad sweep of changes to women's status over widely varied facets of life, such as employment, laws, and sexuality, suggests that the central causes must be effective across these different facets of life or changes in some facets must induce changes in others.

The underlying, enduring causal process that has driven the events eroding gender inequality must have left some kind of telltale footprint, visible behind the specific historic causes of these concrete events. A review of some highlights from women's rising legal and political status and their increasing assimilation by the economy will help shine some light on this footprint.

Policies affecting women's legal and political status developed in three overlapping phases. In the first phase, in the nineteenth century, state laws and judicial interpretations gradually gave married women basic, formal legal equality by granting them independent control of inherited property and earned income and the right to make contracts. In the second phase, the state enacted formal political equality between the sexes by granting women the right to vote. In the third phase, since World War II, policies, laws, and court decisions have furthered women's formal economic equality by banning discrimination against them.

The initiative to extend property rights to married women, in the first phase, came from state legislators and businessmen seeking to ensure the collection of debts and to rationalize the law. These "married women's property acts" began to appear about the middle of the nineteenth century. The laws of the state of New York were representative. In 1848 New York State passed "an act for the more effectual protection of the property of married women," which held that "the real and personal property of any female who may . . . marry . . . shall continue her sole and separate property" (Rabkin 1980, 183–87). As more and more states passed such laws, the only apparent role played by a concern for women's status derived from the emergent desire of affluent people to transfer property to their daughters. (This probably reflected a shift to divisible wealth derived from a market economy and the increasing likelihood of having only daughters because of a declining birth rate.)

The second phase, the initiative for woman suffrage, came mainly from middle-class women who made up the suffrage movement, but the process depended greatly on the actions of men, who had complete control of the political apparatus and the votes needed to pass any legislation giving women the vote. In 1848, participants at the Seneca Falls Convention resolved "that it is the duty of the women of this country to secure to themselves their sacred right to the elective vote," and woman suffrage was a publicly contested issue from this point until 1920, when passage of the Nineteenth Amendment to the U.S. Constitution removed all limits on women's voting.

Although the length of this struggle reflects resistance to woman suffrage, the historical record also suggests far more acceptance than we might expect by both ordinary men and politicians (Jackson 1998, 33–46). The first bill proposing a national suffrage amendment was considered in 1868; later Congressional committees repeatedly considered and reported favorably on a suffrage amendment in the 1880s, although prejudice and the fear of political risks combined to prevent its passage by Congress. Obviously, legislators considering suffrage bills were all male. Similarly, in suffrage referenda that occurred in many states after 1890, typically between two-fifths and two-thirds of the male voters supported woman suffrage. Indeed, between 1890 and 1919, through the actions of male legislators and male voters, twenty-six states granted women full or partial suffrage. The reasons that men came to accept woman suffrage are complex, but the historical record suggests that a key role was played by the accumulated knowledge that giving women the vote had little immediate impact on either women's place or the political process.

In the most recent phase, feminist activists seized the initiative to achieve legal and political equality for women. The legislation against discrimination was preceded by a long history of disputes over unequal pay rates for women that stretch back to World War I (U.S. Department of Labor, Women's Bureau 1951) and intensified during World War II. After many states adopted equal pay laws, Congress adopted equal pay for equal work through the Equal Pay Act in 1963; the following year, women were written into the Civil Rights Act of 1964. Later statutes and policies declared discrimination against women illegal in education expenditures, housing, credit, employment, police protection, and divorce—laws preceding modern feminism that became weapons for women fighting discrimination. Women's role in politics and government expanded. Although women remain a minority in electoral offices, between 1970 and 2002 the number of women in the U.S. House of Representatives rose from twelve to sixty; the number in the Senate went from one to thirteen; the percentage of representatives serving in state legislatures who were women increased fivefold, to almost 25 percent; and women's share of the mayoral positions in cities of 30,000 or more went from 1 to 21 percent. These changes reflected the advocacy efforts of the modern women's movement, the maturing effects of woman suffrage, and the long-term accumulation of organizational power's disinterest in gender. Feminist advocates, politicians seeking votes, and officials pursuing rationalization all contributed to these changes.

Across the three phases in which women's legal and political status changed, the principal initiative shifted from men in power to women empowered by past improvements. Men of influence largely motivated and directed the extension of legal rights in the nineteenth century. While the woman suffrage movement provided the voice for suffrage, the transition was implemented by men with exclusive and unchallenged power, as politicians looked for competitive advantages and ordinary men increasingly wavered between neutrality and weak support. In the third phase, the modern feminist movement, broadly conceived, has most often and most consistently taken the initiative, although many important changes show independent influences of rationalized government and political competition (such as the equal pay acts), and most reflect the relative absence of coordinated male opposition. Along the way, behavioral changes by ordinary men (as when they supported suffrage) and ordinary women (as when they supported female politicians) was crucial.

The long-term assimilation of women into the economy was a more decentralized process than legal or political changes, involving even more diverse actors (Jackson 1998, 71–124). Over the nineteenth century, employers hired an ever-rising proportion of the nation's unmarried women, until more than one half of all unmarried women between the ages of fifteen and forty-five earned a wage by 1890 (Jackson 1984, 148, n26). Many women also found employment outside industry in such occupations as agricultural labor, domestic service, and teaching (Hooks 1947). This female labor market was created by unmarried working-class women seeking a mixture of wage supplements and independence (Kessler-Harris 1982; Weiner 1985). Whether they had never married or had lost their husbands, these women had neither the restrictions nor the advantages of marriage. They were hired by male employers, both large and small, who sought cheap labor or gender-specific skills.

This pattern of ever more women seeking jobs and ever more employers seeking to hire them continued through the twentieth century. During the first half of the century, new jobs opening in low-level, white-collar occupations and manual service-sector jobs accounted for much of this gain. Employers hired women as secretaries, clerical workers, telephone operators, beauticians, factory operatives, and store clerks. Middle-class women received employment particularly as teachers but also in other positions demanding education, such as nursing and social work. Employers seeking new labor sources found women a good, lower-paid alternative, particularly for jobs that seemed to fit their education or female-identified skills, such as caretaking or communication (Hooks 1947, 42). By the end of the century women held close to one half of all jobs. For over a century, women's share of jobs in the modern economy rose at a much steadier pace than many historical references suggest (see figure 7.1).[2] The most important change in the pace occurred in the two decades preceding World War II, when employers' dependence on women to fill jobs added by the expanding economy shifted from hiring women for around one-fourth of the new jobs to over one-half, where it remained for the rest of the century.

The long-term continuity of women's rising employment disguises a number of separate underlying causes of this development. In particular, women's move-

FIGURE 7.1 / Women's Rising Share of Paying Jobs, 1870 to 2000

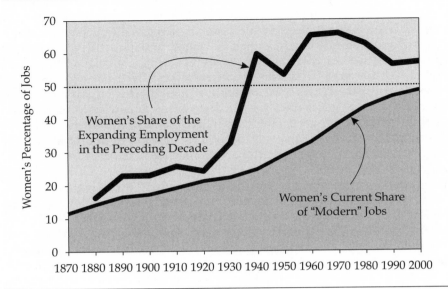

Source: Author's compilation, data from: U.S. Bureau of the Census and Edwards (1943); U.S. Bureau of the Census (1975, 129, 132, 139–40); U.S. Department of Labor (1984, 12, 14, 55, 56); U.S. Bureau of the Census (2004, 391); Hooks (1947, 34, 222, 238).

ment into high-status jobs, to which they previously had little access, from the 1960s forward involved several agents. Whereas most of the preceding rise in women's employment furthered employers' self-interests, to gain high-status jobs women had to fight against resistance ranging from unsympathetic indifference to hostile opposition. The modern feminist movement emerged as a champion of women's rights that could credibly threaten retaliation via effective political mobilization. The government contributed antidiscrimination and affirmative-action policies. Corporate employers responded to these external pressures by rapidly extending the organizational logic of impartial standards. Educational institutions largely did the same.

The Fundamental Sources of Gender Inequality's Decline

As stated earlier, the detailed history of gender inequality's decline is more notable for its irregularity than its continuity: the route to change was composed of extraordinarily diverse, independent, seemingly unpredictable events that were produced by all kinds of actors and conditions for an endless array of reasons. The theoretical challenge is to identify an enduring, pervasive causal process that accounts for the disparate events that constitute the aggregate continuity of gender inequality's decline.

The solution to this historical puzzle concerns the links between the macro-level of social structure—the level at which enduring processes altered the social environment—and the micro-level of decision making and action—the level at which people and organizations responding to concrete historical contexts acted out their interests, opportunities, and beliefs. Arthur Stinchcombe (1968, 188) remarked that "the significance of a value for social life depends on whether it is associated with power or not. . . . To have any appreciable effect on social functioning, the correlation [between commitment to a value and having power] has to be quite high." The progressive shifting of social power and resources from families to organizations gradually diminished the association between power and gender inequality, leading to an erosion of interest in its preservation. The gradual elaboration of structurally induced indifference, the ever-declining significance of gender as a consideration in decisions at all levels of power, allowed the always-present efforts of women to better themselves to become ever more successful.

Diverse actors who were not linked directly by causal chains have contributed to women's rising status in unpredictable ways, because gender has become increasing irrelevant to the functional economic and political organization of power and opportunity. Over time, modern economic and political organization resulted in a separation of power from the commitment to preserving gender inequality. Economic and political activities moved out of the household, and power shifted from families to larger, more centralized organizations of businesses and government. These structural changes intrinsic to modern society have transformed interests and redistributed social power in ways such that people and organizations pursuing their individual interests and adapting to ordinary circumstances increasingly choose strategies inconsistent with the preservation of gender inequality.

Complex social processes such as these involve complex causality—not chainlike but, rather, contingent, probabilistic, and often loosely coupled. Specific social events do not bear the stamp of or allow easy attribution to one causal process. Instead, to distinguish the effects of one causal process, one must look selectively for relevant aggregate effects.

The principal engine of change driving the erosion of gender inequality over time involves the interplay of several key factors:

1.   The inherent dynamism of a modern economic, political, and social order.

2.   The transformation of gender-related interests as a result of the movement of social power and resources from families to organizations.

3.   Women's enduring resistance to subordination and the growth of their aspirations for independence and power.

4.   The accelerating effects of women's rising status, which increased the effectiveness of women's strivings while reducing the will and capacity to obstruct them.

The social dynamism of modern history involves continual new generations of individuals, families, businesses, political regimes, and other organizational entities (such as schools) who, possessing varying degrees of freedom in their choices, face new conditions, have to make crucial decisions about the allocations of resources and positions, and often are unable to replicate past strategies or inherited wisdom. The transformation of gender-related interests means that women, men, and organizational entities arrive at decision points with interests that are increasingly indifferent to gender inequality per se (regardless of their prejudices and predispositions) and are increasingly at odds with the choices that would better sustain such inequality. Women's continuous resistance to inequality and their interest in achieving status and success means that they will be a source of constant pressure such that effort is required to sustain a system of inequality. Further, they will take advantage of any opportunities created by the economy, government, education, and other organizations.

These processes combined with the characteristics of modern society mean that new generations of actors will face circumstances requiring gender-relevant decisions, these actors will have diminished interests in actions consistent with preserving gender inequality, and women's efforts at self-improvement will add opportunities and pressures favoring more egalitarian decisions. The result is that a wide range of social actors are increasingly likely to make decisions that erode inequality. The accumulation of these events and their effects, constituting the reduction in gender inequality, furthers the transition in interests and the expansion of opportunities so as to solidify the past pattern of decisions and raise the likelihood of similar decisions in the future.

For example, over time employers offered more jobs to women to solve labor shortage issues and because demand grew rapidly for some female-identified jobs, such as secretaries and clerks. This growing demand for female labor did not fit the argument associated with Gary Becker's *The Economics of Discrimination* (1957), suggesting that competitive markets will expunge the imputed inefficiency of discrimination (Jackson 1998, 104-13). Employers rarely hired women at discriminatorily low wages to avoid being pushed out of business by other firms (Arrow 1973). Even prejudiced businessmen would commonly employ women rather than go out of business or forgo significant profit opportunities, but labor needs loomed much larger than wage savings in their decisions to hire women.

Gender inequality was also subverted by developing individualism: the increasing tendency to make decisions on the basis of what people know or do rather than as a result of their birth origins or group memberships (Jackson 1998, 125-72). As modern economic and political orders absorbed the mechanisms of power, they increasingly treated people as individuals independent of their families. This generates institutional individualism, a phenomenon in which the relations between institutions and people are direct, consensual, and functionally circumscribed. Bureaucratic rationalization, growing out of large organizations' needs for control and predictability, creates interests in impartiality and stimulates indifference to gender. A free labor market, rules governing promotions, grades in schools, standardized entrance exams, and beliefs that jobs should go to the best-qualified applicants all reflect individualism. Institutional individualism stimulates educational systems that subvert ascribed inequalities by exalting achievements and abstract standards, induces the rise of meritocratic ideals, and transforms families from permanent ties of dependence into voluntary ties of companionship. Individualism diffusely erodes commitments to the discriminatory practices and prejudiced expectations that sustain gender inequality, and thus reinforces the principal factors listed earlier.

With each generation, more people acted inconsistently with past gender expectations as they adapted to the emerging pattern of interests. Women sought education, jobs, promotions, and better life styles. Women, like all subordinated peoples, have always individually challenged their status, but historically, the more gender inequality declined, the more effective their challenges became and their capacity for collective action grew. Powerful men—those wielding influence over other men because they controlled economic or political resources—sought competitive advantages for their organizations or themselves; to these ends, they used women in roles such as students, employees, clients, or voters. Ordinary men begrudgingly conceded women's expanding claims in their own generation, and often encouraged their daughters to claim more. In Stinchcombe's terms, the social value of gender inequality lost its significance as it lost its association with power.

Although prejudices against women still ruled many actions of men with power, their institutional interests repeatedly prompted them to take actions that contradicted gender inequality. To employers, the sex of a potential worker became another characteristic to factor into the calculation of the relative advantages of alternative employment strategies. To politicians, the sex of a voter became one more factor in the calculation of public political acts and the molding of images. Those wielding organizational power may have treated women as pawns, but as pawns women became an increasingly important factor in economic and political strategies. The more organizations followed a rationalized search for profit and efficiency or competed for political advantage, the more indifferent they became toward the sex of those they were exploiting or benefiting. Political and economic leaders discovered, gradually and intermittently, that they might gain more by assimilating women than by preserving policies that kept them subordinated to men. Other institutional contexts such as the family and the modern school system also became less hospitable to gender inequality the more they adopted an institutional form of individualism.

Simultaneously, men gradually withdrew their defense of the barriers limiting women's advance. In part, this probably reflected a loss of will and ability, but even more it showed a lack of motive. Of course, men did resist changes, but we should not overlook the resistance that did not occur. No agitation to restore men's relative monopoly of property rights followed the passage of the married women's property laws. Although men's full electoral approval of woman suffrage grew only gradually, it was surprisingly high in many early referenda, and passage of woman suffrage laws did not arouse backlash efforts to rescind those rights. Although men often resisted women's entry into male occupations, they showed little interest in resisting women's movement into other occupations or the general growth in women's employment. Although men may have placed a higher priority on educating their sons, they commonly sought education for their daughters as well, and more generally they did not oppose the rising education of women. Finding evidence of men's resistance is easy, but in fact, the increasing halfheartedness of men's resistance is more historically striking than the fact that they resisted in the past. As Theda Skocpol (1979) suggested of successful political revolutions, the disarray of the powerful lays the groundwork for effective revolts.

The state, sometimes depicted as a simple instrument of male privileges, has played a complex role in the long-term decline of gender inequality. Until recently, those in government were not much concerned with raising women's status, for their collective interest in effective government and their competitive interests in expanding political influence made them largely indifferent to gender inequality. In the course of pursuing general state interests, they enacted some policies (such as granting property rights to women) that accidentally benefited women, and as they competed for political advantage they accepted other policy changes in response to pressure (as with woman suffrage).

By themselves, large-scale organizations' relative indifference to gender inequality and men's declining defense of masculine privileges would not have led us toward gender equality at the historical pace we have experienced, for neither major institutions nor men as individuals became committed to creating gender equality. The push needed to overcome reservoirs of prejudice, discrimination, institutional inertia, and indifference came from women's own efforts to gain higher status, both individual and collective. The altered pattern of women's actions represented a change in opportunities more than a change in interests. Despite the restrictive influence of cultural expectations about women's place, most women tested the limits of their social identities and whenever new opportunities appeared, some women were ready to try them. By taking advantage of these opportunities, they widened the space for more women to follow.

Women's collective efforts to improve their circumstances were particularly important for bringing down barriers that could not be surmounted through individual efforts. The suffrage movement gave progressive women a voice that placed women's political rights on the agenda, showed women's potential impact as voters, and nurtured the efforts of its members to forge a new identity. Similarly, modern feminists, by organizing themselves, were able to place women's economic and social rights on the public agenda, catalyze the government and political party responsiveness to women's potential electoral influence, and nourish the development of new ideas about gender and women's place in the world.

To survive, the social edifice of gender inequality had to stand on a sound foundation, provided by the conditions that reproduce inequality. The institutional contradictions induced by economic and political development changed those conditions—eroding the foundation. Once the conditions sustaining inequality weakened sufficiently, women's pressure could pull down the deteriorating edifice, toppling inequality piece by piece.

COUNTERVAILING TENDENCIES

Despite the extraordinary improvements in women's status over the past two centuries, some aspects of gender inequality have seemed exceptionally resistant to erosion in recent decades, leading to arguments that further reductions in gender inequality may be difficult to achieve. Three important issues in the debate over limits to women's progress are women's child-rearing responsibilities, the limits to women's occupational achievements, and the widespread predisposition to judge the sexes differently, to women's disadvantage. We know that women continue to do more child-rearing and household work, that women's average pay remains less than men's, that people still think about women and men differently, and that men still occupy most of the highest positions of political and economic power.

These facts give rise to an important theoretical question: Do these conditions suggest the presence of countervailing causal processes strong enough to obstruct the causal processes that have propelled gender inequality's decline?

To answer this question, I propose three criteria to test the adequacy of claims about countervailing forces. First, a basic empirical question: Has the relevant obstacle really shown the implied immovability over the past several decades? If the imputed obstacles, such as attitudes toward women, are enduring impediments to progress, they must themselves resist change. If they have been changing in an egalitarian direction, their ability to obstruct other changes or to remain unchanged themselves becomes questionable.

Second, a theoretical test: Has anyone devised a credible analysis showing how the purported barrier will sustain itself and have the power to stop the powerful engines of change that have driven the movement toward greater equality? We have seen how conditions and processes endemic to modern society have cleared the way for and stimulated actions improving women's status. A serious barrier to continued movement toward equality must have some means of pushing back against the powerful forces promoting change.

Third, a deep-historical test: If we project the implied obstructive process back in time, is the argument consistent with what we know about gender inequality's decline over the past two hundred years? If an apparently severe obstacle has been troubling egalitarian advances without stopping them for two hundred years, it is unlikely to become a greater brake now.

Proponents of what are here called "countervailing" forces would not normally use the term "countervailing," for they do not begin with a theory of the forces that have driven the decline of gender inequality. Rather than thinking in terms of conditions or processes that must *stall* a social engine pushing change forward, they largely adopt a more static approach, focusing on the possibility that some aspects of gender inequality seem relatively unchangeable. To give these arguments a fair hearing, we must largely infer the theoretical logic that is the concern of our second criterion.

The diverse efforts to understand countervailing forces, conceived as relatively intractable dimensions of inequality, reflect larger issues in the explanation of women's status. The difficulty of explaining the continued persistence of gender inequality has increased as the barriers to equality have declined. In the mid-nineteenth century, women's inferior legal status, their exclusion from voting and government, exclusion from good jobs or higher education, and institutionalized subordination to husbands were obvious to all. The differential treatment was a given; what was needed was to show that it was neither necessary nor just. By the middle of the twentieth century, women's status had changed considerably (see table 7.1), but gender inequality was still obvious to those who wished to look. Causes of inequality were easy to identify. Discrimination against women was rampant and obvious in most spheres of life, whatever the formal rules might say. "Give women an equal chance" was a cry shared by the diverse voices released by modern feminism. Nearing the end of the twentieth century, the characterization and explanation of gender inequality became more problematic. Overt discrimination against women, greatly diminished, was rejected by public opinion and was, moreover, illegal. Few doors were closed to women and their success in varied prestigious domains was highly visible. Pinpointing and explaining gender inequality became more difficult.

The theoretical problem (and the political one) was to offer an explanation of gender inequality that was not predicated on the presence of direct discrimination. Each of the three countervailing forces we will consider—women's childrearing responsibilities and the household divisions of labor, women's employment disadvantages, and the potential influence of culturally determined differential gender expectations—can be produced by discrimination, but recent treatments of these issues aim more to show how they may have the effect of sustaining gender inequality in the absence of discrimination. They are invoked more as causes than as effects and characterized as threats to further movement toward equality.

Here we want to ask whether convincing theoretical accounts show how and why these three countervailing forces will resist egalitarian change and obstruct the general movement toward greater gender equality. Applying our three criteria of viability and credibility, we want to see whether any of these efforts have assembled empirically and theoretically defensible claims. In light of our argument that a powerful engine of change continues to undermine the supports for gender inequality, claims about potential obstacles, to be considered convincing, must meet the following three criteria:

1. Show empirically that the purported obstruction has held its ground in recent decades.

2. Provide theoretical reasons for the belief that the obstruction can hold off the pressures for change in the future.

3. Possess a theoretical logic that is consistent and plausible when applied against the history of changes that have occurred over the past two centuries.

Any obstruction argument that fails to meet all the criteria is a speculative claim at best.

The Household Division of Labor

Most often mentioned among the reasons people give for believing we are not on a path toward gender equality are women's responsibilities for household labor, child rearing, and other home-based work. Two uncontested observations feed this concern: women still do more of this work, and time invested in family and household is time unavailable for careers and other pursuits.

Unfortunately, we know less about changes in the patterns of domestic labor and child-caring responsibilities than we would wish. Both conceptual and methodological difficulties hamper research on these questions. Domestic labor and parenting do not easily translate into clearly identifiable activities. Also, the time and effort that go into relevant activities is hard to measure accurately. Most data concern the time invested, not the effort expended nor the work accomplished. Domestic activities commonly intermingle different tasks and forms of relaxation in ways that confound efforts to measure work through people's self-reports. So we should interpret all findings warily.

Available data indicate that the proportion of household labor and child rearing done by men has increased significantly, partly as a result of their own greater efforts and partly because of a decrease in the amount women do. The research suggests that by the 1990s husbands spent about half as much time as wives doing household work (see Coltrane 2000, for a general review of the relevant literature). Researchers often distinguish between more female-identified tasks and male-identified tasks, the latter being less routine and more likely to be outdoors. Mary C. Noonan (2001, 1141) found that women and men each did about three-quarters of the tasks identified with their own sex.

Information focused on child-rearing activities is also uneven, but a good study of recent behavior (Yeung et al. 2001) using time-diary data from 1997 shows the time that fathers spend with children to be about two-thirds what mothers spend during weekdays and seven-eighths on weekends, or a bit under three-quarters mothers' time over all. Although the data used in earlier studies was often not comparable, we can safely conclude that this is a significantly higher level of father involvement than was the case several decades earlier, a general trend supported by other research (see Pleck 1996 for a review).

In sum, the available data on the United States, despite some unevenness, suggest that men's contribution to domestic labor has increased significantly over the past several decades. Although women still do more, the best research data leaves little doubt that the division of domestic labor has been moving toward greater equality, even if the pace of change is slower than we might like.

Although the apparent empirical decline of women's domestic responsibilities falls short of our first criterion—the obstacle has not held its ground in recent decades—we still want to see whether the argument meets our second criterion of providing an effective theoretical argument showing how it is likely to obstruct the general movement toward greater gender equality. Ideally, such an argument would show that women's child-rearing responsibilities derail their own egalitarian desires and are robust enough to resist the demands of social forces propelling change.

Those who advance arguments about women's greater domestic responsibilities attribute them to other conditions of gender inequality such as poorer levels of pay, worse job opportunities, and cultural definitions of women as the ones more responsible for children and household. Consistent with these ideas, research has shown that women's contribution to household labor is higher if they are not employed, do not contribute much to family income, have young children, or believe women should be more responsible for the home (see Coltrane 2000; Bianchi 2000). Thus, women's domestic responsibilities are understood to be a reflection of these other conditions, not self-preserving. They could be a steady obstacle to progress if, and only if, some conditions or processes had halted the movement toward better job opportunities, higher pay, and an improved, more egalitarian cultural imagery for women. Unfortunately for the proponents of this argument (but fortunately for women), most analysts agree that improvement of these conditions is likely to continue. If women's disproportionate domestic responsibilities do derive from lower pay, constrained job choices, and cultural imperatives, progress in reducing these differentials will largely dictate the pace at which the domestic division of labor will move toward equality. Thus the logic of these arguments does not show that women's domestic responsibilities can work as a self-sustaining barrier to obstruct further egalitarian changes.

Our third test asks if the idea that household duties obstruct change is consistent with the long-term historical record. In the past, women used to have much more exclusive responsibility for child rearing and other domestic labor than they do now. Moreover, that work demanded more effort and endured over a larger portion of women's lives because people had more children but fewer services and appliances. The farther we go back in time over the past two centuries, the more extreme are the conditions. Yet starting under conditions in which much more demanding domestic responsibilities restrained women, we have made extraordinary movement toward greater equality over a long period. Of course, these domestic responsibilities were a real constraint that restricted women's actions and achievements, plausibly slowing egalitarian changes, but certainly not blocking them. This long-term perspective induces us to ask, how can the domestic responsibilities of modern women act as a more effective barrier to change than did women's much greater domestic responsibilities in the past?

The argument that women's domestic responsibilities will obstruct continued movement toward gender equality therefore does not hold up well when assessed critically. Those responsibilities have been declining (even if at a slow pace), no adequate theoretical logic has been offered to show how these responsibilities can effectively hold off the pressures toward change, and the idea that women's household responsibilities would effectively block women's economic and political assimilation appears inconsistent with the lessons of the past two hundred years. An uneven burden of domestic responsibilities undoubtedly hampers women's chances for getting ahead, but this does not mean that such responsibilities can or will restrain historical progress.

Lower-Status and Lower-Paying Jobs

Pervasive and seemingly intractable limitations to women's economic achievements form the second threat blocking the path to equality. Women's economic progress over the past several decades has produced a peculiar range of contemporary commentaries that go from celebrating the full arrival of women's economic equality to complaining that women are as bad off as ever. Serious scholars recognize that neither of these exaggerated positions matches reality. Much recent scholarly work on women's economic circumstances investigates why some facets of economic inequality between the sexes have declined greatly and others have not. In this uneven intellectual terrain, ideas about economic obstructions to gender equality crop up in many forms.

The diverse arguments about economic obstructions to equality generally operate on the premise that critical economic disadvantages of women consistently elude egalitarian developments and they limit future progress in other areas. Some arguments focus on the idea that jobs disproportionately employing women pay less and bring fewer status rewards (see England 1999) or that having children has a penalty for women not shared by men (Budig and England 2001). This wage differential is viewed as an obstacle to greater gender equality when it is allied with the empirical observation that the sex segregation of occupations seems to resist change (see Preston 1999 for a review). Another potential economic obstacle to greater equality is represented by the "glass ceiling." This popular image refers to a barrier that stops women's rise through the occupational ranks short of the highest positions. These ideas largely grew from efforts to explain current levels of gender inequality and to debate policies for the immediate future. They have not been developed into systematic, rigorous theoretical arguments about barriers to further progress, although they are important concerns, often invoked when people discuss potential obstacles to further improvements in women's status.

Stripped to their essentials, these arguments rest on a belief that several crucial characteristics of the economy have exceptional inertia. In particular, high-status positions of authority remain disproportionately occupied by men and the wages paid in disproportionately female-identified occupations remain lower than those for comparable male-identified positions.

How well do the empirical data support these arguments? Research on the pay gap between women and men generally shows that it has shrunk considerably over the last several decades. After controlling for characteristics of jobs and employers, recent research finds the remaining earnings gap to be between 5 and 15 percent (Blau and Kahn 1999; Budig 2002; O'Neill 2003). Although occupational segregation between women and men remains high, this persistence appears largely to reflect women and men holding different jobs at each pay level (see Blackburn, Brooks, and Jarman 2001; Charles and Grusky 2004). Only a small proportion of gender wage differentials seems related to the sex composition of occupations (Budig 2002; Macpherson and Hirsch 1995; O'Neill 2003). On balance, the research suggests that wage differences between the sexes have reduced considerably and continue to decline, and that the reasons men's jobs give them higher average pay are largely independent of their gender composition.

Moreover, as mentioned, women have also taken a steadily increasing proportion of professional and managerial jobs. The gains have been slowest at the very top, but even there the signs are consistent and suggest that the pattern of women breaking into new positions may now be reaching the top corporate tier. Note that on average, top-level managers are in their fifties, suggesting that they would have received their start in business twenty-five to thirty years earlier. In 1970, the percentage of MBAs awarded to women was about 4 percent, but this figure rose to 40 percent in 2000, which would lead to the expectation that, absent obstacles, the proportion of women in high-level management would show a similar rise in the period from about 1995 to 2025 as more women MBAs ascend the job ladder. Women's slowly rising presence in top management over the past decade is consistent with this projection (Bertrand and Hallock 2001). Another revealing piece of information is that over the past two decades of the twentieth century, the fraction of couples in which the wife earned more than the husband increased from about one-sixth to about one-quarter of all dual-earner married couples (U.S. Census Bureau 2004). In short, the empirical pattern of change over the past few decades shows considerable movement toward egalitarian conditions, although some aspects of employment have shown these changes more and others less.

The employment-obstacle arguments also fall short on our second criterion, concerning theoretical logic. The proponents of these arguments largely focus their theoretical efforts on explaining women's economic disadvantages. In the past, discrimination by employers, male workers, and schools provided an easy explanation. Today, most scholars acknowledge that sex discrimination still exists in the economy, but they do not believe direct discrimination causes most of the sex differences in jobs and they expect direct discrimination to continue to decline. The key problem is to supply an argument showing that even without direct discrimination, women will disproportionately end up in lower-paying, lower-status jobs.

The employment-obstacle arguments commonly attribute gender differences in employment to inequality in another social realm. A common argument is that women are systematically excluded from better-paying, higher-authority positions. Here, the issue concerns not why women's occupations have lower pay scales but why fewer women get into higher-status positions. Because of the need to avoid relying on discrimination as an explanation, proponents of the employment-obstacle theory argue either that women cannot compete equally with men because they cannot offer the same returns to employers (owing to other obligations, experience deficits, or the like) or that women are judged differently, so that employers (and others) do not recognize women's comparable assets. This line of argument pushes the causal issues back a level, to the question: What are the conditions that make women less competitive or induce women to be misjudged. In short, the employment-obstacles argument encompasses concerns with several kinds of gender-related employment disadvantages that are consistently attributed to other components of gender inequality, mainly domestic responsibilities and cultural expectations. However, if women's employment disadvantages are secondary results of conditions outside the economy such as domestic arrangements, then women's continued disadvantaged employment becomes more a result of insufficient progress toward equality elsewhere rather than a barrier to its achievement. This provides no theory showing how employment disadvantages could effectively repel forces of change.

The argument that labor market disadvantages could block the path to greater gender equality is also difficult to reconcile with the long-term history of women's progress. All the economic conditions that work against women's achievements were more severe the further we go back in time over the past two centuries. In the nineteenth century, strong, overt discrimination sustained sharp divisions between women's and men's jobs. Women suffered severely restricted access to schooling and job training. Only low-status jobs were open to women and they paid much less than equivalent male jobs. Women routinely lost their jobs when they married. Yet in the face of all these obstacles in the labor market, women's participation has risen steadily for over a century. A significant part of this egalitarian progress involved the reduction of these economic obstacles.

Thus, while persisting labor-market obstacles still hinder women's achievements, they are considerably less obstructive than conditions in the past and they are under siege by more powerful, institutionalized forces pushing toward egalitarian outcomes. This is true even of the most problematic issue, women's very low presence in the highest levels of corporate power. A continuing source of motives and resources that could counter the ever-increasing pressures toward greater equality would be required for labor-market conditions to persistently block the movement toward equality. No one seems to have a theoretical model that shows such a causal process.

The Shadow of Cultural Expectations

Proponents of the domestic-responsibilities and employment-obstacle arguments typically place great weight on the role of cultural beliefs in maintaining resistance to change. A third line of argument focuses directly on beliefs and cultural expectations.

Ideology has played an important role in many theories about gender inequality, but its role has been narrowed and refined over time. Male prejudice, beliefs about distinctive sex roles, and socialization loomed large in writings about women's condition in the 1960s and 1970s. As direct discrimination against women declined and women's public image rose, an important strain of theoretical work developed a focus on the ways that unrecognized ideas linked to gender influence the perceptions and actions of both sexes to give an advantage to men.

In *Why So Slow? The Advancement of Women,* Virginia Valian (1998b) argued that women's slow progress in the professions was due to unrecognized, unconscious "gender schemas," implicit biases that "skew our perceptions and evaluations, causing us to overrate men and underrate women" (Valian 1998a, 52). Bosses, coworkers, and the women themselves all share these biases, for example expecting men to be better leaders and women to be more emotional. Though their effects on any particular assessment are small, their cumulative effects across time, careers, and people produce a significant disadvantage for women.

Barbara Reskin has recently expressed strong doubts about a long-held assumption that strategic self-interest is the key to discrimination, which guided her earlier scholarship. Instead, she states that now, "I and others suspect that most employment discrimination originates in . . . nonconscious cognitive processes" (Reskin 2000, 326) that lead to an unreflective dependence on cultural stereotypes and in-group preferences when people interpret and judge the actions of others. Because of past gender inequality the larger culture contains stereotypes that disadvantage women and because men happen to occupy more positions of control, male in-group preferences and biases have more impact, again to women's disadvantage.

Cecilia Ridgeway has produced the most comprehensive analysis of the ways that cultural expectations could obstruct continued progress toward gender equality. The dynamic she describes has four principal features (Ridgeway and Smith-Lovin 1999; Ridgeway and Correll 2004). First, an internalized "presumption of men's greater overall competence" causes women and men to act and to assess the actions of others in a way that privileges men and disadvantages women. This effect may be offset or reinforced by the other conditions affecting people in an interaction, such as their organizational position, their age, the composition of the group, or the purpose of the interaction. Second, gender categorization is always present, although people may not be aware of it. Third, when women interact with men in circumstances where men have, independent of gender identification, greater status, authority, or competence, the interaction process will strengthen the hold of differential gender expectations. Fourth, because of male dominance and the roles allotted to women, "Women seldom meet men in status-equal, role-similar interactions," although women and men "interact frequently and intimately" (Ridgeway and Correll 2000, 110).

Thus, the cultural-expectations approach posits a dynamic whereby people internalize divergent perceptions of women and men, sometimes from the content of culture and sometimes from the structurally directed experience of gender-differentiated behavior. These images affect expectations and cause people to anticipate and evaluate the actions of others in gender-differentiated ways. Internalized conceptions about men and women then have a reciprocally causal, mutually reinforcing relationship with external behavior that maintains the norms of inequality.

It sounds like common sense. How does it stand up to analytic criticism?

All approaches arguing the obstructive potential of cultural beliefs and expectations assume their relative stability. Does this assumption meet our first criterion? Does the evidence show change or continuity of the obstruction over the past few decades? An extensive overview of public opinion poll trends shows "the American public shifted from opposition to support of the women's movement in the early 1970s and has continued to support the movement ever since" (Huddy, Neely, and Lafay 2000, 311). Numerous studies of specific populations and age groups have shown that women's and men's attitudes have become increasingly similar and more supportive of equal treatment for women over the past several decades (Thornton and Young-DeMarco 2001; Bolzendahl and Myers 2004; Brooks and Bolzendahl 2004). The one *notable* exception results from research on college students' ideas about feminine and masculine personality traits (Lueptow, Garovich-Szabo, and Lueptow 2001) which may reflect poorly understood processes whereby the sexes are seen as different in kind even if judged equal in relevant abilities and rights. Despite this exception, the data available from a wide range of sources suggest a strong shift toward egalitarian attitudes and expectations over the past several decades.

Even advocates of the cultural-obstacles view seem to agree that beliefs about gender have been changing (Ridgeway and Correll 2000, 119), yet if the beliefs claimed to sustain gender inequality are themselves declining, they provide a shaky foundation on which to build a theoretical argument that these very beliefs drive processes that will obstruct continued progress toward equality. Thus, the cultural-expectations-as-obstruction view does not meet the first criterion, stability over time.

Is it possible that the arguments favoring the cultural obstructions approach have provided such a strong theoretical model of its potential impact, our second criterion, that they overcome the initial empirical weakness? To argue that some aspects of culture or ideology block social change, a theory must show the obstructing processes are substantially more self-preserving and influential than the normal cultural resistance that all significant social changes must overcome. If the mere presence of traditional beliefs effectively prevented social change, we would all be hunters and gatherers still. Traditional cultural beliefs everywhere reinforce traditional behaviors, in times of both stability and change, and their presence is thus not a factor distinguishing the circumstances under which change occurs from those when change does not. Every significant social change involves the displacement of resistant beliefs.

The argument that the routine enactment of gender inequality helps sustain cultural expectations consistent with that inequality is unproblematic but does not identify processes or conditions that would make people's beliefs about the critical gender differences "stickier" or more resistant to change than other cultural beliefs. To get around this, these arguments sometimes try finessing the problem through language, for example calling such beliefs "deeply rooted" or "embedded" in culture, as though these phrases could imbue gender stereotypes with a permanence that need not otherwise be demonstrated or explained. Yet not so long ago, the desirability of female virginity and the undesirability of middle-class women taking jobs seemed to be deep American values. Then young women sought sex and jobs. Then the values changed. This is the heart of the problem. In recent centuries, innumerable "traditional" social practices have been transformed or displaced, showing over and over again that long-lasting and seemingly deep beliefs supporting the displaced practices were not successful barriers to change.

The cultural-obstructions approach does not stand up any better to our third criterion: it must be consistent with the long-term historical pattern of gender inequality's decline. The further we go back in time over the past two hundred years, the greater are the differential expectations about the competence and appropriate roles of the two sexes, the greater the status gap between women and men. According to our criterion, cultural obstructions should have presented even greater obstacles to changes benefiting women's status than the current ones. Yet despite the prevalence of far more negative stereotypes and expectations, inequality did obviously decline over the past two centuries. To be historically persuasive, the cultural-obstructions proponents need a theoretical argument showing why considerably less restrictive beliefs about gender differences facing much more potent forces of change would have greater obstructive potential. So far, such an argument does not seem to have been developed.

The "Combined-Weight" Thesis

As the three obstacles to equality we have considered are complementary, they could plausibly work together as a "combined-weight" obstacle to the decline of gender inequality. Even if no one of the conditions could stop the progress of women's status if it were the sole obstacle, they could have a mutually reinforcing impact that is great enough to obstruct progress, and their reciprocal reinforcement of each other might sustain them against opposing causal forces.

This sounds like a strong argument, but is its appeal merely rhetorical? Does it provide a successful theoretical and empirical analysis? Social causes are not like pails of water; they cannot be poured together to fill a bigger pail. Even if they could, the end result would not amount to much if the original pails were nearly empty.

That the three main proposed obstacles to women's progress are consistent with each other does not by itself make their combined weight a more effective obstacle. In the era before gender inequality began to decline, most aspects of women's and men's lives—including the three countervailing tendencies considered here and other conditions such as high numbers of children, women's lack of legal equality, and the religious support of male dominance—were consistent with a high degree of gender inequality and were mutually reinforcing. These conditions were much more severe than today and did constitute mutually supportive obstacles to gender equality, but they still lost to the engine of change portrayed above. Today, that engine of change continues and the comparable contemporary societal characteristics are mutually supportive facilitators of greater gender equality: a low number of children, women's legal equality, a secular egalitarian ideology, high levels of women's employment, and impartial organizational rationality.

Moreover, as the three countervailing conditions each show significant egalitarian movement over the past several decades, their combined capacity to resist change must be reduced. What, then, is the basis for inferring that their combined weight can overwhelm the strong forces of change today? As far as I can see, there is none.

Limits of Countervailing Tendencies

I have examined several arguments to the effect that countervailing forces threaten to prevent continued progress toward gender equality. These arguments appeal to us because they seemingly fit many personal experiences and make sense of gender inequality's current state. Each starts with some clearly problematic aspect of gender inequality: Women still do more domestic labor. Women's aggregate employment circumstances are still inferior to those of men. People still think differently about women and men. Each of these conditions appears resistant to change and creates disadvantages for women.

Nonetheless, the arguments suggesting that these countervailing tendencies represent significant threats to future equality are incomplete, empirically dubious, and theoretically weak. The best empirical data available show that each of the initial factors—the domestic division of labor, employment differentials, and cultural expectations—has moved significantly in an egalitarian direction. When we examine the logic of each argument, we see that none of them contains a compelling causal theory of processes that would effectively reverse this pattern. Rather, they seem to rely on a problematic logic according to which these phenomena can inhibit further movement toward equality because they themselves somehow seem hard to change. Third, none of the arguments solves the theoretical difficulties that arise from the long-term history of change. Each of them refers to conditions that were more severe the further back in time we go over the past two centuries and were facing weaker processes pressing for greater equality, yet they failed then to stop the progress toward equality. By itself, this long-term pattern does not mean that it is abstractly impossible that one of these conditions could stop further movement toward equality, but it does mean that it is unlikely. It would require some condition or effect that had not been present in the past. None of these arguments reveals a mechanism adequate for this requirement.

CONCLUSIONS

To assess the status of gender inequality today we must decide what standards and comparisons to apply. This is an analytical, not an ideological, requirement (although one's politics may influence analytical choices). Much can be learned from a snapshot in time, from the question: What is women's status today? However, we can see another dimension of such snapshots by comparing them with those that precede and follow, asking why and how women's status changes over time.

The gender inequality we see today is a slice out of a long history of shifting circumstances. To make sense of this slice, I have tried to place gender inequality in the context of a historical trajectory. Complex forces driving us toward greater equality and other forces resisting those changes pushed and pulled continually over the past two centuries, producing this trajectory. Our predictions about the future will be stronger if we see that the trajectory of change from the past to the present has been determined more by the forces of change than by resistance to change.

Using this dynamic perspective, our critical analysis has found flaws in the typical theoretical argument that one or another facet of gender inequality will impede further progress toward equality. First, I suggest that we cannot assess obstacles to change without understanding what propels the changes. The first thing to seek from the history of women's status is not what has held them back but what has moved them forward. Second, I contend that the principal engine of change is a widespread dilution of interests that formerly induced actions preserving gender inequality, particularly in the form of organizational indifference, combined with women's persistent resistance to subordination. This engine of change will continue to erode gender inequality so long as modern economic and political organization retain their essential forms and women continue to resist subordination. Third, I argue that current efforts to show that certain aspects of gender inequality will obstruct further equalization have largely failed to overcome contrary empirical evidence or produce convincing theoretical models. Lacking a theory of what has driven gender inequality's decline, analyses seeking to understand the limits to change in some facets of gender relations have reached conclusions about potential obstructions to future change that are neither empirically nor theoretically defensible.

The long-term causal process that has driven the decline of gender inequality over the past two hundred years will continue, but it is not easily controlled. For those seeking policies to propel us toward gender equality, that is both the good and the bad of it. Unquestionably, government policies can hasten or retard the movement toward equality. However, even when government policies were supportive they have not been the main driving force behind gender inequality's decline and when obstructive they have not been insurmountable obstacles to progress. Because gender inequality is embedded in our institutions and diffused through every nook and corner of our lives, changing it depends unavoidably on the actions and thoughts of people in every social arena. We have every reason to believe that these actions will continue to change toward the conditions favoring gender equality and away from the requirements for sustaining gender inequality. However, the actions that have eroded gender inequality typically have been highly dispersed, decentralized, and often outside public view. Public policies can influence such processes. They cannot control them.

Returning to our starting point, what kinds of answers does this analysis suggest about the why, how, and when of gender inequality's trajectory?

Why will gender inequality disappear? It is fated to end because essential organizational characteristics and consequences of a modern, industrial, market-oriented, electorally governed society are inherently inconsistent with the conditions needed to sustain gender inequality.

How will gender inequality disappear? Since the processes eroding gender inequality are loosely coupled, the causal dynamic does not follow any simple, predictable sequence. Organizational rationalization, political competition, women's individual efforts to advance themselves, men's remoteness from and unwillingness to defend past practices, women's collective efforts to influence policy, the cultural weight of accumulated past changes, and other strands will all continue to push toward greater equality. Their relative contribution and the exact path we will follow over time will depend on unforeseeable historical conditions.

When will we achieve equality? Again, the causal processes do not permit a simple answer. A crude guess, based on the pace and form of past changes and what seems plausible for the future, is that we will largely achieve equality in five generations at the outside and in one to two generations at best. Where we land within that range will depend both on unforeseeable historical conditions (such as the pace of technological progress and the political issues of the future) and on the effort that people put into establishing social policies likely to accelerate (or slow) movement toward equality. In short, if you want your children or grandchildren to see equality, you had better work at it.

Thus, the theoretical argument developed here implies a strong case for both the value of and the need for continued efforts to hasten our movement toward full gender equality. The processes that are decisively moving us toward equality are also inherently indeterminate in the specific path they take and the speed with which they unfold. As a moral and practical objective, we would like to achieve effective gender equality within one generation, not three, or four. To make this happen requires policies that put us on a direct path to equality rather than allowing us to meander toward it. The theoretical model also suggests that such efforts, if well planned and executed, will be successful, because they are working with rather than against the fundamental pressures of modern social organization.

NOTES

1. For a full statement of this theoretical analysis and the evidence that supports it, please consult Jackson (1998).
2. The "modern" economy excludes agriculture and domestic service. Employment in farming and private households is omitted to focus on gender inequities in the modern industrial and service sectors (Jackson 1998, 74-92).

REFERENCES

Arrow, Kenneth. 1973. "The Theory of Discrimination." In *Discrimination in Labor Markets*, edited by O. Ashenfelter and A. Rees. Princeton, N.J.: Princeton University Press.

Becker, Gary Stanley. 1957. *The Economics of Discrimination*. Chicago: University of Chicago Press.

Bertrand, Marianne, and Kevin F. Hallock. 2001. "The Gender Gap in Top Corporate Jobs." *Industrial and Labor Relations Review* 55(1): 3-21.

Bianchi, Suzanne M. 2000. "Maternal Employment and Time with Children: Dramatic Change or Surprising Continuity?" *Demography* 37(4): 401–14.

Blackburn, Robert M., Bradley Brooks, and Jennifer Jarman. 2001. "Occupational Stratification: The Vertical Dimension of Occupational Segregation." *Work, Employment and Society* 15(3): 511–38.

Blau, Francine D., and Lawrence M. Kahn. 1999. "Analyzing the Gender Pay Gap." *Quarterly Review of Economics and Finance* 39: 625–46.

Bolzendahl, Catherine I., and Daniel J. Myers. 2004. "Feminist Attitudes and Support for Gender Equality: Opinion Change in Women and Men, 1974–1998." *Social Forces* 83(2): 759–89.

Brooks, Clem, and Catherine Bolzendahl. 2004. "The Transformation of US Gender Role Attitudes: Cohort Replacement, Social-Structural Change, and Ideological Learning." *Social Science Research* 33(1): 106–33.

Budig, Michelle J. 2002. "Male Advantage and the Gender Composition of Jobs: Who Rides the Glass Escalator?" *Social Problems* 49(2): 258–77.

Budig, Michelle J., and Paula England. 2001. "The Wage Penalty for Motherhood." *American Sociological Review* 66(2): 204–25.

Charles, Maria, and David B. Grusky. 2004. *Occupational Ghettos: The Worldwide Segregation of Women and Men*. Palo Alto, Calif.: Stanford University Press.

Coltrane, Scott. 2000. "Research on Household Labor: Modeling and Measuring the Social Embeddedness of Routine Family Work." *Journal of Marriage and the Family* 62(4): 1208–33.

England, Paula. 1999. "The Case for Comparable Worth." *Quarterly Review of Economics and Finance* 39: 743–55.

Hooks, Janet M. 1947. *Women's Occupations Through Seven Decades*. Washington: U. S. Government Printing Office.

Huddy, Leonie, Francis K. Neely, and Marilyn R. Lafay. 2000. "Trends: Support for the Women's Movement." *Public Opinion Quarterly* 64(3): 309–50.

Jackson, Robert Max. 1984. *The Formation of Craft Labor Markets*. New York: Academic Press.
———. 1998. *Destined for Equality: The Inevitable Rise of Women's Status*. Cambridge, Mass.: Harvard University Press.

Kessler-Harris, Alice. 1982. *Out to Work: A History of Wage-Earning Women in the United States*. New York: Oxford University Press.

Lieberson, Stanley, and Freda B. Lynn. 2002. "Barking up the Wrong Branch: Scientific Alternatives to the Current Model of Sociological Science." *Annual Review of Sociology* 28: 1–19.

Lueptow, Lloyd B., Lori Garovich-Szabo, and Margaret B. Lueptow. 2001. "Social Change and the Persistence of Sex Typing: 1974-1997." *Social Forces* 80(1): 1–36.

Macpherson, David A., and Barry T. Hirsch. 1995. "Wages and Gender Composition: Why Do Women's Jobs Pay Less?" *Journal of Labor Economics* 13(3): 426.

Noonan, Mary C. 2001. "The Impact of Domestic Work on Men's and Women's Wages." *Journal of Marriage and the Family* 63(4): 1134–45.

O'Neill, June. 2003. "The Gender Gap in Wages, Circa 2000." *American Economic Review* 93(2): 309.

Pleck, Joseph H. 1996. "Paternal Involvement: Levels, Sources, and Consequences." In *The Role of the Father in Child Development*, edited by M. E. Lamb. New York: Wiley.

Preston, Jo Anne. 1999. "Occupational Gender Segregation: Trends and Explanations." *Quarterly Review of Economics and Finance* 39: 611–24.

Rabkin, Peggy A. 1980. *Fathers to Daughters: The Legal Foundations of Female Emancipation.* Westport, Conn.: Greenwood Press.

Reskin, Barbara F. 2000. "The Proximate Causes of Employment Discrimination." *Contemporary Sociology* 29(2): 319–28.

———. 2003. "Including Mechanisms in Our Models of Ascriptive Inequality." *American Sociological Review* 68(1): 1.

Ridgeway, Cecilia L., and Shelley J. Correll. 2000. "Limiting Inequality through Interaction: The End(S) of Gender." *Contemporary Sociology* 29(1): 110–20.

———. 2004. "Unpacking the Gender System: A Theoretical Perspective on Gender Beliefs and Social Relations." *Gender & Society* 18(4): 510–31.

Ridgeway, Cecilia L., and Lynn Smith-Lovin. 1999. "The Gender System and Interaction." *Annual Review of Sociology* 25: 191–216.

Skocpol, Theda. 1979. *States and Social Revolutions: A Comparative Analysis of France, Russia, and China.* Cambridge; New York: Cambridge University Press.

Stinchcombe, Arthur L. 1968. *Constructing Social Theories.* New York: Harcourt Brace & World.

Thornton, Arland, and Linda Young-DeMarco. 2001. "Four Decades of Trends in Attitudes toward Family Issues in the United States: The 1960s through the 1990s." *Journal of Marriage and the Family* 63(4): 1009–37.

Tocqueville, Alexis de. 1835/1966. *Democracy in America.* Translated by J. P. Mayer. New York: Harper & Row.

U.S. Bureau of the Census. 1975. *Historical Statistics of the United States, Colonial Times to 1970.* Bicentennial ed. Washington: U. S. Government Printing Office.

———. 2004. *Statistical Abstract of the United States, 2004–2005.* Washington: U.S. Bureau of the Census.

U.S. Bureau of the Census, and Alba M. Edwards. 1943. *Sixteenth Census of the United States: 1940. Population. Comparative Occupation Statistics for the United States, 1870 to 1940, a Comparison of the 1930 and the 1940 Census Occupation and Industry Classifications and Statistics.* Washington: U. S. Government Printing Office.

U.S. Census Bureau. 2004. *Historical Income—Families, (Table) F-22. Married-Couple Families with Wives' Earnings Greater Than Husbands' Earnings: 1981 to 2001 (Selected Years),* July 8, 2004. Available at: http://www.census.gov/hhes/income/histinc/f22.html.

U.S. Department of Labor, Women's Bureau. 1951. *Case Studies in Equal Pay for Women.* Washington: U.S. Government Printing Office.

———. 1984. *Time of Change: 1983 Handbook on Women Workers.* Washington: U.S. Government Printing Office.

Valian, Virginia. 1998a. "Sex, Schemas, and Success: What's Keeping Women Back?" *Academe* 84(5): 50–55.

———. 1998b. *Why So Slow?: The Advancement of Women*. Cambridge, Mass.: MIT Press.

Weiner, Lynn Y. 1985. *From Working Girl to Working Mother: The Female Labor Force in the United States, 1820-1980*. Chapel Hill, N.C.: University of North Carolina.

Yeung, W. Jean, John F. Sandberg, Pamela E. Davis-Kean, and Sandra L. Hofferth. 2001. "Children's Time with Fathers in Intact Families." *Journal of Marriage and the Family* 63(1): 136–54.

Chapter 8

Toward Gender Equality: Progress and Bottlenecks

Paula England

I s the significance of gender declining in America? Are men's and women's lives and rewards becoming more similar? To answer this question, I examine trends in market work and unpaid household work, including child care. I consider whether men's and women's employment and hours in paid work are converging, and examine trends in occupational sex segregation and the sex gap in pay. I also consider trends in men's and women's hours of paid work and household work. The emergent picture is one of convergence within each of the two areas of paid and unpaid work. Yet progress is not continuous and has stalled recently. Sometimes it continues on one front and stops on another. Gender change is also asymmetric in two ways: things have changed in paid work more than in the household, and women have dramatically increased their participation in formerly "male" activities, but men's inroads into traditionally female occupations or household tasks is very limited by comparison.

I consider what these trends portend for the future of gender inequality. Robert Max Jackson argues (see chapter 7, this volume) that continued progress toward gender inequality is inevitable. I agree with him that many forces push in the direction of treating similarly situated men and women equally in bureaucratic organizations. Nonetheless, I conclude that the two related asymmetries in gender change—the sluggish change in the household and in men taking on traditionally female activities in any sphere—create bottlenecks that can dampen if not reverse egalitarian trends.

TRENDS IN PAID WORK, OCCUPATIONAL SEGREGATION, AND THE PAY GAP

The story of women's increasing employment for pay is familiar, although the explanations are debated. Economists attribute rising women's employment to rising wages, which increased the opportunity cost of being a homemaker (Bergmann 2005). This was aided by disproportionate employment growth in the service occupations that had always hired mostly women (Oppenheimer 1970). Many believe that women's increased employment was motivated by the increased need for two paychecks—in other words, by a decline in men's real wages. It is true that, adjusted for inflation, men's wages in the United States are lower today than they were in the early 1970s (Bernhardt et al. 2001), so this may have motivated the employment of some wives. However, during most of the century, women's employment gains occurred while men's wages were also rising. Moreover, today, employment levels are approximately the same for women with high-earning as with low-earning husbands (Jackson 1998, 98), and highly educated women are *more* likely to be employed than women with less education (Juhn and Murphy 1997). Women's employment is increasingly explained more by how much they can earn than by how much income husbands provide (Cohen and Bianchi 1999). Now that many wives are employed, the increased living standards their paychecks afford create social comparison processes that make other couples perceive a need for comparable income.

Women's labor-force participation has increased while men's has gone down, but men's decline is much smaller than women's increase. The decrease in men's labor-force participation results from staying in school longer, retiring earlier, availability of state payments for those who are disabled, and a growing phenomenon of discouraged workers giving up and dropping out of the labor force. Figure 8.1 maps women's and men's labor-force participation together for the prime employment ages of twenty-five to fifty-four, showing movement toward convergence. However, after decades of increase, women's labor-force participation rates did not change between 1990 and 2000.

Table 8.1 shows more detail on women's employment increases. A snapshot in one week of 1978 showed 56 percent of women employed for pay, and by 1998 this figure was up to 71 percent. The proportion of women working full-time (at least thirty-five hours per week) was 38 percent in 1978, moving to 51 percent in 1998. In both years, wives with children under six were less likely to be employed and, if employed, were less likely to be employed full-time. Yet in percentage terms, wives with young children showed larger increases, moving from 38 percent to 58 percent employed, and from 21 percent to 35 percent employed full-time. If we look at annual hours of paid employment, which reflects both weeks per year and hours per week worked, table 8.1 shows a 41 percent increase for all women (from 1,002 to 1,415) and a 47 percent increase for wives with children under six (from 583 to 1,094).

We can make two generalizations: women's employment has converged toward men's through women's increases and, to a much lesser extent, men's decreases; and married women with small children always have lower employment than other women, but their employment has increased more rapidly than has that of other women.

As women entered paid employment, most went into predominantly female occupations. Men have predominated in management, the most prestigious profes-

FIGURE 8.1 / Labor-Force Participation by Men and Women Twenty-Five to Fifty-Four Years of Age, 1950 to 2000

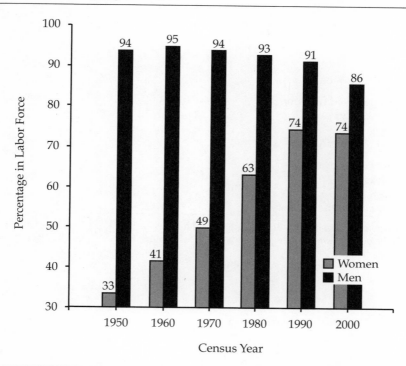

Source: Integrated Public Use Microdata Sample from 1950 to 2000 census data on men and women twenty-five to fifty-four years of age. See Cotter, Hermsen, and Vanneman (2005). Reprinted with permmission.

sions, blue-collar crafts, durable manufacturing work (such as autos, steel), transportation, and construction. Women have numerically dominated professions such as nursing, teaching, and librarianship. Nonprofessional but white-collar occupations of clerical and (noncommission) retail sales work have been largely done by women, as have manufacturing jobs in non-durable-goods industries (electronics, garments), and domestic and child-care work. Most of these patterns of which sex does which job persist, although occupational sex segregation has declined, as shown in figure 8.2.[1] (See also Jacobs 1989, 1999, 2001, 2003; Reskin and Roos 1990.) In particular, many women entered "male" professions (law, medicine, academia, the clergy) and lower and middle management (Cotter, Hermsen, and Vanneman 2004). Yet blue-collar crafts have integrated little; they remain male domains (Cotter, Hermsen, and Vanneman 2004; Jacobs 2003). Similarly, caring labor, such as child care, nursing, and elementary school teaching have integrated little, remaining dominated by women (England, Budig, and Folbre 2002). Segregation declined more in the 1980s than the 1990s.

TABLE 8.1 / Change Between 1978 and 1998 in Indicators of Paid Work of Women Twenty-Five to Fifty-Four Years of Age

	1978	1998	Percentage Change
Percentage employed the week before the survey			
All women	56	71	27
Wives with children under six	38	51	53
Percentage employed full-time the week before the survey			
All Women	38	58	34
Wives with children under six	21	35	67
Annual hours of paid work the previous year[a]			
All women	1,002	1,415	41
Wives with children under six	583	1,094	47

Source: Based on Casper and Bianchi (2002, table 10.1, 290), © 2002 by Sage Publications. Reprinted by permission of Sage Publications, Inc. Data are from U.S. Census Bureau, Current Population Surveys.
[a] Includes women not in the labor force all year.

FIGURE 8.2 / Occupational Sex Segregation, 1950 to 2000

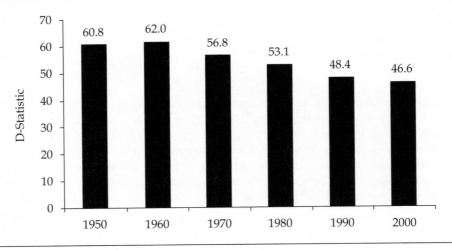

Source: Integrated Public Use Microdata Sample from 1950 to 2000 census data for men and women twenty-five to fifty-four years of age. Segregation is computed using the index of dissimilarity (see note 1) and using the most detailed occupational categories possible while still keeping consistent categories for all decades. See Cotter, Hermsen, and Vanneman (2005). Reprinted with permission.
Note: N = 179 occupations.

FIGURE 8.3   /   Occupational Sex Segregation by Education, 1950 to 2000

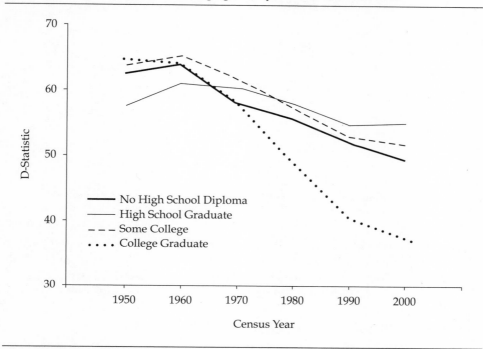

Source: Integrated Public Use Microdata Sample from 1950 to 2000 census data on men and women twenty-five to fifty-four years of age. Segregation is computed using the index of dissimilarity (see note 1) and using the most detailed occupational categories possible while still keeping consistent categories for all decades. Original calculations provided by David A. Cotter, Joan M. Hermsen, and Reeve Vanneman.
Note: N = 179 occupations.

Integration has not happened evenly across the class structure. Much more integration of women into "male" occupations has occurred in managerial and professional white-collar areas than in other jobs (Jacobs 2003). Figure 8.3 shows the trends in segregation separately by the education of the individuals holding jobs. Differences by education level are dramatic. While the segregation of those with a high school degree has declined only about five points (on the hundred-point D scale), the index dropped over twenty-five points for college graduates.

There is no more important indicator of gender inequality than the pay gap. Explanations of the sex gap in pay include sex differences in experience and seniority (Wellington 1994), segregation, and the fact that employers offer lower pay in predominantly female occupations than in male occupations, even relative to their skill demands (England 1992). Trends in pay among full-time year-round workers are shown in table 8.2. The ratio of (median) women to men's pay hovered around .60 for decades preceding 1980. Then within a decade it rose rapidly from .60 to .72. Declining hiring discrimination, declining segregation of jobs, and the declining sex gap in

TABLE 8.2 / U.S. Women's Median Annual Earnings as Percentage of
Men's, for Full-Time Year-Round Workers,
1960 to 2000

Year	Ratio
1960	.61
1965	.60
1970	.59
1975	.59
1980	.60
1985	.65
1990	.72
1995	.71
2000	.73

Source: Institute for Women's Policy Research (2005). Underlying data from
Current Population Surveys.

experience and seniority all contributed to decrease of the sex gap in pay (Blau and
Kahn 1997; O'Neill and Polachek 1993; Wellington 1993). However, there was little
further progress in the last decade of the century; the ratio moved only from .72 to .73.
Thus, here, as with employment and segregation, progress is stalling out.

TRENDS IN UNPAID AND TOTAL WORK HOURS

Women have lower employment rates than men largely because of their responsibility for child rearing and other household work. As more women, including
mothers of young children, work outside the home, we would expect reductions
in their time in household work, but does men's time spent doing household work
increase? How does any such increase compare in size with women's increase in
employment and decrease in household work? We could imagine a set of changes
with complete symmetry by gender and by household versus market sector.
Under such symmetry, we would observe that for every hour of housework
dropped by women, men pick up one, and for every hour of employment increase
by women, men drop one. Is this the pattern, or is it easier to get women into paid
work and out of some housework than to get men into household work?

To answer these questions, consider table 8.3, which contains computations
from two data sets containing time-diary information from probability samples of
Americans. The first study was done in 1965 by researchers at the University of
Michigan, as part of the Multinational Study of Time Use (Converse and Robinson
1980). The 1998 data are from a study by researchers at the University of Maryland
(Bianchi, Robinson, and Sayer 2001; Sayer 2001). Both used time diaries. In the
diary method, participants are asked to recount what they did every period of the
previous day. For each time segment, respondents list what they were doing, and
also if they were doing a second activity simultaneously (for example, cooking
dinner while watching television). Time diaries are a more accurate means of gath-

TABLE 8.3 / Average Hours Per Week Spent in Unpaid and Market Work by U.S. Married Men and Women Twenty-Five to Fifty-Four Years of Age, 1965 and 1998

	Unpaid Work			Market Work			Total Work (Unpaid and Market)		
	1965	1998	Change	1965	1998	Change	1965	1998	Change
Women	50	34	−16	8	31	23	59	65	6
Men	12	21	9	47	39	−8	59	60	1
Difference (Women – men)	38	13	25	−39	−8	31	0	5	5

Source: Calculations provided by Liana Sayer from data described in text (see Sayer 2001). Nonmarket work includes housework, child care, and shopping. Market work includes time in paid employment and travel to work. All figures computed on respondents twenty-five to fifty-four years of age.

ering information on time use than questions that ask respondents how much time they generally spend in some activity per week (Bittman and Wajcman 2000; Sayer 2001). The figures in table 8.3, limited to married women and men in the prime employment and child rearing ages of twenty-five to fifty-four, show gender differences in self-reported time spent in unpaid and market work. Unpaid work includes housework, shopping, and child care. The table uses only the "primary activity" the respondent listed for each time segment to add up total amounts of market and unpaid work time.

As table 8.3 shows, in 1965, sex differentiation was extreme. Men averaged forty-seven hours per week in market work, while women averaged only eight (because most women were not employed). Women did fifty hours per week of unpaid work, while men did only twelve. If we total paid and market work, men and women worked the same number of hours, fifty-nine per week. The gender differentiation was in type of work done, not total hours.

By 1998 things had changed substantially. Women had almost quadrupled their hours of market work from an average of eight to thirty-one hours per week. They had dramatically cut their unpaid work from fifty to thirty-four hours per week. This reflects declining fertility, the increase in employment, and the use of child care during job hours. But since the increase in employment was more than the decrease in unpaid work, women's total work hours had increased by six hours, from fifty-nine to sixty-five hours. By contrast, men increased their total only one hour per week, reflecting the fact that their increase in unpaid work was within about an hour of the magnitude of their decline in market work. Men increased their unpaid work by nine hours per week, a bit more than an hour a day. However, their increase was less than women's decrease in housework (sixteen), and much less than women's increase in paid work (twenty-three hours). Men also decreased their market work by eight hours. Other data suggest that this reduction is not due to a reduction of hours for the typical employed man (which Jacobs and Gerson 1998 show to have been fairly constant for men in recent decades), but rather due to an increased proportion of men out of the labor force (seen in figure 8.1 as well). Labor-force withdrawals in this prime age group resulted in part from more discouraged workers dropping out of the labor force at the bottom of the class structure.

The net effect of all these changes was that, whereas in 1965 married men's and women's total work week (unpaid plus paid) was equal, by 1998, married women worked five hours a week more than men. The evocative title of Arlie Hochschild's 1989 book, *The Second Shift*, suggested this relative and absolute speedup for women. The metaphoric title suggested that in the old days men and women each had one full-time job (him at "work," her at home), but now men have one and women have two (one at "work" and one at home). As table 8.3 shows, this imagery is exaggerated, since the average woman still works fewer hours in the market than men, men have picked up some household work, and total work hours, while greater for women, are certainly not anything remotely like eight hours a day more for women than men. However, Hochschild's metaphor captured something correct in diagnosing a trend toward women's total work burden increasing relative to men's.

Moreover, the gender disparity may be even greater than the figures here suggest, because they use only primary activities. Much child care is recorded by respondents as a secondary activity. For example, Michael Bittman and Judy Wajcman (2000) use Australian time-diary data to show that a higher proportion of women's than men's leisure activities are done while simultaneously doing child care (which is reported as the secondary activity). A higher percentage of men's leisure time is not combined with any work activity. In addition, there are many hours during which a woman at home does not record child care as a secondary activity, but she nonetheless can't leave because she is the one on call for the children. For these reasons, figures undoubtedly understate women's continued disproportionate responsibility for unpaid work. Whether or not the gender gap in total work is greater than indicated in table 8.3, an important point is that changes were not symmetrical. Men took on less traditionally female responsibility than women added in traditionally male responsibility.

HOW INEVITABLE IS MOVEMENT TOWARD GENDER EQUALITY?

What is the trajectory of change in gender? Is a move to equality inevitable? A thoughtful and provocative 1998 book by Robert Max Jackson argues that it is. In *Destined for Equality: The Inevitable Rise of Women's Status*, Jackson documents the many arenas in which women's opportunities have increased, relative to men's, in the past hundred fifty years in the United States. He chronicles women's advances in such areas as the right to vote, rights to property ownership, legislation making sex discrimination in pay and hiring illegal, increasing educational attainment, and employment. Similar trajectories can be seen in most affluent nations. Why did women gain opportunities and rights in all these spheres? He sees the key to be the shift of activities and power out of the household into modern business, political, and educational institutions. While individual men retain an interest in retaining patriarchal control over women and children in their own families, the logic and structure of modern bureaucratic organizations gives men less interest in women's subordination. Modern ideologies of equal opportunity and meritocracy also work against sexism in these institutions. (See chapter 7, in this volume, for Jackson's most recent statement of this position.)

Although Jackson does not draw on them, neoclassical economists offer an analogous argument that suggests that labor-market discrimination by sex should erode if competitive market forces are allowed to operate. Economists argue that competition in labor and product markets erodes discrimination because employers who won't hire women pay more than they need to for labor. Eventually this should make it hard for them to stay in business, as they need to charge higher prices (which may result in reduced product market share), or take lower profits (which should make it hard to borrow money in competitive capital markets). Even if discriminators don't go out of business, they should come to represent a smaller share of employment. (For an overview of economists' views of discrimination, see Arrow 1998; for a critique, see England 1992, chapter 2.)

Both Jackson's arguments and the economic thesis suggest that the trend toward gender equality should continue, at least outside the household and where the issue is allowing women into formerly "male" jobs or reward levels. I agree with Jackson and with economists that modern bureaucratic forms and competitive markets push against treating equally qualified men and women differently. However, the U.S. trends considered above show that progress toward gender equality sometimes falters. We see this in the slowdown of women's employment, desegregation of occupations, and convergence in pay since 1990.

The reason that I do not see "modernizing" trends as creating an inexorable move to gender equality lies in two related asymmetries that create bottlenecks to gender change: the greater tenacity of gender as an organizing principle in household and family behavior (relative to behavior in other "public" or "market" settings), and 2) the greater resistance to change that involves men taking on traditionally female activities than to change that involves women taking on traditionally male activities. Some concrete patterns, such as the limited involvement by men in the care of their children, illustrate both principles simultaneously. My point is not merely that the modernizing forces discussed by Jackson do not produce change directly in the household or in increasing men's involvement in previously "female" activities, but also that these factors feedback onto progress in other spheres, impeding women's ability to enter and succeed in traditionally male careers. I consider these two asymmetries in turn.

First, as Jackson's own thesis says, sexism dies hard in the family. This is not to deny the profound changes in family behavior. Indeed, the changes are dramatic—increases in the age at marriage, more cohabitation, more nonmarital childbearing, more divorce, longer spaces between divorce and remarriage, more single motherhood, a large increase in the hours married mothers spend in paid labor, and a more modest increase in men's participation in household work and child care. (Useful overviews of recent trends are provided by Casper and Bianchi 2002 and Blau 1998.) But the changes more often take the form of men and women living apart than of a diminution in the extent to which gender structures family life. The retreat from marriage, high divorce rates, and single motherhood are examples of a trend away from men and women living together. But gender structures the life of single parents as much as or more than that of married parents. Mothers generally have custody of children when the parents have broken up (whether they were ever married or not). Single mothers now do a higher proportion of the child rearing than wives in traditional 1950s breadwinner-homemaker families! What has changed is that mothers also take most of the responsibility for financial support of children. In 2001, on average, single mothers between the ages of eighteen and sixty-five drew 76 percent of their household income from their own earnings, 6 percent from child support and alimony, and 6 percent from welfare and public assistance (not including Social Security or EITC).[2] What seems most resistant to change is the social assignment of the primary responsibility for child rearing to women. Put another way, it is men's participation in child rearing and other household work that seems the slowest to move.

It is important not to overstate the case here. The huge increase in the employment of mothers and the more modest increase in dads' participation in unpaid work (seen in table 8.3) *are* reductions in gender as an organizing principle in the family. But reductions in the proportion of the typical adult lifetime spent coresiding with a person of the other sex seems the more dramatic change. This is seen in increasing age at marriage and continuing high divorce rates. This juxtaposition of the two possible responses was well put by Frances K. Goldscheider and Linda J. Waite (1991), who titled their book *New Families, No Families*, and argued that unless families change, women may increasingly opt out of having families.

The second asymmetry is that there is greater difficulty in changing men's behavior so that they embrace traditionally female activities than in changing women's behavior to include traditionally male activities. This is true at home and in the labor force. The devaluation of women and, by extension, activities and characteristics associated with women, is deeply inscribed in cultural norms. It is reflected in the greater esteem and reward associated with male activities. Thus, when women seek to enter traditionally male activities—employment, male occupations, roles of political or religious or military leadership—they are entering roles that are well respected and well rewarded. The notion that these activities are inappropriate for women may deter them, and men may sometimes conspire to keep them out, but the rewards and respect associated with the activities nevertheless encourage movement in this direction. On the other hand, there is little incentive for men to enter female activities. The notion that the activities are inappropriate for men may deter them, and in addition, they lose respect and money for doing so. While women's opportunity to access rewarded roles has increased, there is little evidence that the cultural devaluation of female roles has decreased. I know of no evidence that the esteem associated with the unpaid roles of being a full-time homemaker, or with the activities of unpaid housework or child care, have gone up. Neither has the pay penalty for being in female occupations or in occupations involving the quintessentially female-associated tasks of caring labor (jobs such as child care, therapy, teaching) declined (England, Thompson, and Aman 2001).

We can think of the two kinds of changes going on in the family, the degendering of family life and the decline of men and women living together, as examples, respectively, of two broader trends that we might call "exit" and "voice."[3] In this view, consistent with game theory or exchange theory, women's increased access to earnings gives them more bargaining power within marriage to negotiate for whatever they want in relationships (which might include greater male participation in household work) and more ability to leave marriages if they cannot successfully negotiate for wanted change (England 2000; England and Kilbourne 1990; Lundberg and Pollak 1996). Indeed, this theoretical perspective sees the possibilities of exit and voice to arise from the same resources: employment and increased earnings give women the possibility of leaving marriage and still supporting themselves and their children, and this makes it more plausible for them to strike better bargains within marriage. But some things may be harder to bargain for than others. I suspect that it is easier for women to bargain for a greater say in family expenditures than it is to enlist men in traditionally female activities such as household work, child care, and the emotional work of relationships. This is because of the deep cultural devaluation of activities associated with women, and the resistance of men to taking on these activities. The fact that the gender gap in total hours of work increased (table 8.3) suggests this bargaining difficulty. When attempts at "voice" fail, women may leave. The fact that two thirds of divorces are initiated by women is consistent with this interpretation (England 2000).

In both gendered marriages and single-parent families, women do most of the work of child rearing. What is the consequence of this for labor-market inequality? Clearly, women's child-rearing responsibility has a disparate impact on their ability to participate in the job world on an equal footing with men. This is what Jackson's (1998) thesis ignores. His argument hinges on the (unintentional) egalitarian impulse in modern bureaucratic institutions that erodes differential treatment based on sex. While agreeing that this impulse has important consequences, I see nothing in the fundamental structure or logic of these institutions that erode policies that have an adverse impact on those who spend considerable time caring for children. Employers have little incentive to accommodate employees' family responsibilities, particularly when they can make higher profits by hiring and promoting workers with no family responsibilities beyond making money. Indeed, rationalization and profit maximization push employers to try to avoid costs such as health care for children, sick-child leave, parental leave, and so forth, except when a shortage of labor makes such policies pay. (It is, in my view, an open empirical question whether such policies decrease or increase profits.) Given this, as long as families assign child rearing disproportionately to women (even when the couple has broken up), or absent vigorous state and other collective action to change norms and employer policies in a more parent-friendly direction, achieving gender equality in the labor market is by no means inevitable. Employers are sure to resist changes in policies that in essence ask them to absorb more of the costs of child rearing currently borne by individual parents and disproportionately by mothers. I agree with the moral argument that they *should* bear more of these costs, since they benefit from a well-reared next generation of employees, and equity requires that they contribute to the availability of these benefits, but it is in their immediate interest to keep these costs borne by others, and there is nothing in bureaucratic or market logic that pushes them to change these policies.

If motherhood hurts gender equality, as I am arguing, we should see that mothers fare worse in the labor market than women without children. Recent research documents a "motherhood penalty" in wages (Budig and England 2001; Waldfogel 1997, 1998). Some of it results from women's exits from employment when children are young, which reduces the experience and seniority that employers' wage systems reward. Some of the penalty results from mothers' working in part-time employment while their children are young, which generally leads to lower hourly wages and less wage growth. Even after controlling for all these factors, and many measures of the type of job held, there remains an additional unexplained portion of the motherhood penalty. This may reflect effects of motherhood on productivity, or employers' discriminatory treatment of mothers. Recent experimental work suggests that at least some of it is caused by discrimination against mothers (Correll and Bernard 2005). Both married and single mothers suffer the motherhood wage penalty (Budig and England 2001). The fact that motherhood creates differentials among women implies that the sex gap in pay is driven in part by differences between men and women's responsibility for children. This is consistent with prior research showing the role of experience, seniority, and part-time work in the sex gap in pay (Blau and Kahn 1997; O'Neill and Polachek 1993; Wellington 1993). Clearly, many widely accepted policies of employers, policies that may well be rational for profit maximization, have an adverse impact on those women with significant child-rearing responsibility.

"Adverse impact" is language from Title VII discrimination case law, which distinguishes between differential treatment and adverse impact (sometimes called "disparate impact"). Differential treatment involves treating similarly qualified men and women differently on the basis only of sex. Adverse impact involves rules or standards that are applied equally to men and women but disadvantage women because of their characteristics or situation. For example, a rule that barred people under a given height from a job has a disparate impact—an adverse impact—on women since they are shorter than men, on average. Here I am interested specifically in rules and criteria that have an adverse impact on anyone who has extensive child-care responsibilities; such criteria de facto will impact women much more than men, given the current gender division of labor in the family and the fact that women generally have custody of children after couples break up. Examples of policies that are fully consistent with bureaucracy, meritocracy, and profit maximization as usually understood, but that have a disparate impact on those who care for children include raises based on seniority, promotions contingent on putting in long or unpredictable hours of work, the unavailability of health insurance in many part-time jobs, and the lesser availability of part-time work in high-level jobs (Williams 2001).

The 1971 U.S. Supreme Court decision in Griggs v. Duke Power Co. stated that where plaintiffs show that an identifiable policy has a disparate impact on a protected class (for example, women), the burden of proof, which otherwise remains with plaintiffs, is shifted to defendants to show that the policy is a "business necessity." Thus, courts will sometimes strike down as illegal discrimination policies that have a disparate impact, even though the policies apply equally to men and women. Often, however, it is sufficient for the defendant to provide some evidence that the policy helps them hire more productive employees or lower their costs for the court to conclude that the policy is not illegal discrimination, despite its disparate impact. (For a review of cases in which discrimination against mothers has been contested using disparate impact and other doctrines, see Williams and Segal 2003. These authors are optimistic that the courts under some circumstances will rule that policies having a disparate impact on mothers or fathers with significant caretaking responsibility are discriminatory.) Even if court cases can sometimes be won in this area, there is nothing inexorable leading employers to get rid of many policies that have a disparate impact on responsible parents. While it is possible that restructuring work to get rid of these barriers would increase productivity, as Joan Williams (2001) argues, and this "business case" can be used to get employers to make policies more "mother-friendly," employers apparently don't think such changes are in their interest or they would be making them voluntarily. Thus, I don't see any broad structural trend eroding the portion of gender inequality in the labor market that results from the sex gap in parenting responsibility. To change this, either women will have to negotiate their way out of an unequal share of parenting responsibility (and the child-care status quo seems particularly resistant to change), or it will take a major push of collective action to force employers to adopt more parent-friendly policies, or both. Another possibility is continued declines in fertility to levels substantially below replacement levels, as we see in Japan and some countries in Europe now (McDonald 2000). Without these changes, this combination of family arrangements in which women do most of the parenting, and employer policies that have an adverse impact on those with parenting responsibility will continue to disadvantage women.

The resistance to change in men's roles in the family is part of a larger picture of asymmetry of gender-role change. There has long been more stigma for men adopting women's roles than vice versa. For example, as ideas about gender have changed, more parents have started to encourage daughters to participate in sports than have encouraged sons to play with dolls. Women get more approval for integrating male professions or trades than men do for entering female fields. This asymmetry results, as I argued above, from an underlying devaluation of women and, by extension, activities associated with women. Both peer pressure and economic incentives mitigate against men taking on traditionally female activities. This is most true for those quintessentially female-identified activities of unpaid child care and housework. But even outside the household, male resis-

tance to participation in traditionally female jobs is an impediment to sex integration and thus to gender equality. Basing their investigation on a series of case studies of occupational change in the 1970s, one pattern Barbara Reskin and Patricia
Roos (1990) identified was the "tipping" of occupations. The idea is that in an occupation that women start to enter, when a certain percentage female is reached,
men no longer want to stay in or enter the job. Men may shy away from jobs that
are in the process of "feminizing" because they fear the wages will decline, or they
fear the stigma of doing a "girl" thing. This asymmetry makes it hard to achieve a
stable, integrated equilibrium in jobs. One recent analysis of academic fields from
1971 to 2001 has shown this phenomenon (England et al. 2003); increases in the
number of women entering academic fields in the humanities and social sciences
led to fewer men choosing those fields for doctoral study five years later. However,
another analysis of whether rising female participation between 1983 and 2001 deterred male entry into occupations in the economy at large failed to find evidence
of such tipping (England et al. 2004). Men's abandonment of or disinclination to
enter a field when it gets "too female" does not violate nondiscrimination laws or
the rules of any bureaucratic institutions. Yet it is hard to see how integration can
be achieved through one-way movements of women into male jobs. This asymmetry, stemming from a disinclination of men to enter female spheres, is further
reason for doubting that progress toward gender integration is automatic.

CONCLUSION

I have reviewed trends in selected indicators of gender inequality, looking at the
last half century, and offered some speculations about future trends. Women's employment has increased and segregation and the pay gap have decreased, but all
three trends have slowed down since about 1990. Men's participation in unpaid
work increased nine hours per week between the 1960s and 1990s, but this increase was not enough to replace the decrease in women's unpaid work, and was
substantially less than the increase in women's employment over the period.

I considered Jackson's claim that continued progress to gender equality is inevitable (Jackson 1998, and chapter 7, in this volume). I agree with him that the
logic of modern organizations moves us toward sex-blind treatment of individuals
by employers and governments. However, as he concedes, these structural forces
do not directly dislodge gender as an organizing principle of family life. They do
little to change the informal assignment of child rearing to women. Nor do they do
much to change employer policies that have a disparate impact on whoever has
primary responsibility for child rearing—still mostly women. Such policies reward seniority, favor one full-time over two part-time workers, and reward workers who can work long, unpredictable hours. Women's responsibility for child
rearing, combined with these policies, leads to significant gender inequality in
earnings.

The largest bottlenecks to gender equality are the continuing organization of
families by gender (especially the assignment of child-rearing responsibility to

women), and the resistance of men to taking on traditionally female activities in the family or workplace. Neither of these are eroded by the forces of bureaucracy and institutional universalism. Both are serious contemporary impediments to gender equality. While I agree with Jackson's thesis that most of the momentum for increased gender equality to date came as an unintended result of structural changes rather than feminist organizing, it is likely to take feminist organizing for state action to remove these remaining barriers to gender equality.

What policies would break the bottlenecks inhibiting gender equality? The problems are not amenable to policies as straightforward as those appropriate to job discrimination against women seeking to enter male occupations and to be paid equally in them, although vigilant enforcement of antidiscrimination laws would be helpful here. How can legislation change men's disinclination to enter predominantly female jobs? Perhaps comparable-worth policies would help this (England 1992); if female jobs didn't pay less, men might be less averse to sharing jobs with women. But to the extent that social stigma is what stands in the way of men working in fields with many women, cultural education that challenges the devaluation of everything associated with women is needed. It is hard to imagine legislating men's equal participation in household labor and child rearing. But there are policies that could help. In Sweden, the state replaces a portion of a parent's pay after the birth of a child, and recently instituted a policy so that couples who have the entire leave taken by one parent receive less paid leave. The "use it or lose it" rules are increasing male take-up somewhat (Gornick and Meyers 2003). One can imagine a regulatory (rather than spending) approach to getting rid of parent-unfriendly policies; the Family and Medical Leave Act embodied this approach, requiring that large employers hold a worker's job for a six-week unpaid leave after a birth. The time could be extended, employers could be forced to pay as much per hour for part-time as full-time work, to prorate benefits for part-time workers, and so forth. These things might reduce the motherhood wage penalty if combined with vigilant enforcement against discrimination in hiring mothers (since regulations making employers accommodate employees' child rearing would increase incentives for simply not hiring mothers).

A spending rather than regulatory approach would assume that people who care for children will inevitably be penalized by the market, and would use state subsidies to make up for this. A rationale for such policies is that the work of caring for children has positive externalities; many third parties benefit when children grow up to be good friends, workers, spouses, and neighbors to others who did not contribute to the costs of their upbringing (England, Budig, and Folbre 2002; England and Folbre 1999). (Pro-natalism might also be a rationale for such policies, though I would argue on ecological grounds in favor of increasing immigration instead of attempts to increase the fertility of the native-born.) Policies subsidizing those who deliver care might provide a family allowance to anyone doing unpaid care of a child at home (universal family allowances are common in Europe) and credits toward Social Security (based on child rearing rather than on marital history, as is currently the case in the United States). Wages for paid caring labor might be state-subsidized in recognition of their positive externality-producing function (England, Budig, and Folbre 2002). Such policies providing state funding for those who do currently paid and unpaid care work would collectivize some of the costs of rearing children, reduce the ability of men and nonparents to "free ride" on women's caring labor, and in so doing, redistribute resources from men to women (England and Folbre 1999; Folbre 1994).

Policies that seek to increase the rewards of traditionally female work are not without their critics. One argument against comparable worth, the effort to increase the relative pay of predominantly female occupations, or paid parental leave, is that these policies may encourage women to stay in traditionally female roles—at home as child rearers or in "female" jobs. Of course, the same programs increase the incentives for men to enter female jobs or to take parental leave, but if the cultural stigma is such that few men can be induced, then the net effect might be to further entrench gender differentiated roles and jobs. While increasing the incentives for women to remain in traditionally female roles, the policies would simultaneously decrease the penalty for doing so, so it is unclear, on balance, whether women would gain or lose in earnings in the long run. We see here the split between liberal feminism and what Nancy Folbre (2001) has called social feminists. Liberal feminists, such as Barbara Bergmann (2005, especially chapters 9 and 10) argue against anything that might decrease incentives for women's employment and movement into male-typical occupations. Social feminists such as Folbre (2001) recognize these dangers, but also see a danger in underinvestment in (paid or unpaid) caring labor. The dangers are not just in the unfair economic penalty paid by those who contribute to the public good through care, but also in the possible inefficiencies for the economy and society of an undersupply of care (England and Folbre 2003). (See Gornick and Meyers 2003 for discussion of how to structure parental leave to make it more likely to reduce than increase gender inequality.) One policy that both groups can agree on is state-supported child care. This redistributes resources to parents, including single mothers, from others. It also unambiguously increases female employment. It is unclear under what conditions state policies providing replacement wages for paid parental leave increase or decrease women's continuity of employment relative to men's, so some parental leave policies may reduce and some increase gender equality.

I believe that movement toward a society in which women don't do more than their share of child rearing and in which those who do child rearing are not penalized for this is both possible and desirable. However, unfortunately, there is nothing inexorable in the logic of either markets or rationalized bureaucratic organizations that will get us there. It will take persuasion, education, and collective action.

NOTES

1. The statistic used to measure segregation is the index of dissimilarity, D, which, roughly speaking, tells us what percentage of men or women would have to change occupations in order for the proportion in each occupation of males and females to match that of all

employed persons. More precisely, D is a ratio in which the numerator is the proportion of women (men) who would have to change occupations from the current distribution in order to integrate occupations and the denominator is the number of moves women (or men) would have to make to integrate occupations if, instead of the current distribution, occupations were maximally segregated such that all occupations were entirely of one sex or the other. Occupations are considered to be integrated when women's (men's) proportion of each occupation is the same as women's (men's) proportion of the labor force as a whole. D is self-weighting; that is, occupations employing more people count more than smaller ones. This is appropriate if we want to know how segregated the job experience of the average person is. For discussions of how much of the decline comes from integration of specific occupations and how much from disproportionate growth of more integrated occupations, see Francine D. Blau, Patricia Simpson, and Deborah Anderson 1998; David A. Cotter, Joan M. Hermsen, and Reeve Vanneman 2004). Maria Charles and David B. Grusky (2004, chapter 2) have criticized D and proposed an alternative log-linear-model-based measure, A. This measure also shows a decline over recent decades with some slowdown in the 1990s (this author's own calculations, using Current Population Surveys).

2. Author's calculations from 2001 Current Population Survey, March supplement.
3. I am borrowing the terms "exit" and "voice" from Albert O. Hirschman (1970), who argued that when people are dissatisfied with what a firm or the state does, they have three options—to leave and go elsewhere (exit), to bargain with the authorities (voice), or to accept the status quo (loyalty).

REFERENCES

Arrow, Kenneth. 1998. "What Has Economics to Say About Discrimination?" *Journal of Economic Perspectives* 12(2): 91–100.

Bergmann, Barbara. 2005. *The Economic Emergence of Women.* 2nd edition. New York: Basic Books.

Bernhardt, Annette, Martina Morris, Mark S. Handcock, and Marc A. Scott. 2001. *Divergent Paths: Economic Mobility in the New American Labor Market.* New York: Russell Sage Foundation.

Bianchi, Suzanne M., John P. Robinson, and Liana C. Sayer. 2001. *Family Interaction, Social Capital, and Trends in Time Use Study Project Report.* College Park, Md.: University of Maryland, Survey Research Center.

Bittman, Michael, and Judy Wajcman. 2000. "The Rush Hour: The Character of Leisure Time and Gender Equity." *Social Forces* 79(1): 165–89.

Blau, Francine D. 1998. "Trends in the Well-being of American Women, 1970–1995." *Journal of Economic Literature* 36(1): 112–65.

Blau, Francine D., and Lawrence M. Kahn. 1997. "Swimming Upstream: Trends in Gender Wage Differentials in the 1980s." *Journal of Labor Economics* 15(1): 1–42.

Blau, Francine D., Patricia Simpson, and Deborah Anderson. 1998. "Continuing Progress? Trends in Occupational Segregation in the United States over the 1970s and 1980s." *Feminist Economics* 4(3): 29–71

Budig, Michelle, and Paula England. 2001. "The Wage Penalty for Motherhood." *American Sociological Review* 66(2): 204–25.

Casper, Lynne M., and Suzanne M. Bianchi. 2002. *Continuity and Change in the American Family*. Thousand Oaks, Calif.: Sage.

Charles, Maria, and David B. Grusky. 2004. *Occupational Ghettos: The Worldwide Segregation of Women and Men*. Palo Alto: Stanford University Press.

Cohen, Philip N., and Suzanne M. Bianchi. 1999. "Marriage, Children, and Women's Employment: What Do We Know?" *Monthly Labor Review* 122(December): 22–31.

Converse, Philip E., and John P. Robinson. 1980. *Americans' Use of Time, 1965–1966*. Ann Arbor, Mich.: Inter-University Consortium for Political and Social Research.

Correll, Shelley, and Stephen Bernard. 2005. "Getting a Job: Is There a Motherhood Penalty?" Paper presented at Wharton Conference on Careers and Career Transitions. Philadelphia (June).

Cotter, David A., Joan M. Hermsen, and Reeve Vanneman. 2004. *Gender Inequality at Work*. New York: Russell Sage Foundation.

———. 2005. "Gender Inequality at Work." In *The American People: Census 2000*, edited by Reynolds Farley and John Haaga. New York: Russell Sage Foundation.

England, Paula. 1992. *Comparable Worth: Theories and Evidence*. New York: Aldine de Gruyter.

———. 2000. "Conceptualizing Women's Empowerment in Countries of the North." In *Women's Empowerment and Demographic Processes: Moving Beyond Cairo*, edited by Harriet B. Presser and Gita Sen. Oxford: Oxford University Press.

England, Paula, Paul Allison, Su Li, Noah Mark, Jennifer Thompson, Michelle Budig, and Han Sun. 2003. "Why Are Some Academic Fields Tipping Toward Female?" Paper presented at the meeting of Research Committee 28 of the International Sociological Association, New York University. New York (August).

England, Paula, Paul Allison, Yuxiao Wu, and Mary Ross. 2004. "Does Bad Pay Cause Occupations to Feminize, Does Feminization Reduce Pay, and How Can We Tell with Longitudinal Data?" Paper presented at the annual meeting of the American Sociological Association. San Francisco (August).

England, Paula, Michelle Budig, and Nancy Folbre. 2002. "The Wages of Virtue: The Relative Pay of Care Work." *Social Problems* 49(4): 455–73.

England, Paula, and Nancy Folbre. 1999. "Who Should Pay for the Kids?" *Annals of the American Academy of Political and Social Sciences* 563(May): 194–209.

———. 2003. "Contracting for Care." In *Feminist Economics Today*, edited by Julie Nelson and Marianne Ferber. Chicago: University of Chicago Press.

England, Paula, and Barbara Kilbourne. 1990. "Markets, Marriage, and Other Mates: The Problem of Power." In *Beyond the Marketplace: Society and Economy*, edited by Roger Friedland and Sandy Robertson. New York: Aldine de Gruyter.

England, Paula, Jennifer Thompson, and Carolyn Aman. 2001. "The Sex Gap in Pay and Comparable Worth: An Update." In *Sourcebook on Labor Markets: Evolving Structures and Processes*, edited by Ivar Berg and Arne Kalleberg. New York: Plenum.

Folbre, Nancy. 1994. *Who Pays for the Kids? Gender and the Structures of Constraint*. London: Routledge.

————. 2001. *The Invisible Heart: Economics and Family Values*. New York: New Press.

Goldscheider, Frances K., and Linda J. Waite. 1991. *New Families, No Families? The Transformation of the American Home*. Berkeley: University of California Press.

Gornick, Janet, and Marsha Meyers. 2003. *Families That Work: Policies That Reconcile Parenthood and Employment*. New York: Russell Sage Foundation.

Griggs v. Duke Power Co. 1971. 401 U.S. 424 (U.S. Supreme Court).

Hirschman, Albert O. 1970. *Exit Voice and Loyalty: Responses to Decline in Firms, Organizations, and States*. Cambridge, Mass.: Harvard University Press.

Hochschild, Arlie Russell. 1989. *The Second Shift: Working Parents and the Revolution at Home*. New York: Viking.

Institute for Women's Policy Research. 2005. "The Gender Wage Ratio: Women's and Men's Earnings." *Fact Sheet*. Available at: http: /www.iwpr.org/pdf/c350.pdf (updated August 2005).

Jackson, Robert Max. 1998. *Destined for Equality: The Inevitable Rise of Women's Status*. Cambridge, Mass.: Harvard University Press.

Jacobs, Jerry A. 1989. *Revolving Doors: Sex Segregation and Women's Careers*. Palo Alto: Stanford University Press.

————. 1999. "Sex Segregation of Occupations: Prospects for the 21st Century." In *Handbook of Gender in Organizations*, edited by Gary Powell. Thousand Oaks, Calif.: Sage.

————. 2001. "Evolving Patterns of Sex Segregation." In *Sourcebook of Labor Markets: Evolving Structures and Processes*, edited by Ivar Berg and Arne L. Kalleberg. New York: Plenum.

————. 2003. "Detours on the Road to Equality: Women, Work and Higher Education." *Contexts* 2(1): 32–41.

Jacobs, Jerry A., and Kathleen Gerson. 1998. "Who Are the Overworked Americans?" *Review of Social Economy* 56(4): 442–59.

Juhn, Chinhui, and Kevin M. Murphy. 1997. "Wage Inequality and Family Labor Supply." *Journal of Labor Economics* 15(1): 72–79.

Lundberg, Shelly, and Robert A. Pollak. 1996. "Bargaining and Distribution in Marriage." *Journal of Economic Perspectives* 10(4): 139–58

McDonald, Peter. 2000. "Gender Equity, Social Institutions, and the Future of Fertility." *Journal of Population Research* 17(1): 1–16.

O'Neill, June, and Solomon Polachek. 1993. "Why the Gender Gap in Wages Narrowed in the 1980s." *Journal of Labor Economics* 11(1): 205–28.

Oppenheimer, Valerie. 1970. *The Female Labor Force in the United States*. Berkeley: University of California Institute of International Studies.

Reskin, Barbara, and Patricia Roos. 1990. *Job Queues, Gender Queues*. Philadelphia: Temple University Press.

Sayer, Liana C. 2001. *Time Use, Gender, and Inequality: Differences in Men's and Women's Market, Nonmarket, and Leisure Time*. Ph.D. diss., Department of Sociology, University of Maryland.

Waldfogel, Jane. 1997. "The Effects of Children on Women's Wages." *American Sociological Review* 62(2): 209–17.

————. 1998. "Understanding the 'Family Gap' in Pay for Women with Children." *Journal of Economic Perspectives* 12(1): 137–56.

Wellington, Allison J. 1993. "Changes in the Male-Female Wage Gap, 1976–1985." *Journal of Human Resources* 28(2): 383–411.

———. 1994. "Accounting for the Male/Female Wage Gap Among Whites: 1976 and 1985." *American Sociological Review* 59(6): 839–84.

Williams, Joan. 2001. *Unbending Gender: Why Family and Work Conflict and What to Do About It.* London: Oxford University Press.

Williams, Joan, and Nancy Segal. 2003. "Beyond the Maternal Wall: Relief for Family Caregivers Who Are Discriminated Against on the Job." *Harvard Women's Law Journal* 26(Spring): 77–162.

Chapter 9

Gender as an Organizing Force in Social Relations: Implications for the Future of Inequality

Cecilia L. Ridgeway

Although it has hardly disappeared, gender inequality in the labor market has declined noticeably in recent decades, by most standard indicators. Inequality is declining in labor-force participation rates, wages, and occupational sex segregation, even though considerable sex segregation remains, especially at the job and firm level (Jacobs 1999; Petersen and Morgan 1995; Reskin and Padavic 1999). A debate now centers on the nature of the forces behind these changes and their implications for the future. Are the forces that have been and are undermining gender inequality now unstoppable, as recent arguments posit (Jackson 1998)? Is the significance of gender as an organizing principle of inequality in society declining as a consequence? If there are forces that continue to reproduce gender inequality, what do they consist of and what is their future?

With others (Jackson 1998; Reskin 2000), I am persuaded that the growth of bureaucratic and economic rationalization and the consequent spread of universal legal rights and organizational procedures are major forces underlying the recent erosion of gender inequality. My view, however, is that gender inequality is not declining as rapidly as it would be if these forces were not slowed by powerful processes that conserve gender inequality, even if in reduced form (Ridgeway 1997). Robert Max Jackson (1998), too, recognizes that resistance to the decline of gender inequality is present in contemporary society, but he argues that this resistance must lose in the long run because no compelling force continually reproduces gender inequality. I argue, however, that Jackson has overlooked a powerful set of ongoing social processes that work to maintain gender inequality in the face of equalizing forces. These processes derive from the deep-seated role gender plays in the fundamental organization of social relations between individuals and from the stereotypes, status assumptions, and cognitive biases that result from that role. Such processes, I argue, underlie resistance to change in the household division of labor, the persistent gender labeling of new jobs, and continuing resistance to the authority of women. As Paula England (see chapter 8, this volume; Budig and England 2001) argues, unless the household division of labor changes, gender inequality in the labor market will persist even if discrimination in hiring and promotion disappears entirely.

None of us can tell whether the power of the forces conserving gender inequality is sufficient to actually derail, rather than merely slow, the ultimate decline of gender as a principle of inequality. I hope it is not. I have described elsewhere how the forces conserving inequality might be undermined so that progress toward equality is accelerated (Ridgeway and Correll 2000). However, I believe these conserving forces at present remain powerful enough to suggest that the road to gender equality will be a rough one without a completely assured end.

GENDER AS A STATUS INEQUALITY

Before proceeding, a few general considerations about gender as a form of inequality may be helpful. Like Jackson (1998), I view gender as primarily a status inequality rather than a positional inequality. Status inequality is based on relationships between different types of people who distinguish themselves by personal characteristics. Positional inequality is based on relationships between roles within a social structure that carry unequal rights, resources, and responsibilities (see Jackson 1998, 12–13).

Few sociologists would disagree with Jackson's (1998, 249) major contention that "to be effective, all systems of status inequality, including gender inequality, must be embedded in positional inequality." But this states only one side of the issue in understanding the effectiveness and persistence of status inequalities. A status inequality such as gender gains range and effectiveness by being embedded in specific positional inequalities such as those based on economic or political positions. Yet a status inequality such as gender loses effectiveness and significance if it ever becomes fully or completely embedded in another system of positional inequality other than that created by its own independent processes. As Peter M. Blau (1977) pointed out, when dimensions of inequality completely overlap, such that they become fully consolidated rather than intersect, they lose their independent significance and become unrecognizable as separate forms of inequality. Thus status inequalities, including gender inequality, are most effective when they are partially, but not wholly, embedded in positional inequalities in economic and political structures. This, of course, was Max Weber's (1922/1968) point in his delineation of status as a distinct form of inequality that is related to but not the same as wealth and power.

Gender inequality has persisted as a distinct, recognized form of inequality in Western societies for some time. By this analysis, then, it must have done so through some combination of embeddedness in economic and political positional inequalities and its own autonomous productions of inequality that are not fully reducible to economic and political power. What might be the sources of gender inequality separate from access to economic or political power? Most would point for an answer to gender's role in organizing heterosexuality, reproduction, and the family. While not disagreeing, I consider this a partial answer because it does not fully address gender's effects as a status inequality. I will focus my own analysis of gender inequality's independent staying power on a set of intermediate processes that partially result from gender's role in reproduction and the family but that carry gender to relationships beyond the family and sustain it as a status distinction.

GENDER AS AN ORGANIZING FORCE IN SOCIAL-RELATIONAL CONTEXTS

The driving force behind gender as a distinct system of difference and inequality is gender's deep-seated role as an organizing force in social relations. Sex categorization, which is the routine process of labeling others as male or female, is a fundamental cultural and cognitive tool that people use to frame an even more fundamental human activity—relating to another, be it in person, on paper, on the Internet, or even in imagination.

Primary Cultural Frame for Social Relations

From the perspective of individuals, social life and society in general are enacted through multiple social-relational contexts. These are contexts in which individuals define themselves in relation to others in order to comprehend the situation and act. Everyday interactions, whether in person or through some other medium, are by definition social-relational contexts, but contexts where individuals act alone are social-relational as well if the individuals feel their behavior or its consequences will be socially evaluated. In such situations individuals must still implicitly define themselves in relation to relevant others in order to anticipate the reactions of those others and act accordingly.

To successfully manage social-relational contexts, people need at least some shared cultural systems for categorizing and defining self in relation to others in the context so that they can correctly anticipate behavior and act in response. Studies of social cognition suggest that a small number of such category systems, perhaps three or four, serve as primary categories of person perception in a society (Brewer and Lui 1989; Fiske 1998). Primary categories define those things that a person must know about another to render that other sufficiently meaningful in cultural terms so that the person can relate to the other. Possibly because sex category is a simple dichotomous (male or female) classification with relevance to heterosexuality and reproduction, evidence suggests that sex category is virtually always one of a society's primary category systems (Brewer and Lui 1989; Glick and Fiske 1999a). In the United States, race and age are primary category systems as well (Fiske 1998).

In fact, social-cognition research has shown that people automatically and unconsciously sex-categorize any concrete other that they cast themselves in relation to. They do this even when, as is often the case, more relevant and informative institutional roles, such as boss and employee, are readily available to define self and other in the context. Evidence indicates that actors in a relational context first sex-categorize one another and do so almost instantly (Brewer and Lui 1989; Stangor et al. 1992). This evidence suggests that actors' subsequent categorizations of each other according to institutional roles are nested within their prior understandings of each other as male or female and take on a slightly different meaning as a result (compare a male clerk and female customer versus a female clerk and male customer). We can think abstractly about an ungendered boss or employee, but we can never actually relate, even in imagination, to any specific boss or employee without gendering him or her first.

We may speculate that the origins of the sex category as a primary cultural category system lie in its relevance for heterosexuality and reproduction. Whatever the origins, sex category's role as a fundamental cultural tool for framing any social relation carries sex and gender far beyond home, reproduction, and the family. Since we cannot comprehend another sufficiently to relate to the other without sex-categorizing him or her first (and making salient our own sex category by implication), as a consequence, sex and gender are pulled in some degree into every sphere of social life that is enacted through social relations. By this analysis, sex and gender's status as a primary framing device for social relations is what causes gender to be a force in all social institutions, including those that make up the labor market (Ridgeway 1997). It is the use of sex and gender as a relational framing device that embeds (and, I will argue, continually re-embeds) gender in positional inequalities in political and economic as well as familial institutions. Yet, driven by its own logic as a framing device, gender brings its own dynamics to social relations so that it is never fully encapsulated by any given structure of positional inequalities.

Gender Beliefs as Difference and Inequality

Although we tend to assume that sex categorization is "natural," in everyday social relations it is a thoroughly social process that relies on cues of behavior and appearance that are culturally presumed to stand for physical sex differences (Kessler and McKenna 1978; West and Zimmerman 1987). In fact, sex and gender is a cultural system for framing self–other relations precisely because it is based on widely shared beliefs that describe the distinguishing characteristics of typical males and females and the way they are expected to behave. An actor may hold such descriptive gender beliefs whether or not he or she ideologically endorses them as the way men or women should be (Blair and Banaji 1996; Rudman and Kilianski 2000; Spence and Buckner 2000).

We often think of such shared, descriptive gender beliefs as stereotypes. They are that, but they are more as well. Widely shared gender beliefs are, in effect, the cultural rules for perceiving and enacting gender as a distinct system of difference and inequality. It is these beliefs that constitute gender as a status inequality in society.

Studies show that roughly consensual gender beliefs do indeed exist in the contemporary United States (Fiske et al. 2002; Lueptow, Garovich-Szabo, and Lueptow 2001; Spence and Buckner 2000; Williams and Best 1990; see Eagly, Wood, and Diekman 2000 for a review). Because gender stereotypes have status beliefs at their core, they have a hierarchical as well as horizontal dimension and imply inequality as well as difference (Conway, Pizzamiglio, and Mount 1996; Eagly and Mladinic 1994; Wagner and Berger 1997; Williams and Best 1990). Status beliefs define members of one group as more status-worthy and generally competent than those of another group, while granting each group its specialized skills (Wagner and Berger 1997). Similarly, gender beliefs view men as more agentic and competent overall and more competent at the things that "count most" in society (for example, instrumental rationality) than women. Women are viewed as less competent in general, but better at more feminine, communal tasks, even though these tasks are themselves less valued (Conway, Pizzamiglio, and Mount 1996; Eagly and Mladinic 1994; Fiske et al. 2002). Such gender stereotypes are consensual in that most people know them and recognize them as the social "rules of the game" by which most others will judge them, whether or not the people themselves personally endorse these stereotypes. In fact, the likelihood that people hold consensual stereotypes as descriptive beliefs is only modestly correlated with their ideological beliefs about gender egalitarianism (Blair and Banaji 1996; Rudman and Kilianski 2000; Spence and Buckner 2000).

As a cultural device for framing social relations, gender is above all a system of social difference whose utility lies in the assumption that actors classified in one category may be expected to behave differently from those classified in another category. Yet, as an extensive body of research on social cognition and social identity theory has demonstrated, the mere classification of another as different evokes an evaluative response (see Brewer and Brown 1998 for a review). The most basic form of evaluative response to difference appears to be in-group favoritism. That is, if you and I are different, then my group is better and I will act to favor those from my group over those from your group. Thus, difference alone creates cognitive biases that are conducive to discrimination and to the development of a hierarchical as well as difference dimension in group stereotypes.

Notice, however, that the basic evaluative response to difference effectively creates competing views of the proper hierarchical relation between the two groups. Members of each group evaluate their own group above the other. If gender is a system of social difference for framing social relations among individuals and facilitating the coordination of their joint behavior, then competing views of who is "better" are an impediment to mutual relations that may be difficult to sustain over the long run. Under conditions of long-term mutual dependence between groups, competing in-group preferences tend to be transformed by one means or another into shared status beliefs (Jackman 1994). That is, members of both groups come to agree (or concede) that, as a matter of social reality, one group is more respected and status-worthy than the other. In an achievement-oriented society such as our own, status evaluations are expressed and legitimated by corresponding assumptions about differences in general competence and instrumental expertise (Glick and Fiske 1999b).

Social distinctions that are important for organizing social relations within a society tend to demarcate groups with considerable mutual dependence on one another (Jackman 1994; Ridgeway and Erickson 2000). Not surprisingly, then, important social distinctions in our society such as age, race, occupation, education, as well as gender are each associated with widely shared beliefs about the status rankings of the groups these distinctions delineate. In comparison to the groups created by other distinctions, however, there is an exceptional degree of mutual dependence between the sexes. Heterosexuality, reproduction, the way that sex cross-cuts kin relations, and the division of the population into two roughly equal-sized gender groups all increase contact and dependence between the sexes. Virtually all men and women must regularly and repeatedly enter into cooperative relations with members of the other sex to achieve what they want or need. These conditions put unusually strong structural pressures on gender as a system of shared beliefs about difference to be simultaneously a system of shared beliefs about the status ranking of men and women. Given men and women's mutual dependence, then, beliefs about gender difference and beliefs about status inequality co-determine each other, giving a characteristic structure to gender stereotypes.

Although this analysis suggests that cultural beliefs about gender difference tend to foster gender-status beliefs about inequality—beliefs about the relative status of the two genders—it does not presume male dominance. From a logical point of view, the result could also be female dominance. The historical origins of male- rather than female-status dominance are unknown. However, research shows that when some factor gives members of one group a systematic advantage in attaining influence and power in their mutual dealings with members of another group, people from both groups develop shared status beliefs favoring the advantaged group (Ridgeway et al. 1998; Ridgeway and Erickson 2000). Many theories about the origins of male status dominance posit some factor, such as superior male strength or the physical constraints faced by lactating mothers, that could have given men a systematic influence advantage in their dealings with women at some time in the past (see Wood and Eagly 2002). Whatever their origin, once status beliefs favoring men become culturally established, they root male advantage in group membership itself and thus advantage men even over their female peers who are just as strong as they and are not, say, lactating mothers. Because gender-status beliefs root inequality in group membership, they constitute gender as a distinct organizing principle of inequality that is not fully reducible to other differences in power or material resources.

Gender Interests

As a primary cultural system for framing social relations that implies both difference and hierarchy, gender creates a distinct set of interests for actors. These interests are central to the staying power of gender as a significant dimension of inequality. They affect the energy with which actors enact gender in different social contexts and resist challenges to existing gender arrangements. Since people are never just men or women but are also a myriad of other social identities, however, actors' gender interests always coexist with multiple other, often competing interests. As a consequence, men's and women's behaviors and judgments in social relational contexts are almost never determined by gender processes alone.

The gender-status beliefs contained within the current framework of gender beliefs obviously give men an interest in maintaining the presumption of their greater competence and status worthiness compared to similar women. Such a presumption advantages them in access to privileged positions within a wide variety of social institutions (Reskin 1988). Some heterosexual women also benefit from the current framework because their intimate association with higher-status men gives them material resources or access to power that they might not have in a society without male privilege. Yet, as Jackson (1998) notes, even these men and women often have other economic and political interests in the contemporary situation that cause them to take actions that, perhaps unintentionally, undermine men's privileged access to superior economic and political power. Furthermore, the interests of most women in bettering themselves in society cause them to continually push against the constraints of the current gender framework.

Although the current framework of male status dominance does create interests in maintaining male privilege, in my view these are not likely to be the most powerful interests that sustain gender as a system of difference and inequality, especially since most women have a countervailing interest in resisting that inequality. Gender creates another, deeper set of interests as well. Gender is so deeply embedded in social relations that few people are likely to tolerate serious disruptions to the basic system of sex labeling that sets the gender system in motion. Gender is one of the three or four identities that are central to the process by which people render themselves comprehensible to themselves and others in terms that are socially valid within their society (Ridgeway and Correll 2000; West and Zimmerman 1987). As a result, both men and women have deep cognitive interests in maintaining a clear and reasonably stable framework of gender beliefs that define "who" men and women "are" by differentiating them.

To gain a sense of the power of the cognitive interests gender creates, consider a series of skits that played on *Saturday Night Live* a few years ago. In these skits, "Pat," a completely androgynous person, wreaked havoc in even mundane interactions because the other interactants could not place Pat as a man or a woman. The social vertigo that the interactants experienced in the skits was revealing of the importance of sex categorization as an organizing force in social relations. The depth of the resulting interests people have in maintaining a stable system of sex differentiation was revealed by the audience reactions to these skits. Invariably, audience members engaged in extreme nervous laughter and an intense kind of social anxiety and discomfort.

Certainly, actors may have strong economic and political interests, but they also have very strong interests in knowing "who" they are in social terms and who others are in relation to them. These strong interests create a deep reservoir of resistance to any real erasure of gender difference. As we have seen, the preservation of beliefs in gender difference, given the mutual dependence between men and women, also tends to foster beliefs in status inequality.

IMPACT ON LABOR-MARKET INEQUALITY

Job searches, hiring, the development of job skills, job performance and evaluation, promotion, and the everyday conduct of worklife are largely carried out through social-relational contexts. Individuals acting in these contexts automatically sex-categorize one another. Research shows that sex categorization in turn automatically activates gender stereotypes that provide implicit, usually unconscious cognitive lenses through which self and other are perceived and evaluated (Banaji and Hardin 1996; Blair and Banaji 1996; Stangor et al. 1992). As we shall see, the extent to which such gendered lenses bias a person's behavior and evaluations can vary from negligible to substantial, depending on the context. There is increasing consensus among several researchers, however, that the cognitive biases that typically result from the automatic activation of gender stereotypes in work-related contexts are the fundamental, underlying cause of gender inequality in the labor market (Bielby 2000; Reskin 2000; Reskin and McBrier 2000; Ridgeway 1997).

The framing assumptions toward work and workers embodied in these gender biases can become embedded in the organizational structures, authority lines, job classifications, institutional rules and administrative procedures of firms (Baron, Jennings, and Dobbin 1988; Nelson and Bridges 1999; Reskin and McBrier 2000; Steinberg 1995). As this occurs, the implicit biases of gender stereotypes acquire a solidity and institutional force that shapes the work process and acts as an agent of inequality. On the other hand, organizational structures and administrative procedures can also suppress the biasing effects of gender stereotypes on the behavior and judgments of actors in firms. Bureaucratic accountability for equity, formalized personnel procedures, and open information about reward structures have all been shown to reduce the extent to which actors' behaviors and judgments in the work process are biased by gender or racial stereotypes (see Bielby 2000; Reskin and McBrier 2000; Ridgeway and Correll 2000 for reviews). It is precisely the growth of such rationalizing, universalistic organizational forms and procedures that Jackson credits with reducing gender inequality by disembedding it from positional inequality in the labor market. By my account, such forms and procedures have their effect by suppressing the biasing effects of stereotypes on the behaviors and judgments of workplace actors.

Social-Relational Processes and the Maintenance of Workplace Inequality

Since organizational forms and administrative procedures mediate the effect of actors' gender stereotyping on men's and women's labor-market outcomes, Barbara

Reskin (2000; Reskin and McBrier 2000) refers to these forms and procedures as the proximate cause of gender inequality in the labor market, even while cognitive bias is the ultimate cause. My arguments here focus on stereotyping and cognitive bias because these processes are key to assessing the staying power of gender inequality in the labor market. Reskin is correct that in bureaucratically well-ordered work contexts, the degree of gender inequality that results is largely a function of the organizational structures and administrative procedures that enact or suppress it. However, in less well-ordered work contexts, such as those at the interstices of organizations (for example, an interdepartmental task force), in some types of work, in start-ups, in newly developing forms of work, or in newly forming occupations, social-relational processes among individuals come to the fore. The impact of gender stereotypes activated by sex categorization in these social relations, I have argued, are sufficient in themselves to create gender inequality in workers' outcomes without the intervention of biased bureaucratic practices (Ridgeway 1997). There is some evidence to support this assertion: for example, the gender gap in wages and the gender typing of job assignments in television screenwriting, an organizationally chaotic, interpersonally brokered occupation, is comparable to that found in bureaucratically well-structured jobs (Bielby and Bielby 1995).

The primary significance of this assertion, however, is not its ability to account for gender inequality in established but atypical jobs that are outside well-ordered bureaucratic contexts. Instead, the significance of the ability of social-relational processes to create gender inequality lies in its implications for work that occurs at the cutting edge of economic, technological, and social-organizational change. The work sites and start-ups where new industries, new types of work, new occupations, and new forms of organizational structure and business practices are developed are not bureaucratically well-structured sites. Frequently such work sites are initially ordered primarily through interpersonal relations and informal procedures. Workers in these settings not only lack established bureaucratic rules and procedures, they often lack well-defined institutional roles. As result, the workers are especially likely to draw on personal attributes, including gender, to define themselves and others in the context and organize their interpersonal relations. Consequently, gender's effects as a framing device for interpersonal relations is likely to implicitly draw gender stereotypes into the work process at such sites, shaping in some degree workers' relations, assumptions, judgments and behavior. As this occurs, gender inequality is likely to emerge in the work site. More significant, however, is that the actors involved are likely to rewrite gender-biased assumptions into the new organizational practices, divisions of labor, job definitions, lines of authority, and occupations that they develop through their activities. In this way, social-relational processes in work sites at the edge of ongoing economic and technological transformations maintain gender inequality in the face of change by translating it into new organizational forms and work structures (Ridgeway 1997).

Note that this maintenance of gender inequality occurs in contexts that are somewhat shielded, at least for a formative period, from the bureaucratic accountability and formalized universalistic procedures that suppress the biasing effects of stereotypes. By this argument then, social-relational processes in work sites springing up at the edge of ongoing change continually reinstitutionalize gender assumptions and gender hierarchy into newly emerging work structures. This process in turn slows the gender-equalizing effects of bureaucratic rationalization and universalistic personnel procedures in the labor market.

Gender Status Effects in the Workplace

Having argued that gender effects in social-relational contexts constitute an important force that preserves gender inequality over economic and technological transformations, it is now time to describe more specifically the nature of these gender effects. Automatic sex categorization activates gender stereotypes in all social-relational contexts in the workplace and elsewhere, but the impact of these stereotypes on actors' behaviors and judgments can vary from imperceptible to substantial, depending on the nature of the context. Thus, the social-relational effects of gender are not invariant but, rather, context-dependent. I will describe these effects as they operate when they are not suppressed by administrative procedures and bureaucratic accountability.

Recall that gender stereotypes in the United States describe men as more status-worthy, instrumentally competent, and agentic, whereas women are seen as less competent overall but more communal and skilled at caregiving. Sex categorization in social relations activates all aspects of gender stereotypes, but I shall concentrate on the impact of their status and competence contents (which I refer to as gender-status beliefs), since these have the greatest relevance for inequality in the labor market.

The impact of gender stereotypes on actors' behavior and evaluations depends on gender's salience in the context as a distinction that is diagnostic of behavior and on gender's relevance to the central goals or tasks of the setting (Deaux and LaFrance 1998). Although gender's very diffuseness as a social identity allows it to function as an all-purpose orienting frame toward any other person in relation to self, by the same token it virtually never offers sufficiently detailed instructions for action in a specific situation. In defining a situation for action, people categorize one another in multiple ways and quickly focus on institutional roles (for example, file clerk or manager) that carry specific, context-relevant implications for action (Fiske, Lin, and Neuberg 1999). In work-related contexts, institutional roles are in the foreground of actors' perceptions of "who" they and others are in the situation, whereas gender generally acts as a less salient background identity.

As a background identity, gender nevertheless can be (although is not always) effectively salient for actors in a situation, meaning that it is sufficiently salient to measurably affect their behaviors and evaluations. When effectively salient, the status and competence implications of gender stereotypes bias, or modify, the behaviors and evaluations that actors undertake in the performance of their foreground roles as institutional actors. Thus gender can operate as a kind of ghostly presence in work-related contexts, one that subtly colors behaviors and judgments that are not ostensibly gender-related. Workplace actors themselves are often quite unconscious of the background biases affecting their behaviors and evaluations, even if these effects can be measured by observers.

Indeed, actors' routine unawareness of the background biases of gender stereo-types are key to their effects. Actors are capable of suppressing stereotype biases in their behavior and evaluations, but only under demanding motivational circum-stances. To suppress stereotype bias, actors must be alert to its possible presence in their behavior at a given moment, must be motivated to suppress it, and must have the time and energy to do so. Of course, women's own interests in bettering themselves suggests that they will more often be sufficiently motivated to resist the biasing effects of stereotypes in their own behavior than will men (Fiske, Lin, and Neuberg 1999). When acting routinely or pressured to act quickly, however, even committed egalitarians often act in implicitly biased ways (Blair and Banaji 1996; Kunda and Sinclair 1999; Plant and Devine 1998).

Evidence suggests that gender-status beliefs are effectively salient and likely to bias behavior and evaluations in a least two types of contexts: mixed-sex con-texts—work settings with both males and females present—and gender-typed contexts (Wagner and Berger 1997)—those whose tasks, goals, or activities are cul-turally linked to a given sex. A wide variety of work contexts are either mixed sex or gender-linked, but not all. Once gender-status beliefs are effectively salient, the strength of their impact on actors' expectations and behavior is proportional to gender's relevance to the goals and tasks of the setting. Consequently, we should expect the effects of gender-status beliefs to be strongest in gender-typed work set-tings such as engineering and the military (male-linked) and nursing and elemen-tary education (female-linked).

When gender is effectively salient in a context, theory and evidence suggest a distinct pattern of biases in the expectations actors form for each other's compe-tence and status in the situation (for reviews, see Ridgeway 2001; Ridgeway and Smith-Lovin 1999; Wagner and Berger 1997). These gender-biased expectations are consequential because they tend to have self-fulfilling effects on actors' behaviors and evaluations (Harris and Rosenthal 1985; Miller and Turnbull 1986; Jussim and Fleming 1996). In mixed-sex contexts that are not gender-linked, expectations for competence and status should modestly favor men over women who are other-wise similar to them. In male-linked contexts, competence and status expectations will more strongly favor men over similar women. In female-linked contexts, men's advantage will disappear and biases may slightly favor women.

Gender-biased expectations for competence and status have been shown to af-fect men and women's relative willingness to assert themselves in task-oriented settings and offer their opinions; the extent to which others ask for their opinions; the evaluations that their opinions and task performances receive; the inference of ability from a performance of acknowledged quality; the development of influ-ence over others; and the likelihood that they will emerge as leaders (for reviews, see Biernat and Kobrynowicz 1999; Deaux and LaFrance 1998; Eagly and Karau 2002; Foschi 2000; Ridgeway 2001; Ridgeway and Smith-Lovin 1999; Wagner and Berger 1997). Once a person is in a leader or manager role, gender-biased expectations affect perceptions of the manager's competence and legitimacy in that role and the manager's ability to wield directive authority without encountering a "backlash" of hostility and resistance (Heilman, Block, and Martell 1995; Eagly and Karau 2002; Rudman and Glick 2001). Such resistance to women's authority helps create a "glass ceiling" for women who seek top positions. Finally, there is evidence that gender-biased expectations for competence can also inhibit or boost actual performance, independent of ability, by arousing anxieties or instilling confidence (Shih, Pittinsky, and Ambady 1999; Spencer, Steele, and Quinn 1999; Wheeler and Petty 2001).

These effects of gender-status beliefs on actors' behaviors and evaluations of self and others set in motion both demand- and supply-side factors that affect gender inequality in the labor market. On the demand side, gender-biased competence expectations on the part of employers, supervisors, and fellow workers can create a variety of forms of discrimination in the workplace (see Ridgeway 1997; Ridgeway and Correll 2004). Gender-status and competence beliefs also encourage the process by which employers seek and prefer employees of one sex or the other, depending on the status and sex typing of the job. This process in turn supports the sex segregation of jobs and resegregation by specialty within jobs (Reskin and Roos 1990). The continual activation of gender-status beliefs in the workplace by actors' automatic sex typing of self and others contributes as well to the persistent tendency to gender-type jobs, including newly developing jobs, and to associate status value with them accordingly.

On the supply side, the activation of gender-status beliefs in work- or training-related contexts can bias individuals' expectations for their own competence in the situation relative to others'. This in turn can affect individuals' willingness to pursue a particular line of work or training and persist at it in the face of difficulties compared to otherwise similar people of the other sex. It can affect the assertiveness with which individuals conduct themselves in the workplace and the level of rewards they demand in compensation (Bylsma and Major 1992; Major 1989).

Self-expectations that are biased by the activation of gender-status beliefs in a work or training situation can also affect actual performance, independent of ability (Spencer et al. 1999). Even more insidiously, biased self-expectations can affect the level of ability individuals attribute to themselves, given a certain performance. For instance, Shelley J. Correll (2004) has shown that when a task is presented as male-typed, activating gender-status beliefs, men attribute more ability to themselves on the basis of the same performance than women attribute to themselves. When the same task is specifically disassociated from gender so that gender-status beliefs are not effectively salient, there are no differences in the ability men and women attribute to themselves when performances are similar. Noting that math is a male-typed task in the United States, Correll (2001) shows how women's tendency to attribute less math ability to themselves than men do to themselves, when both groups have the same mathematical performance, acts as a barrier to women's pursuit of careers in science and engineering. This in turn helps preserve the masculine dominance of these fields.

Both the demand- and supply-side effects of the gender-status beliefs that are activated in work- or training-related contexts by automatic sex categorization occur through implicit cognitive biases. These cognitive biases shape behaviors and evaluations in ways actors are rarely conscious of. Consequently, such effects on either the demand or supply side of the equation are not best characterized as the intentional results of people's explicit choices in the workplace. They do, however, result from people's active pursuit of their interests in rendering themselves and others as socially meaningful and, therefore, gendered actors in social-relational contexts.

The cultural beliefs about gender status and competence that people draw on to define themselves and others in work contexts occasionally cause actors to explicitly assert or defend their gender-status interests. Most commonly, however, the effects of gender-status beliefs on behavior and evaluations in any given context are more subtle and modest. It can sometimes be difficult to explicitly recognize or detect these effects in a single setting, but when such implicit biasing effects are repeated over multiple work-related contexts, they accumulate over the course of a career to result in substantial differences in men's and women's lifetime outcomes in the labor market. Enforced universalistic administrative procedures and bureaucratic accountability can suppress some biasing effects on the demand side, especially in hiring and promotion. Motivated vigilance on the part of committed egalitarian actors can also suppress such biasing effects on both the demand and supply side of the process. However, the routine background effects of gender-status beliefs will continue to bias supply-side processes as long as gender-status beliefs continue to imply significant competence differences between men and women and continue to be widely held in society. Furthermore, and somewhat paradoxically, the biasing effects of gender-status beliefs are likely to operate fairly freely in the less bureaucratically structured work sites at the forefront of economic and technological change. In these sites, status-based gender inequality may be re-embedded in emerging economic and organizational structures.

IMPLICATIONS FOR THE FUTURE

By this account, the driving force behind gender inequality is sex and gender's role as a primary framing device for social relations. Automatic sex categorization in all social-relational contexts, including the workplace, activates gender stereotypes that in turn shape people's behavior and evaluations in situationally varying degrees. To intervene in this process directly, one must either disrupt sex categorization as an automatic activity or modify the stereotypes sex categorization evokes. In my view, sex categorization is too deeply rooted as a system of relational sense making for people to tolerate a serious effort to disrupt it. A reduction in inequality is more likely to develop from a reduction in the status and competence differences implied by gender stereotypes (Ridgeway and Correll 2000). Such changes could occur through the erosion of cultural assumptions that link gender to specific workplace-relevant skills, such as technical-mathematical expertise or management ability, as well as through a reduction in presumed differences in general competence. Changes like this in stereotype content would reduce the diagnostic value and task relevance of gender for actors in work-related contexts and thus reduce its impact on their behavior and evaluations in the workplace. As a result of such stereotype change, gender would be effectively (that is, measurably) salient in fewer and fewer workplace contexts. There are, however, reasons to believe that stereotype change of this sort will be a difficult and lengthy process.

Widely shared cultural beliefs about gender are only sustainable in the long run if the terms on which most men and women encounter one another confirm these beliefs for them, at least as a representation of the way "most people" are (Eagly 1987). In particular, current gender stereotypes require that men and women routinely experience one another as sufficiently different in ways that justify men's greater power and status. Thus, social changes that systematically rearrange the terms on which most men and women relate to one another in everyday contexts put pressure on stereotypes to change accordingly (Ridgeway and Smith-Lovin 1999).

It is exactly such a set of systematic social changes that Jackson points to in his discussion of increasing bureaucratic rationalization and universalism as forces that irretrievably undermine gender inequality. I've argued that such changes do indeed suppress the biasing effects of gender-status beliefs in workplace contexts, allowing and encouraging women to push past the subtle demand and supply barriers that result from gender-status beliefs. As they have for generations, women continue to push past these barriers through a combination of the determined pursuit of their own interests in bettering themselves and the intentional efforts of men and women committed to gender egalitarianism. Intentional egalitarian motivations and ambition in women are in turn fostered by the social changes Jackson describes. As women move into formerly male occupations and into higher-status positions in the workplace, social-relational contexts at work provide both men and women with experiences of one another that are increasingly at odds with traditional stereotypic assumptions about status and competence differences between the sexes. This is the process that pushes for gradual but accumulating changes in stereotypes that allow for sustainable reductions in gender inequality.

Impediments to Stereotype Change

What are the forces that blunt the process of stereotype change and slow the erosion of assumptions about status and competence that undergird inequality? Organizational processes in the labor market, such as the continuing sex segregation of jobs within firms and specialties within occupations, play an important role by recasting women's gains within an institutional frame that reaffirms cultural stereotypes about gender difference and men's greater status significance (Kilbourne et al. 1994; Reskin and Roos 1990). And there are other forces that are likely to slow, although not stop, changes in gender stereotypes in the face of changes in men's and women's workplace experiences. Some of these forces derive from the tendency for any cultural belief system to lag behind changes in corresponding experience. Others draw more specifically on gender's distinctive role in organizing social relations.

Widely held stereotypes about socially significant distinctions among people in a society, such as gender or race stereotypes, have several characteristics that buffer them somewhat from the impact of disconfirming experience. Studies of social cognition have shown that individuals have powerful tendencies to perceive and interpret people and events in terms that confirm their prior expectations and concerns (Fiske, Lin, and Neuberg 1999). Such confirmation biases, as they are called, cause people to selectively attend to events and experiences that confirm what they want or expect to see and to fail to notice, to ignore, or to discount events and information that disconfirm their expectations. The deeper people's emotional and cognitive commitments to their prior expectations, the more they unconsciously distort what they see to fit those expectations.

Most people's deep investment in gender as a fundamental cultural dimension for understanding self and other potentially fuels powerful tendencies either to not recognize stereotype-disconfirming events as such or to reinterpret them in stereotype-confirming ways. Evidence shows that people find it easier to cognitively encode, and thus to recognize, think about, and remember information that matches gender-stereotypic expectations (Von Hippel, Sekaquaptewa, and Vargas 1995). People also spontaneously fill in unspecified details of male and female behavior to make an experience consistent with gender expectations (Dunning and Sherman 1997). Indeed, given the actual diversity and range of men's and women's real behavior and traits, it is likely that the reason shared cultural stereotypes about "men" or "women" in general are sustainable at all is by dint of such expectation-confirming cognitive distortions.

Given such stereotype-confirming biases, men's and women's gender-atypical workplace experiences with one another will likely have only modest effects on their taken-for-granted assumptions about gender status and competence, although these modest effects will slowly accumulate over longer periods of time. Studies of stereotype change show that even when confronted with a person who forcefully disconfirms cultural stereotypes, most people react first by cognitively reclassifying the person as "an exception" with little import for what can be expected of most others (see Hewstone 1994 for a review). The more "exceptions" people encounter, however, the greater pressure they are under to modify their underlying stereotypes.

A second process that buffers people's widely held stereotypes from their disconfirming experiences derives from people's taken-for-granted presumption that these stereotypes are consensual in society (Zelditch and Floyd 1998). As we have seen, evidence indicates that people in the United States do in fact presume that people generally know and accept gender stereotypes as descriptive of most people (see Eagly, Wood, and Diekman 2000 for a review). When people presume cultural beliefs are consensual, they assume others will treat them according to these beliefs. Consequently, they must take these beliefs into account in their own behavior, whether or not they personally accept these beliefs as descriptive of themselves or consider them ideologically preferable or obnoxious. Gretchen B. Sechrist and Charles Stangor (2001) have shown that the assumption that others hold a stereotype has a substantial impact on the likelihood that individuals act, or refrain from acting, in accord with that stereotype. The presumption of consensus about gender stereotypes buffers them from disconfirmation by encouraging people to act in accord with established stereotypes even when their own and perhaps others' conviction about these stereotypes has begun to waver. Thus, even if disconfirming experiences raise doubts in growing numbers of individuals, these individuals may often inadvertently act to confirm established stereotypes. This blunts the impact on stereotypes of people's self-conscious ideological belief in gender egalitarianism.

Given the processes that blunt the impact of changing workplace experiences on gender stereotypes, we should expect that changes in gender stereotypes will lag substantially behind changes in labor-market inequality and in explicit gender ideology, which will slow the erosion of that inequality. Lagging gender stereotypes continue to inject into relational contexts cognitive biases and behaviors that support both supply and demand aspects of labor-market inequality unless these biases are suppressed by organizational procedures or demanding acts of individual vigilance. This will occur even in the face of countervailing forces that work against inequality. Furthermore, since these lagging gender stereotypes are less likely to be suppressed in institutionally less-scripted work sites such as those at the edge of economic and technological change, these work sites continue to propel gender stereotypes into the future. These less-structured work sites write lagging gender stereotypes into the developing organizational forms and procedures of emerging industries, even as these stereotypes are increasingly suppressed in established, bureaucratically well-ordered industries.

Stability and Change in Contemporary Stereotypes

Not surprisingly, studies of contemporary gender stereotypes show that they have indeed lagged substantially behind declines in workplace inequality. Current and longitudinal studies of gender stereotypes show that descriptive beliefs about the attributes of the typical man or woman are still largely shared and largely unchanged in the United States since the 1970s (Lueptow, Garovich-Szabo, and Lueptow 1995, 2001; Spence and Buckner 2000; Twenge 1997). This relative stability has been maintained despite substantial declines in labor-market inequality during the same period. It has also been maintained despite growing egalitarianism in people's conscious gender ideologies, as reflected in increasing percentages of people who report a willingness to vote for a woman for president (National Opinion Research Center 1998).

Despite the overall stability in beliefs about the typical man or woman, there nevertheless have been some hints of change in other aspects of people's descriptive gender beliefs during this period. People's self-reports of their own instrumental and expressive traits are usually less gender-typed than are their beliefs about the typical man or woman. In many social contexts, people's estimates of gender stereotypes are more important determinants of their behavior than their own self-reported traits because gender stereotypes represent the rules by which people assume they will be judged by others (see Milkie 1999). Still, according to two studies (Spence and Buckner 2000; Twenge 1997), people's self-reports of their own gender traits, while also generally stable over recent decades, have changed more than their gender stereotypes as applied to others, although a third study disagrees (Lueptow, Garovich-Szabo, and Lueptow 2001). In general, both men and women describe themselves as more instrumental than earlier cohorts did, but the effect is stronger for women. As a result, there seems to be a narrowing of the gender gap in men's and women's self-descriptions of their instrumental abilities. It is, however, interesting that there have been either no differences in men's and women's self-reported expressive traits or an increase in expressive traits reported by women. Consistent with the relative stability in the household division of labor, women still attribute much stronger expressive traits to themselves than men attach to themselves. Other studies show that women are evaluated more positively and less negatively than earlier and are now seen by both sexes as similar to men in overall favorability, even though these gains are due to women's being seen by both sexes as "nicer" than men. Men are still rated more highly on the socially valued dimension of instrumental competence (Eagly and Mladinic 1994).

Overall, then, the core structure of cultural beliefs about gender is still intact in both its hierarchical and difference dimensions. The gap on the hierarchical dimension, reflected in beliefs about valued instrumental competence, shows encouraging signs of narrowing. However, the ordinal evaluation of most men as better than most women in valued competence has not yet been eroded.

A Reservoir of Resistance

If a narrowing of the gap between the status and competence ascribed to men and women seems to be occurring, can we extrapolate that a virtual closing of this gap is simply a matter of time, even if a lengthy time? In my view, this may occur. However, we cannot yet be confident that it will because of the capacity of fundamental changes in gender beliefs to activate people's deep seated interests in maintaining clear cultural understandings of gender difference. Modest changes in cultural understandings of men and women can be incorporated into widely shared gender beliefs without evoking much resistance if they do not threaten the core structure of these beliefs that establishes both difference and ordinal hierarchy. Indeed, the Western system of gender inequality has not persisted over centuries through unchanging cultural conceptions of men and women, but through ongoing evolutions of these conceptions in ways that nevertheless continue to reaffirm basic gender differences that justify male dominance (see Bem 1993; Cancian 1987). I suspect that this pattern of change within stability has occurred partly because people react to deep threats to the core structure of their understandings of gender difference by reinterpreting events and behavior in ways that reestablish that core structure, even if in an altered, more moderate form.

This resistance process, motivated by people's investment in gender as a fundamental cultural tool for framing social relations, has a powerful capacity to push back against the gender-leveling effects of economic and political change and the motivated actions of ambitious women and gender egalitarians of either sex. For instance, people's deeply held beliefs that men and women are separate categories of people may cause them to implicitly resist beliefs that there are absolutely no instrumental competence differences between men and women in the "things that count." This resistance may facilitate cultural redefinitions of "what counts" as a sign of high-status instrumental competence. It used to "count" to be a pediatrician, for instance, but it no longer counts as much now that many pediatricians are women.

Furthermore, as widely held gender beliefs attribute fewer and fewer differences to men and women in instrumental competence, these changes not only begin to undermine the legitimacy of the hierarchical dimension of gender stereotypes, but they also cause the stability of cultural conceptions of gender difference to depend increasingly on assumptions about women's distinctive communal or expressive skills and traits. If it is harder to believe that men and women differ in instrumental competence, it may be more important to believe that men cannot and should not do caregiving in the way that women do. Recall that beliefs in women's greater expressive or communal traits are the aspects of gender beliefs that have changed least in recent decades, both in terms of gender stereotypes and self-attributions (Spence and Buckner 2000).

In a sense, the cultural battleground over the maintenance of gender as a system of difference and status is shifting toward the feminine arena of nurturance and away from the masculine arena of instrumental competence as a result of progress toward workplace equality (Ridgeway and Correll 2004). To the extent that this shift occurs, however, it activates a deep cultural reservoir of resistance to fundamental changes in the household division of labor or to changes in the status evaluation of caregiving activities. This resistance can be seen in men's persistent unwillingness to take on primary responsibility for caregiving tasks and in some women's unwillingness to relinquish these responsibilities. It can also be seen in the way that women and men who openly represent themselves in the workplace as caregivers as well as workers (say, by taking parental leave) are judged to be less competent and committed workers (Ridgeway and Correll 2004; Williams 2000). As Paula England (chapter 8, this volume) points out, persistent inequalities in the household division of labor are sufficient in turn to maintain gender inequality in the labor market, even if gender discrimination in hiring and promotion disappears.

The dynamic, almost devilish ways that cultural understandings of difference and status inequality support and reconstitute one another in widely shared cultural definitions of gender make the core structure of taken-for-granted gender stereotypes difficult, although not impossible, to erode. Without substantial changes to this core structure, gender will continue to persist as a significant organizing principle of inequality in society, even if the degree of inequality that it produces is reduced in a growing range of workplace contexts. As the degree of inequality that gender produces becomes less and less, however, the cultural foundations of gender difference are also undermined. Basic threats to gender difference in turn threaten people's deep interests in sex and gender as a fundamental tool for rendering themselves and others meaningful as socially valid actors in society. It is difficult to estimate the power of the resistance to full equality that such interests create. I remain hopeful that we can come considerably closer to equality than we have so far. Achieving greater equality will require not only the economic and legal changes that Jackson points to but also the continuing efforts of committed gender egalitarians who call for accountable procedures in the workplace that suppress stereotype bias (see Bielby 2000). Yet the depth of people's interest in gender as a category of meaning for self and other causes me to believe that we dare not be sanguine about the final outcome of the economic and political changes that we are now seeing.

REFERENCES

Banaji, Mazarin R., and Curtis Hardin. 1996. "Automatic Stereotyping." *Psychological Science* 7(3): 136–41.

Baron, James N., P. Devereaux Jennings, and Frank R. Dobbin. 1988. "Mission Control? The Development of Personnel Systems in U. S. Industry." *American Sociological Review* 53(4): 497–514.

Bem, Sandra L. 1993. *The Lenses of Gender*. New Haven: Yale University Press.

Bielby, William T. 2000. "Minimizing Workplace Gender and Racial Bias." *Contempary Sociology* 29(1): 120–28.

Bielby, William T., and Denise D. Bielby. 1995. "Cumulative Versus Continuous Disadvantage in an Unstructured Labor Market: Gender Differences in the Careers of Television Writers." In *Gender Inequality at Work*, edited by Jerry A. Jacobs. Thousand Oaks, Calif.: Sage.

Biernat, Monica, and Diane Kobrynowicz. 1999. "A Shifting Standards Perspective on the Complexity of Gender Stereotypes and Gender Stereotyping." In *Sexism and Stereotypes in Modern Society*, edited by William B. Swan, Judith H. Langlois, and Lucia A. Gilbert. Washington, D.C.: American Psychological Association.

Blair, Irene V., and Mazarin R. Banaji. 1996. "Automatic and Controlled Processes in Stereotype Priming." *Journal of Personality and Social Psychology* 70(6): 1142–63.

Blau, Peter M. 1977. *Inequality and Heterogeneity: A Primitive Theory of Social Structure*. New York: Free Press.

Brewer, Marilynn, and Rupert J. Brown. 1998. "Intergroup Relations." In *Handbook of Social Psychology*, edited by Daniel T. Gilbert, Susan T. Fiske, and Gardner Lindzey. New York: McGraw-Hill.

Brewer, Marilynn, and Layton Lui. 1989. "The Primacy of Age and Sex in the Structure of Person Categories." *Social Cognition* 7(3): 262–74.

Budig, Michelle J., and Paula England. 2001. "The Wage Penalty for Motherhood." *American Sociological Review* 66(2): 204–25.

Bylsma, Wayne H., and Brenda Major. 1992. "Two Routes to Eliminating Gender Differences in Personal Entitlement." *Psychology of Women Quarterly* 16(2): 1993–2200.

Cancian, Francesca M. 1987. *Love in America: Gender and Self-Development*. New York: Cambridge University Press.

Conway, Michael, M. Teresa Pizzamiglio, and Lauren Mount. 1996. "Status, Communality, and Agency: Implications for Stereotypes of Gender and Other Groups." *Journal of Personality and Social Psychology* 71(1): 25–38.

Correll, Shelley J. 2001. "Gender and the Career Choice Process: The Role of Biased Self-Assessments." *American Journal of Sociology* 106(6): 1691–1730.

———. 2004. "Constraints into Preferences: Gender, Status, and Emerging Career Aspirations." *American Sociological Review* 69(1): 93–113.

Deaux, Kay, and Marianne LaFrance. 1998. "Gender." In *Handbook of Social Psychology*, edited by Daniel T. Gilbert, Susan T. Fiske, and Gardner Lindzey. New York: McGraw-Hill.

Dunning, David, and David A. Sherman. 1997. "Stereotypes and Trait Inference." *Journal of Personality and Social Psychology* 73(3): 459–71.

Eagly, Alice H. 1987. *Sex Differences in Social Behavior: A Social-Role Interpretation*. Hillsdale, N.J.: Erlbaum.

Eagly, Alice H., and Stephen J. Karau. 2002. "Role Congruity Theory of Prejudice Towards Female Leaders." *Psychological Review* 109(3): 573–79.

Eagly, Alice H., and Antonio Mladinic. 1994. "Are People Prejudiced Against Women? Some Answers from Research on Attitudes, Gender Stereotypes, and Judgments of Competence." In *European Review of Social Psychology*, edited by Wolfgang Stroebe and Miles Hewstone. Volume 5. New York: Wiley.

Eagly, Alice. H., Wendy Wood, and Amanda B. Diekman. 2000. "Social Role Theory of Sex Differences and Similarities: A Current Appraisal." In *The Developmental Psychology of Gender*, edited by Thomas Eckes and Hanns M. Trautner. Mahwah, N.J.: Erlbaum.

Fiske, Susan T. 1998. Stereotyping, Prejudice, and Discrimination. In *The Handbook of Social Psychology*, edited by Daniel T. Gilbert, Susan T. Fiske, and Gardner Lindzey. 4th edition. Volume 2. Boston: McGraw-Hill.

Fiske, Susan T., Amy J. Cuddy, Peter Glick, and Jun Xu. 2002. "A Model of (Often Mixed) Stereotype Content: Competence and Warmth Respectively Follow from Perceived Status and Competence." *Journal of Personality and Social Psychology* 82(6): 878–902.

Fiske, Susan T., Monica Lin, and Steven Neuberg. 1999. "The Continuum Model: Ten Years Later." In *Dual Process Theories in Social Psychology*, edited by Shelley Chaiken and Yaacou Trope. New York: Guilford.

Foschi, Martha. 2000. "Double Standards for Competence: Theory and Research." *Annual Review of Sociology* 26: 21–42.

Glick, Peter, and Susan T. Fiske. 1999a. "Gender, Power Dynamics, and Social Interaction." In *Revisioning Gender*, edited by M. Myra Ferree, Judith Lorber, and Beth B. Hess. Thousand Oaks, Calif.: Sage.

———. 1999b. "Sexism and Other 'Isms': Interdependence, Status, and the Ambivalent Content of Stereotypes." In *Sexism and Stereotypes in Modern Society*, edited by William B.

Swan, Judith H. Langlois, and Lucia A. Gilbert. Washington, D.C.: American Psychological Association.

Harris, Monica J., and Robert Rosenthal. 1985. "Mediation of Interpersonal Expectancy Effects: 31 Meta-Analyses." *Psychological Bulletin* 97(3): 363–86.

Heilman, Madeine E., Caryn J. Block, and Richard F. Martell. 1995. "Sex Stereotypes: Do They Influence Perceptions of Managers?" *Journal of Social Behavior and Personality* 10(6): 237–52.

Hewstone, Miles. 1994. "Revision and Change of Stereotypic Beliefs: In Search of the Elusive Subtyping Model." In *European Review of Social Psychology*, edited by Wolfgang Stroebe and Miles Hewstone. Volume 5. Chichester, England: Wiley.

Jackman, Mary R. 1994. *The Velvet Glove: Paternalism and Conflict in Gender, Class, and Race Relations.* Berkeley: University of California Press.

Jackson, Robert M. 1998. *Destined for Equality: The Inevitable Rise of Women's Status.* Cambridge, Mass.: Harvard University Press.

Jacobs, Jerry A. 1999. "The Sex Segregation of Occupations: Prospects for the 21st Century." In *Handbook of Gender in Organizations*, edited by Gary N. Howell. Newbury Park, Calif.: Sage.

Jussim, Lee, and Christopher Fleming. 1996. "Self-fulfilling Prophecies and the Maintenance of Social Stereotypes: The Role of Dyadic Interaction and Social Forces." In *Stereotypes and Stereotyping*, edited by C. Neil Macrae, Charles Stangor, and Miles Hewstone. New York: Guilford.

Kessler, Suzanne, and Wendy McKenna. 1978. *Gender: An Ethnomethodological Approach.* New York: Wiley.

Kilbourne, Barbara S., Paula England, George Farkas, Kurt Beron, and Dorothea Weir. 1994. "Returns to Skill, Compensating Differentials, and Gender Bias: Effects of Occupational Characteristics on the Wages of White Women and Men." *American Journal of Sociology* 100(3): 689–719.

Kunda, Zivr, and Lisa Sinclair. 1999. "Motivated Reasoning with Stereotypes: Activation, Application, and Inhibition." *Psychological Inquiry* 10(1): 12–22.

Lueptow, Lloyd B., Lori Garovich-Szabo, and Margaret B. Lueptow. 1995. "The Persistence of Gender Stereotypes in the Face of Changing Sex Roles: Evidence Contrary to the Sociocultural Model." *Ethology and Sociobiology* 16: 509–30.

———. 2001. "Social Change and the Persistence of Sex Typing: 1974–1997." *Social Forces* 80(1): 1–36.

Major, Brenda. 1989. "Gender Differences in Comparisons and Entitlement: Implication for Comparable Worth." *Journal of Social Issues* 45(4): 99–115.

Milkie, Melissa A. 1999. "Social Comparison, Reflected Appraisals, and Mass Media: The Impact of Pervasive Beauty Images on Black and White Girls' Self-Concepts." *Social Psychology Quarterly* 62: 190–210.

Miller, Dale T., and William Turnbull. 1986. "Expectancies and Interpersonal Processes." *Annual Review of Psychology* 37: 233–56.

National Opinion Research Center. 1998. *General Social Survey, 1972–1998: Cumulative Study.* CD-ROM. Storrs, Conn.: Roper Center for Public Opinion Research.

Nelson, Robert, and William Bridges. 1999. *Legalizing Gender Inequality: Courts, Markets, and Unequal Pay for Women in America.* New York: Cambridge University Press.

Petersen, Trond, and Laurie A. Morgan. 1995. "Separate and Unequal: Occupation-Establishment Sex Segregation and the Gender Wage Gap." *American Journal of Sociology* 101(2): 329–65.

Plant, E. Asby, and Patricia G. Devine. 1998. "Internal and External Motivation to Respond Without Prejudice." *Journal of Personality and Social Psychology* 75(3): 811–32.

Reskin, Barbara. 1988. "Bringing the Men Back In: Sex Differentiation and the Devaluation of Women's Work." *Gender and Society* 2(1): 58–81.

———. 2000. "The Proximate Causes of Employment Discrimination." *Contemporary Sociology* 29(2): 319–28.

Reskin, Barbara, and Debra Branch McBrier. 2000. "Why Not Ascription? Organizations' Employment of Male and Female Managers." *American Sociological Review* 65(2): 210–33.

Reskin, Barbara, and Irene Padovic. 1999. "Sex, Race, and Ethnic Inequality in United States Workplaces." In *Handbook of the Sociology of Gender*, edited by Janet S. Chafetz. New York: Kluwer/Plenum.

Reskin, Barbara, and Patricia A. Roos. 1990. *Job Queues, Gender Queues: Explaining Women's Inroads into Male Occupations*. Philadelphia: Temple University Press.

Ridgeway, Cecilia L. 1997. "Interaction and the Conservation of Gender Inequality: Considering Employment." *American Sociological Review* 62(2): 218–35.

———. 2001. "Gender, Status, and Leadership." *Journal of Social Issues* 57(4): 637–55.

Ridgeway, Cecilia L., Elizabeth Heger Boyle, Kathy Kuipers, and Dawn T. Robinson. 1998. "How Do Status Beliefs Develop? The Role of Resources and Interactional Experience." *American Sociological Review* 63(3): 331–50.

Ridgeway, Cecilia L., and Shelley Correll. 2000. "Limiting Gender Inequality Through Interaction: The End(s) of Gender." *Contemporary Sociology* 29(1): 110–20.

———. 2004. "Motherhood as a Status Characteristic." *Journal of Social Issues* 60(4): 683–700.

Ridgeway, Cecilia L., and Kristan G. Erickson. 2000. "Creating and Spreading Status Beliefs." *American Journal of Sociology* 106(3): 579–615.

Ridgeway, Cecilia L., and Lynn Smith-Lovin. 1999. "The Gender System and Interaction." *Annual Review of Sociology* 25: 191–216.

Rudman, Laurie A., and Peter Glick. 2001. "Prescriptive Gender Stereotypes and Backlash Toward Agentic Women." *Journal of Social Issues* 27(4): 743–62.

Rudman, Laurie, and Stephen E. Kilianski. 2000. "Implicit and Explicit Attitudes Toward Female Authority." *Personality and Social Psychology Bulletin* 26(11): 1315–28.

Sechrist, Gretchen B., and Charles Stangor. 2001. "Perceived Consensus Influences Intergroup Behavior and Stereotype Accessibility." *Journal of Personality and Social Psychology* 80(4): 645–54.

Shih, Margaret, Todd L. Pittinsky, and Nalini Ambady. 1999. "Stereotype Susceptibility: Identity Salience and Shifts in Quantitative Performance." *Psychological Science* 10(1): 80–83.

Spence, Janet T., and Camille E. Buckner. 2000. "Instrumental and Expressive Traits, Trait Stereotypes, and Sexist Attitudes: What Do They Signify?" *Psychology of Women Quarterly* 24(1): 44–62.

Spencer, Steven J., Claude M. Steele, and Diane M. Quinn. 1999. "Under Suspicion of Inability: Stereotype Threat and Women's Math Performance." *Journal of Experimental Social Psychology* 35(1): 4–28.

Stangor, Charles, Laurie Lynch, Changming Duan, and Beth Glass. 1992. Categorization of Individuals on the Basis of Multiple Social Features." *Journal of Personality and Social Psychology* 62(2): 207–18.

Steinberg, Ronnie J. 1995. "Gendered Instructions: Cultural Lag and Gender Bias in the Hay system of Job Evaluation." In *Gender Inequality at Work,* edited by Jerry A. Jacobs. Thousand Oaks, Calif.: Sage.

Twenge, Jean M. 1997. "Changes in Masculine and Feminine Traits over Time: A Meta-Analysis." *Sex Roles* 36(5-6): 305–25.

Von Hippel, W., Denise Sekaquaptewa, and Patrick Vargas. 1995. "On the Role of Encoding Processes in Stereotype Maintenance." In *Advances in Experimental Social Psychology*, edited by Mark Zanna. Volume 27. San Diego: Academic Press.

Wagner, David G., and Joseph Berger. 1997. "Gender and Interpersonal Task Behaviors: Status Expectation Accounts." *Sociological Perspectives* 40(1): 1–32.

Weber, Max. 1922/1968. *Economy and Society.* Edited by G. Roth and C. Wittich; translated by E. Frischoff et al. New York: Bedminster Press.

West, Candace, and Don Zimmerman. 1987. "Doing Gender." *Gender and Society* 1(2): 125–51.

Wheeler, S. Christian, and Richard E. Petty. 2001. "The Effects of Stereotype Activation on Behavior: A Review of Possible Mechanisms." *Psychological Bulletin* 127(6): 797–826.

Williams, Joan. 2000. *Unbending Gender: Why Family and Work Conflict and What to Do About It.* New York: Oxford.

Williams, John E., and Deborah L. Best. 1990. *Measuring Sex Stereotypes: A Multinational Study.* Newbury Park, Calif.: Sage.

Wood, Wendy, and Alice H. Eagly. 2002. "A Cross-Cultural Analysis of the Behavior of Women and Men: Implications for the Origins of Sex Differences." *Psychological Bulletin* 128(5): 699–727.

Zelditch, Morris, Jr., and Anthony S. Floyd. 1998. "Consensus, Dissensus, and Justification." In *Status, Power, and Legitimacy: Strategies and Theories,* edited by Joseph Berger and Morris Zelditch, Jr. New Brunswick, N.J.: Transaction Press.

Index

Boldface numbers refer to figures and tables.

Abbott, E., 82
academia, 6, 174–75
accounting industry, 47, **168**
adverse impact, 256–57
adverse selection, 31n14
affirmative action, 19
African Americans, pay gap, 112
age: as category system for social relations, 267; and earnings, 105, 110; and family obligations, 194–95; at first marriage, 80, 95, 254; labor-force participation by, **109**; and occupational rank, 181–82; and work experience, 170–71
Aigner, D., 12, 29–30n3
Akerlof, G., 31n15
antidiscrimination legislation. *See* federal antidiscrimination legislation
Arrow, K., 29, 99n43
ascription, 15
Asian Americans, PSID sample, 151n5
asymmetries in information, 92–93
Australia: child rearing data, 252; employment status of men and women, **110**; pay gap, **111, 115**
Austria, pay gap in, **111**

baby boom, 95, 100n52
banking industry, 46
bargaining power, 255
Barnett, W., 173, 174
Baron, J., 173, 174
Baum, C., 112
Baxter, J., 206n4
Becker, G., 9, 12, 13, 29n1, 42–43, 46, 152n15, 226
Belgium, pay gap in, **115**
beliefs, about gender, 268–70, 281–82
Belkin, L., 119, 121n15
"benign circle," 10, 22, 28
Ben-Porath, Y., 102
Berger, M., 112

Bergmann, B., 43
Berkman v. City of New York, 99n48
Beyard, K., 63n14
Bianchi, S., **248**
Bible, gender wage gap justification in, 103
biological differences, 164
Birkelund, G., 206n4
birth cohort effects, 196–203, 204
birth rates, 91, 95, 163, 257
Bittman, M., 252
Black, D., 13
Black, S., 46
blacks, pay gap, 112
Blau, F., 13, 30n8, 43, 50, 56, 99n45, 110, **111**, 115, 121n11, 162–63, 167
Blau, P., 266
BLS (Bureau of Labor Statistics), **108, 109,** 117, 126, 151n2, 165. *See also* Current Population Survey (CPS)
blue-collar jobs: "brawn" jobs, 69, 81–85; male predominance, 3, 50, 52, 247; trends, **70**; women employed in, **71**
BNT codes, 175
Brainerd, E., 46
brain jobs, 69, 82, 85–88, 94–95. *See also* white-collar jobs
brawn jobs, 69, 81–85. *See also* blue-collar jobs
Breen, R., 204
Brett, J., 174
Budig, M., 112
bureaucratic personnel practices. *See* personnel policies
Bureau of Labor Statistics (BLS), **108, 109,** 117, 126, 151n2, 165. *See also* Current Population Survey (CPS)
Burtless, G., 58
business administration, 190, **192, 200–201**
business colleges, 98n28
Butterfield, D., 173
buyers, **169**

Cain, G., 12, 30n3
California, family-friendly policies, 148
California Civil Service, 174
Canada: employment status of men and women, **110**; female labor-force participation, 107–8; pay gap, **115**
Cancian, M., 58
Carnevale, A., 135
Casper, L., **248**
Catalyst, 105–6, 108, 119, 121n15
categorization, by sex, 267–68, 269, 272, 274, 277
Catholic Church, 149
causal model, 7–8
Census Bureau: earnings by education group, 56; earnings of full-time workers, **113**; labor-force participation by marital status, **107**; labor-force participation of men, 120n1; occupation group distribution, **71**; occupation vs. employment question, 76; wage-gap data, 126, 151n2; women's share of paying jobs, **224**; work hours, 151n1. *See also* Current Population Survey (CPS)
Central Confederation of Employers, 175
CEOs, 147
chemists, **168**
child care: availability of, 104, 163, 165, 204; employer-provided, 10; public provision of, 158, 260. *See also* child-rearing activities
child-care subsidies, 10
child-care workers, 247
childlessness, 148, 254
child-rearing activities: before 1950, 91; government policies, 259–60; of mothers vs. fathers, 231, 250–52, 254, 255, 258; time spent on, 149; value of, 127